A Search for Stability: U. S. Diplomacy Toward Nicaragua, 1925–1933. William Kamman.

Freedom and Authority in the West. George N. Shuster, ed.

Theory and Practice: History of a Concept from Aristotle to Marx. Nicholas Lobkowicz.

Coexistence: Communism and Its Practice in Bologna, 1945–1965. Robert H. Evans.

Marx and the Western World. Nicholas Lobkowicz, ed.

Argentina's Foreign Policy 1930–1962. Alberto A. Conil Paz and Gustavo E. Ferrari.

Italy after Fascism, A Political History, 1943–1965. Giuseppe Mammarella.

The Volunteer Army and Allied Intervention in South Russia 1917–1921. George A. Brinkley.

Peru and the United States, 1900–1962. James C. Carey.

Empire by Treaty: Britain and the Middle East in the Twentieth Century. M. A. Fitzsimons.

The USSR and the UN's Economic and Social Activities. Harold Karan Jacobson.

Chile and the United States: 1880–1962. Fredrick B. Pike.

East Central Europe and the World: Developments in the Post-Stalin Era. Stephen D. Kertesz, ed.

Soviet Policy Toward International Control and Atomic Energy. Joseph L. Nogee.

INTERNATIONAL STUDIES OF THE

COMMITTEE ON INTERNATIONAL RELATIONS

UNIVERSITY OF NOTRE DAME

The Russian Revolution and Religion, 1917–1925. Edited and translated by Bolesław Szcześniak.

Soviet Policy Toward the Baltic States, 1918–1940. Albert N. Tarulis.

Introduction to Modern Politics. Ferdinand Hermens.

Freedom and Reform in Latin America. Fredrick B. Pike, ed.

What America Stands For. Stephen D. Kertesz and M. A. Fitzsimons, eds.

The Representative Republic. Ferdinand Hermens.

Theoretical Aspects of International Relations. William T. R. Fox, ed.

Catholicism, Nationalism and Democracy in Argentina. John J. Kennedy.

Christian Democracy in Western Europe, 1820–1953. Michael P. Fogarty.

The Fate of East Central Europe. Stephen D. Kertesz, ed.

German Protestants Face the Social Question. William O. Shanahan.

Soviet Imperialism: Its Origins and Tactics. Waldemar Gurian, ed.

The Foreign Policy of the British Labour Government, 1945–1951. M. A. Fitzsimons.

Diplomacy in a Whirlpool: Hungary between Nazi Germany and Soviet Russia. Stephen D. Kertesz.

Bolshevism: An Introduction to Soviet Communism. Waldemar Gurian.

A Russian

European

Paul McConnox.

A Russian

European

Paul Miliukov in

Russian Politics

By THOMAS RIHA

 UNIVERSITY OF NOTRE DAME PRESS
NOTRE DAME — LONDON

Library of Congress Catalog Card Number: 68–27582
Manufactured in the United States of America

PREFACE

This is not a full biography of Paul Miliukov (1859–1943). I have chosen to relate only the major part of his political fortunes and have left to others the task of analyzing Miliukov's contribution as a distinguished historian of Russia. I have stressed that aspect of Miliukov's politics which appeared to me to be central. Space did not permit a fuller discussion of many other topics closely related to my concern—the fortunes of the Kadet party, the status of the Russian middle class and of Russian liberalism, or the performance of the four Russian Dumas in the first two decades of the twentieth century.

I wish to thank several persons who helped me in the course of this study. Ludmila Patrick first suggested Miliukov as a subject of investigation. Martin Malia supervised my work in two seminars devoted to Miliukov and has since discussed the topic with me on several occasions. Richard Pipes was my dissertation adviser at Harvard and helped to improve that first version of this book. Nicholas Riasanovsky was its second reader and pointed out some pitfalls in my thinking. Mark Vishniak suggested the title for this work and proved a stimulating source on Miliukov's Russia, which he remembers well. Nathan Smith has shared with me his insights into the nature of Russian constitutionalism in the first years of our century. Boris Elkin, Miliukov's literary executor, corresponded with me about the materials in his possession and his recollections of Miliukov's career. Lazar Volin, William Rosenberg, and Robert Feldman were kind enough to give me copies of documents which I found useful. Michel Confino read the first part of this study, and made valuable suggestions for its improvement. Arcadius Kahan read the entire manuscript, and offered his advice on several points. Donald Fanger gave an inspiring example as friend and scholar. Hanushka S. urged me on with sympathy and tact when these were most needed. Ruth Jensen typed several versions of the manuscript with her customary zeal and competence and caught many errors and inconsistencies.

A scholar is always dependent on libraries. I owe a debt to several of them. I began my work in the University of California collection at Berkeley. I continued it at the Widener Library of Harvard, always an ideal place for research. An academic year in the Soviet Union made it possible to work in the libraries of Moscow and Leningrad. I was not permitted to use the rich Soviet archival collections on Miliukov and the Kadet party. I regret this. I did use some unpublished material by and about Miliukov at the Hoover Library in Palo Alto and recall a summer spent there with great pleasure. Philip Mosely admitted me to the collections of the Columbia University Archives of Russian History and Culture of which Lev Magerovsky is the tirelesss guardian and stimulating interpreter. The Miliukov Collection under his care is the richest source of unpublished materials about Miliukov and the Kadets outside the Soviet Union, although it yields little information about the personal life and private views of a man who always preferred to be reticent. The University of Chicago library was most helpful, and I made use of the Samuel Harper Papers deposited in its Special Collection.

I am grateful for financial assistance toward the completion of this study. The Ford Foundation Foreign Area Program supported me for two years. The Inter-University Committee on Travel Grants made possible an unforgettable year at Moscow State University. The University of Chicago gave me a Willet's Teaching Fellowship and granted me additional funds to free me from teaching duties for a year. Peter Scheibert invited me to his *Seminar für Osteuropaische Geschichte* at Marburg and proved to be the ideal academic host. Harvard's Russian Research Center gave me a home for a semester.

Dates used in this work are Old Style, except when they relate to events outside Russia. To convert dates from the Julian to the Gregorian calendar, twelve days should be added in the nineteenth, and thirteen in the twentieth century. The Cyrillic alphabet is transliterated according to the Library of Congress system, without its diacritical marks.

CONTENTS

ABBREVIATIONS

A	*Athenaeum* (London).
ARKHIV	Konstitutsiono-Demokraticheskaia Partiia, "Arkhiv 1920–1924"; two-volume unpublished collection at the Hoover Library, Stanford, California.
ARR	*Arkhiv Russkoi Revoliutsii* (Berlin).
ASEER	*American Slavic and East European Review* (New York).
ATL	P. Miliukov, "Present Tendencies of Russian Liberalism," *Atlantic Monthly* (Boston), March, 1905, pp. 404–14.
BAL	P. Miliukov, *Balkanskii krizis i politika A. P. Izvol'skago* (St. Petersburg, 1910).
BALK	P. Miliukov, "The War and Balkan Politics," in J. Duff (ed.), *Russian Realities and Problems* (Cambridge, Eng., 1917), pp. 1–24.
BE	*Entsyklopedicheskii slovar' Brokhauz-Efron* (St. Petersburg).
BEL	I. Belokonskii, *Zemstvo i konstitutsiia* (Moscow, 1910).
BES	I. Bestuzhev, *Bor'ba v Rossii po voprosam vneshnei politiki, 1906–1910* (Moscow, 1961).

BLOK   N. Lapin (ed.), "Progressivnyi blok v 1915–1917
                gg.," *Krasnyi Arkhiv* (Moscow), L–LI (1932), 117–
                60; LII (1932), 143–96; LVI (1933), 80–135.
BOL   P. Miliukov, "Bolgarskaia konstitutsiia," *Russkoe
                Bogatstvo* (Moscow), 1904, No. 8, pp. 193–216;
                No. 9, pp. 26–69; No. 10, pp. 28–59.
BOLSH   P. Miliukov, *Bolshevism: An International Danger*
                (London, 1920).
BROWKER   R. Browder and A. Kerensky (eds.), *The Russian
                Provisional Government, 1917* (Stanford, Cal.,
                1961), 3 vols.
BUCHANAN   G. Buchanan, *My Mission to Russia* (Boston,
                1923), 2 vols.
CASE   P. Miliukov, "The Case of the Second Duma,"
                Contemporary Review (London), XCII (October,
                1907), 457–67.
CHER   E. Chermenskii, *Burzhuaziia i tsarism v revoliutsii
                1905–1907 gg.* (Moscow, 1939).
CONST   P. Miliukov, *Constitutional Government for Russia*
                (New York, 1907).
CRI   P. Miliukov, *Russia and Its Crisis* (Chicago, 1905).
DAN'   M. Vishniak, *Dan' proshlomu* (New York, 1954).
DENIKIN   A. Denikin, *Ocherki russkoi smuty* (Paris-Berlin,
                1921–26), 5 vols.
DNEVNIK   P. Miliukov, "Dnevnik." Unpublished diary, May
                28, 1918–January 20, 1920 (MSS in the Miliukov
                Papers, Russian Archives, Columbia University).
EZH   *Ezhegodnik Gazety Riech'* (St. Petersburg).
FIRST   V. Maklakov, *The First State Duma* (Bloomington,
                Ind., 1964).
FIS   G. Fischer, *Russian Liberalism* (Cambridge, Mass.,
                1958).
GES   I. Gessen, *V dvukh vekakh* (Berlin, 1937).
GM   *Golos Minuvshago* (St. Petersburg).
GMCS   *Golos Minuvshago na Chuzhoi Storone* (Paris).
GOD   P. Miliukov, *God bor'by* (St. Petersburg, 1907).
GOL   F. Golder (ed.), *Documents of Russian History,
                1914–1917* (New York, 1927).
GOS   P. Miliukov, *Gosudarstvennoe khoziastvo Rossii v*

pervoi chetverti XVIII veka i reformy Petra Veli-kago (St. Petersburg, 1892).

GRABUR B. Grave (ed.), *Burzhuaziia nakanune fevral'skoi revoliutsii* (Moscow, 1927).

GRAKLAS B. Grave (ed.), *K istorii klassovoi borby v Rossii v gody imperialisticheskoi voiny: Iul' 1914–fevral' 1917* (Moscow, 1926).

GUR V. Gurko, *Features and Figures of the Past* (Stanford, Cal., 1939).

HAR S. Harcave, *First Blood: The Revolution of 1905* (New York, 1964).

HARP S. Harper, *The New Electoral Law for the Russian Duma* (Chicago, 1908).

HSS *Harvard Slavic Studies* (Cambridge, Massachusetts).

IAKHONTOV I. Iakhontov, "Tiazhelye dni: Sekretnyia zasedaniia soveta ministrov 16 iuliia–2 sentiabria 1915 g.," *Arkhiv Russkoi Revoliutsii* (Berlin), XVIII (1926), 5–136.

ISTORIIA P. Miliukov, *Istoriia vtoroi russkoi revoliutsii* (Sofia, 1921–24), 3 vols.

IZ *Istoricheskiia Zapiski* (Moscow).

JCEA *Journal of Central European Affairs.*

JUB P. Miliukov, *Ocherki po istorii russkoi kul'tury* (Jubilee ed.; Paris, 1930–37), 3 vols. in 4 parts.

KA *Krasnyi Arkhiv* (Moscow).

KAD B. Grave (ed.), "Kadety v 1905–1906 gg.," *Krasnyi Arkhiv* (Moscow), XLVI (1931), 38–68; XLVII–XLVIII (1931), 112–39.

KAL F. Kalinychev (ed.), *Gosudarsvennaia duma v Rossii v dokumentakh i materialakh* (Moscow, 1957).

KER A. Kerensky, *Russia and History's Turning Point* (New York, 1965).

KIZ A. Kizevetter, *Na rubezhe dvukh stoletii* (Prague, 1929).

KOK V. Kokovtsov, *Out of My Past* (Stanford, Cal., 1935).

KONST E. Adamov (ed.), *Konstantinopol' i prolivy po*

	sekretnym dokumentam byvshego ministerstva inostranykh del (Moscow, 1925–26), 2 vols.
KRY	S. Kryzhanovskii, *Vospominaniia* (Berlin, n.d.).
LEN	V. Lenin, *Sochineniia* (3d ed.; Moscow, 1935–37).
LEV	A. Levin, *The Second Duma* (New Haven, Conn., 1940).
LMS	*Le Monde Slave* (Paris).
MAR	A. Martynov, "Istoriia konstitutsionno-demokraticheskoi partii," in L. Martov, et al., *Obshchestvennoe dvizhenie v Rossii v nachale XX veka*, III (St. Petersburg, 1914), 1–85.
MB	*Mir Bozhii* (St. Petersburg).
NABOKOV	V. Nabokov, "Vremennoe pravitel'stvo," *Arkhiv Russkoi Revoliutsii* (Berlin), I (1921), 9–96.
NEK	A. Nekludoff, *Diplomatic Reminiscences before and during the World War* (London, 1920).
NUZ	P. Miliukov, "Vvedenie," in K. Arsen'ev, et al., *Nuzhdy derevni po rabotam komitetov o nuzhdakh sel'sko-khoziaistvennoi promyshlennosti* (St. Petersburg, 1904), I, 1–40.
O	P. Miliukov, *Ocherki po istorii russkoi kul'tury*. References to Vol. I are to the 5th ed. (St. Petersburg, 1904); Vol. II to the 1st ed. (St. Petersburg, 1897); Vol. III to the 3d ed. (St. Petersburg, 1909).
OKH	Paris Okhrana Archive, Hoover Library, Stanford, Cal. File XVII: "P. N. Miliukov."
OS	*Osvobozhdenie* (Stuttgart-Paris).
PAD	P. Shchegolev (ed.), *Padenie tsarskogo rezhima* (Moscow, 1926–27), 7 vols.
PAL	M. Paléologue, *La Russie des Tsars pendant la Grande Guerre* (Paris, 1921), 3 vols.
PAPERS	The Samuel N. Harper Russian Papers, Harper Library, University of Chicago.
PETR	I. Petrunkevich, *Iz zapisok obshchestvennogo deiatelia* (Berlin, 1934).
PN	*Posledniia Novosti* (Paris).
PNM	S. Smirnov et al., *Pavel Nikolaevich Miliukov: Sbornik materialov po chestvovaniiu ego semidesiatiletiia, 1859–1929* (Paris, n.d.).

POST	Konstitutsionno-Demokraticheskaia Partiia, *Posta-novleniia II-go s"ezda 5–11 ianvaria 1906 g. i programma* (St. Petersburg, 1906).
RB	*Russkoe Bogatstvo* (St. Petersburg).
REP	P. Miliukov, "The Representative System in Russia," in J. Duff (ed.), *Russian Realities and Problems* (Cambridge, Eng., 1917), pp. 25–46.
RM	*Russkaia Mysl'* (Moscow).
ROK	P. Miliukov, "Rokovye gody," *Russkia Zapiski* (Paris, 1938–39).
RR	*Russian Review* (Hanover, N.H.).
RUS	P. Miliukov, *Russia Today and Tomorrow* (New York, 1922).
RV	*Russkiia Vedomosti* (Moscow).
RVS	*Russkiia Vedomosti, 1863–1913: Sbornik statei* (Moscow, 1913).
SEER	*Slavonic and East European Review* (London).
SHA	D. Shakhovskoi, "Soiuz osvobozhdeniia," in *Zarnitsy* (St. Petersburg), No. 2 (1909), Part 2, pp. 81–171.
SHI	D. Shipov, *Vospominaniia i dumy o perezhitom* (Moscow, 1918).
SID	S. Sidel'nikov, *Obrazovanie i deiatel'nost' pervoi gosudarstvennoi dumy* (Moscow, 1962).
SM I	N. Smith, "The Constitutional-Democratic Movement in Russia, 1902–1906" (Ph.D. diss., University of Illinois, 1958).
SM II	C. J. Smith, *The Russian Struggle for Power* (New York, 1956).
SO	Russia. Gosudarstvennaia Duma. *Stenograficheskiia otchety* (St. Petersburg).
SUKHANOV	N. Sukhanov, *Zapiski o russkoi revoliutsii* (Berlin, 1922–23), 7 vols.
SZ	*Sovremenniya Zapiski* (Paris).
TAK	P. Miliukov, *Taktika Partii Narodnoi Svobody vo vremia voiny* (Petrograd, 1916).
TR	D. Treadgold, *Lenin and His Rivals* (New York, 1955).
TRI	P. Miliukov, *Tri popytki* (Paris, 1921).

TSENTR   Otchet tsentral'nogo komiteta Konstitutsionno-
            Demokraticheskoi partii za dva goda, s 18-go oktia-
            bria 1905 g. po oktiabr' 1907 g. (St. Petersburg,
            1907).
VE   Vestnik Evropy (St. Petersburg).
VES   Vestnik Partii Narodnoi Svobody (St. Petersburg-
            Petrograd).
VIN I   M. Vinaver, "Konflikty v pervoi dume," in N.
            Borodin et al., Pervaia gosudarstvennaia duma (St.
            Petersburg, 1907), I, 184–279.
VIN II   M. M. Vinaver i russkaia obshchestvennost' nachala
            XX veka (Paris, 1937).
VIN III   M. Vinaver, Istoriia vyborgskago vozvaniia (Petro-
            grad, 1917).
VLAST'   V. Maklakov, Vlast' o obshchestvennost' na zakate
            staroi Rossii (Paris, 1936).
VOI   V. Voitinskii, Gody pobed i porazhenii (Berlin,
            1923–24), 2 vols.
VON   T. Von Laue, Sergei Witte and the Industrializa-
            tion of Russia (New York, 1963).
VOSP   P. Miliukov, Vospominaniia (New York, 1955),
            2 vols.
VOSR   Velikaia Oktiabrskaia Sotsialisticheskaia Revoliut-
            siia. Dokumenty i Materialy. Revoliutsionnoe dvi-
            zhenie v Rossii posle sverzheniia samoderzhaviia
            (Moscow, 1957).
VTO   P. Miliukov, Vtoraia duma (St. Petersburg, 1908).

INTRODUCTION

> *I am, to be sure, a European among Russians; but I wish
> to remain a Russian—and to be considered as such—among
> Europeans.*[1]

I

It was March 4, 1929. The halls of the Lutetia on the Boulevard
Raspail, the second largest hotel in Paris, were buzzing. But not in
French. Hundreds of Russians were assembling for a banquet upstairs.
Among the guests were the ministers in Paris of Bulgaria, Yugoslavia,
Czechoslovakia, Estonia, and Latvia. But not of the Soviet Union. It
was an occasion for Russians, but not for Soviet citizens. This was the
second day of celebrations. On the previous afternoon some one thou-
sand persons had crowded into the Paris Oceanographic Institute lec-
ture hall to celebrate the same occasion. In other European capitals
Russians were banqueting for the same reason: in Warsaw on March
2, in Riga and Sofia on March 3, in Berlin on March 5, in Prague on
March 6. Jubilee committees had been organized in Belgium,
Yugoslavia, Bulgaria, Finland, Rumania, Latvia, Estonia, Lithuania,
Czechoslovakia, Germany, Poland, England, and even in the U.S.A.

In the Lutetia, telegrams from all over the world were read. They
came from President Thomas Masaryk of Czechoslovakia, the chairman of the Bulgarian parliament, the International Union of Journalists, Ivan Bunin and Alexander Kuprin, André Mazon and Jules Cam-

[1] PNM, p. 271.

1

bon, Sir Bernard Pares and the senate of Cambridge University, Nicholas Murray Butler of Columbia and Lawrence Lowell of Harvard, Sebastien Charlety of the Sorbonne and Lyman Wilbur of Stanford, Maurice Paléologue and the senate of Oxford University, the Bulgarian Academy of Sciences and Alexander Kaun of the University of California in Berkeley. But there were no telegrams from Moscow or Leningrad.[2]

The object of all this attention in Paris and elsewhere outside of Russia was Paul Nikolaevich Miliukov. He had become seventy in January, but the doctors had advised him to avoid excitement at that time. So the jubilant took a leave of absence from the editorship of the Paris daily *Posledniia Novosti* and went to the Pyrenees for a rest. He was now back, sun-tanned and relaxed, and enjoying himself very much. It was an occasion to please his heart. At the Lutetia he could speak in several of the languages he knew well. The personal representative of the president of the French senate heard him in French, the minister of Yugoslavia in Serbo-Croatian, the gentlemen from Sofia in Bulgarian.

The rest of the evening he spoke his native Russian. "I am simply overwhelmed," he admitted, "by this avalanche of greetings, kind words and appraisals."[3] He may have derived most pleasure from the fact that his most popular work, *Outlines of Russian Culture*, was to be reissued in a revised translation. There had been seven editions in Russia, the last in 1918. Now the work of a political émigré, the book was ignored by the Soviet reading public and had become a bibliographical rarity abroad. It would be available again. The funds had been appropriated by a unanimous vote of the Bulgarian parliament "in recognition of your work on behalf of the recreation of young Bulgaria."[4] Sofia University, where he had taught thirty years earlier, elected him doctor *honoris causa*. The Sofia City Council voted to name Rouen Street Paul Miliukov Street.

Miliukov the historian was thus very well pleased. Miliukov the journalist, editor of the emigration's largest newspaper, could not but regret that his *Free People* (the title of his first newspaper in 1905) were no longer free and that his *Speech* (the title of his influential

[2] PN, March 5, 1929, pp. 2–3.
[3] PNM, p. 258.
[4] By 1937 four revised volumes had appeared. A fifth remains in manuscript. There is a recent, much abridged, paperback edition in English in three volumes.

second newspaper) was now forced into silence.[5] But, as always, he remained an optimist in politics. His erstwhile political comrade and now bitter critic, Vasilii Maklakov, had disassociated himself from the celebrations. "While Russia is in mourning," he had written Miliukov, "demonstrative public celebrations should be avoided. . . . I feel, perhaps more strongly than I should, the responsibility not only of the Right and the Left, but of all of us, that is also of those who followed you, for what happened in Russia." Miliukov, on the other hand, believed that it was "precisely at this moment, when humanitarian ideals are denied in our fatherland, that we must prove that they are alive elsewhere, and that the future belongs to these ideas."[6]

II

Miliukov's old party and newspaper colleague Iosif Gessen ended his message from Berlin with the wish that the next jubilee be celebrated on the banks of the Neva or Moscow River. Miliukov himself, observing the troubles that the Soviet regime was having with the beginnings of the new Five-Year Plan and the brutal collectivization campaign, thought that the emigration was not destined to remain away much longer. The future belied these hopes. The Soviet regime remained. Or was it perhaps that the Russian people wanted no part of this Russian European and his solutions? Fully half a century earlier, in 1878, Dostoevsky had predicted just that to the high-school student Miliukov. The great writer had become, in Miliukov's words, "our oracle"; his *Diary of a Writer* had aroused the young people's enthusiasm for the Slavic cause against the Turks.[7] For Miliukov it was the beginning of that lifelong attachment to Bulgaria for which he was honored in the Lutetia.

But something had gone wrong with the relations between the students and the Moscow population in the 1870's. During a parade in downtown Moscow some students failed to take off their caps to

[5] PNM, p. 271. See my article, "*Riech*': A Portrait of a Russian Newspaper," *Slavic Review*, XXII (1963), 663–82.

[6] Maklakov quoted in L. Liubimov, *Na chuzhbine* (Moscow, 1963), pp. 159–60. The message was not quoted in the Miliukov memorial volume; I have taken it from the interesting memoirs of a Russian émigré who returned to the Soviet Union. For Miliukov, see PNM, p. 259.

[7] VOSP, I, 68.

the national standards. The butchers of Okhotnyi Riad beat them up mercilessly, and a mild pogrom had ensued in the streets. Young Miliukov and his friends, who had watched this with dismay, decided to ask the great Dostoevsky's opinion. "To what extent are we students guilty?" they inquired. They were being accused of "intellectual and moral decline." Was it true? "Our teachers are silent and are losing their right to call themselves teachers." Would Dostoevsky answer their queries? The great writer replied that a real answer would require a book but that he would risk the students' displeasure by giving them a short explanation. "You are guilty of nothing," he began, "but you do not wish to know anything about Russia; do not attempt to deny it. A student turns not to the people but somewhere abroad, to 'Europeanism.' And yet all our salvation is in the people."[8]

Miliukov, then aged nineteen, and his young friends disagreed. "This contrasting of the people and Europe astounded us. . . . We could not give up Europe, and not only saw no contradiction between the people and Europe, but expected this Europe to raise the people to a higher cultural level. . . . I cannot say whether I already had a ready answer: Russia too is Europe. But all my thoughts moved in that direction."[9]

[8] F. Dostoevskii, Pis'ma (Moscow, 1959), IV, 353–57, for Miliukov's letter of April 8, 1878. Pp. 16–19 for Dostoevsky's answer of April 18, 1878.
[9] VOSP, I, 62–63.

1: THE MAKING OF A HISTORIAN

I was younger than the generation of the "seventies" but older than that of the "eighties" and "nineties" and, in my youth, had not lived through the hypnosis of one or another doctrine.[1]

I

Paul Miliukov was born on January 15, 1859. On the same day the future kaiser of Germany, William II, was born in Berlin. The two men were never to meet; but for Miliukov Germany and, particularly, her foreign policy were to become a lifelong preoccupation. Closer to home, in 1859 the Editorial Commission, under the chairmanship of the liberal Count Iakov Rostovtsev, was discussing the emancipation of Russia's serfs with land. The agrarian problem, which was to beset Miliukov's party throughout its existence, was about to receive its decisive stamp. In London, on the pages of *The Bell* of 1859, Alexander Herzen and Nikolai Kostomarov debated the future of the Ukraine; they envisaged a free federation with Russia, a solution which was to bedevil Miliukov and his party in 1917 and to contribute to their downfall.

The boy was born in a period of transition. His mother had a small property in Yaroslavl province; he could remember the peasants who, as they had done from time immemorial, still brought annual gifts to their mistress in Moscow: greasy but infinitely tasty flat cakes which the children adored. "We got acquainted with the end of serf-

---

[1] ROK, XI (1938), 138.

dom from this tasty side," he recalled.[2] There must have been less
pleasant memories in the family though; his mother, born a Sultan-
ova, had first married a certain Baranov who was so hated by his serfs
that they had killed him one day in the fields. On the father's side the
family traced its origin to a grant of nobility by Tsar Aleksei Mikhailo-
vich in the seventeenth century. The family coat of arms and seal
were kept in the house; but since certain formal proofs were lacking,
the Tver nobility refused Miliukov's grandfather's request that his
name be entered in the local nobility roll.

The Miliukovs had not been prosperous or successful in the last
generation. Miliukov's father tried his luck with Siberian gold, without success. He had returned, bringing with him his mother and
various uncles and aunts whom he had to support. His wife, Miliukov's mother, considered her marriage a bad match, and let her husband know it. He was an architect who taught in a Moscow architec-
tural school and served as inspector in another one. Later he became
Moscow's municipal architect, which provided some pleasure for his
children. For the many Moscow fairs it was he who approved all temporary structures erected in the streets and squares of the old capital.
Little Miliukov and his younger brother naturally got free passes to
all the marvellous shows and booths. On those days they came home
late, but excited and grateful.

After private lessons at home the eleven-year-old boy was enrolled
in Moscow's First Gymnasium, where he spent seven years (1870–
77). At first he did not do particularly well, dropping from fourth to
twentieth place in the class. But a new teacher of Greek aroused his
interest, and eventually Miliukov graduated with the highest honors;
no gold medal was granted that year, but he received a silver one.
This was the era of classicism; the Minister of Education, Count
Dmitrii Tolstoi, sought to make the schools politically innocuous by
curtailing current and practical subjects, instituting two daily lessons
of both Greek and Latin. One day, brought to Miliukov's class by the
director, he was told: "This student, Your Highness, made very poor
progress; now, thanks to the classicism introduced by you, he is one
of the first." The old bureaucrat mumbled something about how the
Scriptures had foretold "that the least would become the first."

Miliukov's best friend at the gymnasium was Mikhail S. Zernov,

[2] The details of Miliukov's early life are drawn from VOSP, unless otherwise
cited.

the son of a priest. At age twelve Miliukov had a brief spell of religious devotion, but there was no one at home to encourage him; there was not even a copy of the Bible. The gymnasium required formal proof of yearly confession and Holy Communion. But other forces were at work; Miliukov discovered Voltaire, "who gave meaning to my rejection of the formal side of religion." To this was added Herbert Spencer "who sowed more seeds of doubt." Miliukov was never to be religious again. But Misha Zernov was a wonderful friend and remained so into the Paris emigration days. Zernov had a private teacher who taught Miliukov his lifelong love of books. He also took him fishing below Sparrow Hills, where Moscow University skyscrapers today dominate the river. When Miliukov's father built a dacha in nearby Pushkino, Miliukov and his younger brother Alexei would go fishing in the little river Serebrianka. The parents were often absent, and the boys grew up very much by themselves. Alexei eventually lived separately from the family, but Miliukov "felt sorry for mother" and did not want to break with home yet. "There was no harmony in our family," he recalled. His mother was "a passionate and imperious woman," who played first fiddle in the family. All this was not conducive to the parents having much moral or intellectual influence over their children. "Without exaggerating much," Miliukov recalled, "I could say to myself that I owe everything to my own efforts."

During his last year at the gymnasium (1876–77) the Russo-Turkish War broke out in the Balkans. Miliukov was then a member of a gymnasium circle in which pro-Slav feelings were quite strong. It was in this circle that the idea of the letter to Dostoevsky was born. A leading member of the circle was Prince Nikolai D. Dolgorukov, a scion of a great and ancient Moscow family. His brothers Paul and Peter were to become Miliukov's intimate friends and colleagues in the Kadet party of later days. When the Moscow nobility organized a volunteer medical unit to be sent to the front, young Dolgorukov invited his friend Miliukov to come along; they would leave after their gymnasium examinations and return before the beginning of the autumn semester at Moscow University. To Miliukov's initial regret the unit was sent, not to Bulgaria "where I dreamt of going," but to the Caucasus, far from the front, in Suram, some distance from Tiflis.[3]

[3] The episode is described in VOSP, pp. 67–76, 83, 93.

Miliukov was captivated by the beauty of the mountains. Though he had no idea of bookkeeping, he served as the unit's cashier, while Dolgorukov was the group's troubleshooter. There was a third member of the team who, however, spent his time reclining on a divan and complaining of the intolerable summer heat. This was Nikolai A. Khomiakov, son of the famous Slavophil leader and future chairman of the Third Duma in which Miliukov was to be a deputy for five years. Khomiakov had brought with him Nikolai Danilevsky's *Russia and Europe*, which the young men discussed with much passion. There were long arguments with the wounded about the meaning and goals of the war, trips to broiling Tiflis for cash from the bank, and long horseback rides to the Turkish frontier. In September the two friends returned to Moscow. It was the closest that Miliukov ever came to army service.

II

Miliukov's five years at Moscow University (1877–82) were spent in the historical-philological faculty. In his first year he heard Sergei Solov'ev, who died the following year. He was not much impressed by the rest of his professors. To earn extra money he took down the lectures of some of them for sale and use among the students. In the process he discovered that some professors were in the habit of paraphrasing certain books; sometimes they even repeated the text verbatim. During Miliukov's second year at the university his father died of a heart condition. "This death," he recalled, "did not make a strong impression on either mother or myself." The estrangement within the family had grown too deep. But now finances became a paramount issue. Miliukov had earned some money in his gymnasium years by giving private lessons to less talented students. Now much more income would be needed not only for himself but also for his mother and his younger brother. Miliukov increased the number of his private lessons. There was to be no financial crisis. In the summer of 1879 he hired himself out as a tutor to the family of Princess Dolgorukov, the widow of Prince Vasilii Dolgorukov, Minister of Justice under Alexander I. He was treated with some haughtiness but consoled himself by reading Auguste Comte, whose historical scheme he was to use in his future *Outlines of Russian Culture*.

Coming back in the fall of 1879, he found two new teachers on the faculty. They were Paul Vinogradov in ancient and medieval history and Vasilii Kliuchevskii in Russian history. Both were to exercise a major influence on his intellectual formation. Vinogradov had just returned from abroad as a young *Privatdocent*. Only five years older than Miliukov, he seems to have treated him with great informality. This was not true of Kliuchevskii. Born in 1841 he belonged to another generation and never permitted his students to come close to him. Partly as a result of this, Miliukov did far more work for Vinogradov, though he had already decided that his future efforts would be devoted to Russian history. This, however, was to wait, while Vinogradov taught him historical method. "It was impossible to work with V. O. Kliuchevskii," he recalled. Not that the professor was unfriendly or unkind. He had just come from the Theological Academy, and Miliukov was among his first students at Moscow University. He taught his first course there while his great work on the Boyar Duma (later his doctoral dissertation) began to appear in the pages of *Russkaia Mysl'*. In 1880–81 his seminar met at his home. After the sessions tea would be served, and the students would "most unceremoniously" pump Kliuchevskii for his views on current affairs. These he refused to give but produced entire "salvos of jokes and paradoxical remarks" which kept the students in stitches.[4] But despite his humor and little tea parties he never became Miliukov's real master. His was an intellectual but not a personal inspiration.

In addition to his studies and tutoring Miliukov became active in student affairs. This was the era of the "dictatorship of the heart" or, as Miliukov himself called it, "a favorable moment of government liberalism."[5] Miliukov was elected chairman of the student court. He also represented his class in the student self-help organization, created to assist students without means. Most Moscow University students were dependent on some form of aid. Thus in the academic year 1875–76 only 376 of the 1,259 students paid the rather low tuition. All others were either granted a stipend or excused from all payments on the grounds of their poverty. Remembering his work on behalf of other students, Miliukov recalled: "I cannot say that the post was a sinecure."[6] Inevitably, this job involved Miliukov in politics as well.

[4] P. Miliukov, "V. O. Kliuchevskii kak lichnost'," PN, January 24, 1932, pp. 2–3.
[5] VOSP, I, 97.
[6] Data on student aid in V. Ger'e, "Svet i teni universitetskago byta," VE, February, 1876, p. 694; VOSP, I, 96.

One of his organization's charges, Iakov Ludmer, was sent by administrative order into exile in Arkhangelsk province. Miliukov began to correspond with him; in his letters he condemned certain government policies, blamed the zemstvo for weakness, and the Left organizations for their irreconcilability. "I am sorry," wrote Miliukov in his memoirs, "that this correspondence disappeared." He did not give the Okhrana enough credit. They read all his letters to Ludmer and made copies of them, which probably remain in Soviet archives. His contacts with a political suspect led to three searches of his apartment; but nothing incriminating was found, and his first brush with the secret police was inconclusive.[7]

Then came the assassination of Alexander II on March 1, 1881. All student meetings were forbidden. But the more radical students called a meeting to protest the government's measures. Miliukov went "to convince the meeting to disperse of its own accord." The police came and arrested all those present. Everyone was released the morning after, but each student was called individually before the rector, Professor Nikolai S. Tikhonravov, to explain his attendance. It soon became clear that the rector wanted to hear only one thing: the student had attended by mistake. He would then excuse the student and close the matter. Miliukov had been Tikhonravov's favorite student and would undoubtedly have been excused. But he chose to stand on his principles. When Tikhonravov, with a smile, asked him: "You, of course, did not know why the meeting was called?" Miliukov replied that he had known and had gone nevertheless. Miliukov was expelled from Moscow University until the following autumn, when he was to enrol again, with the loss of one year of study.

It was an unfortunate incident, but he made the best of it. A certain Krechetov, a friend of his brother's and a wealthy merchant's son, asked Miliukov to accompany him on a trip to Italy. Miliukov agreed to borrow the necessary funds from Krechetov and used his enforced vacation for educational purposes. Now he would get material for his study of ancient and Renaissance history with Vinogradov. At twenty-two Miliukov was going abroad for the first time. "My plan was not to admire, not to fall into raptures, but to learn." He was destined to travel through Italy alone. His companion remained in

[7] VOSP, I, 99–100; OKH, August, 1897. Report on Miliukov to the Paris branch of the Okhrana.

Vienna, seduced by its charms. Armed with Jakob Burckhardt's books, Miliukov moved from north to south: Venice, Padua, Bologna, Pisa, Florence, and Siena. Then a month in Rome, living in a cheap room on the Via Sistina above the Piazza di Spagna. It was July, and the indefatigable student almost suffered sunstroke. "Daily I walked around practically the entire present-day Vatican State." One day he was so taken by the collections of the Capitol Museum that he stayed after closing hours and would have been locked in for the night. Finally a guard was called, and Miliukov was searched before being released. From Rome he went to Naples and Pompei, and then home by boat, filled with marvellous impressions of his three months in the West.

III

Coming back to the university was almost an anticlimax. Miliukov's old friends had graduated, and he had little in common with the new group. Yet one of them remembered Miliukov with admiration. This was Prince Dmitrii I. Shakhovskoi, who had come to the university in 1881. He was to become a prominent Zemstvo-Constitutionalist and Miliukov's political colleague in the Kadet party. For Shakhovskoi, Miliukov was a champion of student rights:

> I well remember the calm and resolute figure of Miliukov who was risking his entire brilliant future in the name of one conviction: that rights left undefended when threatened will never be consolidated. This discussion in a group of students on the high porch of the Anatomy Auditorium in the courtyard of the old university has remained brightly in my memory.[8]

Vinogradov's seminar now included new members, with whom Miliukov would have many political and scholarly debates. They were Alexander Guchkov, the future leader of the Octobrists, and Mikhail Pokrovskii, future dean of Soviet historians. The fiery Pokrovskii of later days was not yet in evidence; in Vinogradov's seminar "he behaved modestly, remained silent most of the time, and wore the expression of one perpetually offended and not properly appreciated.[9] While the others wrote their seminar papers, it was time for

---

[8] D. Shakhovskoi, "Avtobiografiia," *Russkiia Vedomosti 1869–1913* (Moscow, 1913), pp. 196–97.
[9] VOSP, I, 117.

Miliukov to prepare for the final examinations. He did very well in all his fields.

Next came preparations for his magister's examination which preceded the writing of the magister's dissertation. He would be examined in his major field, Russian history, as well as in two minor subjects, European history and political economy. Again he did well. To be retained at the university he was now expected to deliver a public lecture on a subject of his own choice. He delivered the lecture in 1885, choosing "The Juridical School of Russian Historiography" as his theme. Russian historiography was a subject which would continue to occupy him and result, eventually, in his valuable survey of the subject for the eighteenth and early nineteenth centuries, a work which has not been superseded yet. The lecture was well received and was printed in the Moscow *Russkaia Mysl'* the following year. With this began Miliukov's career as an author. *Russkaia Mysl'* became his first journalistic home; henceforth his articles and book reviews appeared in that highly respected journal on an ever-growing scale.[10]

Miliukov had now crossed the boundary from student to specialist. To his surprise Vinogradov insisted that he specialize in European history, while it was Miliukov's clear aim to devote himself to Russian history. At the time he did not perceive the root of the trouble. It appeared only later that Kliuchevskii had not been eager to retain him. Vinogradov, as a loyal friend, had stepped into the breach. Somehow the matter was settled, however, and Miliukov was retained with a specialty in Russian history. As a candidate for the magister's degree, he could now abandon his private tutoring and begin secondary school teaching. His recommendations were excellent, and he secured two positions as a history teacher. The first was in the Moscow Fourth Gymnasium for Women, where he remained until 1894; not only his supervisors and inspectors but the daughters of the Moscow bourgeoisie were evidently satisfied with him. He also taught history at the Agricultural School on Smolensk Boulevard.

It was fortunate that Miliukov had this employment since he obviously would have starved as a *Privatdocent*, which he had become in

---

[10] The survey is *Glavnyia techeniia russkoi istoricheskoi mysli* (Moscow, 1897). The lecture appeared as "Iuridicheskaia shkola v russkoi istoriografii (Solov'ev, Kavelin, Chicherin, Sergeevskii)," RM, June, 1886. For a bibliography of Miliukov's printed works beginning with this article and ending in 1930, see B. Evreinov, "Bibliografiia pechatnykh trudov P. N. Miliukova," PNM, pp. 313–51.

1886. "I remember one semester," Miliukov told the Duma in 1914, "when my salary was ninety-eight kopecks. Seldom did it go beyond a few dozen rubles."[11] In 1896, for example, of the ninety-five *Privatdocents* at St. Petersburg University sixty did not receive even the three hundred rubles which constituted the standard student stipend, while eighteen received no pay at all. *Privatdocents* almost never taught required courses, and enrolment in the elective ones was very small. There was, in any case, a drop in the number of students attending the historical-philological faculty; it had decreased from 11 per cent of the university total in 1880 to 4 per cent in 1899. This was the result of the new university statute of 1884 which, in line with the classicism of the gymnasia, aimed to turn this faculty into a special school for classical languages, where history and literature would be only supplementary subjects.[12]

In the foreseeable future Miliukov would obviously not be rich, yet he decided to marry. He had met Anna Sergeevna Smirnova at the Kliuchevskiis. She had been Kliuchevskii's student at the Women's Courses, which she had now completed, and was working on a problem in Russian history suggested by the professor. Her father, Sergei K. Smirnov, was the rector of the Trinity Theological Academy, where Kliuchevskii taught Russian history two days a week. She came from a church-oriented family. Her brother was a priest, and five of her sisters married priests or theologians. But Anna Sergeevna, like Miliukov, was an individualist and had early in her life decided to live independently. She moved away from the family and supported herself by giving private piano lessons. The Kliuchevskiis had become her Moscow patrons, and the professor called her his "golden-haired girl."[13] He obviously approved of the match, and after a brief courtship the two were married in 1887.

The young couple first lived with Miliukov's mother, but this soon became impossible. His mother evidently disapproved of her son's choice, and the Miliukovs moved to a modest apartment in the Denezhnyi Pereulok. The literary specialist, Professor Nikolai I. Storozhenko with his family, lived in the same house, and this proved the beginning of a pleasant friendship. The Storozhenkos did a good deal of entertaining, and Miliukov became part of a group of university

[11] SO, Chetvertyi Sozyv, Sessiia II, Zasedanie 109, June 12, 1914, pp. 1138–39.
[12] P. Miliukov, "Universitety v Rossii," BE, LXVIII (1902), 797, 799.
[13] A. Zhikhareva, "Anna S. Miliukova," PN, April 5, 1935, p. 2.

people. He was accepted as a desirable ally in a circle to which he gave
the rather unflattering description of "moribund liberalism"; it was,
despite this, the only political position acceptable to him.[14] He was
not interested in the extremes on the Left and the Right and found
the mild professorial progressivism to his liking. There were the jur-
ists, like Ivan Ivanovich Ianzhul, Maksim M. Kovalevskii, and Sergei
Muromtsev. Nikolai V. Bugaev, dean of the mathematical faculty,
was a regular and disputatious visitor. Of the literary people there
was Viktor A. Gol'tsev, editor of *Russkaia Mysl'*, who introduced
Miliukov into that large literary and intellectual family. Konstantin
Bal'mont came to read his poetry, and Vladimir Solov'ev came to
philosophize. Andrei Belyi has left us a rather satirical portrait of
these Sunday afternoons. He was then the little boy Boren'ka (his
real name was Boris Bugaev, the son of the mathematician) who drew
much attention because of his popular father and his own precocious
talents. "My image of the Storozhenkos," he recalled, "was that they
were real windows to Europe." They subscribed to many Western
journals, which were displayed in the anteroom. The great symbolist
writer appreciated his host's kindness but had no respect for his literary taste. Of Storozhenko's monographs he observed, "I learned how
one should not write, and how one should not interpret literary phenomena." Even Miliukov, who had enjoyed the hospitality so much,
admitted of Belyi that "his observer's talent enabled him to note
much which was really ludicrous in that tiny universe of ours."[15] It
was tiny and perhaps a little pompous, but it was welcome to a
young *Privatdocent* who was just starting out.

IV

Storozhenko, that "real window to Europe," had also a hand in
introducing Miliukov to the art of book reviewing. He passed on to
the young historian his regular survey of Russian literature in the British weekly, *The Athenaeum*. Beginning with 1889, Miliukov wrote
the yearly survey until 1896. He thus made his modest European
debut. "This participation," he recalled, "was, so to speak, symbolic;
but it had major significance for me." It taught him, among other

[14] VOSP, I, 134.
[15] A. Belyi, *Na rubezhe dvukh stoletii* (Moscow, 1930), pp. 110, 119. VOSP, I, 133.

things, to pay attention to the way in which the Russian literature of his day concerned itself with the civic issues of the moment. "Politics," Miliukov discovered, "seeped through the literary forms."[16] It was significant that Miliukov should begin in a British journal; England would always remain his political model. Miliukov was following in a noble tradition by writing for *The Athenaeum*, where Alexander Herzen had made his English debut two decades earlier.

In his first article for the London journal, he recorded the death of the great satirist Mikhail Saltykov-Shchedrin, of whom he observed that "he was one of the most influential reflectors and directors of public opinion." Miliukov clearly preferred him to Gleb Uspenskii, "the idol of our youth. . . . [whose] artistic conception is generally excellent, but it is frequently spoilt by his subordinating it to his moralizing purposes."

But the *engagé* writers seemed to be dying out; the following year, 1890, Miliukov recorded the death of Nikolai Chernyshevskii, praising his "remarkable power of work, and his journalistic vigour." Individualism in literature was now in the ascendant, and, Miliukov complained, "every year the task of reviewing the literary movement of Russia grows more and more difficult." As examples of such individualism, Miliukov gave Leo Tolstoy's *Kreutzer Sonata* and Anton Chekhov's *A Melancholy Tale*. In plays, he complained, "the plot is generally based on adultery." Only in philosophy was a new and talented writer, Prince Sergei Trubetskoi, "preparing to found a system of his own."

Miliukov was more pessimistic in his review for 1891. "The barrenness of our literature," he wrote, "is merely a reflection of the emptiness of our daily life." He saw few prospects for his own generation: "The decade that recently came to a close presented most unfavorable conditions for the social development of the generation which has now attained the ages of twenty-five to thirty-five. . . . The generation which has just attained maturity . . . is remarkable for its premature senility and indifferentism." Fortunately, the situation was to change the same year. The famine of 1891 aroused the Russian public out of its lethargy, and Miliukov noted in his next review "a rise of the social temperature." The famine, he observed, had "called forth an interest in the people in circles and corners into which such

[16] *Ibid.*, I, 155.

sympathies could not have penetrated under normal conditions." He himself had attended several banquets to raise funds for the peasants and had observed with pleasure that even professors who normally remained aloof from politics could now be involved. Once aroused they could even be made to sign protests against the forcible removal from Moscow, in the same year, of some twenty thousand Jews.[17] In his 1893 review, Miliukov wrote that "the rise in the social temperature, which I recorded last year, continues unmistakably." For the first time since 1880 there was public debate. "The controversy between the liberals and the radicals," he reported, "seems to have occupied the attention of our larger public more than anything else."[18]

Miliukov was still to be found with the liberals, though most of his time was devoted to scholarly work. He had, after all, his various teaching jobs and the preparation of his dissertation. At home there were both sad and happy events. His mother died in Iaroslavl, without having made peace with her son and daughter-in-law and leaving behind no message other than some money for her burial. In 1889 Miliukov's first son, Nikolai, was born. There was great pleasure in the house and new contacts with Miliukov's younger brother who had small children of his own. The work at Moscow University was going well; Miliukov's classes were small, but his students were loyal. One of them, Alexander Kizevetter, later himself a prominent Moscow historian and Miliukov's political colleague, left us a description of the beginning teacher:

> Miliukov's lectures . . . made a strong impression because the lecturer introduced us to the current work in his laboratory. . . .
> He was young, and by no means experienced in public speaking.
> . . . Not infrequently he would blush deeply during a lecture. We found this appealing. The young lecturer became friendly with us, and soon we began to visit his apartment. . . . His modest quarters resembled the premises of a used-books dealer. One could not make a move without knocking into some book. . . . In such surroundings we spent many evenings in pleasant and interesting conversation.[19]

[17] VOSP, I, 162–63.

[18] Citations from the annual reviews are A, July 6, 1889, No. 3219, pp. 27–29; July 5, 1890, No. 3271, pp. 25–27; July 4, 1891, No. 3323, pp. 29–32; July 2, 1892, No. 3375, pp. 25–27; July 1, 1893, No. 3427, pp. 27–30.

[19] KIZ, p. 87.

But while Miliukov was popular with the students, his relationship with the sensitive Kliuchevskii did not improve. "Major trouble" began over a special Miliukov course on Russian colonization. It was no wonder since, according to Miliukov, it "thoroughly contradicted" Kliuchevskii's theory of a mass movement of the Russian population from south to north after Kievan times. Miliukov noticed "a certain coolness" toward himself on Kliuchevskii's part. He regretted this but stuck to his views: "I could not, of course, sacrifice my freedom of research," was his remark. The pleasant visits to the Kliuchevskii home and to their dacha near Podol'sk now came to an end.[20]

V

Miliukov had plunged heart and soul into research for his dissertation, to which he devoted a large part of the years 1886–92. He had decided to investigate Russia's economic history during the reign of Peter the Great. In choosing the economic approach, he was sensitive to the tenor of the times. "I began my investigation of the reform," he recalled, "at a time when historical materialism represented the fashion of the day." By choosing Peter he was also joining the debate between the Westernizers and the Slavophils, but he was doing it on his own terms: "It was my thesis," he claimed in his memoirs, "that Russia's Europeanization was not the product of borrowing, but an inevitable result of internal evolution, identical, in principle, in both Russia and Europe, but held back in Russia by the conditions of the environment."[21]

His archival work took him to St. Petersburg, where he spent two summers examining the unpublished records of the early eighteenth century and becoming acquainted with the capital's historians. They were divided into two groups. The larger, "official," school consisted of the young Sergei Platonov, Evgenii Shmurlo, Nikolai Pavlov-Sil'vanskii, and Alexander Lappo-Danilevskii. Of these Platonov was the most useful to Miliukov. He arranged for the publication of Miliukov's research results in the journal of the Ministry of Education; the

[20] VOSP, I, 136–38.
[21] See P. Miliukov, "Pierre le Grand et sa Reforme," Le Monde Slave (Paris), February, 1925, p. 163, and VOSP, I, 138.

monograph began to appear serially in September, 1890.²² The "left" group of Petersburg historians consisted of Vasilii Semevskii and his sole student, Venedikt Miakotin. Semevskii, who had been too outspoken on the peasant question, was refused a position at St. Petersburg University and defended his dissertation in Moscow. Eventually, he was appointed a *Privatdocent* at St. Petersburg but was not long after dismissed by the Minister of Education. Miliukov could do little more than sign an address of appreciation that was sent from Moscow. Miakotin, another historian of the peasantry, particularly in the Ukraine, and a Narodnik, also not acceptable to the regime, became a lifelong friend. When he came to work in the Moscow archives in the early 1890's, he lived with the Miliukovs. Through Miakotin, Miliukov gained entry to Narodnik circles, to their patriarch Nikolai Mikhailovskii and to their journal *Russkoe Bogatstvo*.²³

When Miliukov returned from St. Petersburg, loaded with his archival discoveries, he went eagerly to Kliuchevskii. But the master poured cold water on the researcher's enthusiasm and advised him to save his discoveries for the doctoral dissertation; the documents of one of the northern monasteries, he said, would be sufficient for the magister degree. It was only much later that Miliukov began to understand his professor's lack of sympathy. Kliuchevskii had never liked Peter and his successors and, throughout his life, preferred pre-Petrine history. In a most perceptive and warm essay written after his master's death, Miliukov said of Kliuchevskii: "While he feels 'at home' in the Moscow world, he is an 'alien' in that of Petersburg." It was not accidental that the "European" Vinogradov was Miliukov's best friend, while Kliuchevskii could not, and would not, become "European." A small incident illustrated this vividly. The famous Danish critic Georg Brandes came to Moscow for a series of lectures. A dinner was given in his honor to which Kliuchevskii was invited. But he did not speak foreign languages and, though pressed by several

²² The first installment of GOS appeared in *Zhurnal Ministerstva Narodnogo Prosveshcheniia* (St. Petersburg) in September, 1890; the last (ninth) installment in February, 1892. The revised work of some seven hundred pages appeared in book form in 1892. There was a second edition in 1905.

²³ M. Petrovich, "V. I. Semevskii, Russian Social Historian," in J. Curtiss (ed.), *Essays in Russian and Soviet History* (Leyden, 1963), p. 70. P. Miliukov, "Pamiati V. A. Miakotina," PN, October 8, 1937, p. 2.

guests, including Miliukov, would not speak to the famous visitor from the West. "I was terribly embarrassed for my teacher," recalled Miliukov.[24]

By February, 1892, the last instalment of Miliukov's work, entitled "Russia's State Economy in the First Quarter of the Eighteenth Century and Peter the Great's Reform," had appeared. It was now time for the public defense of the dissertation, which was set for May 17, 1892. Rumors of Kliuchevskii's disagreements with his foremost student had spread in the university, and the crowd was large. One eyewitness recalled that the students were on Miliukov's side and came to the dispute in a frame of mind hostile to Kliuchevskii. Miliukov's speech was very moderate in tone; he limited himself to a brief outline of his methods of research and a summary of his conclusions. Kliuchevskii spoke with reserve; this was evidently intentional and was to become his manner at all disputes. V. N. Speranskii, who knew Kliuchevskii well, recalled that the master did not like to give public recognition to his students and disapproved of those professors who did. Besides he evidently felt that his star pupil's nerves were excellent: "One could always feel assured and calm for Miliukov," he asserted.

"Your book," he began, "needs commentaries more than objections." A compliment as regards content, this was a reproach on the matter of form. Kliuchevskii, the masterful stylist, was doubtless offended by the heavy burden of Miliukov's statistics and the rather raw nature of his complex commentary. Pointing out various minor deficiencies, he ended his speech with the rather icy formula that the work "provides an adequate basis for the granting of the magister's degree." There had hardly been a question of that in anyone's mind. Miliukov's friends had hoped for more; since one of his elder colleagues had been granted the magister and doctor's degrees simultaneously, the same result was expected in Miliukov's case. This was Vinogradov's argument, but Kliuchevskii objected: let Miliukov write another dissertation for the doctor's degree, scholarship would only gain thereby. Following Kliuchevskii's speech, there was a brief debate which, the official chronicler noted, was led by Miliukov "with great

[24] See P. Miliukov, "V. O. Kliuchevskii," in V. O. Kliuchevskii, kharakteristiki i vospominaniia (Moscow, 1912), p. 206, and VOSP, I, 154–55.

tact and moderation," for which he was rewarded "by the friendly applause of a large public."[25]

The dispute was over. All of Miliukov's professors present congratulated him and embraced him as was the tradition. Kliuchevskii, in a very formal way, merely shook his hand. There was a party to celebrate the event, but Kliuchevskii was not invited. There seemed to be a formal break, but the two men were to become very good friends again. Nevertheless, the first seeds of doubt about a scholarly career may have been sown in Miliukov's mind. He was obviously offended by not having been granted the doctor's degree and swore that he would never seek that honor, though Platonov was prepared to arrange for the award at St. Petersburg University.[26] Something seems to have snapped in Miliukov's eagerness for the professor's calling. When he abandoned it for politics, the pain was minimal.

For the time being, regardless of Kliuchevskii's lack of enthusiasm, the world of scholarship had unquestionably gained by Miliukov's monograph. In a recent bibliographical survey, Nicholas Riasanovsky calls the book "one of the most famous and best argued interpretations of the entire reign of Peter the Great." An excerpt from the work is included in a 1963 anthology on Peter, seventy years after the book first saw the light of day. The Marxist historian Pokrovskii, no friend of Miliukov's, called the work "a superb book for its time." Moreover, the work plays a very important part in the development of Miliukov's conception of Peter's role. Over the years Miliukov's view of Peter's reforms was to undergo a change; as he became more "European," he was more willing to excuse Peter. In 1892 he had written that "Russia had been raised to the rank of a European power at the cost of the country's ruin." In 1925 he was far more conciliatory: "Not everything was justified at the time," he now felt, "but everything was justified by the subsequent march of events."[27]

[25] On the defense of the dissertation, see V. Maklakov, "Kliuchevsky," SEER, XIII (1935), 323; PNM, pp. 254–55; and V. Storozhev, "Istoricheskaia khronika," Istoricheskoe Obozrenie (St. Petersburg), V (1892), 198–215. The text of Miliukov's speech is in RM, July, 1892, pp. 57–66. The full text of Kliuchevskii's speech is in V. Kliuchevskii, Sochineniia, VIII (Moscow, 1959), 177–83. All of the book reviews of Miliukov's work are cited on the first page of Storozhev, loc. cit.

[26] VOSP, I, 142–46.

[27] Judgments of Miliukov's work are in reference to P. Horecky (ed.), Basic Russian Publications (Chicago, 1962), p. 78; M. Raeff (ed.), Peter the Great

VI

After six years of work on the thesis and the ordeal of the dispute, Miliukov felt in need of a vacation, and he took his family for a short visit to the Crimea. Gol'tsev of *Russkaia Mysl'* was in the same train and in Yalta proved to be a wonderful connoisseur of wines. The Miliukovs fell in love with the Black Sea coast; eventually they would buy some property there and become regular visitors. Upon their return to Moscow Miliukov, now liberated from the burden of the dissertation, felt freer to pay attention to the world outside the university. His work for *Russkaia Mysl'* alone would have kept another man busy enough. He was now in charge of the entire bibliographical section of the journal, while he personally reviewed all historical works on a monthly basis and wrote several articles. But the journal was, politically, more or less neutral, and his sympathies were definitely with the *Vestnik Evropy* ("Messenger of Europe"), the established organ of Russian liberalism. During the reign of Alexander III, it was this journal's "Public Chronicle" section which, he recalled, "unfolded before us the program of Russian liberalism from issue to issue with irresistible inner logic." Of the editor, Konstantin Arsen'ev, Miliukov remarked that he was "a European, and a Westernizer" who untiringly urged a return to the noble aims of the Great Reforms of the 1860's.[28]

Politically, these years (1892–96) were a rather peaceful interlude at the universities. Students were required to sign a statement that they would join no organization; their *zemliachestva* ("fraternities") of earlier days were now illegal. Nothing, however, could stop the young people from gathering under one pretense or another. A Moscovite of the time recalled a meeting during 1892 called to promote "co-operation between students and professors," though the ostensible purpose of the gathering was a dance. Those who could dance were made to do so in one room, while a discussion was held in another room in the presence of several professors, including A. I. Chuprov,

(Boston, 1963), pp. 32–34; and M. Pokrovskii, *Istoricheskaia nauka i bor'ba klassov*, I (Moscow, 1933), 206. Arcadius Kahan, who has done extensive work in Russian economic history, confirms my impression that Soviet scholars quote and use Miliukov's data with much respect to this day. Miliukov's own comments are from GOS, p. 546, and P. Miliukov "Pierre le Grand et sa Reforme," *Le Monde Slave* (Paris), February, 1925, p. 183.

[28] P. Miliukov, "K. K. Arsen'ev," PN, May 4, 1929, pp. 2–3.

I. I. Ianzhul, Vinogradov, and Miliukov. Vinogradov left after a
false alarm announcing the police, but Miliukov remained to argue
with the students until three in the morning. These debates were not
always friendly; another participant, enrolled in the medical faculty,
recalled a vehement dispute between Miliukov and a group of young
Marxists, led by D. P. Kalafati, who were critical of Miliukov's views
on Russia's historical development.[29]

In addition to such secretive gatherings, Miliukov also developed
his views from a public forum. On January 22, 1893, he lectured in
the large auditorium of Moscow's Historical Museum on "The Dissolution of Slavophilism." The movement, he thought, had not yet
died in Moscow, and he wished to expose its unsuitability for the
present. Vinogradov had lectured from the same platform a year earlier on the Slavophil Ivan Kireevskii. Thus Vinogradov and Miliukov,
the two "Europeans," presented views opposed to those who ideal-
ized Russia's past. Though the lecture was a historical survey, Miliukov made topical references to the Westernizers who had now
given way to "democratic liberalism of the newest type." Even the
Slavophils had been unable to do without Europe; their intellectual
roots lay in European Romanticism. Miliukov included the philosopher Vladimir Solov'ev among the Slavophils; the latter objected wittily against being counted in that company, though he
agreed with Miliukov about the ultimate fate of the doctrine.[30]

Miliukov was becoming known in wider circles, and soon an unex-
pected honor came his way: he was invited to a discussion with Leo
Tolstoy. The great writer had begun to summon various Moscow per-
sonalities to question them about their beliefs and theories. Thus,
Professor Chuprov was invited to talk about political economy, and
Miliukov's gymnasium colleague, Stepan F. Fortunatov, was asked to

[29] V. Eliashevich, "Iz vospominanii starogo moskovskogo studenta," *Pamiati
russkogo studenchestva: Sbornik vospominanii* (Paris, 1934), pp. 106–14; S.
Mitskevich, *Revolutsionnaia Moskva, 1888–1905* (Moscow, 1940), p. 138.

[30] P. Miliukov, "Razlozhenie slavianofilstva (Danilevskii, Leont'ev, Vl. Solov'ev),"
Voprosy Filosofii i Psikhologii (Moscow), 1893, No. 3, pp. 46–96; reprinted in
P. Miliukov, *Iz istorii russkoi inteligentsii* (St. Petersburg, 1903), pp. 266–306,
which also includes (pp. 307–8) Miliukov's reply to Vladimir Solov'ev. Also V.
Solov'ev, "Zamechaniia na lektsiiu P. N. Miliukova," *Sobranie sochinenii V. A.
Solov'eva*, V (St. Petersburg, n.d.), 458–62. See also N. Skif (pseud.), "G.
Miliukov i slavianofilstvo," *Russkii Vestnik* (St. Petersburg), CCLXXXIII (1903),
No. 1, 269–317.

provide historical facts about the life of Jesus and Buddha. Miliukov
was to discuss theories of history, a rather large order to be sure. Many
years later he described his first personal encounter with Tolstoy:

> I recollect having had once a two hours' debate with him in his
> poorly furnished mansard room in his house at Khamovniki. He
> wished me to talk to him—not politics, which he abhorred—but
> science, and the theory of evolution. He listened very attentively,
> discussing the details. Then we were asked to tea, downstairs, in
> the well-furnished drawing room. Tolstoy took a tart and a knife,
> and summed up our discussion the following way: "This is what
> your science is: if I wish, I will cut the tart like this, or, if I wish,
> I will cut it like that."

This left Miliukov somewhat bewildered, and he concluded: "I saw
then that I would never understand Tolstoy."[31]

Miliukov's first year of university teaching was drawing to a close.
Unexpectedly, the dissertation brought tangible fruit: it had been
submitted for the Sergei Solov'ev Prize and had won, bringing in a
fairly substantial sum of money. The Miliukovs could do what they
wished: they decided to spend the summer of 1893 in France. Miliukov had made friends with the French Slavists, Jules Legras and
Paul Boyer. The Miliukovs went to the coast of Brittany, not far from
Brest and had a relaxing time by the sea. In Paris Miliukov met Peter
Lavrov; it was his first and last encounter with the famous philosopher
and ideologue of Russian populism. He could hardly foresee that he
would be jailed for an outspoken speech in honor of Lavrov's memory
a few years later. Mikhail Dragomanov, the leader of the Ukrainian
national movement, was also in Paris and made a deep impression on
Miliukov.[32]

Before returning to Russia, Miliukov paid a short visit to England.
He had become interested in the English experience of university
extension and home reading, methods of bringing education to a
wider audience outside the schools, particularly in the provinces. His
attention had been drawn to the matter in Moscow by Elizaveta N.
Orlova, the Russian pioneer of the movement. She provided him with
letters of recommendation to people in Cambridge, where he was to

[31] VOSP, I, 153–54; P. Miliukov, "Leo Tolstoy and the Russian People," *The
New Russia* (London), III, No. 45, (December 9, 1920), 459.
[32] VOSP, I, 146–48.

observe the summer extension courses in operation. He noted that not
everyone was in favor of the program: a debate in the University
Union on the topic "that extension courses are undesirable" suggested
that more than half of those present agreed with the motion. He also
discovered that the Cambridge working class displayed a very negative
attitude toward the movement, though it had been one of the movement's original aims to attract workers in large numbers. Workers'
participation, he reported, remained "the most painful question" of
university extension. And yet, he concluded, it was in Russia, "more
than anywhere else," that this movement was needed.[33]

VII

Miliukov was evidently eager to break out of the confines of teaching and an occasional debate to greater activity on behalf of his ideals.
Russia, he told his *Athenaeum* readers, was suffering from two ills:

> Misrule and ignorance—these are the principal plagues of con-
> temporary Russia. For this reason the reign of legality in all
> branches of life and a wide diffusion of popular education have
> become aims for which people of the most diversified opinions
> are uniting.[34]

Economic ills, it should be noted, are not listed by Miliukov. He was
well aware of them and wrote about them, as we shall see in another
connection; but in his own program of action the political and cultural factors played the first role. It was to remain thus throughout his
political life. For the time being, he would let "the reign of legality"
rest, while concentrating on what he knew best—education. This, he
probably thought, would arouse a minimum amount of interference
from the authorities. In this hope he was disappointed, but at first all
went well with the Moscow action to promote home education.

It was launched immediately after Miliukov's return from England.
He recruited some of his university friends for the work—Vinogradov, Storozhenko, Chuprov, Veselovskii. After a private campaign of
persuasion, Miliukov and Orlova called a meeting in the large hall of
the Moscow Polytechnical Museum. The flower of the city's intelligentsia was present, and a four-year program of reading courses was
approved. Those who agreed to serve as consultants included Nikolai

---

[33] P. Miliukov, "Letnii universitet v Anglii," MB, May, 1894, pp. 194–206.
[34] A, July 6, 1895, No. 3532, p. 24.

Umov in physics, Mikhail Menzbir in zoology, Lev Lopatin in philosophy, Storozhenko in literature, Chuprov in the social sciences, and Vinogradov and Miliukov in history. The Moscow publisher Sytin agreed to produce a series of textbooks, the "Self-Education Library," to begin with four volumes. Through the efforts of Orlova, the organization—called the Commission for the Organization of Home Reading—received the sponsorship of a technological institution patronized by one of the Grand Dukes. With such an exalted protector there would be no trouble from the authorities.

Miliukov was charged with supervising the preparation of the first-year handbooks. They were all delivered on schedule, except the one on physics: Professor Umov complained that he had no time. Miliukov was not to be defeated so easily. He went to Umov's house with pencil and paper, asked questions for several hours, took diligent notes, and left with an outline which saved the day. Once the handbooks were ready and printed (the text totaled thirteen-hundred pages of small print) the first contacts with future readers were made. The results were heartening. By the end of 1895 the Commission's program had 382 subscribers; there were 585 in 1899. By then over four-thousand books had been sent to subscribers. Almost 60 per cent of the subscribers lived in rural areas, where educational opportunities were least available. Fifty libraries bought the Commission's books. The proportion of women (27 per cent) among subscribers was lower than in England, but workers were still absent from the list. This was obviously not a program for the wide masses of the population. But the Moscow example was catching, and similar commissions were founded in St. Petersburg, Kazan, Odessa, Kharkov, and Kiev.[35]

So far the authorities had not disturbed the Commission; its activities were innocent enough as long as they were restricted to correspondence courses. For long after Miliukov's enforced departure from Moscow, the Commission continued its useful work and Orlova published a journal until 1909. In his recent memoirs Soviet Acad-

---

[35] The commission's full title was Kommissiia po Organizatsii Domashnego Chteniia, Sostoiashchaia pri Uchebonom Otdele Obshchestva Razprostranenia Tekhnicheskikh Znanii. Its beginnings are described in KIZ, pp. 287–94. For additional data on the Moscow commission, see two articles by Miliukov: "Razprostranenie universitetskogo obrazovania v Anglii, Amerike i Rossii," RB, 1896, No. 3, pp. 79–121, and "University Extension," BE, LXVIII (1902), 803–9. See also "Kommissia po Organizatsii Domashnego Chteniia v Moskve," MB, May, 1894, pp. 231–36.

emician N. M. Druzhinin recalled how useful the Commission's work had been to him in 1904:

> I made extensive use of the *Programs of Home Reading*, that unique attempt by progressive figures . . . to create some sort of correspondence university open to the people. The recommended readings and test questions in this publication greatly assisted my independent reading both prior to and during my university course.[36]

Not satisfied with mere correspondence courses, Miliukov now proposed to undertake a more daring enterprise. A lecture series was offered to any provincial center to ask for it. This would help accomplish the true purpose of university extension which, in Miliukov's words, was "the democratization of higher education, an attempt to bring the universities closer to the people, and to make education the possession of the entire nation, and the task of a whole lifetime." The lecture series would also employ young *Privatdocents* who, as Miliukov knew from bitter experience, spent years getting degrees while giving private lessons to earn their daily bread.[37]

The Commission's new activity was likely to arouse the vigilance of the authorities. Miliukov and his colleagues, however, had been emboldened by the events of the day. The reactionary Alexander III had died on October 20, 1894; and the public expected a change in the political temperature. As Miliukov told his *Athenaeum* readers: "We do not know whether we are on the eve of reforms, of reactionary measures, or of a regime of no principles."[38] The Commission took a chance, and Miliukov was used as a guinea pig. In November, 1894, he gave a course of six public lectures in Nizhnii Novgorod on "Social Trends since Catherine II." A member of the audience recalled that the very title astounded the provincial town; such words had not been used publicly before. The Nobility Hall was packed every evening, and the applause was deafening. All of local "society" was there, from the deputy-governor, Chaikovskii (brother of the composer), to dozens of gymnasium students who could find only standing room. Two persons who refrained from applause were the bishop, whose social

---

[36] M. Druzhinin, "Recollections and Thoughts of a Historian," *The Soviet Review* (New York), IV (1963), No. 1, 25. The journal was *Kriticheskoe Obozrenie* (Moscow, 1907–9), edited by B. A. Kistiakovskii.

[37] P. Miliukov, "Razprostranenie . . .," RB, 1896, No. 3, pp. 79, 114–18.

[38] A, July 6, 1895, No. 3532, p. 24.

station did not permit it, and the colonel of the gendarmerie who was, for good reason, all ears. The text of the lectures is not available, but they dealt with such explosive figures of the Russian past as Nikolai Novikov, Alexander Radishchev, the Decembrists, and Alexander Herzen. Miliukov had overstepped the boundaries of the politically permissible. He was to hear of the consequences in a few weeks. Poor Chaikovskii, for his applause, failed to get his promotion, while the bishop had some difficulties for having been present at all. The colonel was soon made general because he had been properly watchful.[39]

VIII

Miliukov returned to Moscow with no knowledge that his days in the old capital were numbered. Soon he would be exiled to the provinces, then abroad; he would not again live permanently in his native city or teach at his university. Immediately upon his return there was trouble at Moscow University; on December 1 Kliuchevskii made a speech commemorating Alexander III as the tsar of peace. The students, who expected criticism of the monarch they hated, showed their displeasure too loudly. The police made many arrests and exiled fifty-five persons. Miliukov joined in editing a petition of professors on behalf of the students. It was a futile gesture and gave the authorities further ammunition against Miliukov. Then another group of students was arrested for a campaign against the existing university statute. The investigation disclosed that the students had been in touch with Miliukov. He was also in demand as chairman of debates between Narodnik and Marxist student groups. The future Socialist Revolutionary leader, Viktor Chernov, since 1892 a student in the law faculty, wanted Miliukov to write a pamphlet on behalf of the Narodniks, to be distributed illegally. Miliukov, whom the police would accuse of exercising "a harmful influence" on students, wondered with amusement "who had had a harmful influence on whom?"[40]

On January 17, 1895, the new emperor, Nicholas II, told a delegation of zemstvo leaders: "I shall maintain the principle of autocracy

[39] The incident is described in I. Demidov, "P. N. Miliukov kak uchitel'," PNM, pp. 154-55.

[40] L. Tikhomirov, Vospominaniia (Moscow, 1927), p. 499; KIZ, pp. 244-46; V. Chernov, Zapiski Sotsialista-Revoliutsionera (Berlin, 1922), pp. 172-75; and VOSP, I, 162.

just as firmly and unflinchingly as did my unforgettable father." The hopes of some zemstvo men that their voice might be heard were, in the Emperor's famous phrase, "senseless dreams."[41] It was as if Nicholas were speaking to Miliukov also; two of the tsar's ministers now took action against him. The Minister of Education dismissed Miliukov from all his teaching posts and forbade his employment in any educational institution. The Minister of Interior ordered his exile from Moscow for two years, with the privilege of choosing the provincial town in which he wished to reside. The Nizhnii Novgorod colonel had done his job well, and the secret police had put Miliukov under observation as a man "politically highly suspect, and with harmful influence on student youth."[42]

On February 23, 1895, Miliukov was informed that he was to leave Moscow immediately. His wife and children (he now had a second son) were to follow him in due course to Riazan', which he had chosen as the provincial capital closest to Moscow. His numerous friends made every attempt to guarantee him a steady income. The newspaper *Russkiia Vedomosti* gave him a monthly salary as a correspondent; the monthly *Mir Bozhii* contracted to print Miliukov's *Outlines of Russian Culture* serially. *Russkaia Mysl'* gave him a farewell banquet, at which his old friend Gol'tsev predicted that Miliukov would become the historian of the autocracy's downfall.

When Miliukov arrived at the railroad station, the platform was filled with young people who had come to see him off. (This demonstration would only add weight to the police charge of "harmful influence" on youth, though Miliukov was this time entirely innocent in the matter.) Even the young gymnasium ladies were there, despite the strict prohibition of the directress. Miliukov's friends were more upset by his enforced departure than the victim himself; while they saw his exile as a catastrophe, Miliukov recalled leaving "with a feeling of some sort of liberation. . . . I had long ago overstepped the boundaries of the university because they had become too narrow for me."[43] Not only had Kliuchevskii effectively blocked his university career, but Miliukov had become interested in the world outside academic circles. That world was soon to absorb him altogether.

<hr>

[41] The speech is partially printed in G. Fischer, *Russian Liberalism* (Cambridge, Mass., 1958), pp. 74–75.

[42] Quoted in an Okhrana report of August, 1897, OKH.

[43] VOSP, I, 164–67, has an account of Miliukov's exile from Moscow.

2: FROM SCHOLAR TO POLITICIAN

> The years 1895–1905 were a turning point in my life and career.[1]
>
> Abroad I became an observer of the political life and the foreign policies of the democratic countries. At home events were taking place which demanded the application of these observations—and demanded them particularly from me, as there were very few Russian observers. . . . I could take comfort from the fact that, in my case, observations on the life of the advanced democracies were combined with premises acquired in the study of Russian history. The former pointed out the goal, the latter determined the limits of possible achievements.[2]

I

Riazan' was to be Miliukov's home from February, 1895, to early spring, 1897. It turned out to be a rather pleasant and productive exile. His old friends and former students came to visit from nearby Moscow. Riazan' society opened its doors to him, and he acquired new friends among the local zemstvo and archive employees. He now had more time for music and played first violin in the local quartet. When the group gave concerts outside the province, the governor gave his consent to the exile's travel. Miliukov acquired a new passion —archaeology—and found plenty to excavate in the neighborhood. The local archaeologists appreciated their new collaborator and made him their delegate to Russia's Tenth Archaeological Congress in Riga. The family lived in a pleasant house, to which Miliukov moved his substantial library. Here, in the quiet of his study, with a view of a large garden and orchard, he had the leisure to write some of his best works.[3]

Of the lesser ones, surely the most charming was a series of feuille-

[1] ROK, VIII–IX, 108.
[2] VOSP, I, 255.
[3] Ibid., I, 166–68.

tons for *Russkiia* Vedomosti. These were devoted to the affairs of the heart of Nikolai Stankevich, Vissarion Belinsky, and Alexander Herzen, and gave a touching picture of these young "idealists," as Miliukov called them, of the 1830's. The sketches were skilfully woven from the correspondence of his three subjects and breathed sympathy, delicacy of feeling, and perception. They belong to the very best written on these men. Miliukov was proving his ability to read human feelings.[4]

Romantic love did not make Miliukov forget current Russian politics, which he described for *Athenaeum* readers. In 1895 he noted that the Populists "are losing their intellectual supremacy more and more, and are becoming a sharply defined separate group." The Russian Marxists, on the other hand, were gaining new popularity. Of these he singled out Peter Struve, his future colleague in the Kadet party: "Struve," he noted, "has many partisans among our young men, especially in the provinces." In 1896 Miliukov told his English readers about George Plekhanov, the leader of Russian Marxism who had just published, under the pseudonym of Volgin, an attack on the Populist leader Vorontsov. "Volgin," he noted, was "the hero of the day."

> The old facts and experiences, supplied in part by Vorontsov, are handled with great skill to prove that our village commune as well as our home industries, the principal forms of popular industrialism in the opinion of the Populists, have already actually been drawn into that very process of "capitalist development" against which they were to act as a barrier, according to the Populist programme. . . . Once you have proven that within the village commune neither our home industries nor our agriculture can become the bases for new collectivist forms of society . . . all interest in them disappears. The collectivists of the future must again be sought in the town and the factory.[5]

These lines summarize not only the conflicts of the nineties but the future of party alignments in Russia in which Miliukov would take active part.

Himself neither a Populist nor a Marxist, Miliukov now turned to work which, though historical in nature, was to touch upon con-

---

[4] "Liubov u idealistov tridtsatykh godov" appeared in RV, in 1895–96; reprinted in P. Miliukov, *Iz istorii russkoi intelligentsii* (St. Petersburg, 1903), pp. 73–168.

[5] A, July 6, 1895, No. 3532, p. 25; July 4, 1896, No. 3584, p. 26.

temporary Russian issues to a much greater extent than his earlier monographs. In 1895 began to appear his *Outlines of Russian Culture* (*Ocherki po istorii russkoi kul'tury*), a unique work of historical synthesis. Russian historians had heretofore not considered it possible or desirable to analyze the present along with the past; Miliukov, to some extent "expelled" from the profession, felt free to be present-minded. He was no longer an academic; in the *Ocherki* he saw himself as "an intermediary between specialized scholarship and the broad circles of the educated public." The goal of the book, which grew to three large volumes, was "to communicate to the reader those *basic* processes and phenomena which characterize Russian social evolution." "Cultural" history, in Miliukov's eyes, "encompasses all aspects of internal history: economic, social, political, intellectual, moral, religious and esthetic."[6]

In these statements we have the Miliukov of the extension movement. The *Ocherki* were, in fact, his personal contribution to the popular education campaign which had led to his being in Riazan' in the first place. Unable to conduct the campaign in person, he launched it from his historian's desk. The *Ocherki* had their origin in an invitation extended to Miliukov in 1892 to give a series of lectures on the history of Russian culture for the Moscow Pedagogical Courses. His models for this work of "popularization" were the books of the Englishman Donald Mackenzie Wallace and the Frenchman Anatole Leroy-Beaulieu. Both had written books on Russia which, Miliukov noted, "made the strongest impression on me, particularly Leroy-Beaulieu." The structure of the *Ocherki* was modeled on the four volumes of François Guizot, *Histoire de la Civilisation en France*.[7] The lithographed text of the lectures fell into the hands of the geologist Valerian Agafonov, a popularizer of science who had published a very successful work, *The Past and Present of the Earth*. It was he who chose the title for Miliukov's work and arranged for its serial publication in *Mir Bozhii*.[8]

This "thick journal" had become the organ of the Legal Marxists, particularly Peter Struve and Mikhail Tugan-Baranovskii. Miliukov, who had earlier written for the liberal *Russkaia Mysl'* and the Populist

[6] O, I, 3, 18; emphasis in the original.
[7] VOSP, I, 160.
[8] P. Miliukov, "Segodniashnemu iubiliariu," PN, February 24, 1939, p. 2.

Russkoe Bogatstvo, was now, in some minds, identified with the Russian Marxists. Since much of the first volume of the *Ocherki* dealt
with Russia's economic structure ("In the first part of the *Ocherki*,"
wrote Miliukov in the second volume, "we assigned a significant role
to the economic factor[9]"), it was easy to see why this misunderstanding arose. The censors, for their part, were baffled and assigned Miliukov to the camp of "economic materialism," as they had with Leo
Tolstoy. M. P. Solov'ev, head of the Ministry of Interior's press department, wrote the minister in 1897: "Marxism reaches out [*podaet
ruku*] to the so-called economic materialism which pretends to be a
basic principle for the study of history, and of which our chief expo-
nents are Count L. Tolstoy, Professors Miliukov, Erisman, Andrei A.
Isaev, and others."[10]

In fact, Miliukov was of another persuasion. "Economic materialism," he wrote in the *Ocherki*, "is destined to play an important, but
a temporary role."[11] In his dissertation, as in the first volume of the
Ocherki, he was merely a pioneer of Russian economic history. It
should be noted that Tugan-Baranovskii's basic history of Russian
industrialism appeared only in 1898. An attentive reading of the
Ocherki would have shown that Miliukov was not impressed by economic determinism. The economic base, in his eyes, did not deter-
mine the superstructure, at least not in his homeland. "In Russia,"
he wrote, "the State had an enormous influence on the social organization, whereas in the West the social organization determined the
State structure." The second volume of the *Ocherki* must finally have
disappointed those who counted Miliukov among the *Mir Bozhii*
school. Here Miliukov spoke of the Russian church and school and
affirmed that "the evolution of the so-called 'spiritual' needs has its
own inner natural development [*zakonomernost'*]."[12]

Throughout the *Ocherki* he was concerned with Russia's place in
European history. Was her development unique, or was she destined
to follow the Western pattern? Miliukov took a stand between the
Slavophils (or the "nationalists," as he called them) and the Westernizers. "In all spheres of life," he wrote,

[9] O, II, 4.
[10] Quoted in V. Polianskii (ed.), "Marksistskaia periodicheskaia pechat' 1896–
1906 gg.," KA, No. 9 (1925), p. 258.
[11] O, II, 4.
[12] O, I, 133–34; II, 5.

our historical development proceeds in the same direction as it has proceeded everywhere in Europe. This does not mean that it will carry us, in every detail, to identical results; but then we do not find such identical results among the various states of the West—each one of them represents major variations.[13]

Russia did belong to Europe, then, but she would not copy the West. Rather she would develop her modern life from that of her past. But she must be free to do this, and the last sentence of the first volume of the *Ocherki* calls for "the creation of a new Russian cultural tradition corresponding to contemporary social ideals."[14] Miliukov was to discuss these ideals in the third volume of his work, which appeared only after the turn of the century.

II

By the end of 1896 the prolonged administrative investigation of Miliukov's "crimes" ended, and a verdict was ready: one year of jail in distant Ufa. Just then an invitation arrived from Bulgaria to fill the teaching position left vacant by the death of Mikhail Dragomanov. Miliukov's wife began a campaign in the ministries: if the official goal was to remove her husband temporarily from the scene, allow him to accept the Sofia position. Anna Sergeevna and her friends were successful, and the verdict was changed to two years of "exile abroad." It was a masked permission to teach ancient and Slavic history to Bulgarian youth. The police made Miliukov sign a statement that he would not engage in political activities, and he was free to go. It was the spring of 1897, and his teaching was to begin that autumn.[15]

Since Russia was now closed to him for two years and since he wished to prepare his lectures in a good library, Miliukov went to Paris. Several years before he had met Dragomanov there. The Bulgarians, evidently, had heard of him from Dragomanov, and they calculated that a scholar in provincial exile would respond to their invitation. Miliukov settled in Paris for a few months of research. While he stayed in Jules Legras' apartment on the Boulevard Port Royal, his family spent the summer in Switzerland. Miliukov joined them

[13] O, I, 272.
[14] *Ibid.*, I, 275.
[15] VOSP, I, 169; OKH, 1897 report.

for a few days of sightseeing, and then all four left for their new home in exile. The Bulgarian authorities made every effort to make their stay pleasant. Miliukov's salary was higher than that received by Bulgarian professors, and he feared resentment. But he was met with great friendliness and curiosity. He had learned some Bulgarian, and though he lectured in Russian he could chat with his students in their native language and understand their questions. Most Bulgarian textbooks were Russian books, and the director of the only public library in Sofia, filled with Russian works, was a Russian émigré. Miliukov met the Bulgarian professor, Ivan Shishmanov, who was married to Dragomanov's daughter, and through him made many new friends.[16]

Miliukov's Bulgarian teaching career came to an abrupt end. He had disregarded his promise not to engage in political activities. He forgot that even in Bulgaria there were Russian police agents who observed him. He had made friends with several Bulgarian oppositional figures, including Alexander Malinov, leader of the Democratic party.[17] Even worse was his correspondence with Russian revolutionaries in London; he sent contributions to the London Fund of the Free Russian Press, founded, decades earlier, by Alexander Herzen. The Okhrana intercepted a letter to Miliukov from Nikolai V. Chaikovskii, the leader of the People's Will, who asked Miliukov for articles on Russia to be printed by the Free Russian Press. Chaikovskii told Miliukov that he had been offered Dragomanov's chair "at the suggestion of our comrades" because he had opposed the Russian regime. "It would be more than pleasant for us," wrote Chaikovskii, "if you would take part in our publication. We are sure that you will regard this work in the same way as we do.[18] It was an invitation to continue in Herzen's footsteps. Miliukov sent only money, no articles.

Then he committed a new "crime," for which he was made to pay. On December 6, 1897, the Russian colony in Sofia celebrated the Emperor's birthday. Miliukov made the concession of going to the official church services but failed to visit the residence of the Russian agent in Sofia, IU. P. Bakhmetev. This was interpreted as an insult to the Emperor, and Bakhmetev, in an official note to the Bulgarian authorities, demanded Miliukov's dismissal from his post. The Bul-

[16] VOSP, I, 170–73.
[17] P. Miliukov, "Pamiati A. P. Malinova," PN, March 24, 1938, p. 2.
[18] OKH, 1897 report, undated copy.

garians offered some resistance, but Bakhmetev enlisted the help of St. Petersburg. Sofia did not wish to endanger her relations with Russia and yielded. Bakhmetev had his way.

The Bulgarians, however, were generous and paid Miliukov's salary for the entire year. He had come to like the small Slavic country. He would devote the rest of his exile from Russia to the study of Bulgaria, particularly of her foreign relations. This was the beginning of Miliukov's lifetime preoccupation with foreign policy, particularly in the Balkans. It was 1897, the year of an important agreement between Russia and Austria providing for the maintenance of the status quo in the Balkans. Few in Russia were well enough informed on the problems of that peninsula. On the spot and with the means and leisure to analyze the problem, Miliukov began by a study of Macedonia, contested for by Bulgaria, Serbia, and Greece, and always in the forefront of any Balkan disturbance.

To visit Macedonia, then under Turkish administration, without exciting suspicion, Miliukov proposed to do some archeological excavations there. He made a visit to Constantinople and was granted the patronage of the local Russian archeological institute. Its director, the famous Byzantinist F. I. Uspenskii, obtained for Miliukov official permission for the digging; half the finds were to be turned over to the Ottoman Museum. Having learned some Turkish and modern Greek, Miliukov was ready in June, 1898, for his first expedition into the Macedonian hinterland.[19] It began in the city of Bitola, somewhat north of the present Greco-Yugoslav border. Miliukov was accompanied by a whole caravan, consisting of the Russian consul, Rostkovskii, two armed Turkish soldiers with rifles, a photographer, a cook, Bulgarian servants, and portable beds and other equipment. Miliukov was not used to horseback riding, and he must have been quite exhausted by the steady mountain climbing of some ten hours every day.

Crossing into Albania, they reached Korce, an area where life was dominated by violence and feuds; even ploughmen went to their fields with rifles over their shoulder. Miliukov was expected to eat elaborate meals without knives and forks and heard his Albanian host complain that he could not leave his fortified house because of numerous blood feuds against him. The population of two Bulgarian villages asked Miliukov when Russia would liberate them from the Turkish yoke;

[19] VOSP, I, 173–76.

he let the counsul handle that particular question. Turning north to Lake Okhrid they came to villages where the inhabitants had never seen matches and had not the slightest notion of Russia's existence or its location. Returning to Bitola for a short rest, Miliukov started on a second expedition, north to Skoplje. The roads were beyond belief; as Miliukov remarked, "bad roads contribute to the permanence of the Turkish Empire." In two days of riding the caravan did not meet a single traveler.

The last leg of the journey was made by train. Miliukov arrived in Skoplje during a Serbo-Bulgarian incident. Bulgarian students were throwing rocks at Serbian women teachers. Such outbreaks, Miliukov was told, took place at least once a month. Though Bulgarians represented the vast majority of the city's population, the Serbs were beginning to exert influence through their schools. The Turks, with their policy of divide and rule, were glad to assist the weaker party. Nevertheless, Miliukov came away with a good deal of respect for the Turkish administrators who, he discovered, were often more honest than the Christian population of these regions. As for Russia's diplomatic agents in the Balkans, Miliukov found them poorly informed.[20]

Coming from Sofia, Miliukov was considered a Bulgarophile and he thus found Serbian leaders distrustful or hostile. But his aim in Macedonia had been a fact-finding one, and he later defended himself against charges of partiality. "I have never been and never will be," he wrote, "a friend of the Bulgarian nation against the Serbian, or of the Serbian against the Bulgarian." He thought of Macedonia as an end in itself, not a means of domination in the Balkans. If the happiness of the Macedonian people was the aim, then, he wrote, "I have the right to judge which of these means, the Bulgarian or the Serbian, better serve the realization of this aim."[21]

His experiences in the Balkans were valuable to him in Russia later. One of the more concrete results of his trip was a small atlas of Macedonian ethnography, which he published in 1900 and which brought together all the available evidence gathered by the disputants and French and other Western observers. His two years of exile were ending and he telegraphed for permission to return to Russia. This

---

20 P. Miliukov, "Pis'ma iz Makedonii," RV, January 7, 1899; January 15, 1899; January 21, 1899; February 5, 1899; and March 2, 27, 1899.
21 P. Miliukov, "Pis'mo v redaktsiu," RV, 1900, No. 356.

obtained, he made his way to the 1899 Archaeological Congress in
Kiev. From there he and his family proceeded to St. Petersburg.[22]

III

Four years earlier Miliukov had been expelled from Moscow. Henceforth he was to live in St. Petersburg, with its more active political
life. A scholarly career was closed to him, and his recent past was now
determining his future. "Exile," he wrote, "fixed my public reputation
as a politician of a particular orientation; a number of consequences
followed from this."[23] One of these was that he joined the editorial
board of *Mir Bozhii*, which had so successfully promoted his *Ocherki*.
By 1899 the first volume was in its third edition, and the second in
its second edition. The third volume was appearing in the journal;
there had been a German translation in 1898.[24] The book and the
editorial work were bringing in income, which was supplemented by
Miliukov's participation, as coeditor with S. N. Iushakov of the
Bol'shaia Entsiklopediia, a Russian version of the famous German
Meyers Lexikon. It was to be a popular encyclopedia, in contrast to
the more serious work of Brokgauz-Efron for which Miliukov had
written several lengthy and scholarly articles beginning in 1895.
Iushakov proved an uncongenial partner, however, and Miliukov
withdrew from the project in its early stages.[25]

The work for *Mir Bozhii* went well at first. If the censor's description of the journal was accurate, it would seem to have been ideal for
Miliukov. "In its orientation," wrote the censor, "it is a liberal journal, attempting, as far as this is possible for a publication subject to
the censorship, to criticize the contemporary political structure and
to adhere to the principles of cosmopolitanism."[26] With sixteen thousand subscribers, it was Russia's most widely read journal. Miliukov
worked in both the political and fiction departments.[27] All went well

[22] VOSP, I, 184–88. The atlas is P. Miliukov, *Piat etnograficheskikh kart
Makedonii* (St. Petersburg, 1900).
[23] VOSP, I, 188.
[24] P. Miliukov, *Skizzen russischer Kulturgeschichte* (Leipzig, 1898).
[25] The *Bol'shaia Entsiklopediia* appeared in St. Petersburg in twenty-two volumes from 1900 to 1909. For Miliukov's articles in it, see Evreinov's bibliography,
PNM, pp. 322, 325, 326.
[26] KA, No. 18 (1926), p. 179.
[27] O. Gruzenberg, "Staromu drugu," PNM, p. 182.

at first, but then disagreements arose with the chief editor, Angel
I. Bogdanovich. A former member of the People's Will he had become a "Legal Marxist" and apparently disagreed with Miliukov on
many issues. Miliukov withdrew from the journal, which, however,
continued to print his *Ocherki* until 1905.[28]

Marxism, even when "Legal," was evidently too strong a medicine
for him. Though certainly not a Populist, Miliukov felt more at home
with the *Russkoe Bogatstvo* group, where he had his personal friend
Miakotin. Though he did not write or work for the journal, he appreciated its "arduous efforts to steer a middle course between the Scylla
of Marxism and the Charybdis of Populism."[29] It was in that middle
region that Miliukov himself was operating; his reputation, however,
continued to be more radical than his actual beliefs, particularly
among the students. Again they invited him to their meetings, and
again this led to trouble with the police. But, he told his American
readers in 1905, "to be branded as a political criminal by the police
is a mark of distinction, gradually becoming a quite necessary qualifi-
cation for everybody who claims to advocate liberal public opinion."[30]

The secret police reported that he frequented meetings where
"exclusively radical youth debated and defended revolutionary programs."[31] Then in December, 1900, he was asked to chair and speak
at an illegal meeting in the Mining Institute in honor of the People's
Will leader, Peter Lavrov, who had died that year in Paris. Miliukov
traced the history of the Russian revolutionary movement since the
seventies. The secret agent present must have noted his conclusion
that "any revolutionary movement which fails to reach its goal ends
in terror." Some must have thought this prophetic, since only a few
weeks later, on February 14, 1901, the Minister of Education Nikolai
Bogolepov was assassinated by a student. By then Miliukov was
already in jail.[32] His arrest was part of a large police roundup in which
some two hundred political suspects were seized. The investigation
proceeded slowly, and the preliminary detention lasted six months.
Prison conditions, however, were not unpleasant. His wife came to
visit him regularly, and the public library sent all the books needed

[28] VOSP, I, 190–92.
[29] A, July 7, 1894, No. 3480, p. 24.
[30] CRI, p. 516.
[31] OKH, report of July, 1902, describing Miliukov's activities in 1900.
[32] ROK, IV, 112–13.

to continue his work on the third volume of the *Ocherki*. Sentence
was to be determined by administrative procedure; in the early summer of 1901 he was released and forbidden to reside in St. Petersburg.
He was free again until further notice.[33]

The Miliukovs spent the summer in Finland. In the fall they
moved to Udel'naia, some eighteen minutes by train from St. Petersburg, outside the city limits. It was a pleasant suburb, and friends
from the capital dropped in with the news. Soon Miliukov disregarded the rules and began to visit the city illegally. During one of
these expeditions, while visiting Professor Fedor Batiushkov, he was
introduced to two guests from Chicago. These were President William R. Harper of the University of Chicago and Charles R. Crane,
the Chicago industrialist. Crane had become interested in the Slavs
and had contributed funds to bring representatives of the various
Slavic countries to lecture at the University of Chicago. In 1901
Maksim Kovalevskii came to speak on Russian political institutions.[34]
Professor Thomas Masaryk of Prague was scheduled to lecture on the
Czechs in the summer of 1902, and Miliukov was asked to speak on
"Russian Civilization" in the summer of 1903. His former teacher,
Kovalevskii, may have recommended him to Harper and Crane. Miliukov was delighted to accept. "My American lectures," he recalled,
"were a repetition of the *Ocherki* for foreigners—they stood on the
borderline between history and politics."[35] He was chosen to follow
Kovalevskii and Masaryk because, like his predecessors, he represented
a certain political trend: "Mr. Crane had turned to us as representatives of progressive tendencies in the Slavic world; his aim was to
make clear to the American public not only the actual situation of our
two countries, but also the possibilities of their future."[36]

The lectures were to be published. Miliukov, always challenged by
languages, decided to write the text in English and hired a certain
Miss Hughes as a tutor. She came to Udel'naia daily and helped
with the text and English conversation. To improve the latter, Miss
Hughes, her friend Miss Patterson, and Miliukov planned a bicycle

[33] VOSP, I, 195–97.

[34] For a brief sketch of Crane, see A. Parry, "Charles R. Crane, Friend of Russia
(1858–1939)," RR, V (1945), 20–36. Maksim Kovalevskii wrote "American Impressions," RR, X (1951), 37–45, 106–117, 176–184.

[35] VOSP, I, 235.

[36] P. Miliukov, "De Masaryk a Benes," LMS, XIII (1936), No. 1, 384.

tour of England during the summer of 1902. The police proved remarkably understanding and permitted Miliukov to leave on condition that he return in the fall to begin a six-month term in jail, the penalty determined upon for his speech at the Lavrov meeting. The bicycle tour was a great success and achieved its aim. Upon his return to St. Petersburg, Miliukov reported, pillow in hand, to the Kresty jail on the Vyborg Side and began his prison term.[37]

IV

One wonders whether the police would have been as co-operative had they had full knowledge of Miliukov's activities in the spring of 1902. He had then become involved in a major activity of the Russian liberals, their illegal journal *Osvobozhdenie* ("Liberation"). So far he had been a lone wolf in politics, with no permanent commitment to any political group. The time had come to join in an action which was bound to arouse his full sympathy and co-operation—the founding of a liberal journal which would speak for neither Populists, Marxists, nor supporters of the old regime. Miliukov was clearly none of these. He described himself at this point in his life as follows:

> I succeeded in remaining independent of the influence of both major currents which dominated the minds of Russia's intelligentsia in the last quarter of the nineteenth century—Populism and Marxism. . . . I belong to a generation younger than that of the seventies, carried away by Populism, but older than the generation of the eighties and nineties which swore by Marx. . . . On the other hand, in my student years, I was influenced by the two founders of contemporary sociology—Auguste Comte, the creator of positivist philosophy, and Herbert Spencer, the creator of synthetic philosophy.[38]

He would now put his beliefs to the test in collaboration with the group to which, in the Russian situation, he had been most likely to gravitate. These were the zemstvo liberals around Ivan Petrunkevich.[39]

By the turn of the century, Russian liberalism, heretofore dominated by the gentry, was beginning to turn for support to the Russian

[37] VOSP, I, 199–201.
[38] JUB, I, 5.
[39] See F. Rodichev, "The Veteran of Russian Liberalism—Ivan Petrunkevich," SEER, VII (1928–29) 316–26.

intelligentsia and the free professions.[40] Zemstvo veterans like Petrunkevich were beginning to call on unattached liberals like Miliukov.
The two met briefly in Moscow in the early nineties but had lost contact. Both had been persecuted by the government, but while Miliukov went abroad Petrunkevich remained in zemstvo work in Tver
province. When he and his zemstvo friends decided to publish a journal, they thought of Miliukov as a possible editor. The journal was to
be issued abroad, to escape the censorship, as were the Social Democratic *Iskra* and the Socialist Revolutionary *Revoliutsionnaia Rossiia*.
Its aim was the promotion of constitutionalism in Russia.

Miliukov was first asked to edit the journal in 1891. Though interested, he was not inclined to go abroad again and risk becoming a
permanent émigré. Petrunkevich understood his reluctance and wrote:

> No matter how desirable his editorship of a newspaper intended
> as a continuation of *The Bell* might be, we were decidedly opposed
> to condemning Miliukov to Herzen's fate, that is condemning him
> to lifelong emigration, and thus deprive ourselves of such an enor-
> mous talent, for whom a great role in the struggle with the govern-
> ment for Russia's freedom might be in store.[41]

The former Legal Marxist, Peter Struve, had decided to emigrate in
any case, and the editorship was entrusted to him. Miliukov would
be one of the paper's chief ideologues. In the spring of 1902, he
went to Mashuk, the Petrunkevich estate in Tver province, to write
the leading article for the journal's opening issue. The die had
been finally cast for politics as against all else. "My relationship to
Osvobozhdenie," recalled Miliukov, "pulled me, once and for all,
into the most active participation in current politics."[42]

At Mashuk Miliukov found, in addition to the host who was his
senior by some sixteen years, two men slightly younger than himself.
These were Prince Dmitrii Shakhovskoi and Alexander Kornilov.
Shakhovskoi, it will be remembered, had heard Miliukov lecture at
Moscow University. He had since been active in the Tver and Yaroslavl zemstvos and was a convinced constitutionalist. Kornilov, a historian of Russia by training, had worked for various ministries in Russian Poland and in Irkutsk. In 1901 he had been exiled to Saratov

[40] FIS, p. vi.
[41] PETR, p. 337.
[42] VOSP, I, 235.

where he worked for the local newspaper.[43] Together the four men at Mashuk represented the nucleus of the future central committee of the Kadet (Constitutional Democratic) party. In their persons they also illustrated the alliance of the liberal zemstvo (Petrunkevich and Shakhovskoi) with the non-revolutionary intelligentsia (Miliukov and Kornilov) which was to be the foundation of the future party of Russian liberalism. Miliukov's draft was first approved at Mashuk and, having been examined and slightly amended by another group of constitutionalists in Moscow, it appeared in the first issue of *Osvobozhdenie*, published in Stuttgart on June 18, 1902. Though written by Miliukov, it represented the views of a group of men and was entitled, "From Russia's Constitutionalists."[44]

It was a program designed to give Russia free political institutions while avoiding a revolution. If accomplished (and here is echoed the voice of Miliukov the Russian European and the author of *Ocherki*), it would "mark Russia's decisive entry to a higher stage of political and cultural existence." It addressed itself not to the entire nation but to that segment of it which had not joined the conservative or the socialist camp. "Our organ," wrote Miliukov, "differs from others published abroad in that we propose to unite those groups of Russian society which do not find it possible to express their indignation by means of either the class or the revolutionary struggle."

Miliukov's program consisted of the following points: personal inviolability, equality of all before the law, freedom of the press, of assembly and of association, the right of petition, the calling of "a classless representative body," the annulment of "administrative growths" such as rules, circulars, administrative exile, and a "broad amnesty."[45] It was a program at once narrow and ambitious. It was narrow in the sense that no economic or social demands were included; it was daring, since the autocracy could not be expected to give in to such demands. Nor were the steps necessary to achieve these aims spelled out. These deficiencies, Miliukov tells us, were deliberate.[46] Economic and social demands were omitted since they were

[43] For Shakhovskoi, see his autobiographical sketch in RVS, pp. 196–200; for Kornilov, see A. Kizevetter, " A. A. Kornilov," GMCS, IV (1926), 234–40.

[44] VOSP, I, 236–38; "Ot russkikh konstitutsionalistov," OS, No. 1 (June 18, 1902), pp. 7–12. There is a brief comment on the document in FIS, pp. 132–35; SM I, 41–57, has a detailed analysis.

[45] "Ot russkikh konstitutsionalistov," pp. 7, 9–11 passim.

[46] VOSP, I, 236–37.

the province of the already organized Social Democratic and Social-ist Revolutionary parties; they would, moreover, though Miliukov did not mention this, tend to frighten the majority of the zemstvo men who, it must be remembered, were not as yet committed even to con-stitutionalism. Tactics were not spelled out, since much was being left to local initiative and there was as yet no broad national liberal move-ment which could be centrally directed.

The program was meant to be "feasible" for the particular time and place.[47] Three steps were envisioned for its realization. The Emperor was to proclaim the personal and civil liberties demanded. The zem-stvos and municipal dumas would then send representatives to an assembly (the "classless representative body") which would draft an electoral law. A popularly elected parliament would then legislate on the issues left untouched by the program. The third step was clearly a matter for the future. The immediate goals depended on the assent of the Emperor (which was doubtful) and on the co-operation of the zemstvo men, which was the chief aim of the program. Clearly, Miliu-kov regarded the nucleus of the zemstvo liberals as a vanguard of the Russian liberal movement. He had formulated a program which was sure to meet with their support but which went no further. It was characteristic of his future tactics that, at the very outset of his politi-cal career, he exercised those qualities of restraint, caution, and com-promise which were to characterize much of his future political activity.

V

We left Miliukov in the fall of 1902 in the Shpalernaia jail of St. Petersburg, and we must return to him there. His prison existence was tolerable. Books were again available to him, and he continued to write the third volume of the *Ocherki*. His wife came for regular visits, and the Miakotins sent his beloved hyacinths. "It was," he recalled, "a kind of temporary change of apartments," and he could patiently await the end of his six-month term. *Osvobozhdenie* did not forget him and reported on his jail "activities" in two issues.[48] Even his old master, Kliuchevskii, reappeared on the scene; the out-come of his intervention was surprising. Late one evening Miliukov

[47] "Ot russkikh konstitutsionalistov," p. 8.
[48] OS, No. 9 (October 19, 1902), p. 132; No. 10 (November 2, 1902), p. 168.

was taken from his cell and driven to the Ministry of Interior on the Fontanka Canal. He expected nothing good. Taken directly to the office of the minister, he was seated opposite the all-powerful Konstantin Plehve.

The successor of the murdered Sipiagin had a reputation as an arch-reactionary. But Plehve behaved like a polite host; the prisoner was served tea, and the Minister praised the *Ocherki*. This broached the subject of the unusual interview. Kliuchevskii, tutor of the Emperor's brother George, had told Nicholas that Miliukov was needed for scholarship and should be released. The Emperor had instructed Plehve to get acquainted with Miliukov and release him if his impression was favorable. Plehve now asked Miliukov to tell him in detail about his troubles with the police. Miliukov was recounting his fate since 1895 when, unexpectedly, Plehve asked: "What would you say if I offered you the post of Minister of Education?" The prisoner was rather taken aback by this turn of the conversation. When he recovered he answered in the negative: "Nothing can be accomplished in that post. Now if Your Excellency were to offer me your position, I would think about it."[49]

With no visible reaction Plehve sent Miliukov back to his cell; he would be called back as soon as the Emperor had been told of their interview. A week later he was summoned again. This time there was no tea and no compliments. Plehve informed him that he was free but warned him against continuing to oppose the government: "You will not make peace with us. At least do not start an open struggle against us. If you do we shall smash you."[50] History was to rule otherwise, and it was Plehve who would be assassinated in 1904. But luck had smiled at Miliukov, and in December, 1902, he was free again to return to Udel'naia. *Osvobozhdenie* reported on his release, and he would remain in Russia until June, 1903, when he was due at Chicago. While he was still in jail the paper had printed an article of his (he wrote under the pseudonym *cc*, presumably unknown to the

---

[49] VOSP, I, 201–3. In another place Miliukov recalled further details of the interview: "M. Plehve himself understood that something must be done to conciliate public opinion. He told the present writer that in his opinion a country like Russia could not be ruled by a ring (he used the Russian word *shaika*), and that the more active elements were to be gradually admitted to the Government" (ATL, p. 409).

[50] VOSP, I, 203–4. For an assessment of Plehve, see GUR, pp. 107–30.

police) directed against Plehve. He had warned the zemstvo men not to make any compromises with the Minister who was rumored to plan to appoint some of them as advisors to various government departments. "Zemstvo representatives," Miliukov wrote, "should not and cannot be satisfied with the role of experts and specialists."[51] There was to be no retreat from the program announced in June.

The journal had become a success and was being read quite widely. Its circulation in 1903 was eight thousand copies inside, and four thousand copies outside Russia, which compared favorably with the thirteen thousand circulation of *Iskra* and the ten thousand circulation of *Revoliutsionnaia Rossiia*.[52] Though it was an illegal publication, polemics with it appeared in pro-government newspapers such as *Grazhdanin*, *Moskovskie Vedomosti*, and *Novoe Vremia*. It was being read not only by the liberals but by the Left and even by the bureaucrats. According to a Social Democrat, *Osvobozhdenie* "was read in the same way as the Social Democratic *Iskra*, by the same persons, and with the same pleasure."[53] The bureaucrats, for their part, liked to read the criticisms, complete with name and date, of the transgressions of their colleagues. Anatolii Nekliudov recalled that when he had been first secretary of the Russian legation in Stuttgart he read the journal regularly:

> My chief (the lamented Prince Gregory Cantacuzene) and I used to read [*Osvobozhdenie*] with enormous interest and intense pleasure. It was the very free enunciation of sincere and serious opinions on what was going on at the time in Russia. The first numbers were of palpitating interest . . . there was no bureaucrat who had not got a number on his table. Several genuinely profited by it; others delighted in reading about the blunders and "indelicacies" therein disclosed.[54]

For Miliukov the more important function of the journal was the propagation of Russian constitutionalism. The spring of 1903, when he was out of jail again, seemed to be a propitious moment for this. The zemstvists' dissatisfaction with the government was on the rise.

---

[51] OS, No. 14 (January 2, 1903), p. 248; the pseudononymous article is in No. 11 (November 18, 1902), pp. 178–79.

[52] Figures for *Osvobozhdenie* in FIS, p. 144 n.; for *Iskra* in TR, p. 276, n. 36; for *Revoliutsionnaia Rossiia* in CRI, p. 498.

[53] VOI, I, 13.

[54] NEK, p. 376.

New recruiting grounds for constitutionalism had been created in 1902 and had been in operation while Miliukov sat in jail. These were the local committees of the Special Conference on Rural Needs which had been called by the government in early 1902 under the chairmanship of Finance Minister Sergei Witte. The creation of five hundred local committees with a total membership of eleven thousand persons proved an unexpected boon to the constitutionalists. The movement was about to profit from the rivalry between Plehve and Witte. The former was an enemy of local initiative; this made the latter, temporarily, its warm proponent. Witte was hoping to undermine Plehve's position by getting the local committees to express their dissatisfaction with his policies. The discussion of agricultural needs became an opportunity to examine many aspects of Russian life critically. It was a perfect setting for testing Osvobozhdenie's ideas.[55]

The committees met during the summer and fall of 1902. Troubles arose wherever the local men were too outspoken. The most fearless speakers were usually actual or potential constitutionalists. For this reason Miliukov agreed, when the history of the committees was being compiled, to write the introduction to the work. "The members of the committees," he wrote, "left the meetings as different people from what they had been when they entered them—they became better informed, better educated, and developed in the public spirit."[56] Many committeemen raised issues only vaguely related to the ostensible purpose of the meetings; they realized that the questions being asked were too narrow. "You can't begin fighting mosquitoes," said one delegate, "till you have removed the vampires." The committees of six guberniias voted for the introduction of universal compulsory education. Delegates from non-zemstvo areas asked for the institution of the zemstvo as "an essential precondition for the revival of agricultural activity." In other committees the demand was made for an all-Russian zemstvo organization which alone could deal with the problems at hand. Though only ameliorative measures

[55] The performance of the local committees is described in VON, pp. 223–26, and SM I, 80–101.

[56] NUZ, p. 39. Though the volumes were published in 1904, Miliukov's Introduction was written in the spring of 1903. Describing the "declarations of hundreds of local assemblies summoned in 1902" to an American audience in 1904, Miliukov called them "the answer of Russian liberalism" (CRI, pp. 476–79).

were to be considered, two committees went so far as to discuss compulsory expropriation of land in the interests of the peasantry.[57]

Some committee chairmen were not in sympathy with such heretical thoughts. In August, 1902, major conflicts broke out in the Voronezh committee. The opposition was led by Andrei Shingarev, a local physician and future leader of the Kadet party. In the Sudzhansk committee of Kursk guberniia there was trouble the following month, led by Prince Peter Dolgorukov, brother of Miliukov's gymnasium comrade and soon to be prominent in Osvobozhdenie ranks. Dolgorukov, who was a prominent zemstvist, was deprived of all his offices and forbidden to engage in any public work for five years. But his cause was persuasive enough to compel the entire committee of seventy-four members to resign. In Tver Petrunkevich protested in January, 1903, that the evidence submitted by his district committee had been suppressed; he and a group of supporters resigned from the committee in protest.

Similar troubles were reported from Tula, Tambov, Chernigov, and Moscow. "The temperature was rising," Miliukov recalled, "but it had not yet reached the boiling point. At this stage I was prepared to consider a rise in temperature as only useful."[58] He would turn to the pages of Osvobozhdenie where the political issues could be discussed. The committee experience had shown that the government permitted local initiative only by accident, never by design. The Witte committees had been useful, but it was an illusion to think they had taught the government anything; the effective jurisdiction of public initiative had not increased. And yet many zemstvists were still under the spell of the old illusion that the government could be changed by appeals to its reason. It was time, Miliukov reasoned, to explode this dangerous fallacy. In February, 1903, he wrote a new programmatic article for Osvobozhdenie.[59]

His aim was to indicate that a Russian liberal party would have to be built without what he called "partisans of ideal autocracy." He had in mind zemstvo leaders such as Dmitrii Shipov, Nikolai Khomiakov,

[57] NUZ, pp. 21–22, 25–26, 29, 37–38.

[58] The troubles are reported in BEL, pp. 86–92, 95, and NUZ, pp. 29–31, 33, 35–36. Miliukov's remark is in ROK, VI, 119.

[59] "K ocherednym voprosam," OS, No. 17 (February 16, 1903), pp. 289–91. It is analyzed in FIS, pp. 136–37, and SM I, pp. 108–17. It was written in Russia and not abroad, as Miliukov erroneously reports in VOSP, I, 239.

and Mikhail Stakhovich. In a previous issue of the journal, Struve had
urged their inclusion in the broad liberal front. Miliukov was convinced that this would be a major error. We saw that he had never
had any use for Slavophiles in politics. Times had changed even further since his lecture on the subject in the nineties. And yet there
was a danger that the soft whisperings of the Shipovites (Shipov led
the moderate zemstvists as Petrunkevich led its left wing) would take
the sting out of the constitutionalists' demands. Shipov had made his
position clear in a talk with Plehve in July, 1902: "I am," he said, "a
convinced supporter of the principle of autocracy. I believe that
the autocratic form of government best suits the Russian people.
In my view justice can be done and people can be more secure under
autocracy than under a parliamentary regime."[60]

Shipovites would clearly not make partisans of Miliukov's ideals.
All they aimed for was "to bring the entire truth before the Emperor." That would suit Plehve, but not the interests of Russian liberalism. Miliukov hoped that the zemstvo circles would not "play the
role of political clowns who are to entertain the public in the political
masquerade being prepared by Mr. Plehve." The lines of the liberal
party would have to be drawn more exactly on the right than had
been done in the past. Miliukov, the strategist, considered it his task
to do so. He was also convinced that little reforming activity could be
expected of the Emperor. In another *Osvobozhdenie* article, his last
one before leaving for Chicago, he commented on the Imperial Manifesto of February 26, 1903.[61] Published on the birthday of Alexander
III, it had inaugurated a series of acts which, in the next three years,
were to define the government's reform plans. Miliukov pointed out
that no concrete improvement had been decreed. The Manifesto
spoke of promoting religious tolerance "within the terms of the Fundamental Laws of the Russian Empire": what improvement was
likely to come of that? A promise was made of further local work on
improvements in agriculture; but, Miliukov asked, would local men
again be treated as they had been in the agricultural committees? He
expected nothing of the Manifesto, and addressing its author, Plehve,

[60] GUR, p. 694. For a sketch of Shipov, see FIS, pp. 23–27.

[61] "Derzhavnyi maskarad," OS, No. 19 (March 19, 1903), pp. 321–23. GUR,
pp. 217–21, has a partial text of the document. See also CRI, pp. 123–29, where
the Manifesto is discussed.

he concluded: "You, and those like you, are still asleep and dreaming, while all around everything has awakened and acts." Subsequent Miliukov articles for *Osvobozhdenie* were written from abroad.[62] He was soon to leave for America.

VI

It was the first of Miliukov's ocean voyages; he was to come to the United States five times between 1903 and 1928, his last visit. On this journey he had armed himself with Mothersill Seasick Pills, and they evidently helped. Still he was glad when, on the sixth day, he could admire the Statue of Liberty. He was rather less impressed by the skyscrapers but evidently liked Charles Crane's Fifth Avenue residence where he stayed for a few days. He met Crane's father, the founder of the family fortune, and his two daughters, one of whom subsequently married the Czech statesman Jan Masaryk. The Crane family became Miliukov's best American friends, and he remained in contact with them throughout his life.[63]

He arrived in Chicago for the opening of the University's Summer Quarter. He was housed in what he considered an elegant dormitory and was issued a cap and gown, which the faculty then wore for lectures. He was grateful, for he could hide his "inadequate clothing" underneath; the heat was "intolerable;" but he was still expected to wear evening dress for dinner in the faculty club. There Miliukov made friends, the best of whom was William Muss-Arnolt, the compiler of an Assyrian dictionary. Arnolt took to Miliukov and helped him with the still wooden text of his lectures. Miliukov did not wish to be left behind: Professor Toyokichi Iyenaga was lecturing on "The Oriental Countries and the Situation in the East" and was drawing larger crowds than he.[64]

Beginning on June 23, 1903, and for the next six weeks, four times per week, Miliukov lectured on "Russian Civilization." It was the first such course at an American university and a very thorough one indeed. Miliukov was presenting the most important findings of his

---

[62] The next one was to appear a year later in March, 1904.

[63] VOSP, I, 206–9. See Miliukov's obituary of his American patron, "Charles R. Crane," PN, February 18, 1939, p. 2.

[64] VOSP, I, 209–11.

Ocherki. But, in America, he could do more than that; not having the censor to fear, he commented on Russian developments right up to 1903. During his second visit to the United States he was to bring the account up to Bloody Sunday. Thus, *Russia and Its Crisis*, the printed version of his lectures, is an indispensable supplement to his *Ocherki*, which did not cover political developments of the nineteenth and twentieth centuries. Particularly interesting are his views on Russian liberalism, which receive extended attention in the lectures.[65]

There were two Russias, Miliukov told his audience, that of Leo Tolstoy, and that of Plehve:

> The former is the Russia of our "intellectuals" and of the people; the latter is official Russia. One is the Russia of the future, as dreamed of by members of the liberal professions; the other is an anachronism, deeply rooted in the past, and defended in the present by an omnipotent bureaucracy. The one spells liberty; the other, despotism. . . . I shall not be expected to discuss Russian affairs from the point of view of Plehveism. It is the cause of the other, the "greater Russia" that I have made mine.[66]

"The Russia of the future" belonged, politically speaking, to the liberals and the socialists. In the process of describing these two movements, Miliukov noted features of their past and present which were full of implications for his own political future. Unlike the West, "Russian liberalism was not *bourgeois*, but *intellectual*—to use the French terms." Russia "did not possess such a bourgeoisie as that of Western Europe, and such as it did possess was neither wealthy nor enlightened, nor numerous and influential enough to have any political weight in the country."

Thus Alexander Radishchev, whose *Journey from St. Petersburg to Moscow* "contains the first political program of Russian liberalism," was a gentry intellectual. The Decembrists represented the second stage of Russian liberalism influenced, as in Radishchev's case, by a foreign model: "The new oppositionary current originated in fresh foreign impressions produced on men of the gentry class by European events." Even the statutes of the Decembrists' societies

---

[65] The chapter on liberalism is the longest in the book (112 pages); the socialist movement gets somewhat less attention (98 pages), while the conservatives receive only scant mention (34 pages).

[66] CRI, pp. viii–x.

were copied from those of the German Tugendbund. These first stages of Russian liberalism produced no concrete results. The next stage in its development coincided with the reforms of the 1860's. These were liberal but carried out by the bureaucracy without recourse to public opinion. This "caused the liberal elements of the provincial gentry to disown their liberal colleagues in the St. Petersburg chanceries," a split which was to hamper the liberal movement in the twentieth century as well, with even more dire results.[67]

The reforms had been liberal, but insufficiently so. Political liberty had not been achieved; liberalism in Russia had not fulfilled its major function. This was to affect its very nature:

> In more advanced countries the battle of political idealism had been won first of all; its practical results made up the level upon which the latter systems of political realism began to build. Political liberty was settled when the social questions arose. Social radicalism simply accepted the results of a struggle won by political radicalism, its predecessor, without endorsing its theory, but also without repudiating its achievements. In Russia alone it so happened that social teachings prepossessed the more active spirits at a time when the work of political liberalism had yet to be done; and the Russian socialists, not satisfied to consider this liberal work superfluous, went even so far as to deem it dangerous for the people.[68]

Two consequences followed from this situation. The first was that Russian liberalism had lost a good deal of credit with the public, and the term itself was becoming rather meaningless:

> Now, in Russia the meaning of the term "liberalism" is at once extended and worn out. It is extended to the more radical groups, particularly in the press, for the simple reason that every more advanced term would be provoking to the censor and thus would incur prompt suppression. . . . At the same time, however, the term "liberalism" is worn out in Russia. This, of course, is not because the liberal program is already realized. Far from being so, this program presents now the first step to be attained; and this is recognized and accepted by all parties in Russia. But, of course, this first step is not acknowledged to be the only one. . . . The greater num-

---

[67] The specific references to passages from CRI are pp. 225–26 (emphasis in the original), 253–55, 265–66.

[68] CRI, pp. 281–82.

ber of such as call themselves liberals in Russia in fact hold to the more advanced opinions. That is why the term, as I said, is worn out, without having actually served.[69]

The second consequence of the peculiar Russian political situation was that "Russian liberalism and Russian socialism were not at all mutually exclusive. Russian liberalism was always tinged with democratism, and Russian democratism has been strongly impregnated with socialistic teachings and tendencies ever since socialism made its appearance."

Miliukov was going much further in America than he had ever gone in the pages of *Osvobozhdenie*. His American lectures might have shocked the liberal party forming in Russia. But the Russian public was not to hear from Miliukov directly until the drastic events of 1904–5 prepared the ground. In America he also gave Russian socialism more credit than he would have granted it in St. Petersburg. "Socialism in Russia," he noted, "more than anywhere else, represents democracy in general. This is what makes its political role much more important than it is in countries with a more extensive and earlier developed democracy." He admitted that "nearly all of the young Russian people who have passed through the schools of Demetrius [sic] Tolstoy are socialistic." If true, this was not an encouraging prospect for his party. Yet he was optimistic about its future; its chances grew with the influx into it of members of the liberal professions and the zemstvo "Third Element." "These men," he said, "filled with red blood the anemic body of Russian liberalism. And at the same time they gave it a more advanced and democratic character."[70]

VII

Miliukov was lecturing at the very moment (July, 1903) that the socialists and the liberals were organizing themselves for future action. The Social Democrats had divided into Mensheviks and Bolsheviks at their Second Congress—a split which was to have momentous consequences in the future. Simultaneously, Russia's constitutionalists held meetings in Switzerland which resulted in the formation of their first formal organization—the Union of Liberation. This group of

[69] *Ibid.*, pp. 224–25.
[70] *Ibid.*, pp. 218, 290, 335, 340.

twenty zemstvists and intelligentsia leaders included Petrunkevich and his wife, Shakhovskoi, Peter Dolgorukov, and Struve. There were additional zemstvo men and university professors, and also revisionist socialists, such as Vasilii Vodovozov, Sergei Prokopovich, and his wife Ekaterina Kuskova. The inclusion of this more radical element was a graphic illustration of Miliukov's Chicago thesis that Russian liberalism needed Russian socialism. The Union of Liberation, conceived at these Swiss meetings, was to be, not a party, but a coalition of groups with similar goals, a wide oppositional front including liberals, constitutionalists, and socialists not affiliated with the Social Democratic or Socialist Revolutionary parties. The Union was to be a semi-conspiratorial organization with branches all over Russia, using the zemstvo and other legal organizations for its own purposes. By November the first such "front organization" was organized in Moscow—the Zemstvo Constitutionalists, or Novosiltsev group, named after Iurii Novosiltsev in whose house they gathered. Osvobozhdenie, having moved from Stuttgart to Paris in the fall of 1903, would be the Union's tribune. The local branches of the Union held their first congress in 1904.[71]

Miliukov, in faraway Chicago, was not part of these first moves, but they could not take him by surprise, as his lectures, now drawing to a close, indicated. The University and Crane were pleased with the results, and Miliukov was invited to return. Chicago had now heard about the Czechs (from Masaryk) and the Russians (from Miliukov). The Balkan Slavs remained, and Miliukov could do the job. Crane and he agreed on another visit to the Balkans and then a series of lectures on the subject during the Winter Quarter of 1905. Crane also arranged that Miliukov give a lecture series for the Lowell Institute in Boston in the autumn of 1904. Miliukov was evidently enjoying himself abroad, for he did not return to Russia in the interim. He spent part of the two summers in the Balkans and the rest of the year in London. In the British Museum he prepared his lectures and the rest of his Ocherki.[72]

Before settling down in London, Miliukov visited the Balkans. After a short stay in Sofia he spent several days of September, 1903,

[71] The beginnings of the Union of Liberation are discussed in FIS, pp. 140–45, and SM I, 130–37.
[72] VOSP, I, 212. Miliukov erroneously dates his Boston lectures in 1903. They were delivered in November–December, 1904.

on the Macedonian border. There was a rising in Macedonia, the
Turks had brought fresh troops to the area, and refugees were stream-
ing into Bulgaria. The aim of the Macedonian partisans was to make
Bulgaria fight for Macedonian autonomy. But Macedonian leaders
told Miliukov that they preferred an intervention by the European
powers. Miliukov, describing his impressions to the Russian public,
urged European intervention as soon as possible.[73] His Balkan research
had begun dramatically. In London he met two British authorities
on the area. Henry Noel Brailsford knew the Macedonian problem,
on which he published a book in 1906; during the Balkan Wars of
1912–13 Miliukov and he were colleagues on a Carnegie Commission
in the area. Robert Seton-Watson, the other Britisher knowledgeable
on the subject, was to make a lasting reputation in both academic
and political circles; he and Miliukov became lifetime friends.[74]

But the most important result of Miliukov's London stay were
his observations of English political life. "These observations," he
recalled, "helped me to a very considerable extent in working out my
own political world view—and it was only subsequently that I could
evaluate the full importance for myself of my London observations."[75]
He was frequently in the House of Commons, and his favorite newspaper was the *Westminster Gazette*, which maintained a consistently
liberal point of view. He made friends with the Fabians, particularly
Ramsay Macdonald, who had just begun his parliamentary career.
The radical journalist George Herbert Perris, who was to write a book
on the Russian Revolution of 1905, arranged a banquet in Miliukov's
honor. He was beginning to feel at home in England. Bernard Pares
recognized this when he said of Miliukov that "his views never
seemed to me to diverge much from what one could hear at any time
at the National Liberal Club in London."[76]

The Russian colony in London included such patriarchs of the
revolutionary movement as Nikolai Chaikovskii, Peter Kropotkin, and
Ekaterina Breshko-Breshkovskaia. Lenin, too, was in London and
asked Miliukov to come and see him "in his miserable cell." It was
the only time that the two met. They quickly got into an argument,
and Lenin did not make a favorable impression on Miliukov—"a

[73] P. Miliukov, "S makedonskoi granitsy," RV, October 1, 1903.

[74] VOSP, I, 217.

[75] Ibid., I, 219.

[76] B. Pares, A Wandering Student (Syracuse, 1948), p. 126; VOSP, I, 217, 221.

stubborn debater and a slow-thinking scholar, as I found him to be."[77] Other émigrés proved more congenial. Miliukov met them through Isaak Shklovskii (Dioneo), the English correspondent of *Russkiia Vedomosti*. Miliukov had been his faithful reader, for Shklovskii also admired "the political mores of a free country."[78] Shklovskii's London house was one of the centers of the émigrés. It was there that Miliukov witnessed a charming scene: Breshko-Breshkovskaia, "the grandmother of the Russian Revolution," did the Russian national dance with Prince Kropotkin, the uncrowned king of European anarchism. "Babushka," Miliukov describes the mood, "floats along the room, coquettishly waving her kerchief, and the Russian brave Kropotkin skilfully winds his way behind her, stamping the rhythm with his feet." Babushka, too, was going to the United States, to raise money for the revolutionary movement or, as Miliukov put it, "to prepare the revolution which I was predicting." She tried to convert Miliukov to revolutionary ways, but he told her that he already had his own "grandfather of Russian constitutionalism," Petrunkevich.[79]

London's damp and chilly winter made Miliukov's boarding house less than pleasant, and he caught the inevitable colds. But the riches of the British Museum made up for much, and he completed his *Ocherki* there. Thus ended an undertaking which had engaged him since the early nineties and which remains his most enduring contribution to Russian historiography. The third volume is his masterpiece. Here he analyzed, in an original and profound way, the beginnings in the eighteenth century of what he called "nationalism and public opinion." In the beginning of that century, it was the government which stood for progress: Miliukov spoke of "the official victory of the critical elements over the nationalistic ones." Even Catherine the Great began her reign in the "critical spirit." But due to the Pugachev Rebellion and the French Revolution she abandoned her reforms, and the government "turned from an ally to a determined foe of the critical elements. . . . From this moment begins the unbroken tradition of Russian public critical thought." The government

[77] RUS, p. 48, where the date of the meeting is erroneously reported as 1901; VOSP, I, 258.

[78] P. Miliukov, "Privet staromu drugu," PN, April 2, 1932, p. 2, and "Pamiati I. V. Shklovskago-Dioneo," PN, March 10, 1935, p. 3.

[79] P. Miliukov, "E. K. Breshko-Breshkovskaia," PN, January 26, 1929, p. 1, and "Pamiati E. K. Breshko-Breshkovskoi," PN, September 28, 1934, p. 2.

would henceforth be a hindrance to progress, which it would oppose not only by force but by an "idealization of the past." The Russian intelligentsia was born in response to this betrayal by the government of the role assumed for it by Peter, and, with Catherine's reign, "Russian public life enters a new phase, which has not yet been completed."[80]

Though he did not carry his analysis beyond the eighteenth century, Miliukov was thus indirectly commenting on his own day. The government continued to block political, social, and economic progress, and the reforming role belonged to that section of public opinion which was not nationalistic. He stressed the intelligentsia's leadership of this otherwise formless public opinion, a leadership which he traced back to the era of Catherine. "The seventies and eighties of the eighteenth century represent the moment," he wrote, "from which begins the unbroken history of an intelligentsia public opinion in Russia."[81] Miliukov's historical scholarship explained and sanctified his political views and activities. The continued success of his *Ocherki* in Russia—the last, seventh Russian edition appeared in 1918—was in part explainable by his successful synthesis of past and present.

VIII

While Miliukov was at work in the British Museum, his political colleagues in Russia made progress. The Union of Liberation held its first congress in St. Petersburg on January 3–5, 1904. Some fifty delegates represented more than twenty branches of the organization. They elected a Council of ten members to direct the group's activities. It consisted of five representatives each from the zemstvo liberals and the intelligentsia. Miliukov, had he been in Russia, would doubtless have been part of the second group. He would have, just as surely, felt more at home with the men of the zemstvo group. These included his old friends Petrunkevich (who was elected chairman), Shakhovskoi (who became secretary), and Peter Dolgorukov (elected

---

[80] It is interesting to note that, in the 1929 Jubilee Edition, Miliukov changed the subtitle "Nationalism and Public Opinion" to "Nationalism and Europeanism." The "official victory" is the heading of chapter i, Part 2, Volume III. The "new phase" is treated in O, III, 250–51.

[81] O, III, 335.

treasurer). The intelligentsia representatives included no one particularly close to Miliukov. The program adopted by the Union included the following points:

> The first and main aim of the Union of Liberation is the political liberation of Russia . . . the Union will seek before all else the abolition of autocracy and the establishment in Russia of a constitutional regime. . . .
> It recognizes as fundamentally essential that the principles of universal, equal, secret, and direct elections be made the basis of the political reform. . . .
> In the realm of social-economic policy, the Union of Liberation will follow the same basic principle of democracy, making the direct goal of its activity the defense of the interest of the laboring masses.
> In the sphere of national questions, the Union recognizes the right of self-determination of different nationalities entering into the composition of the Russian state.[82]

This was a radical advance over the program written by Miliukov for the first issue of Osvobozhdenie. Conditions had changed, to be sure; still the demands regarding "the interests of the laboring masses" and, even more clearly, those regarding the national question went beyond Miliukov's own desires in 1904, as he was soon to demonstrate.

He tended to find himself in a middle position between the Zemstvo-Constitutionalists (to whom he gravitated by preference, though he often found them too cautious) and the left intelligentsia, whose political radicalism he shared but whose socio-economic programs he did not yet support. The outbreak of the Russo-Japanese War made him formulate his position. The Japanese attack aroused much latent nationalism, which spread even to liberal circles and tended to soften their oppositional attitude toward the regime. Osvobozhdenie mirrored the new division in the liberal camp. In a "Letter to Students" Struve suggested that patriotic demonstrations be organized with slogans such as "Long live the army" and "Long live Russia." Miliukov was sure that such advice was not practical. "Down with autoc-

---

[82] The intelligentsia representatives were Nikolai Annenskii, Vasilii Bogucharskii, Sergei Prokopovich, Aleksei Peshekhonov, and Sergei Bulgakov. Of these, Miliukov knew only Peshekhonov, who was a Populist not a liberal. For the program, see FIS, p. 147. For a description of the congress, see ibid., pp. 146–49, as well as SM I, 137–43, and SHA, pp. 109–17.

racy," he suggested, "is no less patriotic. Let us be patriots for ourselves, and for a future Russia." In his reply Struve asserted that the
Russian public was not as indifferent to the war as Miliukov implied.
Besides it might be wise to have the army on one's side: "Who
knows if the moment will not come when the shouts 'Long live the
army' . . . will summon against the chief enemy of the Russian people
—the autocracy?" Struve wrote from Paris, while Miliukov replied
from London; Shakhovskoi, who was on the spot, took Miliukov's
side, when he said in regard to Struve's suggested demonstrations
that "in Russia this formulation of the problem was not even discussed, so clear was its practical impossibility."[83]

But the right wing of the liberal camp did modify their oppositional tone in face of the external danger. This made Miliukov
remind the movement of the goal which must not be lost sight of. In
his "Current Tasks of the Russian Constitutionalists," he insisted that
the Plehve regime could not last and that the liberals must be prepared to state their aims when his successor appeared. As a minimum
program acceptable to both wings, he suggested: (1) a national representative body "which will have legislative power and the right to
inspect the budget," and (2) this body to be elected directly by the
population. As in 1902 this was again a purely political program which
omitted the additional demands made by the Union of Liberation
in January. It was a program acceptable to the Zemstvo-Constitutionalists, who published a statement to the Russian public along such
lines earlier in the year.[84] Miliukov was learning the art of the politician: in a coalition of forces never forget the lowest common
denominator.

He turned out to be a prophet in regard to Plehve. By the time
his Osvobozhdenie article appeared, the Minister had been killed
by a bomb. The news found Miliukov in the Adriatic resort town
of Abbazia; he was making a trip through the Western Balkans in
preparation for his Chicago lectures. His family had come to Abbazia,
and the children saw their father after a year's absence. He soon left
them again to begin his explorations. "The chief aim of my journey,"
he wrote, "was a search for what could not be found in the books: the

[83] For the debate, see Struve in Listok Osvobozhdeniia No. 1 (February 11,
1904), and Miliukov in OS, No. 43 (March 7, 1904), pp. 329–30. SHA, p. 118.
[84] OS, No. 52 (July 19, 1904), p. 38. The text of the statement is in SHA, pp.
120–21, translated in SM I, 194–95.

national movement of the Slavs which was beginning to grow among the popular masses." He had learned Serbo-Croatian, but often had to resort to German, "the common language of the Slavs."[85]

In Sarajevo, as in Moscow and St. Petersburg, the chief slogan of the opposition was "a constitution." Austrian spies followed him into the cafes where he met with representatives of the dissatisfied. But he found that the Austrians had done a great deal in the occupied territory; "it was a long step forward in comparison to the patriarchal Turkish ways." Modernization was in full swing, at least economically. Yet the Austrian enemy was clever and exploited the longstanding friction between Croatians and Serbs. It was a stimulating lesson in nationalism, and the journey was going to bear fruit in Miliukov's later Duma and ministerial career.

Before leaving for America, Miliukov undertook two missions on behalf of Russian liberalism. The first took him to Paris, the second to St. Petersburg. In both cases he performed a function for which he was uniquely qualified—that of a well-informed constitutionalist with an independent point of view and with a knack for compromises among divergent groups with generally similar aims. In Paris he participated in a conference of Russian oppositional groups which met between September 30 and October 8, 1904. Along with Struve, Bogucharskii, and Peter Dolgorukov, Miliukov represented the Union of Liberation; it was his first direct participation in the Union's activity. Petrunkevich, too, was in Paris, bringing additional funds for *Osvobozhdenie*.[86] Miliukov was the author of the conference declaration proclaiming the aims of this uprecedented coalition of liberal, socialist, and national groups. The document stated:

> None of the parties represented at the meeting, in uniting for concerted action, thinks for a moment of abandoning any point of

[85] The journey is described in ROK, V, 110–19, and VOSP, I, 223–34. Miliukov's language abilities were exceptional. On his eightieth birthday a well-wisher pointed out that he had a command of eighteen languages (I. Polonskii, "Miliukov-chitatel'," PN, March, 1939, p. 6). Assembling all the information on the subject, I concluded that this meant the following languages, besides his native Russian: Latin, Greek, Sanskrit, Lithuanian, French, and German (all learned at the gymnasium and at the university); English, Bulgarian, Serbo-Croatian, Turkish, Finnish (for his travels); Czech, Polish, Ukrainian, Norwegian, Armenian, and modern Greek (for study purposes).

[86] PETR, p. 348.

its particular program, or of the tactical methods of the struggle, which are adapted to the necessities, the forces, and the situation of the social elements, classes, or nationalities whose interests it represents. But, at the same time, all declare that the principles expressed below are recognized by all of them:

1. The abolition of the autocracy; revocation of all the measures curtailing the constitutional rights of Finland.

2. The substitution for the autocracy of a democratic regime based on universal suffrage.

3. The right of every nationality to decide for itself; freedom of national development, guaranteed by the law; suppression of all violence on the part of the Russian government, as practiced against the different nationalities.[87]

In annotating the document for his American readers Miliukov asserted that "the declaration of the oppositionary and revolutionary parties certainly marks the climax of the political movement in Russia. Its practical result is to isolate the government in its struggle with the Russian opposition." But he also recognized the many ambiguities hidden behind the general phrases. He noted that " 'a democratic regime' is understood as a constitutional monarchy by the moderate parties, while a republic is the only regime consistent with the socialistic claims." Nor was there any consensus on the implications of the program as regards nationality rights.[88]

It was surprising that a gathering of such diverse origins and aims could agree on anything at all. Had the Russian Social Democrats attended, there might have been no joint declaration; but, though invited, they stayed away and made Miliukov's conciliatory mission easier. Of the eight organizations represented three were non-socialist (The Union of Liberation, the Polish National League, and the Finnish Party of Active Resistance). There were five socialist groups, including the Latvian Social Democrats, the Socialist Revolutionaries, the Polish Socialist party, the Georgian Socialists-Revolutionaries-Federalists, and the Armenian Revolutionary Federation. It was Miliukov's first opportunity to meet several political figures: Koni Zilliacus and Leo Mekhelin of Finland, Roman Dmowski of Poland, and Victor Chernov and Evno Azef of the Russian SR party. Dmow-

[87] CRI, pp. 524–25.
[88] *Ibid.*, pp. 526–28.

ski and Chernov would remain on the Russian political scene until the end of Miliukov's political career in Russia.

Since no economic demands were made in the declaration, it was the national issue that aroused the most heated debates.[89] The conference spent two days discussing the Polish problem, which proved to be the thorniest. It was the first time that Miliukov had to take a stand on the national problem. "Between the two generations," he recalled, "my personal position was difficult. I never shared the one-sided cosmopolitanism of the older generation, which ignored the very existence of the national problem. At the same time I was unable to sympathize with the equally one-sided spirit in which the national problem was solved by the generation of the end of the century."[90] It seemed clear to outside observers, however, that he had little sympathy for nationalism in the Russian Empire, whatever his tolerance for it in the Ottoman and Austro-Hungarian empires. "Pavel Nikolaevich," wrote the Polish leader Alexander Lednicki, who was Miliukov's lifetime friend and political colleague in the Kadet party,

> found himself, in his views on the national question, under the influence of prejudiced ideas about state structure which were deeply imbedded in his mind. He was therefore prone toward largely unitary and unionistic tendencies in the solution of the national problem and paid little attention to existing historical preconditions and to national feelings based on national instincts.[91]

Of the Russian delegates in Paris he was least willing to make compromises on the national question. Remembering "my cautious views of the Polish demands at the Paris conference of 1904," he speculated in his memoirs that "perhaps the reserved attitude of the Poles toward me could be traced back to this period."[92]

[89] "It would evidently be hopeless," Miliukov noted, "to discuss a common platform for economic and social reform. This is tacitly admitted by the silence on the subject of such reform of the document of the Paris agreement" (CRI, p. 527). The Union of Liberation, however, printed its January, 1904, program alongside that of the Paris conference to show that it was interested (even if Miliukov was not) in "the defense of the interests of the laboring masses" (Listok Osvobozhdeniia, No. 17, November 19, 1904, p. 2).

[90] RUS, p. 78.

[91] "P. N. Miliukov i pol'skii vopros," PNM, p. 214.

[92] VOSP, II, 76. Russia and Its Crisis indicates that Miliukov attached little importance to the national question in Russia at the time. Only some five pages

The conference affected Miliukov in two respects. It tended to
blind him for the next year to the real differences between the liberals
and the revolutionaries. The common declaration seemed to suggest
that it was possible to co-operate with the Left. As Miliukov put it,
rather optimistically: "Both groups have learned better than to fight
each other while opposing the common enemy. . . . The revolutionists
having become more practical, and the liberals more democratic and
more advanced in their demands, a direct agreement between the two
groups has become possible."[93] Miliukov returned to Russia with this
illusion and paid for it politically on several occasions. In addition to
this misunderstanding, he had created another one in the minds of
those to his right. His collaboration with the revolutionaries tainted
him with an extremist brush. When he became the leader of the
Kadet party his past sins—and this was a major one—would be held
against him. The Okhrana was fully informed about the conference
through Azef, who submitted a report in his double capacity as SR
delegate to the conference and agent of the secret police. The whole
story was to be told publicly in the Third Duma.[94]

IX

From Paris Miliukov went to St. Petersburg to attend two gatherings: the second congress of the Union of Liberation in October,
1904, and the meeting of the Zemstvo-Constitutionalists in early
November. After that he would have to hurry to his Boston lectures.
He had been absent from Russia since the spring of 1903. The most
important change in internal politics since his departure was the
appointment in August, 1904, of Prince Peter Sviatopolk-Mirskii as
the new Minister of Interior. Mirskii was no Plehve, and his regime
was hailed by some as a season of political "spring." Petrunkevich and
Peter Dolgorukov were reinstated in their political rights; this was a
good sign. But there was no indication of a movement forward; rather,

---

(of almost six hundred) are devoted to the problem. The work also underestimates
the forces of Great Russian nationalism, which were to come to full flower under
Stolypin and his successors.

[93] CRI, p. 523.

[94] For a report to the Okhrana by the head of its Paris branch, see "Doklad
Rataeva," in L. Menshikov (ed.), Russkii politicheskii sysk za granitsei (Paris,
1914), pp. 182–95.

as Miliukov put it, it was a restoration of "the status quo ante Plehve." For the constitutionalists this was not enough; "The issue," wrote Miliukov "remains open for further solution." Reform was "the issue," and Mirskii was not its agent; rather "a man has been found who represents not the programme but the momentary disposition of the Government."[95] Reminding the waverers of the program that had been formulated in the first issue of *Osvobozhdenie*, Miliukov asserted: "The new course has as yet nothing in common with this program. . . . *There are no intermediate positions between autocracy and consistent constitutionalism.*" He would adhere to this point of view throughout the next two years. Mirskii was not to be granted any co-operation. Whoever agreed to help the Minister would be discredited: "The moment he becomes yours he ceases to be ours and, therefore, ceases to be useful both to you and to us." "Continue in your course," he said to Mirskii, "but do not depend on us: we will not give you a single one of our people, we will not open up any credit for you, will give you no extension, as long as you do not accept our entire program. Because even in that case we do not know if we shall succeed in saving Russia from your political dilettantism." It was an intransigent attitude, but Miliukov would adhere to it not only with Mirskii but with Witte and Stolypin. He watched Mirskii's actions and was not impressed. The Minister, despite his honeyed words, postponed the coming zemstvo congress because he became frightened of its agenda. The "New Course," so far as Miliukov could see, was not a very firm one.[96]

The zemstvo congress was held despite Mirskii. The Union of Liberation met beforehand (October 20–22, 1904) and decided on a threefold program of action. It would take an active part in the November zemstvo congress; it would raise constitutional questions in the coming zemstvo meetings all over Russia; and it would organize banquets commemorating the fortieth anniversary of the judicial reforms on November 20. The program suggests how dependent the Union remained on the existing zemstvo organizations, which remained the chief recruiting ground for constitutionalism. Union members did not have a majority in any of the provincial or district

[95] P. Miliukov, " 'Novyi Kurs'," OS, No. 57 (October 2, 1904), p. 113; ATL, p. 410.

[96] P. Miliukov, " 'Novyi Kurs'," pp. 113–14 (italics in the original). P. Miliukov, "Fiasko 'Novogo Kursa '," OS, No. 60 (November 10, 1904), pp 162–63.

zemstvo meetings.[97] Only the banquet project was an independent action and succeeded brilliantly. The Union was coming of age. It decided to drop its conspiratorial character and announce its program publicly. The legal weekly *Pravo* began to replace the too-distant *Osvobozhdenie* as the spokesman for Russian constitutionalism. Finally, toward the end of the year, the Union secured control of two daily newspapers, *Nasha Zhizn'* and *Syn Otechestva*. Miliukov would write for all these publications.

Though not a zemstvist, he had a vital role to play in laying the groundwork for the congress. His task was to convince the moderate waverers that constitutionalism was not dangerous. He did it by pointing to the example of Bulgaria, which had been granted a constitution by the Russian tsar, of all people, exactly twenty-five years earlier. "It seems to me timely," he began, "to offer to the public's attention this small attempt at an assessment of Bulgarian political institutions in theory and practice." Bulgaria offered "a contrast between very advanced constitutional institutions and very elementary social and cultural conditions." If the system worked, why should it not be tested in Russia as well? What was needed was confidence, and Miliukov's study ended with a citation from a Bulgarian political figure: "Have more faith in the people, gentlemen."[98] It was decided that, in addition to his articles, Miliukov should present his argument to the zemstvists in person. There is no record of the meeting, but his reasoning must have run along the lines of his Boston lecture on the subject where he said that

> the habitual argument of the conservatives, that Russia is not ready for a constitution, is cut short by this example of Bulgaria. The broad democratic basis of the constitution of that country did not correspond to the degree of political development of the Bulgarian people; but it proved highly valuable as a means of promoting their political education.[99]

[97] SHA, pp. 131–32, 142.

[98] BOL, No. 8, p. 193; No. 10, p. 58. Reprinted as a monograph in Bulgarian, the study remains a useful contribution: "While his treatment of the constitution has been superseded, Miliukov's volume is still interesting for its discussion of the party system, and of the constitutional policy of King Ferdinand" (C. Black, *The Establishment of Constitutional Government in Bulgaria* [Princeton, 1943], p. 286.

[99] CRI, p. 564.

According to Shakhovskoi, who was present at Miliukov's talk to the zemstvists, several crucial votes, including that of Count Peter Heyden, were swayed by Miliukov's logic. "His arguments in favor of a representative system for our country," recalled Shakhovskoi, "exerted a strong influence on the participants. The facts of the Bulgarian situation which he knew well made a particular impact; the Russian zemstvists did not wish to lag behind Bulgaria."[100]

Miliukov made one last contribution to the zemstvo congress, which he could not attend, by suggesting in *Pravo* that "the meeting must, willy-nilly, assume the mission of speaking for the country to the government."[101] He then departed in great haste for Boston, where he commented on the accomplishments of the historic gathering to his American audience. Describing the declaration passed by the congress he said that

> it enumerated all the fundamental rights of the individual and the citizen: the inviolability of the person and of the private home; no sentence without trial, and no diminution of rights except by judgment of an independent court; liberty of conscience and of belief; liberty of the press and of speech; equal rights—civil and political— for all social orders, and, as a consequence, enfranchisement of the peasants; a large measure of local and municipal self-government; and last, as a general condition and guaranty for all the preceding rights, "a regular representation in a separate elective body, which must participate in legislation, in working out the budget, and in controlling the administration."[102]

Labeling the document "The Petition of Rights," Miliukov told his Boston audience that it was "the first political program of the Russian Liberal party, openly proclaimed in an assembly which had full moral right to represent liberalism throughout the empire."[103] And what

[100] SHA, p. 140.

[101] P. Miliukov, "Zadacha zemskago s"ezda," *Pravo*, 1904, No. 48, p. 4.

[102] Friends tried to talk Miliukov out of going to the United States in view of the favorable political situation. "Do not worry," he answered, "I shall return in time, and it is essential to go to America," and he left the same day for Cherbourg (GES, p. 200). CRI, p. 529. The full English text of the document is in FIS, pp. 182–88, and in ATL, pp. 410–12. Miliukov erroneously reports that a zemstvo delegation was received by the Emperor after the congress; no such reception took place.

[103] CRI, p. 530.

a special pleasure for a Russian European to announce such a program before a Boston audience which took such rights for granted but was not prepared to look for them among the subjects of the autocratic tsar!

Russia, Miliukov thought, was maturing politically. The banquet campaign, planned by the Union of Liberation in imitation of the epoch of Louis Philippe in France, was an unprecedented event in Russia: "The freedom of discussion and the boldness of speech in these assemblies surpassed everything that Russia had ever before seen; and the same spirit pervaded the press." It was now the government's turn to respond to this fresh pressure. But the autocrat remained blind, and the Imperial Manifesto of December 12, 1904, offered

> a fatal solution which, instead of ending the conflict, hopelessly enlarged the gulf between the Tsar and his people. . . . All the demands of the Zemstvos, except political reform, were mentioned in the manifesto, but the promised changes were stated in such evasive and ambiguous terms and accompanied with so many "limitations," "possibilities," and other restrictions, that the impression produced was just opposite to what had been expected.[104]

The Tsar was in no mood for concessions and was not about to please the Russian European by becoming a constitutional monarch.

X

Miliukov's Boston experience was particularly gratifying. Having lectured at America's youngest university in the still somewhat culturally raw atmosphere of Chicago, he was now enjoying a taste of American Brahmin culture; he clearly liked it. He was the house guest of President August Lawrence Lowell of Harvard, who introduced him to his first Lowell Lectures' audience. He found his listeners of unusually high caliber: "I must confess," he recalled, "that I hardly ever faced an audience with such high standards as here. . . . I saw with embarrassment that their questions revealed my weakest spots."[105] The Bostonians, for their part, seemed pleased with the gentleman from St. Petersburg: "He spoke good English, and was

[104] CRI, pp. 531, 532–55; the full text of the Manifesto is in HAR, pp. 282–85. The analogy with Louis Philippe is from VOSP, I, 267.
[105] His eight Lowell Lectures were delivered between November 29 and December 23, 1904 (N.S.); ROK, XVI, 129–30.

readily understood by the audience. . . . A very large audience heard this lecture, and the course will undoubtedly be one of the most intensely interesting of the year." The moment for the lectures could not have been better chosen: Russia was in the news not only politically but culturally. During Miliukov's Boston stay, Ivan Pavlov won the Nobel prize in medicine, the first Russian to be thus honored. As if to continue the spirit of the Paris Conference, the legendary Breshkovskaia arrived in Boston to lecture in Faneuil Hall "in the interests of Russian Freedom." In an elegant Boston home, Miliukov served as a translator for Breshkovskaia, who told the ladies how the Tsar had sent her to Siberia. Bostonians were learning about the Russian opposition from authoritative sources. "It is singularly fortunate," wrote the Boston Evening Transcript,

> for those Bostonians who follow the course of European affairs that Professor Miliukov's Lowell Institute Lectures on "The Russian Crisis" coincide with a particularly energetic manifestation of that crisis in Russia. The zemstvo memorial to the Czar . . . illustrates the lectures with a vividness greatly enhancing their interest. Those who have heard Professor Miliukov will have realized that he has unusual qualifications for showing the nature of the forces opposing the Russian autocracy. . . . Professor Miliukov's lecture this evening will be devoted to "The Revolution." No one who can hear it can afford to miss it.[106]

When not lecturing, Miliukov could be found in the Widener Library where he had discovered some rare Russian émigré newspapers of the 'eighties and 'nineties. Harvard's Leo Wiener, whom he knew from Sofia, was his Cambridge cicerone.

The lectures terminated before Christmas, and Miliukov made his way to Chicago where he was to give a course on the Balkans in the Winter Quarter, beginning in January, 1905. Buried in snow, Chicago was a very different place from the humid heat of the summer lectures in 1903. Now there was only a modestly small class of regular students instead of the large summer audience. After a few uneventful weeks, Miliukov read about Bloody Sunday in the Chicago papers.

It was indeed the greatest political outbreak Russia had ever seen. . . . The movement was, however, stifled in blood. Compara-

<hr/>

[106] Boston Evening Transcript, November 30, 1904; December 9, 1904 (editorial); December 10, 1904; December 14, 1904 (editorial); and P. Miliukov, "E. K. Breshko-Breshkovskaia," PN, January 26, 1929, p. 1.

tive and temporary quiet had been reestablished. But it was evident to everybody that for the Russian government it was a Pyrrhus [sic] victory. . . . Nothing short of speedy concessions . . . is likely to prevent further disasters.[107]

Miliukov was sure that he should leave for Russia immediately, without completing the Chicago course. Crane agreed, and it was decided that he would depart as soon as his book was ready for the press. He worked quickly, and the Preface is signed "Chicago, Abraham Lincoln's Birthday, 1905." In Chicago he also found a French translator for the work. It appeared two years later in Paris. Though the book kept him in America two months after Bloody Sunday, he did not regret the time, for he regarded the publication as "a political act of sorts, dependent on me exclusively."[108]

Miliukov's political education, accomplished so largely outside Russia, had come to an end. He was going back to a Russia at the threshold of its first revolution. He was to play a vital role in both the success and the failure of 1905–7. He had prepared himself for that role in ways he found consonant both with the spirit of Russian history and the lessons of Western political life. It remained to be seen whether his formulas would work when applied in his native land in the first decade of the turbulent twentieth century.

[107] CRI, p. 538. For an account of Bloody Sunday, generally considered as the beginning of the 1905 Revolution, see HAR, pp. 88–94.

[108] "If this book," wrote Miliukov in the Preface, "succeeds in creating some new friends for us among a great Allied people my patriotism will be amply rewarded" (La Crise Russe [Paris, 1907], p. iv); VOSP, I, 247.

3: THE BIRTH OF A PARTY

> Our undertaking is too novel for the Russian public which is
> unaccustomed to practical political activity for us to count on
> the full approval of all elements of public opinion. And yet
> our program is, undoubtedly, the farthest to the left of those
> offered by West European political groups analogous to ours.
> This character of our program may not be properly appreci-
> ated at a moment of such high tension as the present—but it
> will doubtless be appreciated later.[1]

I

In April, 1905, Miliukov returned to Russia to stay. The previous decade had been his *Wanderjahre*; he had lived in Europe and America
and, with the exception of a short Russian intermezzo in 1900–1902,
had observed his native land from the outside. He had left Moscow
in 1895 as a historian in exile; he was returning there in 1905 "with
the reputation of a beginning political figure. . . . I was returning as
a kind of new person who was being observed with curiosity—or
interest—in expectation of displaying his political physiognomy."[2]
Even his family must have observed him with curiosity. His wife and
children had seen little of him in those ten years. His oldest son was
already fifteen but, like his brother and sister, had been brought up
almost entirely by his mother. The family home continued to be in
Udel'naia, near St. Petersburg, but at first Miliukov chose to live in
Moscow, where he felt more at home.

Even the old capital had changed in his absence. On his way from
the railroad station to the house of Mikhail Mandel'shtam where he

[1] Miliukov's keynote speech to the founding congress of the Kadet party, October 14, 1905, GOD, p. 101.
[2] ROK, VIII–IX, 109–10.

was to stay whenever he was in Moscow he noticed the city's new look. In the nineties it had been the fashion to build in the pseudo-Russian style. Now the wealthy Moscow bourgeois were building in a mixture of styles, from Gothic to Baroque, but all imitating Europe. Soon Miliukov would be the guest in some of these opulent houses, particularly the "Portuguese" mansion of one of the Morozovs. At first he must have felt rather lost in his native city. But, at the moment, he preferred it to St. Petersburg, where he was to live permanently from 1906 till 1917. In 1905 he was more attracted by Moscow: "The intelligentsia *tonus* of St. Petersburg . . . was too left, too abstract, too theoretical for me," he recalled. "My attention involuntarily passed to Moscow, my old home, where I felt more at home, freer from influences and decisions imposed from the outside."[3]

The "imposed decisions" emanated from the Union of Liberation, which had held its third congress in Moscow on March 25–28, just before Miliukov's return. He had not participated in any of the Union's meetings but sensed that it was moving further left than he would have desired. He had wanted his collaboration with the Union to move in two directions: (1) no part of the program should be surrendered to the government; (2) the program should not move leftward from those political declarations which Miliukov favored. But he admitted that while "it was not hard to reach the first aim it proved impossible to reach the second." The leftist element in the Union was becoming louder. Miliukov had foreseen trouble ahead already in his American lectures, where he stated that "harmonization is hardly possible between a program that tries to 'sharpen,' and one that aims to 'blunt' the social contradictions. One works for 'social peace,' while the other aims at 'social revolution.'" Nor had he sympathized with all the implications of the "banquet campaign" with its "oratorical excesses" that produced "simulations of revolution." "I do not know," he wrote, "whether I would have found a place among our orators had I come back for the 'banquets.'" The Union was in danger of being dominated by the Left at the expense of a balance with the moderates favored by Miliukov. He concluded that "there was more political competition than collaboration. In any case I could not control the influence

---

[3] VOSP, I, 269. Pages 253–62 contain a perceptive self-analysis of Miliukov's state of mind, both psychologically and politically, on his "return home."

emanating from this center, and had to either conform and assimilate, or to start an open struggle." This was not what he had in mind when he had formulated his conciliatory mission between liberals and socialists. He was already enough of a politician to desire to lead, rather than be led. He could not lead the Union of Liberation. He would try elsewhere, among the more moderate Zemstvo-Constitutionalists, who formed the Union's right wing.[4]

The Constitutionalists had met in congress in Moscow on February 24–25 and had made three decisions. They declared that the national assembly should be bicameral (Miliukov was to disagree with this view) and elected by universal and direct suffrage (a minority supported indirect elections). To help solve the agricultural crisis, the group agreed to the principle of compulsory alienation of private land with compensation. A special conference to work out the details of the agricultural program was to be held in April. Finally, the Constitutionalists urged that the zemstvos be allowed to elect representatives to the so-called Bulygin Commission established a few days earlier by an Imperial Manifesto. Alexander Bulygin, assisted by his deputy, General Dmitrii Trepov, had replaced Mirskii as Minister of Interior in January. Miliukov had been sharply critical of their appointment. "The nomination of Mr. Trepov and Mr. Bulygin," he wrote, "can but be taken as a threat of violence and provocation. . . . They received their preparatory training in politics in Moscow, under the auspices of Grand Duke Sergius. It is also known that the policy of the latter is that of unswerving reaction." But Grand Duke Sergei, the Governor-General of Moscow, was assassinated in early February—the first victim of the Imperial house since 1881. It was a great shock to the Emperor and prompted the publication on February 18 of a Manifesto promising, for the first time, at least a consultative assembly designed to assist the government in drawing up legislation. This was the origin of the Bulygin Commission.[5]

Miliukov was quite unimpressed by the Manifesto. "Autocracy," he wrote,

> is to be preserved at any cost, and the role of the representative assembly is to be the same as in that one [sic] planned by Loris Melikov. . . . A study of the "rescript" shows that no time for

[4] VOSP, I, 238; CRI, p. 527; VOSP, I, 267, 269.
[5] The Zemstvo-Constitutionalist congress is described in SHA, pp. 148–49, and SM I, 333–36. CRI, pp. 544–45.

convoking the assembly was set, no definite scheme for the franchise was mentioned, and that previous to putting the promised
assembly into operation, the whole proposition—even as to its possibility—is to be discussed by a special committee. . . . Under these
circumstances it will be clearly seen how illusory the promise
must be.[6]

Another government declaration of the same day had more far-
reaching consequences. An imperial order granted the right of
petition to individuals and organizations, who could now suggest
improvements in the state directly to the Council of Ministers. For
the next few months Russia enjoyed an unprecedented degree of
freedom of speech and assembly under the shadow of this imperial
order. Miliukov profited from it after his return in April.[7]

While the Zemstvo-Constitutionalists were more moderate than
Miliukov, they could be moved leftward, whereas the Union of Liberation could not be moved to the right. Their March congress had
approved a far more ambitious program than that of the Constitutionalists. The Liberators were promising "the broadest regional self-
government" to Poland, Lithuania, the Ukraine, and Transcaucasia.
Miliukov, who in Paris had been stubborn in regard to Poland, must
have had questions about such concessions to other parts of the Empire. He must also have had his doubts about "the introduction of the
eight-hour day immediately where it is possible, and gradually elsewhere"; the Constitutionalists had not made any pronouncement on
the labor question yet. The Liberators also outlined a detailed program of agrarian reform without waiting for the special conference
scheduled by the zemstvists.[8]

II

The Union of Liberation was clearly too heterogeneous and too
leftist to become Miliukov's political home. He was not a socialist,
and it was the socialists who were becoming dominant in that body.

[6] Loc. cit., n. 35.

[7] The text of the government decrees published on February 18, 1905, is in
Pravitelstvennyi Vestnik (St. Petersburg), No. 39 (February 18, 1905), p. 1. A
description of the public reaction is in HAR, pp. 129–36.

[8] The program is printed in HAR, pp. 237–39. SHA, pp. 151–58, is in error
in stating that Miliukov arrived just in time for the congress; he returned to
Moscow in the first days of April. See also VOSP, I, 266–67.

He continued to be friendly with the Populists and, in 1905, continued to write for their *Russkoe Bogatstvo*. But the Populists were friends. Political colleagues were to be found among the Zemstvo-Constitutionalists, particularly in the Moscow group of liberal professors who served as the ideological staff of the group. Maxim Kovalevskii, Sergei Muromtsev, Fedor Kokoshkin, and Paul Novgorodtsev were the members of this brain trust with whom Miliukov had most in common. They were connected with Moscow University, they were liberal, and they were concerned with the political rather than the economic reconstruction of Russia along European constitutional lines. "It was this independent political work which I found in Moscow in a political circle close to me—and I eagerly joined it. Here, finally, I felt fully 'in' at last."[9]

Kokoshkin became Miliukov's closest associate. A Privatdocent in constitutional law, he had made a special study of Western constitutional practice and had twice visited England. Though twelve years younger than Miliukov, he remained an intimate political friend until his murder by Bolshevik sailors in January, 1918. The Moscow brain trust was busy drawing up Russia's future constitution, and Miliukov was enlisted for the work. He disagreed only on the provision for a second legislative chamber, which he regarded with suspicion. Kokoshkin argued that a second chamber was needed for a future federal Russia. Others wanted an upper house based on a more restricted suffrage. Miliukov disagreed with both arguments and feared that "the mere existence of an upper house will serve to prolong the period of theoretic [sic] struggle in politics, as it will always be suspected of defending class interests, and its introduction will undoubtedly be considered as treason to the principle of direct and general representation."[10]

Discussions of the future constitution, however, were not enough. Miliukov had to get acquainted with the Russian public in person. Here the Union of Liberation, with its provincial branches, was indispensable. Though he might prefer the Constitutionalists, Miliukov was not a zemstvist, and they could not provide him with an audience.

[9] V. A. Miakotin had asked Miliukov to join the SR Central Committee in 1902: "He was surprised by my answer that I did not consider myself a socialist" (VOSP, I, 264, and ROK, XI, 139). VOSP, I, 271.

[10] CRI, p. 522. See also P. Miliukov, "Demokratizm i vtoraia palata," RB, July, 1905, pp. 193–210. On Kokoshkin, see VOSP, I, 271–72, and DAN', pp. 69–70; his autobiography is in RVS, pp. 86–90.

The Liberationists could, and Miliukov undertook a speaking tour sponsored by them.

The conciliation mission, which he had chosen for himself in Paris and in his American lectures, was based on certain misconceptions. The workers' movement, for example, appeared to him still as primarily concerned with working conditions and the protection of labor. Some of his audiences, however, particularly in Kursk and Kharkov, would simply not accept such a formulation of the problem. The Bolsheviks in the audience attacked him bitterly; in Kharkov the argument lasted all night, and the contending parties went their separate ways unconvinced. "This," Miliukov recalled, "was quite unlike speaking before American clubs, or lecturing to more or less sophisticated audiences. Here one had to address oneself to a crowd." He discovered that he was no demagogue and depended for effect on calm and logical reasoning. Wherever the audience was properly prepared his speeches, according to witnesses, "had enormous success." There was a good deal of contemptuous heckling. We have a vignette of a Miliukov talk in the Morozov "Portuguese" mansion in Moscow. Asked about the agrarian problem, he emphasized resettling the peasantry beyond European Russia. The Bolshevik Grigorii Aleksinskii replied with sarcasm: "Perhaps the liberal professor would himself like to go to Siberia to plant cabbage and dig for potatoes?" Even the secret police agent present reported that Miliukov had spoken "in a most moderate tone."[11]

Miliukov had now been introduced to the non-zemstvo public. He was next to meet most of the prominent zemstvists, too—an all-Russian congress of the organization met in Moscow on April 22–26, the first such gathering since the November meeting which he had missed. Though he could not participate directly, not being a zemstvist, he was permitted to observe the proceedings. On the lines of the Zemstvo-Constitutionalists the congress approved a bicameral system, with an upper chamber to be elected by the zemstvos. It also approved a preliminary legislative assembly to consist of a single chamber, thus supporting the Liberationist program. The conservative minority, led by Shipov, mustered only eight votes (against 127)

[11] SHA, p. 157; M. Vishniak, "O redaktore 'Russkikh Zapisok,' " PN, March 22, 1939, p. 5. Miliukov's account of his lecture tour is in ROK, X, 135–38, and VOSP, I, 281–84. The Okhrana report is quoted from police archives in CHER, p. 115.

in opposition to universal suffrage. Thereafter, the Shipovites stood apart from their colleagues and, eventually, formed the nucleus of the Octobrist party, while the majority entered the Kadet party. As in the past, Miliukov attacked Shipov's attempts to continue a policy of collaboration with the monarchy. To Shipov's argument that West European constitutions were not applicable to Russia, he answered, with James Bryce, that Russia had to obey "the laws of political biology" which, at certain stages of political evolution, made representative institutions inevitable. "No," he told Shipov, "you better follow your Byzantine path and leave us our West European straightforwardness." The legal weekly *Pravo* agreed with Miliukov in its editorial:

> Our present state order is an exact photographic copy of Western European absolute monarchies of the old regime. . . . Our officials always were and remain convinced Westerners. The whole difference between them and the constitutionalists is that they borrow from European institutions of the old—and the constitutionalists of the new—order.[12]

The Zemstvists, though they could not admit Miliukov to their meetings, wished to hear their ally who had come back from foreign travels. A special meeting was arranged to which "all Moscow" was invited. The audience included Prince V. M. Golitsyn (the mayor of Moscow), the family of Prince Peter N. Trubetskoi (the marshal of the Moscow Nobility), the staffs of *Russkiia Vedomosti* and *Russkaia Mysl'*, in all more than three hundred persons. Miliukov was hospitably readmitted into the Moscow political and social world. After that, invitations streamed in. One of the more interesting came from Margarita K. Morozova, a widow of a wealthy Moscow manufacturer, whose house was frequented by the literary and artistic talents of Moscow. She donated several thousand rubles for Miliukov's future

---

[12] *Pravo*, No. 17 (May 1, 1905), p. 1346, translated in SM I, 341–42. Miliukov's argument against Shipov is from P. Miliukov, "Novyi variant slavianofil'skoi politicheskoi doktriny," RB, April, 1905, reprinted in GOD, pp. 21–26. Miliukov wrote of the Shipovites in another article of the same month: "The presence of such a group in the composition of a constitutional-democratic party would lead to an effacing of its program, and a weakening of its tactics" (GOD, p. 35). Miliukov's account of the zemstvo congress is in ROK, X, 128–31, and VOSP, I, 274–76. See also SM I, 336–42.

political party and had him pose for a portrait by the fashionable
painter Leonid Pasternak.[13]

In addition to such pleasant social duties, Miliukov attended the
agrarian conference of the Constitutionalists at the end of April in
Moscow. The eighty participants included practically all the future
Kadet agrarian experts: Viacheslav Iakushkin, whose agrarian radicalism went back to his grandfather, the Decembrist I. D. Iakushkin;
Nikolai Chernenkov, a zemstvo statistician and a future member of
the Kadet agrarian commission; Aleksandr Kaufman, an expert on
agrarian resettlement; Aleksandr Manuilov, professor of agricultural
economics at Moscow University; and Mikhail Gertsenshtein, the
chief Kadet spokesman on the land problem in the First Duma.
Among such experts Miliukov played a minor role, but he fully
agreed with the general outlines of the solution. Though no formal
program was drawn up, it was clear to all that the land problem was
again on the agenda of the day; the agrarian disorders of 1902 were
being repeated in several provinces, and Constitutionalist radicals,
such as Petrunkevich and Peter Dolgorukov, easily convinced the delegates of the need for compulsory alienation of land, the abolition
of redemption dues, and the lowering of peasant taxes.[14]

III

If formulating economic programs was not Miliukov's forte, there
was one new direction into which his energies were channeled. This
was the "Union" movement, which had gathered momentum in the
spring of 1905. The previous autumn the Liberationists had urged the
formation of unions of professional men to serve as transmission belts
for the passage of political resolutions. The idea began to catch on
after Bloody Sunday, and, by April, a group of unions had met and
endorsed programs of various degrees of radicalism. The movement
aroused Miliukov's interest from the moment of his return to Russia.
Here was a temporary substitute for the political parties which had to
be brought into existence if the constitutional order was to come. The
role of these unions, which should not be confused with the trade

[13] ROK, X, 130–34; VOSP, I, 277–81; the portrait was, apparently, never
completed.

[14] The protocols of the conference are in Agrarnyi vopros: Sbornik statei, I
(Moscow, 1906), 299–355. Miliukov spoke only once, loc. cit., I, 352–53.

unions of a later day, was, in Miliukov's opinion, "to unite such elements as, for one reason or another, could not join the existing political parties. These elements, it so happens, occupy the middle ground between the right and left groupings."[15]

As individual unions formed there was increasing interest in forming a "Union of Unions" to act in the same fashion as the Union of Liberation—as a spokesman for a coalition of groups. The first meeting to form such an organization was held in Moscow on May 8–9; fourteen unions were represented by sixty delegates. They spoke for the union of academic personnel, lawyers, agronomists and statisticians, medical personnel and veterinarians, journalists, the Union for Jewish Equality, the Union for Women's Equality, engineers, accountants, pharmacists, and railroad employees. The Zemstvo-Constitutionalists also sent representatives. It was largely professional men who attended—an important ingredient for the future party of the center. The delegates agreed to meet again at the end of the month, with fuller instructions, for the formation of a united body. Miliukov, who was well satisfied, was to be its chairman.

The Union's congress at the end of May was preceded by an event which mobilized public opinion with renewed force. The Russian Baltic fleet was sunk by the Japanese on May 14 in the Straits of Tsushima. The fresh disaster served as new proof of the government's incompetence in handling the war and produced a reaction among all layers of Russian society. Miliukov was in St. Petersburg at the time and was approached by several members of the Union of Liberation to participate in an anti-government demonstration to be held in the Pavlovsk Park on May 22. The intermission of a concert would be utilized for speeches of protest. Despite misgivings Miliukov agreed to participate, but the attempt proved an utter failure. When the Liberationist Vasilii Vodovozov began to speak, the frightened public dispersed as quickly as possible. Several persons were beaten by the police, who arrested some of the ringleaders. "I left with a feeling of shame for our naïveté," Miliukov recalled. "The incident cured me radically from repeating such demonstrations."[16]

Tsushima brought about a special zemstvo meeting in Moscow on

[15] P. Miliukov, "Politicheskie ili professional'nye soiuzy," GOD, p. 45.
[16] ROK, XI, 143. See also "Demonstratsiia v Pavlovske," OS No. 72 (June 8, 1905), pp. 363–64.

May 24–25. Known as the "coalition congress," it included, in addition to the regular zemstvists and Constitutionalists, representatives of the Shipovite minority, marshals of the nobility, and delegates of the town dumas, some two hundred persons in all. A petition to the Emperor was drawn up asking that a national assembly elected by universal suffrage should, together with the sovereign, deliberate upon the issue of war or peace and draw up necessary governmental reforms. It also demanded the appointment of new ministers and the immediate establishment of civil rights. The congress elected a delegation of fourteen to deliver the petition. These were George and Nikolai Lvov, Petrunkevich, Paul Dolgorukov, Fedor Golovin, Fedor Rodichev, and Shakhovskoi, all future Kadet leaders; N. N. Kovalevskii, Novosil'tsev, Prince Sergi Trubetskoi, and Count Geiden, moderate constitutionalists; and Baron P. L. Korf, A. N. Nikitin, and Mikhail Fedorov, representing the St. Petersburg Town Duma. The Emperor was to receive them on June 6.[17]

The Union of Unions, which met simultaneously in Moscow, was sharply critical of such moderate tactics as a petition to the Emperor. Its mood was far more militant and Miliukov, who was in the chair, seemed to go along with the radicals for the moment. The assembly passed a resolution, written by him, which was directed not to the Emperor, but to the people of Russia. It was cast in unusually strong language:

> We spoke as long as there was a shadow of hope that we would be listened to. This hope has now vanished, and we must seek a new path. We must act. . . . All means are now legitimate against the terrible threat which exists by the very fact of the continued existence of the present government. And all means should be tried. . . . Make every effort immediately to eliminate the brigand gang which has usurped state power, and replace it by a constituent assembly . . . so that it might, as soon as possible, put an end both to the war and to the political regime now in power.[18]

Miliukov had never before so clearly sanctioned revolutionary means. Recalling the event more than three decades later, he said of the reso-

[17] The congress protocols are in OS, No. 74 (July 13, 1905), pp. 403–8.
[18] The text is in OS, No. 72 (June 8, 1905), p. 367, translated in SM I, 366–69.

lution that "*at that time* it seemed neither extreme nor rhetorical, and corresponded fully with the mood of the congress, and my own as well." He probably realized that, given the loose organization of the Union of Unions, he was in any case unable to control its radical members. As for his Constitutionalists—he would protect their tactics from Left attacks; while his meeting refused to express sympathy with the coalition congress it also refrained from condemning the delegation to the Emperor. Miliukov got what he wanted, "benevolent neutrality" toward the methods of the more moderate section of public opinion.[19]

The fourteen-man delegation was received by the Emperor on June 6. Prince Trubetskoi spoke for the zemstvists. He departed from the text of the petition in the direction of a more "fatherly tone," approved at a "rehearsal" at which Miliukov was present. The Russian people, he told the Emperor, continued to trust their Tsar. Trubetskoi condemned both the bureaucracy and "sedition." He refrained from asking for a constituent assembly but warned against representation based on class. After Fedorov, speaking for the cities, reiterated Trubetskoi's sentiments, the Emperor replied. He told the delegates to "cast away your doubts. My will—the Tsar's will to summon representatives of the people—is inexorable." Though the Left was quite critical of Trubetskoi's conciliatory tone and his condemnation of "sedition," Miliukov recalls that he felt a "sense of satisfaction" about the results. Writing about the reception a year later, he saw it as a milestone between the November 1904 zemstvo congress and the October Manifesto. "June 6," he wrote, "occupies a transitional place between November 6 and October 17. On November 6 the country first loudly formulated its desires. On June 6 it heard an equally loud answer to them, one equivalent to an obligation. On October 17 this obligation was embodied in a written document."[20] Miliukov was not above sanctioning revolution, but he also welcomed peaceful pressure on the monarch by the moderates.

---

[19] ROK, XI, 144–46 (italics in the original); VOSP, I, 285–87, 290–93.

[20] P. Miliukov, "Deputatsiia koalitsionnogo s"ezda 6 iunia 1905 g.," *Riech'*, June 6, 1906, reprinted in GOD, pp. 8–12. See also ROK, XI, 143–44. The text of the Trubetskoi speech and the Emperor's answer is in I. Belokonskii, "K istorii zemskogo dvizheniia," *Istoricheskii Sbornik* (St. Petersburg), 1907, pp. 74–77.

IV

"All of Russia is beginning to talk," wrote Miliukov in June.[21] Sometimes it "talked" in very radical terms indeed, as in the mutiny on the battleship *Potemkin* which broke out that month. While the Union of Unions had no branches in the armed forces it did reach out to the peasantry. Miliukov proposed that, henceforth, "all the attention of the unions must be directed toward the provinces." He welcomed the formation of a Peasant Union, which held its founding congress in Moscow July 31–August 1. One hundred delegates represented twenty-two guberniias; an additional twenty-five intellectuals attended. It was not a radical group, since the majority of the speakers favored compensation for confiscated land. Two future Kadets (A. Teslenko and A. Staal') were elected to a central bureau. It looked as if the future liberal party might gain a foothold among the moderate peasantry. A future Kadet leader analyzed the congress in hopeful tones.[22]

Little was heard from the government, except the appointment, at the end of the month, of Witte as the chief Russian delegate to the peace negotiations with Japan. At least the onerous war would be ended. As for internal reforms only the secret Bulygin Commission continued its labors over a future representative assembly. What had been heard of its recommendations inspired no confidence—the proposed assembly was to be elected on the basis of a restricted suffrage and would have very limited powers. At its new congress on July 1–3 the Union of Unions took a largely negative attitude toward elections to such a body. Nine unions voted to boycott the elections, three desired to participate, and four abstained from taking a stand. Miliukov took a rather strange position on the matter. The Union's decision, he thought, "is psychologically and politically correct for the present moment," but he supported participation, for it would make the opposition's power grow, while abstention would weaken it. He feared the radical agitation for a democratic republic which, he said, "must be fought in every way," because it was "illusionary," "politi-

[21] GOD, p. 53.

[22] A. Kornilov, "Fakticheskie dannye o nastroenii krest'ian," *Pravo*, 1905, No. 33, pp. 2689–99. The protocols of the meeting are in OS, No. 77, pp. 470–72, and No. 78–79, pp. 489–95. See also E. Kiriukhina, "Vserosiiskii krest'ianskii soiuz v 1905 g.," IZ, L (1955), 95–141.

cally incorrect," and "dangerous."[23] For the first time he engaged in polemics with the extreme Left, and he was paid back in kind. Lenin, who could not have known who stood behind the initials -cc- in the *Osvobozhdenie* article, attacked Miliukov. "Mr. -cc-," he wrote, "blurted out the hidden 'thoughts' of the landowners and capitalists which we have exposed hundreds of times. 'The chief interest' for them is not giving the vote to the people [this they fear] but in the extent of the Duma's jurisdiction."[24] The Social Democrats, particularly the Bolsheviks, would boycott the Bulygin legislature.

The zemstvists, who assembled for a new congress in Moscow on July 6–9, abstained from taking any direct action on the subject. This was their largest gathering to date, meeting in conjunction with representatives of the town dumas. The latter had also become politically active and, on June 15–16, had held their own Moscow congress, in which one hundred and twenty-six delegates represented eighty-six cities. The congress agreed to join the zemstvists in their future gatherings, and, till the end of the year, the congresses would be joint zemstvo-town duma affairs. Among the town duma leadership were the future Kadet luminaries Nikolai Astrov, Nikolai Shchepkin, and Aleksandr Manuilov. The first joint town-zemstvo congress was attended by two hundred and thirty-five delegates from all over Russia, representing localities as distant as Tiflis, Tomsk, Krasnoiarsk and Irkutsk. During the opening session a police detachment appeared and took down the names of all those present. The delegates were in a defiant mood; all signed the police protocol and cheered when the authorities departed.[25]

The meetings were held in the Dolgorukov mansion where Miliukov, many years before, had prepared for his gymnasium examinations with Nikolai Dolgorukov. This time Miliukov attended the meetings freely, though a few cautious zemstvists objected to his presence. Prince Sergei Trubetskoi, the spokesman of the delegation to the Emperor, resented Miliukov who "incited the radicals" at the

[23] P. Miliukov, "Idti ili ne idti v gosudarstvennuiu dumu," OS, No. 75 (August 6, 1905), pp. 417–18. For some unexplained reason neither Miliukov nor the Zemstvo-Constitutionalists attended the Union congress: VOSP, I, 292–93.

[24] *Proletarii*, August 23, 1905, reprinted in LEN, VIII, 169.

[25] On the town duma congress, see N. Astrov, *Vospominaniia* (Paris, 1940), pp. 303–6; OS, No. 75, pp. 422–23.

congress and "agitated with might and main."[26] But Miliukov was now inseparable from such assemblies, though he still had no legal right to attend and no vote. His influence behind the scenes was undeniable.

The congress heard a report on a substitute for the Bulygin project. This was the "Fundamental Law of the Russian Empire," prepared by the group with whom Miliukov had worked in April—Muromtsev, Kokoshkin, et al. It specified a bicameral legislature, no vote for women, and rather wide powers for the monarch. This "constitution" was approved in principle by the meeting in what Muromtsev called its "first reading"—using the parliamentary terminology of Western countries. There was much more debate over a proposed "Statement to the Public"; some zemstvists hesitated to turn to the people directly. Finally, however, all signed the pronouncement sanctioning peaceful political activity by all groups of the population: "Let us march united to our common goal," said the document. "You must calmly and openly assemble, and discuss your needs and announce your desires without fear that someone will try to stop you."[27]

The Zemstvo-Constitutionalists met immediately afterward. Here Miliukov was more at home and saw progress toward the formation of that constitutional party which he saw as the goal. The Constitutionalists, meeting July 9–10, elected a committee of twenty, including Miliukov who, with another twenty to be chosen by the Union of Liberation, were charged to formulate a program for the crystallizing party. In Miliukov's eyes the general zemstvo congresses, though useful, had held up the formation of a party. The Constitutionalists and Liberationists now had to make up for lost time. It was clear to him that the advanced zemstvists and the Liberationist intelligentsia had to co-operate in the future party. "One thing is certain," he wrote: "namely that 'political power' will remain with the latter group [the zemstvists] only in union with the former [the intelligentsia], and that the conditions of such a union must be fully clarified in a mutual striving for one and the same goal."[28] The question remained, however (and it was not solved till the following

[26] O. Trubetskaia, Kniaz' S. N. Trubetskoi (New York, 1953), p. 148.

[27] The text is in Belokonskii, op. cit., pp. 87–91. The protocols of the meeting are in "Iul'skii s"ezd," OS, No. 76, pp. 447–60.

[28] GOD, p. 33.

year), as to the limits, on both the right and the left, beyond which the party would not go.

This question was debated at the congress in a motion of joining the Union of Unions on a definitive basis. Miliukov defended the affirmative but met with some determined opposition. Several delegates criticized the Union's May appeal (written by Miliukov) sanctioning revolutionary action. "I would never resort to aggressive physical action," protested Count Geiden. Prince Evgenii Trubetskoi did not condemn "organized mass uprisings" but felt quite differently about "individual terroristic acts." If they were condoned now, they could not be opposed "in the future, when they will be applied to us if we do not please someone." Miliukov contended that the situation was too serious to permit such moral scruples:

> It is after all difficult [he said] to depend on a peaceful solution of political problems at a time when a revolution is taking place all around us. Or perhaps you are counting on someone else's physical strength, secretly hoping for certain results, but not wishing to personally participate in acts of physical compulsion? But that would be hypocrisy, and that sort of hypocritical formulation of the problem would be dishonest from the civic point of view.

The man who privately deplored the peaceful Pavlovsk Park demonstration in which he had taken part spoke rather differently in public. Peter Dolgorukov took his side: it was clear, he said, that the "political spring" of Sviatopolk-Mirskii owed everything to the bomb which had killed Plehve. Besides, the Union of Unions, with its forty thousand members, represented a mighty force compared to the slender cadres of the Constitutionalists; in Dolgorukov's district, for example, there were four Constitutionalists but sixty members of the Union of Unions. Miliukov moved the meeting to action by wondering whether the Union of Unions might not "decline the honor of entering into comradely relations with you" in view of what had been said. This decided the issue, and the group voted to join the Union, and not to bind its delegates by any conditions.[29]

The radical turn which the revolution was to take in the autumn seemed to justify Miliukov's summer urgings. In an article written in

---

[29] The protocols are in "Zemtsy-konstitutsionalisty o konstitutsionno-demokra-ticheskoi partii," OS, No. 78–79 (October 5, 1905), Prilozhenie, pp. 1–14. See also ROK, XII, 122–25, and VOSP, I, 296–98.

July he asserted that "Russia finds herself in a condition close to civil war . . . the country is not on the brink of anarchy, as often used to be said in the past, but in anarchy itself." What was needed to deal with chaos was organization; a party was needed which would have moral authority not only among the moderate elements, but with the masses. The zemstvists, he warned, "must remember that public opinion, on which their strength rests, is not 'in their hands,' that they are only a small part of that wave which flows irrepressibly to its limit, and that no pacification is possible before that limit is reached."[30]

V

The Bulygin project, conceived in February, finally bore fruit in July and August. The national representative body promised by the Emperor in June was at last taking shape. The project, prepared by a bureaucratic commission, was considered at a secret conference at Peterhof presided over by the Emperor. Kliuchevskii was invited as a consultant. After the first day's meeting he sent his son Boris to Miliukov with all the papers and a request: would his former student help to orient him in the political situation of the moment? Miliukov responded with pleasure, and every evening after the meetings (July 19–26) the two met in Kliuchevskii's hotel discussing the proceedings. At the end of the conference Kliuchevskii gave Miliukov a copy of the secret protocols, which the latter turned over to the journal *Pravo.* They were published abroad with an introduction by Miliukov's future newspaper colleague Iossif Gessen. It had been a splendid opportunity to reconnoitre the inmost circles of the government. But Miliukov also prized his new relationship with his old teacher. His master in history was now sanctioning his new political career. Kliuchevskii joined the future Kadet party and remained Miliukov's friend till his death in 1911. "My contacts with Kliuchevskii," Miliukov wrote with pride, "were not interrupted from the time of our July meetings till his death. I saw with pleasure and moral satisfaction that Vasilii Osipovich gave all his sympathy to the

[30] P. Miliukov, "Rossiia organizuetsia," OS, No. 74 (July 13, 1905), pp. 396–98; GOD, p. 32.

political group to which I have the honor of belonging."[31]

Kliuchevskii's copy of the protocols gave Miliukov the information he needed to write about the government project which was finally published on August 6.[32] A national representative body had now become law. Despite its imperfections Miliukov saw it as an immense step forward:

> There is no going back from it [he wrote]. There is only an opportunity of moving forward. . . . We think that the very fact of the appearance of national representatives, elected by the population, will bring so new a tone into our political life that the preservation of the old order will remain quite impossible. . . . Now, after August 6, the bureaucratic system in Russia is no more.

The Bulygin Duma was only a beginning: "It will be impossible to restrict the free political life implied by the document within the limits of the Fundamental Laws," he thought, since "Russia's inhabitants are formally acknowledged to be . . . citizens."[33]

But though the Rubicon had been crossed, neither the radicals nor the moderates were pleased with the reform. The Duma was "an institution quite clearly not created 'on a Western model.'" "We did not," Miliukov commented, "get away from Western forms despite all efforts, but only departed from the contemporary and best forms of political life in the civilized world. Or, rather, we have not grown up to them yet." Instead of universal and direct suffrage the law granted only a limited and indirect one. Only males over twenty-five who were peasants, landowners, or propertied city dwellers were to vote in two to four indirect stages. The Duma, far from being an independent legislature, was conceived as an appendage of the State Council.

Instead of a national electorate, the law created "an oligarchy of

---

[31] *Petergofskoe soveshchanie o proekte gosudarstvennoi dumy: Sekretnye protokoly* (Berlin, n.d.). See also B. Pares "The Peterhof Conference," *Russian Review* (London), II (1913), 87–120. Also P. Miliukov, "V. O. Kliuchevskii," in V. O. *Kliuchevskii: Kharakteristiki i vospominaniia* (Moscow, 1912), p. 215.

[32] Miliukov wrote two articles on the Bulygin Duma: a lengthy analysis for *Pravo* and a short newspaper comment for *Syn Otechestva*. They are reprinted in GOD, pp. 54–69 and 69–72. The text of the Imperial Manifesto, the Duma Statute, and the electoral law is in KAL, pp. 30–54.

[33] GOD, pp. 67–68, 71.

electoral colleges" in which the peasants represented 42.7 per cent of
the electors, the nobles 34.1 per cent, and all other categories 23.1 per
cent. The workers and almost the entire intelligentsia were disfranchised by the high property requirements. Miliukov knew that "there
is an enormous gulf between that which the Duma gives the public
and what the public desires," but one could not afford to boycott the
elections: "This is not as little as it seems—to the vanguard of the
fighters," he concluded. Lenin disagreed vehemently:

> If we had a parliament [he wrote] we would definitely support
> . . . Miliukov and Co. . . . But in the epoch of a revolution and not
> of a parliament . . . the support of men unable to struggle in a
> revolutionary fashion is 1. a violation of the independence of our
> party . . . 2. such support is treason to the revolution. There is no
> parliament yet, only the Miliukovs have illusions. We must struggle
> in a revolutionary manner for a parliament, and not in a parlia-
> mentary way for a revolution.[34]

In Lenin's eyes Miliukov was "unable to struggle in a revolutionary
fashion." The government, nevertheless, put him in jail on August
7, the day after the publication of the Bulygin Duma statute. The
authorities considered that its promulgation ended the public debate
about political reform inaugurated in February. They would now
settle accounts with some of those who had taken too much advantage of the relaxation; Miliukov was evidently one of these. Already
in July the police had searched the residence of prominent zemstvists
and confiscated the papers of the last zemstvo congress.[35] They
moved with even more despatch against the Union of Unions, which
had voted to boycott the Duma. When its bureau met in Miliukov's
Udel'naia apartment, the police surrounded the house and took all
those present to St. Petersburg. It was Miliukov's third and last
prison term. He thought that the month in jail "resembled an idyll."
The prison library had the Russian classics, and he read to his fill.
His wife visited him regularly and brought political reading matter.

---

[34] *Ibid.*, pp. 55, 59. It is interesting to note that Sergei Kryzhanovskii, the chief
author of the Bulygin project, asserted he took Speranskii as a model "to avoid
the possibility of being reproached for copying Western models" (KRY, p. 34).
Also GOD, pp. 63–64, 67, 70; and Lenin to Lunacharskii, October 11, 1905,
reprinted in *Leninskii sbornik*, XVI (Moscow, 1931), 276–77.

[35] OS, No. 75, p. 440.

Once a week a friend came to play chess: the game took place in the prison director's office. While the revolutionary storm gathered, Miliukov had a quiet rest in preparation for the harder days ahead.[36]

In his absence the Union of Liberation held its congress in Moscow on August 23–26, their first since March when Miliukov had still been abroad. They followed the example of the Constitutionalists, appointing a commission to join the former in laying the foundations for a political party. They acted in Miliukov's spirit, voting for "an open political party in the European sense of the term," to be called "constitutional-democratic." These foreign words were adopted "as a pedagogical move" to educate the public in Western political terminology. The congress also voted to participate in the Bulygin Duma, not for "organic work," however, but in order "to struggle to achieve truly constitutional freedoms." The Union would continue to exist until the Duma's calling. "It is still irreplaceable," Miliukov had written in July, "and cannot be disbanded."[37]

VI

Miliukov's arrest had created a good deal of concern both in Russia and abroad. Kliuchevskii asked Prince Sergei Trubetskoi to intervene on his behalf and to regain Kliuchevskii's papers, which had been seized during Miliukov's arrest. Political figures urged open protests, much to Lenin's disgust; he thought that other victims of the regime deserved help more urgently.

> We will patiently wait [he wrote bitingly] while Parvus, Petrunkevich, Stakhovich and Martov "organize a popular protest and, if possible, a popular rising" for Miliukov's defense. After all, gentlemen, that is a far more active question in our "almost" constitutional epoch: to defend Miliukov rather than the hundreds and thousands of arrested and beaten-up workers!

The Academic Union, meeting in Moscow August 25–28, expressed, in a special resolution, its "feeling of strongest indignation and most decisive protest" at Miliukov's arrest. The British journalist Henry

[36] ROK, XI, 149; XII, 116–18, 125; VOSP, I, 301–2.
[37] The fullest account of the congress is in SHA, pp. 164–69. See also P. Miliukov, "Soiuz osvobozhdeniia i drugie politicheskie partii," OS, No. 74 (July 13, 1905), pp. 410–12.

Wickham Steed, then a correspondent of the London *Times*, visited Miliukov in jail to bring him the sympathy of his English friends. In his interview with the all-powerful General Trepov, head of the Empire's police, Steed intervened on Miliukov's behalf. Such help might prove embarrassing in the eyes of the Left; after his release in early September Miliukov asserted that "it would be incorrect" to give Steed credit for his liberation. Since the Left might suspect some sort of deal between the police and Miliukov, he assured the public that if his release should mean "a decrease in the activity of Russian society then I would a thousand times prefer to return to the Vyborg jail." It was a wise precaution on Miliukov's part, since even his future Kadet colleagues, such as Mandel'shtam, maintained that "Miliukov was freed for the sake of Europe, not for our sake." Steed had not earned Miliukov's gratitude, particularly when, at a meeting with prominent opposition leaders, he urged them to take seriously the government's concessions of August 6. In his eyes "these forces proposed peace to you." Maksim Kovalevskii, Vladimir Nabokov, Fedor Rodichev and other speakers disagreed with Steed's conciliatory campaign. Miliukov, who served as interpreter at the meeting, rejected Steed's "attempt to combine absolutism with liberalism." The Russian European did not want this sort of European help.[38]

Miliukov had been released in time to attend the Zemstvo-Town Duma congress in Moscow of September 12–15, the last such gathering before the formation of the Kadet party a month later. It was the last opportunity to use the zemstvo arena for the future party's work. Miliukov, who in April had only listened through a half-opened door and, in July, had been merely a delegate of the Union of Unions, was this time elected a member of the congress bureau, together with his old teacher Maksim Kovalevskii. He had become politically indispensable, as the loud applause greeting his election proved. In fact the congress had been delayed while he was in jail and held immediately after his release. The main item of business was the forthcoming Duma election and the platform which the congress wished to present to the voters.

The "Appeal to Voters" which Miliukov presented to the congress

---

[38] Trubetskaia, *op. cit.*, 152 n.; *Proletarii*, September 13, 1905, reprinted in LEN, VIII, 225–26; *Pravo*, 1905, p. 2881. Also P. Miliukov, "Pis'mo v redaktsiiu," RV, September 17, 1905. An account of the meeting appeared in RV, September 17 and 18, 1905.

stressed that political reform "remains the first task on which all must unite"; the Appeal was conceived of as "a non-party program," the last attempt to speak for a coalition of moderate and radical liberals. The "first and chief task of the State Duma" must be "the reorganization of the Duma itself," to provide it with wider powers, and the country with a new electoral law. The economic program was rather brief; it promised the workers a "shortening of the working day," and the right to organize and to strike—a right which they had been exercising vigorously for months. As for the peasants the Appeal stated that "in case of need the government should alienate part of the privately owned land," for "just compensation." The Appeal said nothing about the controversial nationality problem; Alexander Guchkov, who had led the opposition against the bureau's proposal, asserted that this averted a split in the congress.[39] What he really meant was that the Liberationists could push the zemstvists only so far. They had already made them speak in ways to which they were not used—on the labor question and on the land problem. The nationality problem, on which the Liberationists had acted as early as 1904, was too much to swallow at one sitting, and the radical liberals decided to bide their time on the issue.

Guchkov, the future leader of the Octobrists, had opposed concessions to non-Russians in the empire on earlier occasions. The issue, particularly as related to Poland, had been debated in liberal circles since 1904. Miliukov, it will be remembered, had not been overly generous on the subject at the Paris conference. But he knew that concessions to the Poles were unavoidable and wanted to make them while Polish demands were moderate. Aleksander Lednitskii, the popular Polish lawyer who lived in Moscow, made his spacious residence available for a series of Russo-Polish meetings in the spring of 1905. Lednitskii and his political colleagues presented a minimum program of autonomy within the ethnographic boundaries of Poland, with equal rights for Poles living in the so-called Southwest Region. A Russo-Polish meeting in May agreed to their demands, and the Constitutionalists were henceforth committed in this respect. Guch-

---

[39] The "Appeal to Voters" is in *Pravo*, 1905, pp. 3246–48. The bureau expected everyone to vote: "The experience of Western European countries," it said, "shows that abstention from elections leads to no results, while even a weak opposition in the chamber will affect the situation" (*ibid.*, 1905, p. 3047). The congress debates are in *ibid.*, 1905, pp. 3043–64 and 3170–83.

kov had debated the issue with Miliukov in Morozova's "Portuguese" mansion in April, and now came back to it in September.[40]

The border areas, particularly Poland and the Baltic provinces, had been exceptionally active in the liberation struggle throughout 1905. With seven delegates from the Polish provinces present at the congress, the autonomy issue was bound to come up. Kokoshkin presented a detailed "Report of the Organizational Bureau on the Rights of Nationalities and the Decentralization of Administration."[41] Provisions on cultural autonomy aroused no fears; but a proposal to create autonomous political regions with their own legislative assemblies aroused opposition. A substantial minority was not prepared to go that far, and a ballot resulted in a vote of 78:37. The dissenters, Miliukov later pointed out, were the nucleus of the future Octobrist party, led by Guchkov and Count Geiden.[42] Autonomy for Russian Poland was opposed only by Guchkov who argued that concessions to Poland would lead to a federal Russia and to the Empire's disintegration. Rodichev answered with a new argument, to be adopted by Miliukov in the future. Polish autonomy could be used as a weapon against Germany. "Autonomous Poland," he maintained, "will be a barrier against imperialism, against our enemy." The radical liberals wished to strengthen, not to weaken Russia as a great power. Guchkov cast the only dissenting vote against the resolution granting Poland autonomy and its own Sejm while "preserving the state unity of the Empire."[43] The Liberationists had moved the zemstvists to an important new milestone. Miliukov with his middle-of-the-road position could be satisfied with the progress made. The cadres of a party neither radical nor too cautious were now available for the coming elections.

Before that parliamentary test the Russian revolution still had some major surprises in store for that party; its founding congress was held

[40] The Russo-Polish meeting is described in Z. Nagorski, "Alexander Lednicki," Zeszyty Historiczne (Paris), I (1962), 29–30. The debate with Guchkov is related in ROK, VIII–IX, 122–23.

[41] The text is in Pravo, 1905, pp. 3321–42; on Poland, see the informative essay of M. Dziewanowski, "The Polish Revolutionary Movement and Russia, 1904–1907," in HSS, IV (1957), 375–94.

[42] ROK, XIII, 119–21.

[43] Pravo, 1905, pp. 3172, 3176. For an analysis of the congress, see SM I, 407–18.

at the height of Russia's first general strike. Only a few days after the September congress there began in Moscow a strike movement which was to paralyze the entire country. By October 8 all the Moscow railroad lines stopped operating; since the city was the rail center of the empire the result was soon felt in all parts of European Russia. By the sixteenth not a single train moved across the land. With all professions and trades joining in the strike all organized life came to a halt. The government, now headed by Witte, who had been appointed as the country's savior on October 13, was cut off from all its agents. There was no telegraph, telephone, water, electric power, bread, or newspapers. There were only rumors and endless meetings. Under such auspices was born the Constitutional-Democratic (Kadet) party, which held its first congress in Moscow October 12–18.[44]

VII

The Dolgorukov house, where the delegates gathered, was lit by candles. The eighty-one persons who attended were only a fraction of those who had been expected. The rest were stranded because of the railroad strike. There was even some question of whether to hold the congress; but the situation was too drastic, and there had been too much preparation. Even before adopting a program the party, on the fourteenth, issued a statement supporting the general strike in full. The goals of the strike were a constituent assembly elected by universal suffrage and a political amnesty. The party said that "it identifies itself in advance with the popular demands, and deposits on the scales of popular liberation all its sympathy, all its moral force, and it will grant it every form of support."[45] Thus, on the very first day of its existence the party adopted a bold stand which was to cost it much sorrow in future months. But the moment was too overwhelming, and it could not, it thought, act otherwise.

On the same day Miliukov delivered the keynote speech of the congress. "It was," he recalled, "the entrance examination for leadership"; it was also a critical moment in Russian history. "It was particularly difficult," Miliukov wrote later, "to remain calm, and main-

[44] The general strike is described in HAR, pp. 180–91. An incomplete account of the Kadet congress appeared in RV, October 18–20, 1905. For organizational matters connected with the calling of the congress, see TSENTR, pp. 16–20.
[45] The text of the statement is in Pravo, 1905, No. 52, Prilozhenie, pp. 57–58.

tain sober judgment under such circumstances." But the speech was quite moderate, in part for accidental reasons. "My task was made easier," he remembered, "by the absence of several Petersburg members of the Union of Liberation who would have brought an element of irreconcilability." The railroad strike had kept some radicals away. Present were some twenty-four members of the Union of Zemstvo-Constitutionalists and the Union of Liberation; the rest were provincial delegates who had not been infected by the extremism of the capital. The two Unions, Miliukov stressed, were the party's constituent elements. Their programs were not always in agreement; but he was sure that "as long as it will be possible to march to a common goal together both groups of the party will act as a single whole regardless of this difference in motives."

It was important, Miliukov continued, to define the party's relationship to its neighbors on the right and the left. The former, he said, attacked the Kadets as violators of private property and enemies of the unity of Russia. It would be more correct to say, Miliukov asserted, that "we are unalterable enemies of bureaucratic centralization and the Manchester school." Looking for analogies abroad, he asserted that "our party most resembles those Western groupings of the intelligentsia known as 'social reformers.' " While the party desired social justice for all classes, it was itself not a class party and could not subscribe to the slogans of the Left. "We do not," he said, "join their demands for a democratic republic and the socialization of the means of production. . . ." But the Kadets wished to remain friends with the socialists; Miliukov wished to speak "not of rivals but of allies on the left."[46] The future would show whether the Left was equally disposed.

The party program, presented to the congress for approval, was an amalgam of the many pronouncements of the zemstvo and Liberationist meetings. While the political program was largely of zemstvo origin, the economic and nationality provisions came from the more radical intellectuals. Given the conditions of the moment during which it was being adopted, it was a moderate program. On the vital land question the party took a further step, however; the program provided that "insofar as is necessary" land should be "alienated from

[46] ROK, XIII, 122; VOSP, I, 307. The text of the speech is in GOD, pp. 97–101.

private landlords and paid for by the government at equitable, not market prices." The last five words were an addition to the previous stand of the Constitutionalists and were a new concession to the land-hungry peasant. Two issues were left open in order not to antagonize the minority: the old question of one versus two legislative chambers and suffrage for women. It was decided that party policy, which was to extend the vote to women and demand a unicameral system, would not be binding on members who disagreed.[47] Among these was Miliukov, who opposed suffrage for women and debated the issue at the congress with his wife, much to the amusement of the delegates. He thought the provision would hurt the party's chances with the peasants who, he thought, doubted the political maturity of their spouses. The issue was allowed to ride till the following party congress.

The congress elected a Central Committee of thirty. Its composition showed that, though the party consisted of zemstvists and intellectuals, the latter predominated. Of the thirty only ten were zemstvists, and even some of these were professionals employed by the zemstvo. Perhaps as a concession to the weaker partner, the zemstvist Paul Dolgorukov was named chairman of the Committee; but the party's leadership was definitely in the hands of the intellectuals, where it would remain to the end.[48] And it was the moderate intellectuals, for four of the radicals elected resigned immediately after the congress, dissatisfied with the middle-of-the-road program adopted by the party. These were the revisionist socialists Sergei Prokopovich and his wife Ekaterina Kuskova, the Populist Vasilii Bogucharskii,

[47] The Kadet program is available in English in HAR, pp. 292–300 (Article 28 is missing by mistake).

[48] The committee consisted of the persons listed below; as noted above, four members resigned immediately after the congress, altering the ratio of zemstvists to intellectuals to 9:17. Zemstvists are labeled Z, others P (professionals). The source is MAR, pp. 14–16, and Konstitutsionno-Demokraticheskaia Partiia, S"ezd 12–18 oktiabria 1905 g. (Moscow, 1905), p. 26.

Vernadskii, V. (P); Vinaver, M. (P); Gessen, I. (P); Dolgorukov, Pavel (Z); Dolgorukov, Peter (Z); Kablukov, N. (Z); Kokoshkin, F. (P); Koliubakin, A. (Z); Kornilov, A. (P); Kotliarevskii, S. (P); Luchitskii, I. (P); L'vov, N. (Z); Maklakov, V. (P); Maksimov, A. (P); Mandel'shtam, M. (P); Miliukov, P. (P); Muromtsev, S. (P); Nabokov, V. (P); Petrovskii, I. (P); Petrunkevich, I. (Z); Sabashnikov, M. (P); Teslenko, N. (P); Chernenkov, N. (Z); Shakhovskoi, D. (Z); Shchepkin, N. (Z); Iakushkin, D. (P).

and Vasilii Khizhniakov. Their sympathy was with the St. Petersburg Soviet, and they accused the party's leadership of "aiming to become ministers"—an allusion to the negotiations with Witte which we shall examine presently. The Union of Unions had been captured by the Social Democrats, and its former chairman Miliukov was reduced to receiving its inflammatory mimeographed proclamations. Though one writer tried to convince moderate socialists that they could find a home in the Kadet party his was a lone voice, and Miliukov admitted that, "objectively speaking, the congress ended in a schism." But he said nothing to indicate that he regretted the loss of these former allies.[49]

The October Manifesto burst upon the congress without warning. Many were inclined to see it as a complete victory for the opposition, an approval of all its demands. Miliukov, lifted on a table to make a speech, however, "threw a cold douche" on his listeners. The manifesto, he said, "still does not represent the last word of possible concessions and does not even represent that minimum of concessions needed today." The manifesto proclaimed the general ideas that all wished to hear; but the "basic principles must still be embodied in exact legislative norms." The government had made promises before; it remained to be seen whether they were to be taken seriously this time.[50] Despite champagne and cheering Miliukov remained the sober analyst. Out on the street later, he found that his skepticism was not unjustified; a Black Hundreds' procession carrying icons and a large portrait of the Emperor was marching, shouting slogans against the Left. Miliukov disappeared into a side street to avoid having to take off his hat.[51]

Answering the manifesto, the party congress told the public that the party's major task remained the summoning of a constituent assembly; the Duma of October 17 could be "only one of the means

[49] See ROK, XIII, 124, and VOSP, I, 338–43. The appeal to socialists is A. Chuprov, "K.D. partiia i sotsializm," Pravo, November 20, 1905, pp. 3663–76, and is based on Miliukov's speech at the founding congress.

[50] Miliukov describes the banquet scene in ROK, XIII, 125–28; his comment on the Manifesto is in GOD, pp. 72–77. The English text of the Manifesto is in HAR, pp. 195–96. Maklakov, who was present at the banquet, recalls that Miliukov's speech ended with the words: "Nothing has changed, the war continues" (VLAST', p. 431).

[51] ROK, XIII, 128.

toward the realization of this aim." If the government meant what it said in the manifesto it must undertake the following: (1) the immediate establishment of civil rights, and the abolition of exceptional laws; (2) the immediate introduction of universal suffrage; (3) the replacement of the existing government by a "cabinet of experts" until Russia's parliament selected a new government from its majority; (4) the granting of a political amnesty. Commenting on the statement, Miliukov wrote that he did not see why a constituent assembly frightened so many moderates. "In itself," he maintained, "the idea of a constituent assembly means nothing terrifying, and history provides examples of constituent assemblies of the most peaceful character."[52] One might equally well wonder, however, whether the lessons of earlier European history applied to modern Russia in the midst of a violent revolution.

VIII

Miliukov also spoke of Witte's report to the Emperor, which accompanied the October Manifesto. In the Premier's statement, he said, "we find wider perspectives than in the manifesto."[53] Witte recognized that the government must engage in "extensive and active co-operation with society"; on October 18 he began by inviting Shipov to join his cabinet as state comptroller. But Shipov was, as Miliukov put it, "an honest man" and refused to collaborate unless the radical zemstvists were invited as well. On October 21 Witte received a zemstvo delegation consisting of Kokoshkin, Golovin, and Prince George L'vov. Shipov had recommended L'vov, Petrunkevich, and Muromtsev, but others arrived instead. According to Miliukov, Petrunkevich was not then in Moscow, while Muromtsev "was left out intentionally, because of a not unjustified fear of his pliability." As for Kokoshkin, his selection, Miliukov added, "indicated that the bureau did not want to be a party to compromise solutions." Kokoshkin was Miliukov's candidate because "he, almost alone in the Moscow circle of friends, showed the disposition of a genuine politician."[54]

The delegation, all of whom were Kadets, told Witte that "the only

[52] The party's resolution on the Manifesto is in *Pravo*, 1905, Prilozhenie to No. 52, pp. 95–96. Miliukov's comment is in GOD, p. 76.

[53] GOD, p. 73. The English text of Witte's report is in HAR, pp. 289–92.

[54] VOSP, I, 321; TRI, p. 11.

way out of the present situation" was the calling of a constituent
assembly elected by universal suffrage. The civil rights promised by
the October Manifesto "must be put into effect immediately on the
same principles as in West European states" and a full political
amnesty must be granted. Witte was unwilling to talk in such terms.
He said nothing about a constituent assembly; as for universal suffrage
it could be implemented by the future Duma and he would, if still
in power, do everything to help in this. Temporary rules would have
to take the place of laws on civil rights, and the Emperor was willing
to sign only a partial amnesty. In view of the "daily bloody clashes
between various groups of the population," Witte told the delegation
he simply could not undertake "such basic reforms" as they asked
of him.[55]

Witte accomplished nothing with the intransigent delegates. He
was no more successful with Guchkov and Prince Evgenii Trubetskoi,
both of whom were offered cabinet posts. They declined, partly because they knew they represented only the minority of the opposition
movement, but also because they refused to work with men like
Minister of the Interior Petr Durnovo.[56] But Witte continued to
consult representatives of the public, and it was soon Miliukov's
turn to be contacted by the premier. On the face of it the two men
might have had a good deal in common. Witte felt that the government must "win back the loyalty of at least the 'thinking people,' the
moderates, by political Europeanization." For Miliukov, Witte,
"despite his lack of experience and his conceit was the most important
figure among Russian government leaders."

> I came not as a delegate [Miliukov recalled] empowered by any-
> one, but as a private person. . . . I decided to answer according to
> my conscience and personal conviction, not limiting myself to the
> generally accepted political formulas of my partisans. I wished to

[55] He was referring to troubles in many cities such as the anti-Jewish pogroms
which errupted with great violence; the Odessa pogrom claimed over five hundred
lives. The famous Lieutenant Peter Shmidt, who was to have a curious relation
to Miliukov, spoke at the funeral for its victims and vowed a continuation of the
war against the government. The Odessa events are described in L. Greenberg,
The Jews in Russia (New Haven, Conn., 1951), II, 76–78. The zemstvo delegation's report on its visit to Witte is in *Pravo*, 1905, pp. 3473–75.

[56] Shipov's account of his talks with Witte is in SHI, pp. 334–49; his letter to
Witte declining the cabinet post is in *Pravo*, 1905, pp. 3475–76, that of Trubetskoi in *ibid.*, 1905, pp. 3476–77.

bring the dispute from academic heights down to the sphere of
everyday reality.

Were he to answer as a Kadet, Miliukov told Witte, he would repeat
Kokoshkin's demands. But simpler solutions might work, if adopted
immediately. "Decent bureaucrats" would do in lieu of public figures
in the cabinet; they could be found among the deputy ministers.
Witte was delighted with the counsel: "Finally," he said shaking
Miliukov's hand vigorously, "I hear the first sound advice."

The rest of Miliukov's recommendations, however, were not acceptable. Instead of waiting for a constituent assembly, Miliukov advised
Witte to publish a constitution immediately, using either the Belgian
or the Bulgarian ones for his model. The Belgian constitution, he
thought, was "the classical example" for a parliamentary monarchy,
while the Bulgarian one "would be more convincing to a Russian
minister." It doubtless seemed like sensible advice to the Russian
European; Witte, however, would have no part of it; he knew he
could not persuade the Emperor to adopt such a course. Vasilii
Maklakov, then a member of the Kadet Central Committee and
later one of Miliukov's bitterest critics, dismissed Miliukov's advice
on these grounds: "How could Miliukov have thought," he wrote,
"that the Emperor would be convinced by a reference to Belgium
and Bulgaria?"[57]

Witte told Miliukov that the Emperor would not hear of the word
"constitution." Besides, the premier thought, the public would not
accept a charter granted from above; nor did the ordinary Russian folk
have any use for a constitution. Miliukov argued that if the people
felt indifferent to a constitution, they would sooner accept one
granted by the Emperor than one drafted by a constituent assembly.
None of this appealed to the premier, and the two men parted without agreement. Miliukov's first and last contact with Witte had
resulted in mutual disillusionment: Miliukov saw that "the country's
savior" in fact had only limited powers, while Witte remembered

[57] Witte is quoted in T. Von Laue, "Count Witte and the Russian Revolution of 1905," ASEER, XVII (1958), 31; Miliukov's estimate is from VOSP, I,
325. Nikolai Kutler, then Deputy-Minister of Agriculture, and later a Kadet Duma
deputy, was such a person, Miliukov noted in TRI, p. 24. Also P. Miliukov,
"Liberalizm, radikalizm, i revoliutsiia," SZ, No. 57 (1935), p. 312. VLAST', p.
447. Maklakov's withering critique of Miliukov's recommendations to Witte is in
ibid., pp. 440–51.

the Kadet leader as "an extreme leftist, on the borderline of the revolutionaries."[58]

The premier now turned his gaze upon the Zemstvo-Town Duma Congress which met in Moscow on November 6–13. He supposed that the congress would prove less radical than its bureau which, he had found out, was not inclined toward compromise. Witte was destined to be disappointed. The congress was the last one, Miliukov pointed out, which served as a substitute for political parties. No party to the right of the Kadets had yet emerged, and even that party was barely three weeks old. It was, however, strong enough to dominate the congress. The first day's session was presided over by Petrunkevich. The congress was taking place in the midst of unprecedented peasant violence which many described as "worse than the Pugachev uprising." But Petrunkevich did not blame the Left for the drastic turn the revolution had taken. "I am not a socialist," he told the congress, "but if someone were to tell me that the socialists will save Russia I would be the first to extend my hand to them." The socialists, for their part, were in a very different mood. A delegation of Moscow Social Democrats informed the congress that the only way out of the situation was the overthrow of the government by an armed uprising and its replacement by a democratic republic. As for any possible negotiation with Witte the Social Democrats condemned it as "shameful horsetrading of the congress with the tsarist government." The Left had never addressed the zemstvists so directly and so critically. "Here," Miliukov noted, "for the first time, a clearly demarcated political boundary was drawn between us." It was impossible to expect the congress to show sympathy for such goals.[59]

[58] S. Witte, Vospominaniia (Moscow, 1960), III, 166; though Witte describes his negotiations with political leaders, he says nothing of his encounter with Miliukov. The latter wrote several accounts of the interview. They are, in chronological order, GOD, pp. 182–84; TRI, pp. 22–25; ROK, XIV, 128–31; VOSP, I, 324–29. The first appeared six weeks after the meeting. It does not mention the fact that Miliukov spoke only for himself, nor does it reveal the suggestion of a cabinet of "bureaucratic experts."

[59] While there were 72 acts of peasant violence in September, the number increased to 219 in October, and 796 in November; see S. Dubrovskii, Krestianskoe dvizhenie v revoliutsii 1905–1907 gg. (Moscow, 1956), p. 42. Pravo, 1905, pp. 3601, 3615; the account of the congress is in ibid., 1905, pp. 3601–30 and 3699–3727. The Social Democratic resolution is in ibid., 1905, pp. 3617–18; Miliukov's comment comes from VOSP, I, 333.

There were, however, few at the congress who supported the government's punitive expeditions and the indiscriminate use of military courts in dealing with troublemakers in town and village. Miliukov, who introduced the bureau's resolutions, was pleased at the unanimous vote for the abolition of the death penalty. There was a long debate on the question of amnesty; many opposed amnesty for those guilty of theft and arson, but finally a blanket statement urging a political amnesty was adopted, as urged by the bureau. A long debate raged over Poland which had been put under martial law; the bureau asked that this be rescinded and that Poland be granted autonomy. Miliukov and Guchkov again, as in September, found themselves on opposite sides of the question. Guchkov opposed the termination of martial law and wished the future Duma to decide the extent of Poland's autonomy. But the congress was with Miliukov who, to the accompaniment of bravos and loud applause, told Guchkov that "the Polish question is a question of healing a seriously ill person; he must be cured by science, and not by secret home remedies." The vote was 156:12 in favor of Miliukov's resolution.

There was no unanimity on the universal and direct suffrage urged by Miliukov. The majority opposed a constituent assembly and voted instead for a Duma "with constituent functions" which was to work out a constitution to be approved by the Emperor; the zemstvists remained dominantly monarchist. A vast majority urged "the immediate implementation of the constitutional provisions" of the October Manifesto; they would support the government only so long as it undertook to do this. After a long debate the congress agreed to send a delegation to Witte to communicate its decisions to the premier. For once Miliukov disagreed with the bureau's recommendations. Witte had not invited a delegation; he "will read it a little lecture" on what he did not like about the congress resolutions and put the congress "into a ridiculous, even a humiliating position." But the assembly voted (88:57) to send Petrunkevich, Muromtsev, and Kokoshkin.[60]

Miliukov was right; Witte refused to receive the delegates. Having cooled their heels for a week the men returned to Moscow and were followed by the premier's answer to their written communication. The delegates had written Witte that if it retreated from its demands "the

[60] Pravo, 1905, pp. 3715–17, 3724–76.

congress would lose its only strength—its power of moral authority—without in any way increasing the authority of the government." Witte's answer was rather contemptuous. The government did not need the zemstvists, who failed in their patriotic duty to help maintain law and order. The answer did not surprise Miliukov. He pointed out that "the 'support' which Count Witte received from the congress was so hedged with conditions that it resembled a vote of no confidence." But the implications of the premier's attitude toward the public were frightening. Witte had adopted "a new tone, a daring tone. . . . How much new blood, how many victims, moral and material, will this tone cost Russia?" the Kadet leader asked.[61]

IX

There was "much new blood," as Miliukov had predicted; the Moscow uprising, in early December, alone claimed over a thousand civilian dead. But Miliukov had underestimated the government's strength; Witte was now in a position to deal with force by force. Writing on December 1, Miliukov did not yet understand the new correlation of power; the government was no longer on the defensive, as he implied. He suggested that the Witte cabinet always offered too little and too late. "Those were the tactics of Charles I and Louis XVI," he wrote. "Our governmental figures should take a few supplementary lessons in history."[62] But the ministers needed no tutoring; Durnovo showed that he could deal with the Moscow rebels.

Miliukov's comment was printed in the new Kadet newspaper, which was financed by Stanislav Propper, publisher of the prosperous St. Petersburg daily *Birzhevyia Vedomosti*. One of his three daily editions was not doing well; he offered to turn it over to the Kadets if they would make it pay. Miliukov agreed on condition that the paper would get a new name and the party would have a free hand. He and Iosif Gessen were to be editors, while M. I. Ganfman was invited as business manager. Gessen, a member of the Kadet Central Committee, was a lawyer who, since 1898, had been the chief moving force of the weekly *Pravo*. Ganfman, too, was on the *Pravo* editorial board;

---

[61] The delegates' letter and Witte's answer are in *ibid.*, 1905, pp. 3812–13, and 3926–27; also see GOD, pp. 14, 18.

[62] *Ibid.*, p. 164. On the Moscow uprising, see HAR, pp. 233–38.

in addition he was, of the three men, the only experienced newspaper-man, having been a co-editor of *Syn Otechestva* and *Novaia Zhizn'*. Politically he was left of the Kadets and remained so; but the trium-virate got along splendidly and remained newspaper collaborators until 1917.

Svobodnyi Narod, as the new paper was called, appeared for the first time on December 1. It was suppressed on December 2 for print-ing the "Financial Manifesto" of the St. Petersburg Soviet urging the population to stop paying taxes and to withdraw all deposits from government banks. Miliukov hesitated to print the document, but all the capital's editors agreed to do so as a matter of policy. As a conse-quence eight newspapers were confiscated and their editors charged with violating the criminal code. The trial of Miliukov and Gessen was to take place in May, 1906. Their newspaper reappeared as *Narodnaia Svoboda* on December 14 but was again suppressed after six issues for an article by Peter Struve. Propper stopped publishing the paper, claiming that the triumvirate would ruin him. The Kadets had to wait until February, 1906, when, with a different sponsor, they got a permanent daily, *Riech'*. But the brief publishing venture had been useful. For Miliukov the apprenticeship had been a hectic one. "In the first days—or more exactly nights—," he recalled, "I stood at the type case, looked through piles of accumulated copy, corrected galley proofs and, in spare moments, sat down somewhere in a corner to write the editorial or fill up blank spaces with a notice."[63]

The first editorial spoke of the moment's most burning issue—the tactics of the St. Petersburg Soviet. That body, Miliukov felt, was going too far, and would endanger the revolution's victories. "Yes, we are for the revolution," he wrote, as if replying to Trotsky's famous theory, "insofar as it serves the aims of political liberation and social reform; but we are against those who pronounce the revolution 'con-tinuous,' because we consider that a continuous revolution serves only the aims of reaction." Russia's Marxists should draw on the experience of their Western comrades, and not resort to dangerous native tactics. Russian socialism, after all, "is only applying a doctrine very thor-oughly elaborated by the West, and it need only raise its homemade tactics to the level of the borrowed doctrine." In the cities the Marx-

---

[63] VOSP, I, 345; details on the publication of the newspaper are in GES, pp. 218–21, and ROK, XVI, 130–32.

ists proposed to use "homemade tactics"; as for the countryside there were no Western models to follow: "Village socialism is a specifically Russian invention." The latter frightened Miliukov even more than the barricades in the cities. "It is becoming," he asserted, "the most serious threat to the Russian liberation movement."[64]

The arrest of the St. Petersburg Soviet on December 3 made the situation more drastic yet. The Soviet declared a new general strike, the third one since October. Miliukov reminded the Left that the Kadets had supported the first strike and had helped the victims of the second one in November (they had raised funds to pay the postal and telegraph strikers). The October strike, he wrote, had been "a civic feat." The November one had been "a political mistake." As for the December one "it might become a crime—a crime before the revolution." The masses were tired, and the chances for success were minimal. Were the leaders aware of the consequences of their rash directives? "The general staff," he wrote, "must be convinced that it is leading its soldiers to victory, not to the slaughterhouse." But worse was yet to come; in Moscow the strike turned into an armed uprising. Writing from St. Petersburg on December 8, Miliukov raised his voice against the hopeless attempt. "I beg of all those on whom the decision depends," he pleaded, "to reconsider—and to stop, while it is not yet too late."[65]

Henceforth, along with all of Russia, he became a horrified spectator of "the slaughterhouse." On December 14 he wrote: "Moscow is being bombarded by cannon. Bombarded with a fury, with a persistence, with an accuracy with which the Japanese positions were never favored." What was worse was that the Left, in resorting to arms, frightened the moderates and made it easier for the government to deal with the opposition. "Witte," Miliukov wrote in January, "found unexpected support in the Russian revolutionary movement which, by its childish goals of 'armed uprising' and 'a democratic republic' made that frightening impact on the average citizen on which Count Witte relied."[66] In later years Miliukov became an even more severe critic of the Left's tactics. "That the autocracy has not

[64] GOD, pp. 167–69.
[65] Ibid., p. 171.
[66] Ibid., pp. 175, 181.

surrendered since 1905," he wrote in 1920, "and that a kind of sham constitution existed between 1905 and 1917, thus paving the way for a second revolution, we owe to the Bolsheviks of 1905."[67]

At the very height of the Moscow uprising the government issued, on December 11, a new electoral law based on the October Manifesto promise of changes in the suffrage. It granted, Miliukov pointed out, "neither universal, direct nor equal suffrage." The government had not utilized the month since the October Manifesto "to study the textbooks of constitutional law, and the practice of the European powers." It had waited so long only "to deny to Russian public opinion that which constitutes the essence, the nerve center of all its hopes and expectations, the focus of its aspirations and practical plans for the future." Witte was well aware of the meagerness of the government's concessions. "It should be expected," he said at a conference with the Emperor, "that the new electoral law will pacify neither the revolutionary circles, nor the moderate elements. The results will be bad."[68]

There were, nevertheless, improvements in the new law over that of August 6. The vote was now granted to industrial workers, to all persons who paid house and lodging taxes, and to persons who occupied separate lodgings under their name. This increased the tenant franchise from some eighteen thousand to two million. Newly enfranchised were government employees, railway employees, and zemstvo workers. Women, workmen in plants employing less than fifty persons, artisans, craftsmen, casual laborers and landless peasants remained excluded. Voters remained divided into curias, which, Miliukov asserted, set up "limitations of the passive electoral right unprecedented in the annals of West European legislatures." But he admitted that the new law "is more liberal than the Prussian or Austrian one" and concluded that "we must take the electoral law of December 11 and try to make of it everything we can."[69]

[67] BOLSH, p. 21.

[68] GOD, pp. 78, 80; Byloe (Petrograd), 1917, No. 3, pp. 264–65. The protocols of a special conference to consider the electoral law are printed in ibid., 1917, No. 3, pp. 217–65.

[69] HARP, pp. 6–8. The text of the electoral law is in KAL, pp. 94–102. Also GOD, pp. 79, 81, 184.

X

The electoral campaign would be fought on the basis of the December 11 law. The Kadets would have to make the best of it. They were still weakly organized. Yet, considering the situation, remarkable progress had been made since October. By early January forty-two local Kadet groups had been formed in addition to the large Moscow and St. Petersburg branches, and the Central Committee daily received news of fresh provincial beginnings. By January, 1906, the party had approximately one hundred thousand registered members. Moscow remained the party's headquarters; it was the seat of the Central Committee and of the party publishing house, Narodnoe Pravo. Twelve pamphlets and dozens of leaflets with party slogans had been sent into the provinces in large editions. Moscow had organized a "school of orators," under the direction of Vasilii Maklakov, which sent trained speakers into distant localities. The bigger cities had party clubs (there were six in the capital, and two in Moscow) which could be used as recruiting centers. Though Miliukov's daily had been suppressed, there were several Kadet newspapers in the provinces.[70]

The Second Kadet congress, which met in St. Petersburg on January 5–11, 1906, surveyed the progress the party had made so far. It was attended by over one hundred and fifty delegates representing forty-eight localities spread as far as Kazan', Bessarabia, Archangel, Simbirsk, and the Kuban and Don regions. Central Committee member Lev Petrazhitskii was doubtless right when he said that only about one per cent of the population belonged to political parties; but the congress did represent a substantial part of that active one per cent. The main subject of debate was the party's participation in the Duma elections, which had been postponed until March. The overwhelming majority agreed with Miliukov that "the party must not and cannot refuse to take part in the elections even though it might be threatened with a sure defeat; in that case it will play an even more favorable role—that of a political opposition." No matter what the Duma might turn out to be, the party needed the elections to put its own house in order. They would, Miliukov told the congress, give the party

[70] For a report of Kadet activities between October, 1905, and January, 1906, see *Pravo*, 1906, Prilozhenie to No. 4, pp. 5–15, and TSENTR, pp. 21–23. Maklakov describes his "school for orators" in VLAST', pp. 511–20. See also ROK, XVII, 108.

"strengthened local committees, a clear conception of party discipline, a permanent organizational network, tried cadres of organizers and propagandists, and an increased and well-established membership."[71]

The congress made some changes in the party program. In response to the demand that the party name be amended to something more appealing to the masses, it added the words "Party of Popular Freedom" to the original title of "Constitutional-Democratic." The change made no practical difference, however, and the party remained best-known as the Kadets. Article thirteen of the program, which read "The constitutional structure of the Russian state shall be defined by the fundamental laws," was changed to read "Russia should be a constitutional and parliamentary monarchy." This was a concession to those who wished to dissociate the Kadets from the republicanism of the Left. The program slogan of a constituent assembly was defeated by a vote of 137:80 in favor of a formula which stated that "a 'Constituent Assembly' means an assembly of popular representatives with constituent functions, summoned to formulate the fundamental laws, and not an assembly endowed with 'full powers.' " This, too, was a step to the right, undoubtedly brought about by the excesses of the Left in the previous month. The ever-present agrarian issue also received attention. An addition was made to Article 36 of the program stating that the land to be alienated in favor of the peasantry would be valued on a lower basis than the high-lease prices prevalent in areas of land scarcity.[72]

Suffrage for women came up again; the congress ruled that the party's stand granting the vote to women was binding on all members. The issue had remained controversial throughout 1905. At the March, 1905, congress of the Liberationists, women's suffrage passed by only one vote. At the first Kadet congress in October fifty-seven delegates asked for the floor to speak on the subject, and the matter had been included as a non-binding part of the program. Now, at the second

[71] The incomplete minutes of the congress are in Pravo, 1906, Prilozhenie to No. 4, pp. 1–22, and Prilozhenie to No. 7, pp. 25–56. The account breaks off in the middle of a sentence and covers only the first two days of the meetings. See also POST for a record of congress decisions and "Rezoliutsii, priniatyia vtorym s"ezdom-k.d.-partii," Pravo, 1906, pp. 153–58. Miliukov's comment on the congress is in GOD, pp. 102–17. An account in English is SM I, 474–76, and 503–8. Also GOD, pp. 106–7.

[72] POST, pp. 8, 33, and ROK, XVII, 111–12.

congress, fourteen votes were cast against female suffrage; one of these was Miliukov's, who again debated the matter with his wife. We have no account of his speech, but we have a participant's recollection. Evidently a group of Moslem delegates from Kazan opposed women's suffrage; their leader, Iusuf Akchurin, warned the Kadets that they would lose Moslem votes if they insisted on it. Miliukov, we are told, "was twirling his mustache" listening to this unexpected partisan. The Russian European might not have liked this sort of support; perhaps he was thinking of the fact that nowhere in the world, except in Scandinavia, did women have the right to vote in 1906. Our informant, Ariadna Tyrkova, the only woman delegate at the congress, had her own explanation of Miliukov's anti-feminism. Perhaps, she thought, "as a great admirer of female company he was afraid that the prosaic side of politics would becloud women's feminine charm."[73]

Though he lost that particular fight Miliukov was well pleased with the congress. "When we called the first congress," he wrote in February, 1906, "we could only guess as to what the party might become." During the second congress, he felt, "the party had found itself." It had, to be sure, moved somewhat to the right, but "it remained an oppositional party."[74] The new Central Committee was not much different in composition from the old one, though three old members had been dropped and nine new ones added. Of the latter only three were zemstvo men; the intellectual contingent in the party was getting ever stronger.[75] The Kadet general staff still needed an army; it would

---

[73] A. Tyrkova-Williams, Na putiakh k svobode (New York, 1952), pp. 239–43, and the same author's "Pervyi zhenskii s"ezd," Zarnitsy (St. Petersburg), II (1909), 184–85.

[74] GOD, pp. 111, 117; emphasis in the original.

[75] The list below comes from POST, p. 3. Members dropped were N. Kablukov, I. Petrovskii, and D. Iakushkin. Newly elected members are starred, and members are identified as Z (zemstvo) and P (professional). Only four of the thirty-two men were from outside St. Petersburg or Moscow.
Vernadskii, V. (P); Vinaver, M. (P); *Gessen, V. (P); Gessen, I. (P); Dolgorukov, Paul (Z); Dolgorukov, Peter (Z); *Kizevetter, A. (P); Kokoshkin, F. (P); Koliubakin, A. (Z); Kornilov, A. (P); Kotliarevskii, S. (P); *Lomshakov, A. (P); Luchitskii, I. (P); L'vov, N. (Z); Maklakov, V. (P); Maksimov, A. (P); Mandel'shtam, M. (P); Miliukov, P. (P); Muromtsev, S. (P); *Mukhanov, A. (Z); Nabokov, V. (P); *Petrazhitskii, L. (P); Petrunkevich, I. (Z); *Protopopov, D. (Z); *Rodichev, F. (Z); Sabashnikov, M. (P); *Struve, P. (P); Teslenko, N. (P); Chernenkov, N. (Z); Shakhovskoi, D. (Z); Shchepkin, N. (Z); *Shershenevich, F. (P).

get it in the forthcoming elections, to which Miliukov looked forward eagerly. He had every reason to be pleased with the job done since his return from America in April, 1905. In the elapsed nine months he had helped to forge an indispensable weapon for Russia's political westernization: a constitutional party ready to enter the first Russian parliament. An English journalist who interviewed him after the January congress found him hopeful and unafraid of the future. "Reaction?," he replied; "Why, it is already over. The spirit of the thing is dead." The journalist could only marvel: "But then Professor Miliukov is one of those few happy people who have carried with them the glories of youth into middle age."[76]

[76] H. Nevinson, *The Dawn in Russia* (London, 1906), pp. 246–47.

4: A RUSSIAN PARLIAMENT

The country chose the party as its defender but it did not, as a result, become Kadet itself.[1]

Tell me, your Excellency, why does your Emperor not invite Mr. Miliukov to act as head of your government? I believe this would be a good move both from the point of view of satisfying public opinion, and from that of solving many problems.[2]

I

Describing the Revolution of 1905 to a Carnegie Hall audience in 1907, Miliukov divided it into four stages. The first, lasting from November, 1904, to October, 1905, he called the "national" phase, a period during which the whole Russian people strove for change. October to December, 1905, was the "revolutionary" phase, dominated by the socialists. The third, from January, 1906, to the dissolution of the First Duma, was the "constitutional" phase, dominated, in his view, by the Kadets. In the fourth, the counterrevolutionary phase, the bureaucracy and the nobility returned to controlling positions. After June, 1907, the revolution was over.[3] We have now come to the third phase when the Kadets seemingly triumphed, only to lose their leadership to the forces of the old regime. But at first all seemed rosy and promising. The party was growing, it acquired an influential newspaper, it won the largest number of seats in Russia's first parlia-

---

[1] FIRST, p. 4.
[2] KOK, p. 117; the question was asked of Vladimir Kokovtsov by Georges Clemenceau in the spring of 1906.
[3] CONST, pp. 5–7.

ment, it was courted by the government. It was one of Miliukov's great hours; he was to get only one other, in 1917.

The third phase of the Revolution of 1905 was dominated by the First and Second Dumas. Russia's first parliament had not been won easily. When the final legislation establishing a legislature appeared on February 20, 1906 ("The Duma and State Council Statutes"), it failed to satisfy Miliukov. He admitted that the law contained "very significant improvements" over that of August 6, 1905. But the promises of the October Manifesto had not been kept. The Duma was to share legislative power with a reorganized State Council which had not been mentioned in the Manifesto. Miliukov had no love for an upper house which he called "that pre-reform collection of retired pompadours." Only half of the State Council would be elected, and that by a very restricted electorate. The other half would be appointed by the Emperor, a block against the Duma's ambitions. "The fight against the very existence of the State Council," Miliukov promised, "will become a new goal of the liberation movement." As for the Duma, its competence had been limited; the Fundamental Laws were exempt from its consideration. It could not be turned into an assembly with constituent functions. The government had also retained its power to legislate when the Duma was not in session; since the Duma need be called for only two months a year, the government had wide latitude, and the road was open for massive abuse of the Duma's powers.[4]

It was not the kind of parliament that Miliukov had bargained for. But the imminent electoral campaign soon absorbed all his interest; the Duma would be what its deputies would make it. If they were Kadets it might become something the bureaucrats had not forseen. Miliukov entered the elections with a tribune, the party's new newspaper *Riech'*. Unlike the ill-fated attempts of December, the new daily throve from the very first day of publication, February 23, 1906. The old team of Miliukov-Gessen was at the helm, ably assisted by Ganfman. Petrunkevich became treasurer, Vladimir Nabokov joined the board, and a wealthy engineer, Iulian Bak, became publisher. The only troubles that the paper was to have in the next eleven years were difficulties with the censor; in all other respects it was a successful and

---

[4] The text of the legislation is in KAL, pp. 102–23; Miliukov's three articles on the subject are reprinted in GOD, pp. 86–92 and 187–89.

valuable venture. Miliukov wrote almost all the editorials, and these
provide a running commentary on what he thought of as "constitutional" Russia. While he commented on the day's political news in St.
Petersburg, his best friend Kokoshkin often wrote the editorial in the
Moscow *Russkiia Vedomosti;* the Kadet leadership was thus heard
from the pages of two distinguished Russian newspapers in Russia's
most important cities. It was a useful and valuable platform for the
cause.[5] For purely party purposes the Kadets published a weekly, the
Vestnik Partii Narodnoi Svobody, the most solid organ of information
of any Russian political party. The leaders wrote the keynote articles,
but the bulk of the journal was filled with news of provincial branches
and statistics about membership and party activity. There is no better
source for the study of the Kadet movement in the period 1906–8.
Suppressed in 1908, the *Vestnik* was revived only in 1917.

During February and March, 1906, both *Riech'* and the *Vestnik*
were filled with election news. The Kadets were the only party well
prepared for the contest. Those to the right of the Kadets had no
organizational experience, while the Left parties decided to boycott
the elections in view of the restricted suffrage. Thus the Kadets were
the only opposition party openly available to the voter. Miliukov
regretted this, and found it incomprehensible that both the Populists
and the Social Democrats preferred to abstain. His old *Russkoe Bogatstvo* friends opposed the Duma, while only Georgii Plekhanov
urged the Marxists to enter the lists; Miliukov asked "the comrades"
to emulate their wise leader, but neither the Mensheviks nor the
Bolsheviks were persuaded.[6] The Kadets, by contrast, seemed to be in
their element, particularly in the cities. Already in January the party
had run a special Moscow course for "agitators." Miliukov gave the
first and last lectures. Over two hundred persons, many of them from
the provinces, attended. A St. Petersburg series was planned for February, but the authorities made difficulties, and the course was held
in private apartments because, officially, the party was not "registered"
and, therefore, not legal.[7]

[5] VOSP, I, 272, 357–58. His editorials for 1905–6 are collected in his *God
bor'by* (St. Petersburg, 1906); those for 1907 in his *Vtoraia duma* (St. Petersburg, 1908). For more on the newspaper, see T. Riha, "Riech': A Portrait of a
Russian Newspaper," *Slavic Review,* XXII (1963), 663–82.

[6] GOD, pp. 222–23; ROK, XVII, 114–15.

[7] VES, 1906, pp. 33–34.

The fact that the party had not been officially legalized (it remained "illegal" until 1917) was to make endless difficulties. In February a Kadet delegation, headed by Miliukov, went to see the capital's prefect V. E. Von der Launitz, to complain. The prefect told them that Witte had instructed officialdom to make the Kadets' lives hard because "they engage in too much self-advertising," and because they had "crossed the Rubicon"—it was hard to tell where the Kadets ended and revolutionaries began.[8] Minor harassment in the capital gave way to much more insistent administrative restrictions in the provinces. In the first issue of *Riech'* Miliukov annotated a secret government circular which had come into his possession and which instructed land captains on how to handle "anti-government parties" such as the Kadets. Local officials were to explicate the "groundlessness" of party programs; to prevent public meetings where speakers aroused "unrealizable hopes" among the peasants; and to post the names of candidates whose election "will clearly be annulled as suspect." "In Europe," Miliukov commented, "they do not do it that way—and in Asia they do not talk about it." Though such interference seemed dangerous, Miliukov saw also how it could help the cause. "Repressions," he commented, "are a powerful propaganda weapon in our favor. . . . We are convinced once again that that government is our most faithful ally, and we shall let it work in the interests of the Russian opposition."[9]

Speaking for the entire Russian opposition was a dangerous business, for it implied collusion with the revolutionaries. This was a delicate issue, on which Miliukov and the Kadets never spoke clearly; it therefore stimulated repeated attacks from the government and the Right. Witte's organ, *Russkoe Gosudarstvo*, wrote that "there is no doubt that the Kadet left wing is in constant and direct relations with the revolutionaries, and is replenished from their ranks." The paper urged the Kadets to stop their flirtation with the extremists and use their influence to pacify the Left. "Only those with a primitive political understanding," replied Miliukov, "can think that the Russian revolutionary movement can be halted by the Russian 'liberals.'" It was the government's fault that the opposition was forced to resort to

[8] GOD, pp. 134, 138.
[9] *Ibid.*, pp. 90, 135, 217–18.

extralegal means in its political struggle. "The entire Russian opposition," he wrote:

> to the extent that it is an opposition at all, is by necessity revolutionary in its aims since these aims, to a larger or lesser degree, include an element of "the overthrow of the existing order." . . . One can speak of "reform" if a channel is open, if a canal has been dug for a "reform"; but if the way is barred and the aim remains then "reform" comes very close to overthrow.

The bloody struggle would continue, and the Kadets were not about to urge its abandonment. Miliukov could not sympathize with the actual process (by October, 1906, 3,611 government officials of all ranks had been killed or wounded, while 13,381 citizens had been executed or killed by courts-martial, troops, brigands, etc.) but he realized the value of this powerful form of pressure on the government.[10]

II

As it happened Miliukov personally was under litigation for "attempting to overthrow the existing order" through the printed word—the government had not forgiven him the transgressions of *Narodnaia Svoboda* in December; the paper, it will be remembered, had printed the manifesto of the St. Petersburg Soviet. The litigation disqualified Miliukov from the election.[11] But he did more than his share in helping to elect other Kadet deputies; with his customary vigor he spoke wherever possible, both in the provinces and in the capital. One Social Democrat recalled that "Miliukov was our most dangerous opponent. He made an impression on the listeners, and next to the middle-aged professor the defenders of a boycott could not but appear as provocative boys."[12]

At first Miliukov's tone was rather modest. "If the voters send us to the Duma," he wrote, "we shall not dare to call ourselves 'the true voice of the people's will' with the existing utterly incorrect system" of elections. Even when it became clear that the Kadets would carry the cities (of the twenty-eight deputies chosen by twenty cities, twenty-

[10] *Ibid.*, pp. 260, 272; figures on terror are from LEV, p. 21, n. 28.
[11] VES, 1906, pp. 290–91.
[12] VOI, II, 30; ROK, XVII, 109–10.

six were Kadets) he admitted that "this brilliant success" was not due only to the party's merits. The boycott by the Left had contributed heavily to the Kadet success. But as the returns showed the Kadets leading even in the provinces, Miliukov's tone became more arrogant. "There is nothing accidental or artificial in the triumph of the Party of Popular Freedom," he wrote. "Its representatives will have the right to speak in the name of a very considerable majority of Russia's population." It was an exaggerated and dangerous claim. The final party representation would not be clear until the Duma actually met, but Miliukov was already promising too much. "The Kadet party," he wrote, "we say it boldly—perhaps it alone—can lead Russia out of its fateful impasse."[13]

It was in this tone of supreme confidence that Miliukov commented on the three issues before the calling of the Duma: the floating of a large Russian loan in France, the issuance of the new Fundamental Laws, and the dismissal of Witte. All three events took place in early April, only days before the first session of the First Duma. The French loan appeared to Miliukov in a rather illusory light. "The government got the money," he wrote, "and on exceptionally hard terms, in large part because the victory of the constitutional-democratic party gave Europe some hope for a pacification in Russia—a hope that the revolutionary crisis we are witnessing is coming to an end."[14] In fact, of course, much larger issues of European diplomacy were involved, issues which we shall explore in a later context. The Kadets had done little to win foreign public opinion. In fact in early March the party's Central Committee resolved to remain passive in this respect. "Regarding the question," it ruled, "raised by some party members on clarifying the party's physiognomy in the foreign press . . . it was decided that the party as such should not appeal to the public opinion of Western Europe with the aim of undermining the government's prestige."[15]

But if the party as such abstained this did not mean that individual Kadets could not try to win friends and influence people in France. Miliukov admitted "the possibility of personal explanations to influential leaders of public opinion in both countries with the aim of en-

[13] GOD, pp. 216, 225, 234, 247.
[14] Ibid., p. 300.
[15] KAD, p. 57.

lightening them about the true state of affairs. . . ." He saw "nothing
unpatriotic" in such activity, and hoped that the French would see
the light: "If the French public values these considerations of a political group so close to it in its fashion of thinking, and its aims, it will
take them into consideration. . . ." In fact the party was caught in a
dilemma described by Miliukov as follows: "From a strictly constitutional point of view we had to oppose the loan, and from the same
point of view we could not threaten a public bankruptcy. . . . The party
always considered that no government can refuse to fulfill the financial
obligations entered into by its legal predecessor."[16] It was "unconstitutional" to conclude a major foreign loan abroad only days before the
session of a national legislature. On the other hand the Kadets, if they
formed the next government, would honor Russia's financial obligations. When Paul Dolgorukov and Vasilii Maklakov, apparently on
their own initiative, tried to prevent the loan in Paris, the party disavowed them. The Central Committee voted unanimously to take no
steps to prevent the loan though "the Central Committee has a completely negative attitude towards this loan." Maklakov must have
been shocked to hear Clemenceau tell him: "I myself advised my
servants to subscribe to this loan. After all, not every concierge can
engage in politics because of a loan."[17]

The conclusion of the loan signified the end of Witte's career. He
was dismissed by the Emperor in favor of the more pliable Ivan
Goremykin, his old rival of the 'nineties. Miliukov had never been
fond of the "Russian Necker." He described him as "a careerist and a

---

[16] GOD, pp. 294, 298, 302.

[17] KAD, p. 58; VES, 1906, pp. 370–71; VLAST', p. 534. The episode is significant for an understanding of Maklakov's later political evolution. His books
are strongly critical of Miliukov's radicalism. On this occasion, however, he was
more radical than the Kadet Central Committee. In a memorandum of April 18,
1906, to the French Minister of Finance, which he signed as "a member of the
Central Committee of the Constitutional-Democratic party," he advised against
the loan as "a good Russian citizen, and a real friend of the French Republic."
It was "an illusion" to think that the existing Russian government "is susceptible
to agree sincerely to liberal reforms." It had, after all, "annulled all the liberties
promised by the manifesto of October 17" and had "annihilated the Duma's
authority by the creation of an upper chamber." All of this is the purest Kadet
radicalism and should be kept in mind when reading Maklakov's later strictures
against his party and Miliukov. The text of the Maklakov-Dolgorukov memorandum is in O. Crisp, "The Russian Liberals and the Anglo-French Loan to Russia,"
SEER, June, 1961, pp. 508–11.

courtier," not a "genuine statesman." Witte had had a chance to accomplish much, but had missed the opportunities. "Had Count Witte
really known what was necessary 'to save Russia' . . . his name would
take its place along such names as Cavour, Bismarck, Gambetta." But
he preferred ambition to statesmanship, and "he got lost between the
Versailles and the Paris of our contemporary history." The positive
result of his dismissal was that it ended the period of "autocratic constitutionalism" or "constitutional autocracy." "Count Witte's merit
is that he has proven the impossibility of creating the elementary conditions of free political life if autocracy is preserved." On the negative
side the change of premiers made a conflict between government and
Duma much more likely: "Count Witte's dismissal signifies the disappearance of the last chance to come to an agreement, and is therefore
inexpedient—if only the decision has not already been made to provoke a conflict." But Miliukov's eternal optimism won out over the
doubts, and he concluded that "the Duma can rest satisfied. It would
have had to exert itself to push aside the monumental figure of Count
Witte. As for Messrs. Goremykins—they will step aside themselves."
In fact Miliukov interpreted the change of cabinets as, of all things,
the introduction of parliamentary government into Russia: "The
entire cabinet is to resign. Thus, willy-nilly, the principle of pure parliamentarism won out on the very first step of Russia's political life."[18]

Witte's last service to Russian politics had been the preparation
of a new set of Fundamental Laws. Writing of Witte several years
later, Miliukov approved of their publication before the Duma's convocation on the grounds that if the Duma were to be dissolved pre-
maturely (as it was) nothing would remain of "the new order besides
the October Manifesto which, it was clear to Witte, was juridically
not binding."[19] In April, 1906, however, Miliukov was utterly critical;
the laws should have passed "through the laboratory of a popular
representative body." The proposed legislation had been leaked to
Riech' which published them on April 11, twelve days before their
promulgation. "A future conflict is becoming inevitable," Miliukov
warned, "if the Fundamental Laws pass in the proposed form." General Dmitrii Trepov, the palace commandant, had also passed a copy

---

[18] GOD, pp. 180, 193–94, 306, 309.
[19] P. Miliukov, "Witte," *Entsyklopedicheskii Slovar' Granat* (7th ed.; X [Mos-
cow, 1911]), 367.

of the proposed laws to his friend Vladimir Ivanovich Kovalevskii, who invited Miliukov, Muromtsev, Gessen, and Maxim Kovalevskii to submit their suggestions. Their memorandum said the project "makes the most melancholy impression." According to Witte, "this memorandum evidently made His Majesty hesitate, and he did not sign the Fundamental Laws." Certain minor changes were made, but even Witte had to admit that the final product was "a conservative constitution, and without parliamentarism."[20]

The publication came during the third Kadet party congress, held in St. Petersburg on April 21–25, on the very eve of the Duma's convocation. This "congress of victors" could hardly believe that the government would go so far in what was regarded as a violation of the October Manifesto. In his report to the congress Miliukov omitted any mention of the Fundamental Laws on the presumption that all was well on that front. But since the government had acted he felt that "we must answer this deception of the people immediately." Comparing the new constitution with the Austrian one, he asserted that "in these fundamental laws the best is a worsening of the worst features of the worst European constitution."[21]

The mood at the congress was even more militant than such pronouncements. There were voices urging that a new Central Committee was needed; the old one was described as "too diplomatic." Miliukov's more moderate counsels prevailed, however. His proposal to add ten additional members to the committee was accepted; those elected were not all leftists by any means (Golovin, Izgoev, Tyrkova, and de Roberti belonged to the right wing), and there was even a new Moslem member (Akchurin).[22] The tone of Miliukov's report on tactics was cautious. In the Duma the Kadets should move carefully and avoid provoking the government on a minor issue. "Before anything else," he advised, "it is necessary to await the first declaration of the

[20] GOD, pp. 285, 287; S. Witte, *Vospominaniia*, III (Moscow, 1960), 305–6. The Kadet memorandum for Kovalevskii is printed in KA, No. 11–12 (1925), pp. 116–20.

[21] *Pravo*, 1906, p. 1694. A summary of the congress proceedings appears in *ibid.*, 1906, pp. 1667–97. For an English text of the first eighty-two articles of the Fundamental Laws, see W. Dodd, *Modern Constitutions* (Chicago, 1919), II, 181–95.

[22] The new members were (VES, 1906, p. 600): Golovin, F. A., Izgoev, A. S., Akchurin, IU. A., Gredeskul', N. A., de Roberti, E., Tyrkova, A. V., Vasil'ev, D., Shchepkin, E., Lednitskii, A. R., and Chubinskii, M. P.

new cabinet and, in particular, the speech from the throne." It was
dangerous to advocate changes in the Duma's present status: "A sharp
change in this realm might meet with unexpected complications and
can hardly be placed among the immediate tasks of the party's activities in the Duma." Only the abolition of the death penalty and a full
amnesty would be demanded regardless of the consequences: "A conflict is possible on these points . . . but under the circumstances the
party cannot retreat or make concessions."[23]

As usual Miliukov concentrated on political issues which, he felt,
should get priority. He said little on the agrarian problem and nothing
at all on the workers' question. Several delegates pointed out that he
had neglected to mention "the first and chief fighters for freedom,"
the urban proletariat, but the congress was satisfied by the establishment of a special committee on the subject. The land question, however, could not be settled so easily. Many delegates urged that the
party program be radicalized and that "land nationalization" be
adopted as a tenet. Miliukov pointed out the ambiguity of the concept. "Land nationalization" would not be popular with the peasants
when they discovered that it applied not only to the landlord's hold-
ings, but to theirs as well. It would be hardly possible to move farther
left in the land question while "remaining within the bounds of a
legislative solution." After much debate the congress entrusted the
land program to a committee of Duma deputies and adjourned full
of expectations.[24]

III

Though he was not a deputy, Miliukov was in the thick of the
Duma's most important decisions. On April 26, before the chamber's
opening, he presided over a meeting of deputies of various parties in
the Kadet Club which had opened the previous day. It was the first
open political club in Russia. The meeting was intended to set the
tone of the Duma's first session. Miliukov did not attend the ceremony
in the Winter Palace where the Emperor addressed the deputies, but
he waited for them at the doors of the Taurida Palace. For the next
two months the beautiful white building was his second home. He
could be found either in the journalists' box or in the chairman's box,

[23] GOD, pp. 330, 332.
[24] Pravo, 1906, pp. 1671–76, 1685–94; GOD, pp. 335–41.

or at the Kadet table in the buffet, the most convenient place for
quick party consultations. "I will not deny," he recalled, "that I had
genuine influence" in the Duma. Bernard Pares, who observed the
Duma, put it more strongly: "He was the real ruler of the House, and
every important step was referred to him by his party for decision."
This is an exaggeration; Pares is closer to the mark when he stresses
Miliukov's role as the strategist of the unruly chamber. "Tactical unity
was hardly to be expected in the first Russian Parliament, and it is
immensely to the credit of Miliukov that he was even able to keep the
Duma united for so long." He must have been quite a sight as, during
that warm spring, he walked in the Palace grounds under an enormous
brightly-colored umbrella, trying to decide on the next move. "Miliukov, in the simple dress of an English country gentleman, walked up
and down the corridor receiving the suggestions of various party leaders which seldom induced him to deviate a yard from the tactics
upon which he had determined."[25]

It was, of course, not Miliukov alone who determined the party's
Duma tactics. The "general line" was worked out by Miliukov, Petrunkevich, Kokoshkin, and Maksim Vinaver. Vinaver was a lawyer active
in various Jewish organizations who had been elected from St. Petersburg; he remained Miliukov's friend and collaborator into the emigration. The two seemed to have masterminded the Kadet fraction, since
Kokoshkin was often ill and Petrunkevich, though "he stood high
above us all," simply could not keep the murderous pace. "My share,"
Miliukov recalled, "consisted in determining the middle position of a
meeting, and working out a conciliatory formula." Since these meetings involved not only Kadets but also their allies of the moment,
Miliukov was often called upon to act as a conciliator. This led Maklakov to accuse him of not having been a leader at all. According to
him, Miliukov

> belonged to those of whom it was said: *je suis leur chef, donc je
> les suis.* There are men who lead others; for this special character-
> istics are needed which are not granted to all. Miliukov was not a

[25] On the Kadet Club, see VES, 1906, pp. 683–84, and VIN I, 186–87. It
was financed by Prince D. I. Bebutov, who later proved to be in the pay of the
government. In April, 1906, it had a thousand members and was an important
center of party propaganda. Pares' recollections are from his *Russia and Reform*
(London, 1907), pp. 543, .551, 559, and his *My Russian Memoirs* (London,
1931), p. 106. There are some wonderful photographs of Miliukov on the Duma
grounds in *Poslednii samoderzhets* (Berlin, n.d.).

leader of this type. . . . If I speak of him so often it is not because
he led the party. But he most clearly *represented* it, with all its
virtues and shortcomings. He was not the party's *leader* but its
standard-bearer. . . . If the party had a real leader he would not have
been afraid of a split. . . . But the leader of the Kadets was a col-
lective in which both tendencies were intentionally represented.[26]

In Maklakov's eyes the Kadets were merely a loose coalition artificially
held together by a compromising central committee. The experience
of the First Duma will show that this was not quite so, though there
is no doubt of Miliukov's special function as the party's conciliator.

It was often Miliukov in *Riech'* who commented most succinctly
on Duma incidents. It was he alone who stood aside from the hurly-
burly of the excited and often chaotic gathering. He was a leader,
therefore, in the special sense of being a spokesman, a formulator of
views which the outside world would regard as the position of the
Duma's leading party. For the Kadets did not have a majority in the
chamber, and they could lead it only in alliance with other fractions.[27]
Miliukov's help was indispensable for the intricate maneuvering which
was often necessary to achieve a parliamentary majority.

Particularly unpredictable were the one hundred non-party deputies
and the one hundred and two Trudoviks or Laborites, a group which
leaned toward the Socialist Revolutionaries, particularly in their land
program. At the very outset of the Duma, the Trudoviks planned some
drastic reply to the Emperor's colorless speech from the throne. "The
speech from the throne," Miliukov noted, "skilfully avoided all contro-

---

[26] Miliukov described the inner workings of the Kadet leadership in ROK,
XVIII, 113, and VIN II, 21. Maklakov's critique comes from FIRST, pp. 3, 9,
passim. Italics in the original.

[27] There are no reliable figures on the Duma's party affiliations. The latest
monograph on the subject is used here (SID, p. 196). According to this source,
the picture looked as follows in June:

Social Democrats	18 deputies	3.7 per cent of total
Trudoviks	102	21.0
Kadets	176	36.0
Polish Kolo	33	6.8
Autonomists	14	2.8
Democratic Reform	6	1.3
Progressives	12	2.5
Peaceful Reconstruction	26	5.3
Non-party	100	20.6
	487	100.0

The law provided for 524 deputies. When the Duma was dissolved on July 9,
only 499 of these had been elected.

versial topics."[28] Three Kadets (Miliukov, Vinaver, and Kokoshkin) and three Trudoviks formed a committee to pass upon the Duma's answer. The Kadets prevailed upon their allies to support their version, which was then passed by the Duma. It included practically the entire Kadet program as approved by the second party congress in January. It was a very large order indeed, and it was inaccurate to say, as Miliukov did, that the Duma had the right to implement such measures as the abolition of the State Council or the enlarging of its own competence.[29]

Miliukov himself had some moments of doubt. "We are not accustomed to believe in luck," he noted, "and, somehow, at first glance, it is hard to believe that the hothouse plant of a national legislature will survive on a Russian city street where Messrs. Goremykin flourish."[30] Indeed the Emperor refused to receive a Duma delegation bearing the answer to his speech—he was obviously displeased by the demands made therein. Again the Trudoviks threatened retaliation, and again Miliukov went to calm them. He warned the Trudoviks that this was not the time for picking a fight with the government. The population would not understand why the Duma did not concentrate on its chief task: liberty and land. Miliukov's speech met with success, and several peasant deputies remarked: "We don't have a fellow like this who could explain everything clear and smart." The Trudoviks agreed to the Kadet formula.[31]

The government, in its turn, proceeded to answer the Duma's sweeping demands. On May 13 Goremykin, in a barely audible voice, read a government declaration. Many of the Duma demands, including the agrarian program of compulsory alienation of land, were deemed "absolutely inadmissible." The government's own promises were vague and utterly out of keeping with the seriousness of the moment. Even the most moderate Count Heyden, always to the right of the Kadets, was deeply dissatisfied with the cabinet's position. "When I entered the State Duma," he told the chamber, "I supposed that we would be granted the opportunity to work peacefully and profitably, and that we would get the government's full sympathy on this path. Unfortu-

[28] *Riech'*, April 28, 1906.
[29] GOD, p. 407; VOSP, I, 372–74; see also VIN I, 191, 199–200. The texts of the Emperor's speech and the Duma's answer are in *Pravo*, 1906, pp. 1764–68.
[30] GOD, p. 343.
[31] VIN I, 216–17.

nately, however, today's government declaration convinced me of the
exact opposite [Stormy applause]." "May 13," Miliukov noted, "became the date which signified the beginning of an open fight." Again
he chaired a meeting of Kadet and Trudovik deputies to agree on a
formula expressing no confidence in Goremykin's cabinet; it passed
the house with only eleven dissenting votes.[32]

IV

There was now no question of collaboration between Duma and
government. The chamber had made it clear that the Goremykin cabinet had to go. But Russia was not France, and the ministers remained
in office. In April Goremykin predicted that the Duma will make "an
attempt to govern a country suffering the ill effects of revolution by a
system that is a parody on West European parliamentarism."[33] What
seemed a parody to Goremykin appeared as political necessity to Miliukov and his party. The Duma demanded the formation of a cabinet
responsible to the Duma and enjoying its confidence. Henceforth
Miliukov hammered away at this point until the Duma's dissolution;
it was, in his eyes, a precondition of further political progress. To those
who objected that there was no law saying Russian ministers must
resign if the Duma withholds its confidence he replied that England
had no such law either. Parliamentary practice had established it. To
those who pointed to Germany, which did not recognize cabinet
responsibility to the chamber, he replied that "the strong medieval
monarchy of estates of our German neighbors evolves into a consistently parliamentary system much more slowly than our democratically-
patriarchal autocracy."[34] Like some Russian Marxists this Russian
liberal evidently saw his country skipping stages which had seemed
essential in the evolution of other lands.

He wished to enlist England and France on the side of Russian
parliamentarism; as for Germany and Austria they were obviously
friends of the old regime. He was convinced that "a liberal England
can form a durable and solid connection only with a constitutional
Russia." For France money might play a more important role; the

[32] SO, May 13, 1906, p. 349. Pp. 321–24 have the text of Goremykin's speech;
pp. 352–53 have the Duma vote of no confidence. See also VOSP, I, 374, and
VIN I, 229–30, as well as GOD, pp. 412–13.
[33] KOK, p. 124.
[34] GOD, pp. 482, 485.

important daily *Temps* which, at the time of the Russian loan maintained that it dealt only with the Russian government not with the nation, had now changed its tone and recommended a Duma cabinet for Russia. In short "liberal Europe finds itself in a strange position: . . . it seeks a liberal Russia but, instead, finds the same old clumsy, awkward Russia, autocratic, and quite unable to take a new path." Only the Central Powers rejoiced at Russia's predicament:

> At a time when the advanced democracies of England and France concern themselves with strengthening constitutional principles in Russian life and with the pacification of Russia certain other powers prefer to preserve Russia's sources of weakness and internal tension, and they send troops to the Russian frontier in order to take advantage of the country's difficult position when internal trouble reaches its extremes.[35]

While Clemenceau urged that Miliukov be made premier, it was rumored in the Russian press that the Central Powers had offered to intervene on the side of the Russian government in its struggle with its own people.

It was Miliukov's new excursion into foreign policy. Characteristically, it was prompted by Russian political problems and his desire to solve them the "European" way. A crusade for a Duma ministry was combined with concern about Russia's image abroad. "The open conflict between the government and the people," he wrote, "which daily assumes a sharper character and wider dimensions, threatens to deprive Russian diplomacy of its last weight in international questions."[36] In this view he was supported by Russia's Foreign Minister Alexander Izvolsky who, almost alone in the cabinet, desired a change of ministries, a course opposed by the premier, Finance Minister Kokovtsov, and Minister of Interior Peter Stolypin. A perceptive observer wrote that "A. P. Izvolsky posed as an enlightened European who had become thoroughly steeped in Western culture, and attempted to act as an intermediary between Stolypin and the Kadets." Izvolsky himself told Miliukov that "basic political reform will bring us closer to Europe, and ease the foreign minister's task abroad."[37]

A more unexpected, and possibly more influential, ally appeared in

[35] *Ibid.*, pp. 375, 509–10, 516.
[36] *Ibid.*, p. 508.
[37] KRY, p. 91; ROK, XIX, 117.

the person of General Dmitrii Trepov, the former "dictator" of Moscow and St. Petersburg, now palace commandant of Peterhof. A man of most conservative views and unquestioned loyalty to the Emperor he had his sovereign's complete confidence. Nicholas wrote of him to his mother: "Trepov is absolutely indispensable to me; he is acting in a kind of secretarial capacity. He is experienced and clever and cautious in his advice."[38] Why should this man be more inclined toward compromises with the opposition than most of the bureaucrats? Miliukov thought that he was more "far-sighted." Others were more cynical. Witte wrote that Trepov "conceived the idea of applying the 'Zubatov theory' to the Kadets; as he had hoped, in Moscow, to bring the workers over to his side, worming himself into their midst, so he now decided to do the same with the Kadets." One of Trepov's closest associates in the Ministry of the Court reports that the Emperor regarded Trepov's advice on a Kadet cabinet as a temporary derangement due to his ill health—he had had a heart attack prior to his negotiations with Miliukov.[39]

Perhaps the Emperor never took the matter seriously. Others around him, however, negotiated with Miliukov and other Kadet leaders with their sovereign's permission, and, indeed, on his direct order. The initiative came from Trepov, who, in early May, asked Kokovtsov about the possibility of forming a new cabinet composed of Kadets. The minister, who always opposed the project, talked to others about squelching the enterprise, which was beginning to be discussed in governmental circles, and in the press. "When *Temps* abroad, and *Novoe Vremia* in St. Petersburg demand a Kadet ministry," wrote Miliukov, "everyone understands what it means." The Left immediately picked up the scent of a Kadet "betrayal." "One has to keep asking Messrs. Kadets for the same thing," wrote Lenin in answer to Miliukov. "What you do, do quickly. Then, Mr. Miliu-

[38] J. Bing (ed.), *The Secret Letters of the Last Tsar* (New York, 1938), p. 211.

[39] Witte, *op. cit.*, II, 353; A. Mosolov, *Pri dvore Imperatora* (Riga, n.d.), pp. 123–31 *passim*. The most Machiavellian explanation of Trepov's behavior is offered by Izvolsky who claims to have it from Trepov. According to this version, Trepov never wanted any Kadets in the cabinet. Nevertheless, he urged a Kadet ministry, calculating that "such a cabinet, at the very start, would not fail to enter into a violent conflict with the Emperor; as soon as that happened he [Trepov] would take strong measures, with the aid of the troops in the capital, to suppress the Kadet government, and substitute a military dictatorship of which he himself would be the chief" (See A. Izvolsky, *Recollections of a Foreign Minister* (New York, 1921), pp. 217–19.

kov, everyone will definitely soon understand 'what it means.' "[40]
One positive result of Miliukov's new respectability was the fact that
the government litigation against him was terminated. He was, as
we know, charged with attempting to overthrow the government
through the press in his first newspaper, Narodnaia Svoboda. Utilizing the new political climate, his lawyer asked for an immediate consideration of the case. In a private discussion with the judge he
pointed out that it would be highly inconvenient to jail a man who
might, any day, become His Majesty's minister. The judge understood, for the case was dropped, though other newspaper editors
guilty of the same offense had just been sentenced to one year in
jail. It was Miliukov's last legal tussle with the old regime; he would
never sit in its jails again.[41]

Trepov began his campaign by attempting to see Petrunkevich.
The veteran Kadet refused, however, to speak to him, though he said
nothing of the incident to anyone. Trepov then approached Miliukov,
who agreed to see him, again without telling his colleagues about the
matter. "Considering the Kadet fraction's mood," he wrote, "it was
hopeless to get its permission." But since the only alternative to the
negotiations was the Duma's dissolution, and since the chamber had
asked for a Duma cabinet, "I considered it impossible to turn down
the invitation."[42] Trepov proved to be a business-like partner who,
paper and pencil in hand, took down Miliukov's proposals. It was not
a question of individual Kadet ministers, Miliukov insisted, but of
adopting the Kadet program, which he outlined. Trepov then coun-
tered with his understanding of what was possible. A partial amnesty
could be arranged, but "not for the bombists." He saw no reason for
the abolition of the State Council, "since these old men will follow
any government." He agreed to universal suffrage and, most amazing,
to the Kadet land program. As for compensating the landlords, the
Treasury would make up the difference between "a just valuation" of

---

[40] GOD, p. 360; LEN, IX, 325.

[41] See V. Nabokov, "Kaprizy pravosudiia," Pravo, 1906, pp. 1805–6. The transcript of the trial is in ibid., 1906, pp. 1854–60. Miliukov's lawyer tells his tale in
PNM, pp. 183–85. Gessen, also involved, relates the incident in GES, p. 229.

[42] ROK, XIX, 108. It is interesting to note how secretive the Kadet leaders
were about these negotiations. Petrunkevich did not inform Miliukov, the latter
did not inform his colleagues, Muromtsev did not inform the party leaders later,
etc. Both differences of opinion on tactics and private ambitions probably played
their role here.

the land and the market price. But the land reform would be enacted
by Imperial Manifesto, not through the Duma. To this Miliukov
offered no objection. "The simple soldier," Miliukov thought, showed
more "healthy common sense" than the professional politicians who
soon took over the negotiations. "I consider this meeting," Miliukov
added, "as the most serious of all those dealing with the same
question which followed."[43]

Trepov, however, ran into difficulties, for in an interview with
Reuters he went back on his promises to Miliukov. He granted that
"neither a coalition cabinet nor one taken from outside the Duma
will calm the country." The cabinet had to be Kadet "because they
are the Duma's strongest party." But one could speak of a Kadet
ministry and still "unconditionally reject the principle of expropriation." To this Miliukov replied that "those who wish the Kadets to
disarm the revolutionaries must accept the principle of expropriation." As for Trepov's "finding it impossible to speak of a full
amnesty," Miliukov retorted: "Let us stop talking about a Kadet
ministry."[44] Nevertheless, Trepov pressed on and gave the Emperor
a list of candidates which showed Muromtsev as premier, Miliukov
or Petrunkevich as Minister of Interior, Nabokov or Kuzmin-Karavaev
as Minister of Justice, Gertsenshtein as Minister of Finance, N. N.
L'vov as Minister of Agriculture, and Shipov as State Comptroller.
It was a coalition, not a Kadet cabinet, but the very existence of such
a list was a return to the conciliatory Witte days of the previous
autumn.[45]

This could not but arouse the Left which, since those very days,
had always suspected some sort of deal between "the bourgeoisie"
and the government behind "the people's" back. We have seen
Lenin's reaction to the news of a possible Kadet cabinet. To be sure
he represented the extremist position, but much of the Social Democratic press spoke in similar terms. In their eyes "a bourgeois cabinet"
was a betrayal of the popular hopes for change. Miliukov might well
reject their "political abstractions," such as "the dictatorship of the
proletariat," "nationalization," "socialization," or "municipalization
of the means of production," but such slogans were acquiring popu-

[43] P. Miliukov, "Moe svidanie s gen. Trepovym," Riech', February 17, 1909;
ROK, XIX, 108-9.

[44] GOD, pp. 495-99.

[45] KOK, p. 147.

larity. Only Plekhanov and the Mensheviks agreed that a ministry
should be formed from among the Duma majority; even they said
they would fight against a cabinet of "Petrunkevich-Miliukov." Not
unnaturally Miliukov found this hard to swallow. "It is impossible,"
he wrote, "simultaneously to insist on a ministry enjoying the confidence of the Duma and then suspect the private motives of those
who are to enjoy such a confidence. . . . That is a policy of elemental
revolution which leads to a military dictatorship."[46]

V

His party, Miliukov the historian detected, was in danger of becoming another Girondist group—the unlucky middle group destroyed by
pressures from the Left and Right. "If we are speaking about a party,"
he wrote, "which may become the victim of its historical position
between two extremes then the comparison of 'the Kadets' with 'the
Girondists' has a deep meaning." While the Right clamored for the
Duma's dissolution, the Left insisted on turning it into a revolutionary tribune. Even the Trudoviks had little respect for the chamber
as a means of reforming Russia. "How many in Russia believe in
the peaceful results of parliamentary work?" asked their leader Ivan
Zhilkin. "One must be a romantic dreamer, an idealist, to give oneself over to such rosy hopes." To Miliukov, however the "Duma of
national hopes" was still at the center of the people's attention and
should only be used as a tool for peace. "The Duma will be a weapon
of pacifying the country, or it will not exist at all; but it will not
become a weapon toward the establishment of chaos."[47]
Such remarks were directed at the intransigent Social Democrats,
not at the Trudovik group which, Miliukov asserted, "regards the
views of the extreme left parties cautiously, and separates itself from
them in practice, though it might share some of them in theory."
What was more, there was no denying that the Trudovik deputies
were popular among the peasants. "The chief and unmistakeable
merit of the Trudovik group," he wrote, "is the fact that it has helped
powerfully to give the Duma the sympathy of the entire population.
For the Russian peasant any thought of the Russian Duma is doubt-

[46] GOD, pp. 450, 469, 367.
[47] Ibid., pp. 350, 364–66, 396.

less limited to the Trudovik group, and its leaders are quickly becoming popular heroes." As a result the Trudoviks expected that they too
would join the parliamentary cabinet. To this Miliukov's answer was
negative. "Unfortunately," he felt, the group did not have "sufficiently
qualified persons for this role." The Kadets were not about to share
power with their neighbors to the Left, particularly since Miliukov
calculated that he could obtain a parliamentary majority without
relying on the entire Trudovik fraction. Of one thing he was quite
sure; it was impossible, in the First Duma, to get a majority against
the Kadets.[48]

In the meantime the semisecret negotiations for a Kadet ministry
proceeded at full pace. The government leaders now favored a coalition cabinet of bureaucrats sharing power with the opposition, but
keeping control in their hands. Miliukov would not agree to such a
plan; he had rejected it in the Witte days. Some have criticized him
for this position. "The whole plan," wrote Maklakov, "was destroyed
by Miliukov's unyielding stand."[49] In Miliukov's eyes, basic principles of Russian political reform were involved. The efforts for compromise of Izvolsky and Stolypin were, therefore, wasted. Moreover,
Miliukov doubted Stolypin's sincerity and thought that the Minister
of Interior interviewed him "only to find motives for the strengthen-
ing of his own negative opinion of a Kadet ministry."[50] Only
Izvolsky was genuinely interested; for, as he told the Emperor,
"beyond the frontiers of Russia there was unanimous condemnation
of the proceedings of M. Goremykin's ministry, and no one hoped
for the re-establishment of normal conditions in Russia until other
men came into power and other policies were inaugurated." He gave
the Emperor a memorandum in which this passage was devoted to
Miliukov:

> The participation in the Ministry of M. Miliukov would be
> especially well regarded for, although he has no seat in the Duma,
> his influence is very great with the public as well as with the Duma
> itself. In spite of all his defects—an immense ambition and a cer-
> tain tendency toward intrigue—he is a man endowed with a very
> keen perception and an extremely clear political sense. His en-
> trance into the Ministry might even be unavoidable, for he would

[48] *Ibid.*, pp. 385, 400, 493–94.
[49] FIRST, p. 198.
[50] TRI, p. 33.

become the most vigorous defender of the Government against the attacks of the extreme left. He is the only one who would be capable of organizing a Governmental party under conditions that are as novel as they are difficult.[51]

It was, on the whole, a rather flattering description of Miliukov's gifts and usefulness; the Emperor commissioned Stolypin to continue the negotiations. But, in Miliukov's eyes at any rate, the minister had ambitions of his own and realized that his own post would be held by a Kadet. What, he queried, would Miliukov do in his job, which involved supervising the secret police? Miliukov gave the curious reply that "the Kadets' role in the government must not be judged by their behavior as the opposition" but concluded that there was no hope from that quarter. Izvolsky, who was present at the interview, remained silent throughout and could only offer Miliukov a ride home in his carriage. Even that proved to be too much of a risk:

> It was almost morning by that time; we were in an open victoria, and all the way back we passed other carriages, returning from the many pleasure resorts nearby, when it suddenly occurred to me what a strange impression must be produced by the sight of the Minister of Foreign Affairs driving at four o'clock in the morning with the chief of the Kadets. . . . I mentioned it to my companion, who replied that he had just thought of it himself, and that we both ran the risk of being seriously compromised—he in the eyes of the Opposition, and I in those of the Conservatives. There was nothing to do but laugh heartily at the situation.[52]

There was to be one more attempt at a compromise, connected with the candidacy of Shipov as premier. The veteran zemstvo leader was willing to work for a new cabinet on condition that the majority of the seats went to his old rivals, the Kadets. In his long audience with the Emperor, Shipov spoke to Nicholas about the qualifications of various Kadet leaders. He had the following to say about Miliukov:

> With due respect to his capacities, his talents, and his erudition, I thought that his conception of life was mainly that of a rationalist, a positivist; that he had little religious feeling, that is, a realization of every man's moral duty before the Supreme Being and

[51] Izvolsky, op.cit., pp. 188–89, 191.

[52] Ibid., p. 212; ROK, XIX, 115–17. Izvolsky erroneously places the incident after the Vyborg Manifesto; it took place in June.

before humanity. It was my opinion, therefore, that if Miliukov were placed at the head of the government he could hardly be expected to accept moral duty as a basis of his activity, and that his policy would not be likely to lead to that moral development of our people which was so very much needed at the present time. At the same time Miliukov loves power and is autocratic (I used the last word thoughtlessly and I very much regret it) so that if he is placed at the head of the government it is to be feared he will oppress his comrades, and thereby interfere with their independent activities. But the presence of Miliukov in the cabinet as Minister of Interior or of Foreign Affairs would be exceedingly useful, and even necessary, if the cabinet is to be composed of members of the Kadet Party.[53]

Miliukov admits that "there was then circulating an opinion about my tendency toward autocracy." In any case, however, the whole scheme soon collapsed because of developments in the Duma and in the countryside. Soon after the interview with Shipov, the Emperor told Kokovtsov that the enterprise had never really had his blessing; "I can tell you now in perfect composure that I never intended to embark upon that distant and unknown journey which I was so strongly advised to undertake."[54]

VI

What frightened the Emperor more than Miliukov's possible "autocratic" tendencies was the agrarian problem and the Duma's attitude toward it. In the early spring there had been relative peace in the countryside—perhaps the peasants hoped that the Duma would find a quick and just solution to their grievances. But Goremykin had told the Duma that its proposed solution was "absolutely inadmissible"; yet the government itself proposed so little as to offer no hope at all. Alexander Stishinskii, the Minister of Agriculture and an ultra-reactionary, made a speech which, in Izvolsky's words, "was limited to vague promises of an extension of the opera-

[53] GUR, pp. 714–15. I have used the English translation of Shipov's memoirs available in this work in an appendix.

[54] TRI, p. 57; KOK, p. 149. The cabinet negotiations are most perceptively analyzed in R. Tuck, "Paul Miliukov and Negotiations for a Duma Ministry," ASEER, X (1951), 117–29.

tions of the Peasants' Bank and the development of emigration to Siberia. It produced a most deplorable effect."[55]

The number of peasant disturbances across the country, which had stood at forty-seven in April, rose to one hundred and sixty in May, and to seven hundred and thirty-nine in June. "If there are now agrarian disorders in Russia," wrote Miliukov, "then those chiefly responsible for them are Messrs. Gurko and Stishinskii," accusing the Minister and his deputy. "Compulsory alienation," he asserted, "is the only means against a destructive jacquerie."[56] The Kadets introduced their land bill into the Duma early in May. Miliukov admitted that "there is not complete unanimity regarding the details of the land question in the party"; it was an issue on which Russian liberalism would never be unanimous. Petrunkevich was probably right when, at the Kadet party congress in April, 1906, he pointed out that "while in political questions we had the possibility of using the examples of West European experience which cleared the way for all our labors we must clear our own way in the agrarian question, and must struggle with difficulties with which we had not met before."[57]

Drastic as the Kadet solution seemed to the government and the Right it was conservative compared to the Trudovik and other Left programs. Miliukov pointed out that, in the First Duma, the peasantry "was represented in a way in which it has never been represented anywhere."[58] There had never been a parliament with so many peasant deputies; there had never been a peasantry which expected so much in so short a time from so weak a body as the first Russian legislature. Incensed by the Duma debates on the land question, the government, on June 20, published a statement in its official organ, the Pravitel'stvennyi Vestnik, warning the peasants that the Duma legislation would hurt them. The peasants were rather enjoined to expect help from the Emperor and his government. The government's highhanded action aroused the entire chamber; even moderate Kadets were incensed. Miliukov, however, counselled cau-

---

[55] Izvolsky, op.cit., p. 179.

[56] S. Dubrovskii, Krestianskoe dvizhenie v revoliutsii 1905–1907 gg. (Moscow, 1956), p. 42; GOD, pp. 498, 440.

[57] GOD, p. 413; Petrunkevich is quoted by Miliukov in his "Liberalizm, radikalizm, i revoliutsiia," SZ, LVII (1935), 297.

[58] GOD, p. 242.

tion. "The ministerial proclamation was, doubtless, an unconstitutional act," he wrote; "in it the executive assumed legislative power. But it does not follow from this that, in retaliation, the Duma as the legislative power should assume executive functions, and thereby formally abandon strictly constitutional grounds."[59] Such action would be interpreted as "revolutionary" and would serve as the pretext for dissolution which the government needed.

It proved impossible to stop the blow, however, and Miliukov could only try to soften it. On July 6 the Duma finally voted on a statement, prepared by the Kadets and unacceptable to either their Right or Left allies. Miliukov's pleasure at the forestalling of the crisis was premature. "In spite of those who wanted to pull the Duma over to a new tactic the majority remained faithful to its strictly constitutional point of view," he wrote. The Duma statement was a "simple factual denial, and a factual statement about the Duma's intentions in the agrarian question."[60] Factual or not, Stolypin drew his own conclusions, and on July 8 the First Duma was dissolved. When the rumors of dissolution started, Miliukov had illusions that "the country will rise to a man to show Messrs. the ministers that a legally convoked national assembly is not a Soviet of Workers' Deputies." Two days before the dissolution, he wrote: "And so we are on the eve of a civil war. For the Duma's dissolution—there can be no doubt of that—means civil war. Independently of how the Duma will act when it is told to take a rest or disperse altogether its very name will be a banner around which the masses will gather."[61]

Others made the same prognosis. The Minister of the Court Baron V. B. Frederikhs, told Stolypin that "this decision may lead to the most awful consequences, including the destruction of the monarchy." Stolypin, who had now replaced Goremykin as premier, warned all governors to take the strongest protective measures "in view of the expected general disorder." A prominent Social Democrat returning to the capital was sure that he would find "if not barricades then at least a general strike and street demonstrations."[62] In fact there was general apathy, and the first days after the dissolu-

[59] *Ibid.*, p. 381.
[60] ROK, XX–XXI, 103–4; GOD, p. 427.
[61] GOD, pp. 371, 380–81.
[62] KOK, p. 152; CHER, p. 291; VOI, II, 84.

tion passed in absolute peace. Miliukov explained to his readers that "the calendar of popular risings" indicated July to be a dead season. But, he warned, "an upsurge will begin within a month, and toward winter a national rising will be at its zenith." When the news came of the armed uprising in the naval fortress of Sveaborg, dominating Helsinki, he was sure that it was "the first sign of a terrible hurricane." But the expected storm never materialized. He drew some consolation from the reaction of the British; when a Duma delegation, caught in London by the news of the dissolution, went to see the British prime minister, he coined the phrase, "La Douma est morte; vive la Douma." "This happy formula of the head of the English cabinet," wrote Miliukov, "most successfully expresses what, in our opinion, must be the central thought of all defenders of a popular legislature."[63]

Such thoughts might satisfy Miliukov. For other Duma deputies, the sudden dissolution came by surprise, but few would accept it without a show of resistance. It had been presumed that the Duma would be dispersed, but not so soon. The Kadet Central Committee discussed the matter on June 4; Miliukov argued that dissolution was the monarch's privilege and that the Kadets, as a constitutional party, must bow to it. The only proper reaction, he thought, was to disperse and prepare for the new elections. But the majority was opposed to such a solution even then. When the edict actually appeared, the Kadets felt constrained to act if only to prevent the Left from committing a blunder. Miliukov was the first to hear of the dissolution, at four in the morning in the offices of Riech'. He immediately got on his bicycle and rounded up the entire central committee. By eight they met and had charged Miliukov to write the statement that became the Vyborg Manifesto.[64]

It was decided that all deputies who wished to protest should meet, but not in the capital, where police measures were feared. The group traveled to Vyborg, Finland, and met in the hotel Belvedere, beginning July 9. The meeting, presided over by Muromtsev, could not agree on the text of the statement. The Trudoviks and Social Democrats wished to make it much stronger than the Kadets. Miliukov was not permitted to enter the hall (only deputies were admitted). In

[63] GOD, pp. 538, 540, 533.
[64] KAD, p. 64; VIN III, 7, 10.

the morning even the Kadets were divided on the appeal to the population. Only a third of them approved of the passive resistance measures urged in the document. Miliukov, though he would not be a signatory in any case, was not very enthusiastic himself. "I was held back by the fact," he recalled, "that I did not share the general responsibility." It was clear that the government would take action against the rebelling deputies.

Then a *deus ex machina* intervened. The governor of Vyborg told Muromtsev that, if the deputies did not leave immediately, troops would disperse them. In the resulting hurry it was decided to sign the document as it was, though a large number of Kadets did this against their better judgment. A total of one hundred and forty-seven deputies (representing four parties) signed the document, which urged the population to offer passive resistance to the government. "And so," the Manifesto ended, "until the calling of a new popular legislature do not contribute a kopeck to the Treasury or a single soldier to the army." It should be remembered that direct taxes formed an infinitesimal part of the Russian budget. Recruits were due only in October and, as events developed, there was no trouble at the recruiting stations. "The Vyborg Manifesto was," Miliukov felt in retrospect, "the minimum of what could have been done to find a way out of the general situation."[65]

The deputies traveled back to the capital in silence, expecting to be arrested at any moment. There were also rumors that the Black Hundreds were readying an attack on them, and so when Miliukov left the railroad station in St. Petersburg "an energetic Kadet lady" pushed him into a waiting cab and drove him home in safety. There were no immediate arrests, though litigation was initiated against all signatories of the Manifesto. In December, 1907, they were tried and sentenced to three months in jail. A worse penalty was that they were barred from all political activity until 1917. The flower of the Kadet party could no longer participate in the Duma. It was a sad end to Russia's first parliament. In June, when hopes still ran high, Miliukov had forebodings of trouble when he wrote that this was "a rare, a

[65] The official Kadet history of the Vyborg Manifesto is VIN III, from which this account is drawn. The protocols of the meetings in Vyborg are in "Pervaia gosudarstvennaia duma v Vyborge," KA, No. 57 (1933), pp. 85–99, which also has the text of the Manifesto. See also SID, p. 368, and ROK, XX–XXI, 110–11, as well as TRI, p. 63.

heroic time. Soon, perhaps, it will end, and we must treasure its last minutes all the more." The Duma itself was not to blame in his eyes. "The Russian people's political first-born," he wrote, "this Duma will forever remain that beloved child of whom all is expected, and who is forgiven all." Another consolation was the comment of his teacher and friend Kliuchevskii who had written of Russia's first parliament:

> Observing the activities of this Duma I was forced to admit two facts which I had not expected. These were the rapidity with which the people's view was formed that it was the most promising organ of legislative power, and then the unquestionable moderation of the dominant mood expressed by the Duma.[66]

It was enough encouragement to make Miliukov look forward to the Second Duma.

VII

That summer the Miliukov family took a dacha in the resort town of Terioki, in Finland, not far from the capital. It was pleasant to relax in the woods (a photograph shows a comfortable old wooden building surrounded by trees) but there was also a political reason for the move: it would be easier to hold meetings away from St. Petersburg where the police could come at any moment. After the Vyborg Manifesto the Kadets were more than ever under official suspicion though they did practically nothing to implement the document. On July 15 the Central Committee met in the dacha to decide the party's official attitude to the matter; only the parliamentary fraction had committed itself to the Manifesto. The Kadet leadership voted that the party should avoid adopting the Manifesto, should not distribute it among the population, and should not put it into action. It was a complete retreat. A consultation with party representatives from twenty-nine provinces held in Moscow August 2–3 showed that in fact very little had been done by local Kadet groups about the Manifesto. Most delegates were skeptical of its practicality and reported primarily apathy and fear. In the provinces, membership was dwindling, local committees were disintegrating, morale was low: everyone

---

[66] *Riech'*, June 6, 1906; GOD, p. 525; Kliuchevskii's letter to A. F. Koni of June 21, 1906, is quoted by Miliukov in his "V. O. Kliuchevskii kak lichnost'," PN, January 26, 1932, p. 2.

expected directives from the center. All delegates urged the calling of a new party congress to rally the party.[67]

Miliukov was absent from this sad post-mortem. He had gone to western Europe for a different kind of stocktaking: he wished to see the European reaction to the disappearance of Russia's parliament. There were, in England and France, public figures who wished to express their sympathy with the Duma in some tangible way. The idea arose of a "Memorial to the Duma" expressing support for the Russian chamber. It was to be signed by a large number of prominent Frenchmen and Englishmen and delivered to Muromtsev by a British delegation which was to travel to Russia. Over a thousand French leaders signed the document stating that "there is now but one hope for Russia, and but one for the alliance—namely the re-establishment of the Duma."[68]

The English address was signed by two hundred and fifty members of parliament, the editors of twenty-four newspapers, fifty mayors, and the leaders of all important trade unions. It was "a direct message of sympathy and respect" which told Muromtsev that "the complete triumph of liberty in Russia, to which we look forward at no distant date, will at length make it possible for the English and Russian peoples to give formal expression to the friendship already uniting them." Miliukov must have felt elated when a number of the signers gave a banquet in his honor in London. The toast offered by the editor of the *Daily News* was "to the Duma and the Russian people." The *Times* reported Miliukov's response:

> He thought that the memorial to the Duma was well-inspired in acknowledging the simple principle which the Russian government would never understand, that any people, when it reached a certain standard of well-being and of culture and civilization, must of itself develop the same ways of freeing itself, the same ways of higher existence which other nations had developed.[69]

The Russian European was in his element, but there were disappointments later. Many Britishers wondered whether the personal delivery of the "memorial" would not constitute an interference in

---

[67] KAD, No. 46, pp. 67–68; No. 47–48, 113–33 *passim*.

[68] *Times* (London), August 30, 1906, p. 3.

[69] The *Times* of September 6, 1906, has the full text of the "Memorial to the Duma." *Times*, September 12, 1906, p. 7, has an account of the banquet.

internal Russian affairs. Rumblings were heard from Russia that the authorities would not permit any public demonstrations in favor of the dead Duma. The *Times* editorialized that "the projected visit of the English deputies evokes profound misgivings" even though "Professor Miliukov and other prominent reformers have done their best to raise it above the level of partisan or personal considerations."[70] The Russian diplomatic establishment would do nothing to help the enterprise. The Russian Ambassador in London, Count Aleksandr Benkendorf, informed Izvolsky in disapproving tones of Miliukov's performance in London. "When a man like Miliukov," he wrote, "and a party such as his campaign abroad it indicates that the party is desperate for one reason or another. This is what the political sense of the English makes them feel, and from this point of view Miliukov made an error."[71] Finally, both the British and the Russian sides decided to cancel the personal visit. Miliukov, as chairman of the Anglo-Russian Friendship Committee which was to have welcomed the British delegation, wired to London: "The committee is convinced that the time will soon come when the Russian people, through its representatives, will be able to give solemn expression to its real feelings towards the British people."[72] It was only as a member of the Third Duma, as we shall see, that Miliukov kept this promise in 1909.

Now, however, he had to get his party ready for the elections to the Second Duma. The first step was to call a new party congress. This time, unlike April, it proved impossible to meet in the capital: the authorities would not permit the "unregistered" party such a luxury. Miliukov fumed that "nowhere in the world do they 'legalize' such free associations as political parties," but Stolypin thought otherwise. The party's clubs in St. Petersburg and Moscow were closed, and the Kadets again resorted to the hospitality of the Finns. The fourth party congress met in Helsinki on September 24–28, 1906. Even

---

[70] *Ibid.*, October 10, 1906; the Russian reaction is given in "Privetstvie anglichan gosudarstvennoi dume," VES, 1906, 1607–9, 1665–67.

[71] A. Izvolsky, *Au service de la Russie* (Paris, 1937), I, 370–71.

[72] *Times*, October 15, 1906, p. 3, has the text of the telegram. Miliukov recalls in his memoirs that he received the beautifully bound and engraved "Memorial to the Duma" only in 1910 and turned it over to Muromtsev's widow. Note that in the memoirs Miliukov confuses the whole "Memorial" incident, forgetting that he went to London in the summer of 1906 (VOSP, II, 42–43).

there the sessions had to be closed to the public, and to reporters. Very meager accounts of the meetings exist, though reports of angry clashes over Vyborg made their way to Tsarskoe Selo. "How shameful," wrote the Emperor to his mother, "is the behavior of our Dolgorukys, Shakhovskoys and Co. at Helsingfors. Everybody here in Russia laughs at them."[73]

The ridicule was concentrated on the mental contortions connected with upholding the Vyborg Manifesto while doing nothing to carry it out. The congress voted that "it considers the distribution of the Vyborg Manifesto essential in order to acquaint the population with the idea of passive resistance, but not with the aim of arousing the population to its immediate realization." The Manifesto was being buried, of that there was no doubt, but it was to be an impressive funeral, to please those delegates who still believed in some form of open struggle against the government. The party's full verbal fury was next turned against the field court-martials which had been instituted in August, after an unsuccessful attempt on the life of Stolypin. The congress termed the institution "monstrous" and stated that "in a civilized country they represent an unthinkable denial of the basic principles of justice, and have turned the death penalty, unanimously condemned by the Duma, into a daily occurrence. . . . The system must be condemned by a unanimous verdict of all cultured mankind." The final vituperation was reserved for the ministry. "The government of P. A. Stolypin," the congress pronounced, "is a government of such violence and arbitrariness as had not been experienced by Russia in the darkest epochs of unlimited autocracy. . . . Any support of the anticonstitutional ministry, whatever form it might take, is an act aimed against the Russian people."[74]

This was a strong negative program. On the positive side the party announced that its election platform would be constituted of the First Duma's answer to the Throne Speech. Such general pronouncements

---

[73] P. Miliukov, "Obshchii obzor izbiratel'noi kampanii," in A. Smirnov, *Kak proshly vybory v 2-iu gosudarstvennuiu dumu* (St. Petersburg, 1907), p. 9. See A. K., "K zakrytiiu partiinykh klubov," VES, 1906, pp. 1232–35. For an account of the official refusal to register the party, see A. Kaminka, "Otkaz v registratsii partii nar. svobody," *ibid.*, pp. 1461–67. Also J. Bing, *op. cit.*, p. 219. The protocols of the congress were never printed.

[74] The resolutions are taken from "Postanovleniia IV-go s"ezda partii nar. svob.," VES, 1906, pp. 1585–91.

soon were supplemented by more specific campaign strategy. In late October the Kadets called together in Moscow a number of provincial representatives for pre-election indoctrination. The militant tone of the Helsinki congress gave way to a more sober estimate of the situation. The theme of "an orderly siege" was Miliukov's chief tactical recommendation for the Second Duma. The government was too strong to be toppled over easily; the opposition had to prepare for a lengthy and difficult tug of war.

Both the Left and the Right would now compete with the Kadets in a way they had not in the first elections. The Right had won several victories in the autumn zemstvo elections. This proved, said Miliukov, that the Duma must democratize local government. Elections would become genuinely popular only if the implementation of civic freedoms came first on the Duma's agenda. Here, too, there would be less controversy than in the field of economic reform. Nevertheless, the agrarian problem would again come to the fore and, Miliukov was as sure as ever, the Kadet solution was still the best and the most reasonable. Had it not aroused stubborn opposition from the Right? Referring to the murder, in July, of the Kadet deputy Mikhail Gertsenshtein, the leading party spokesman on the agrarian question, by members of right-wing organizations, he maintained that it was "not accidental," since the party's program "fundamentally affects the basic interests of the privileged layers of society." The Duma dissolution, he said, had been "a respite granted to this class by the government," which was utilizing the interim to promulgate its own agrarian legislation. Miliukov spoke only a few days before the chief item of this legislation, Stolypin's decree on dissolving the commune, was published on November 9.[75]

VIII

November and December were dominated by preparations for the new parliament. The government, for its part, was doing everything to ensure a more pliable Duma by weakening the leading parties of the First Duma. Litigation against the signers of the Vyborg Manifesto disposed of the flower of the Kadet and Trudovik parties. Other

---

[75] Miliukov's campaign speech is in *ibid.*, 1906, pp. 1781–93. The text of the Stolypin decree is in KAL, pp. 274–80.

oppositionists were sent into administrative exile; in 1906 thirty-five thousand persons were thus punished. Opposition newspapers and their editors were persecuted; in January, 1907, alone seventy-seven periodicals were squashed, and sixty editors sued by the government. "In no country," wrote Miliukov, "would a citizen tolerate such arbitrariness, and he would demand the restitution of his rights from a higher body, or from a court." But in Russia no legal recourse was open to the persecuted citizen. The Right, too, was active, and in the depth of the countryside many a nobleman made sure that he would influence the elections. "It seems," Miliukov wrote, "that our Russian landowners read all the details of how English and American elections are falsified." The clergy, too, an instrument of conservatism, was enlisted in the election process at the behest of the Holy Synod.[76]

The Kadets came in for their full share of official harassment. Election meetings planned in St. Petersburg with Miliukov's participation were repeatedly forbidden or, if held, closed by the police under one pretext or another. Miliukov was again disfranchised because he had not established full residence in his new apartment. His old teacher Maksim Kovalevskii, who replaced him as a candidate from the same district, was disqualified on identical grounds.[77] The party's "illegal" or "unregistered" status was a convenient pretext to invoke the law against the Kadets all over Russia. In early January, Stolypin invited Miliukov in for an interview. Received in the Winter Palace with all the marks of courtesy, he was taken aback when asked by the premier to become his ally in the fight against the revolutionaries. If the Kadets openly condemned political assassinations, the premier would legalize the party. This had always been a painful matter for the Kadets who, not sympathizing with revolutionary tactics, did not dare to disown them for fear of the political repercussions which would ensue from the Left. Miliukov, who never approved of terror personally, could not but demur and told the premier that the matter represented "political tactics for the party."

Stolypin sensing that Miliukov was not adamant, reduced his

---

[76] The above statements are drawn from Miliukov's essay in Smirnov, op. cit., pp. 10–13, 20, 29–31.

[77] For examples of police harassment, see VES, 1906, p. 1898; 1907, pp. 240–42. Miliukov's removal from the electoral lists is described in D. Protopopov, Ocherk deiatel'nosti S. Peterburgskoi gruppy partii narodnoi svobody (St. Petersburg, 1908), pp. 19–21.

demand. "Write an article," he suggested, "condemning political assassination. I shall be satisfied with that." Miliukov agreed, provided the article appeared unsigned. The premier consented, and Miliukov accepted the bargain, provided the party approved. If the article appeared Stolypin was to act; otherwise, nothing would change. When Miliukov described the arrangement to Petrunkevich, the latter exclaimed: "How could you have agreed to this compromise even conditionally? You are destroying your own reputation, and you will drag the entire party down with you. . . . Better to sacrifice the party than to destroy it morally." Needless to say, Miliukov went no further in the matter. But rumors about the interview had already spread, and Miliukov was forced to describe it in *Riech'*. "The party will not be legalized at the present moment," he wrote of the interview, "because the conversation made it clear that its legalization is made dependent on certain steps which do not follow from the normal course of registration, and which are unacceptable to the party."[78]

The Left, however, refused to believe that a deal had not actually been made. It was too good an election device to overlook, particularly since some Mensheviks and Popular Socialists had agreed to form election blocs with the Kadets. "A socialist," wrote Lenin, "who has a conscience and any shame, will never run on a joint ticket with the Kutlers and the Miliukovs." Of the Stolypin-Miliukov meeting Lenin wrote with biting irony:

> And Miliukov chats at an audience with Stolypin: "As you see, Your Excellency, I disrupted the revolution, and tore the moderates from it. Now for a tip from Your Excellency" . . . Stolypin: "Hm, yes, I'll look into the legalization of your party. You know, Pavel Nikolaevich, you should split up the working rabble, and I'll hit them with a club. That way we'll get them from both sides. . . . It's a bargain, Pavel Nikolaevich."[79]

[78] The interview with Stolypin is described in VOSP, I, 430–31, but is placed incorrectly in March, 1907. Miliukov's article, "Moe soglashenie s P. A. Stolypinym," *Riech'*, January 24, 1907, makes it clear that the meeting took place in early January.

[79] LEN, X, 299, 323. In addition to the two articles of January, 1907, Lenin came back to the matter the following month; see *ibid.*, X, 348–49. A cartoon by Kukryniksy illustrating Lenin's satirical comments appeared in *Krokodil'* (Moscow), April 20, 1960, p. 11.

The Left, which campaigned actively, were proving to be formidable enemies of the Kadets. The population went out of its way to support the extremist parties, partly because they suffered most from the authorities. As Miliukov wrote in the London *Contemporary Review:* "The pressure used by the government, as well as its reactionary rule in the interval between parliaments, brought about so much disaffection in the country that a great number of the members elected were chosen by the exasperated population from the ranks of the Revolutionary Parties."[80]

As in the First Duma, the Left again intended to use the chamber as a revolutionary platform and a springboard for radical action. Even Plekhanov proposed that "a sovereign Duma," meaning a Duma free of all restrictions imposed by the Fundamental Laws, should become the goal of the entire opposition. Miliukov deplored the fact that the Left had learned nothing from the experience of the First Duma. Such a slogan, he claimed, "turns the clock back to the pre-Duma period," when the limitations of the chamber had not yet become clear.[81] The Duma was too fragile an instrument to be used for pounding the old regime into dust, Miliukov argued in his debates with the Left. One of his Bolshevik combatants recalled that

> as in the first campaign the strongest opponent of the Social Democrats was Miliukov. He demanded a clear answer from us: what is the meaning of your tactics of utilizing the Duma for organizing extra-Duma forces? . . . The Duma, he said, is a complicated instrument, and should be used only for specified purposes. Take a violin: it can be played. But it cannot be used to pound nails— for that you use a hammer.[82]

Miliukov, the amateur violinist, must have particularly relished this metaphor of his own making.

Though he saw the Left danger he was, nevertheless, willing to make concessions to his foes. Due to the government's election machinations it became clear that, though the Social Democrats would have thousands of votes in the capital, they would be unable

[80] CASE, p. 458.

[81] P. Miliukov, "Polnovlastnaia duma," VES, 1906, pp. 2132–40, passim.

[82] VOI, II, 138. The author recalls that quite unscrupulous accusations were leveled at Miliukov by the Social Democrats. Many workers, he writes, believed that Miliukov had forty thousand rubles from the banks to buy votes (ibid., II, 133).

to elect a deputy and the Kadets would get all six seats in the capital. The Kadet Central Committee had to vote on the Social Democratic demand that the Kadets yield two of their seats to their opponents. There was much opposition, but Miliukov pushed for the concession. "It is important," he said, "to calm our voter who wants above all that a bloc with the Left be put right." The Kadets yielded one seat which went to the Bolshevik Grigorii Aleksinskii, one of their bitterest critics in the Second Duma. The Bolsheviks did not believe in gratitude.[83]

IX

The election results were not what the Kadets had expected. The Left scored significant victories, as did the Right. Unlike the First, the Second Duma would have a weak Kadet center; the party's hegemony over the parliament was gone.[84] The Second Duma would be even more radical than its predecessor. The government's attempt to sway the elections had produced unexpected results. As Miliukov put it:

> In the West, usually, the people express confidence, or lack of it, in the government. In our country the opposite is true: with us the government condescends to trust the people, or deprives the people of their confidence. The history of our second electoral campaign is the history of a grandiose attempt to make the population say what the government wanted to hear. Its outcome is a loud and solemn confirmation of the fact that the country knows well what it wants.[85]

Although opposition to the government had been demonstrated, the Kadets could not be satisfied; they were no longer the leaders of the opposition. Miliukov put balsam on the wound by suggesting that one could not speak of "a defeat of the party of Popular Freedom since the extreme parties received, chiefly, the votes which would

[83] The deal between the two parties is described in ibid., II, 159–60; Protopopov, op. cit., p. 13; CHER, p. 335.
[84] The 518 deputies were distributed, from Left to Right, as follows (LEV, p. 67): Social Democrats 65; Social Revolutionaries 37; Popular Socialists 16; Trudoviks 104; Polish Kolo 46; Moslems 30; Kadets 98; Cossacks 17; Non-party 50; Democrat. Reforms 1; Octobrists 44; Right 10.
[85] VTO, p. 1.

have most likely been cast for them at the time of the first elections, if they had then participated as rivals." The fact remained that the Kadets would have a much more difficult time in the second Russian parliament then they had had in the first. The now-stronger reactionaries had no sympathy for the chamber at all. "They," Miliukov said, "are going into the Duma in order to destroy it." The Left hung on to its old illusions about the Duma, but Miliukov hoped they might still change their minds. They had, after all, given up the boycott.[86]

For the time being, however, though weakened, the Kadets would still be the Duma's parliamentarians. It would be a hard role. As Miliukov noted, "a chamber, two fifths of which deliberately do not accept constitutional means of struggle, would be in a permanent danger of dissolution even in countries with a more stable constitutional order." The large Social Democratic fraction indicated that it wished to go its own way; Miliukov was rather pleased by this. "The sooner they will separate their affairs from those of the Duma," he wrote, "the more calmly and evenly will the Duma be able to take care of its business."[87]

The Duma's business was to pass as much useful legislation as possible. The Kadet fraction, meeting a few days before the chamber's opening, approved Miliukov's timetable of beginning with bills on civic freedoms and the reorganization of local government. The fraction elected Prince Paul Dolgorukov as its chairman, with Miliukov's *Riech'* colleague Gessen as his deputy. The Kadet Fedor Golovin, former chairman of the Moscow Zemstvo Board, was nominated for Duma chairman, with N. V. Teslenko, the Moscow lawyer, as his deputy. Both were elected by the Duma which thus acknowledged that, though much weakened, the Kadets continued to have a near monopoly on talent and experience.[88] But Miliukov felt that a change had come over his relationship to the fraction. It was all very well to say that if the Second Duma "does not have the youthful fervor of the First Duma it is because it does not have its illusions either." But the illusions had been precious and had made the daily work exhilarating. Now most of Miliukov's closest associates were absent. "A layer of Russian citizens experienced in political

[86] *Ibid.*, pp. 17, 24, 41.
[87] *Ibid.*, pp. 21, 23, 61, 269.
[88] VES, 1907, pp. 531–32.

struggle," mostly the old zemstvo-constitutionalists, were disqualified by Vyborg. "In the fraction," Miliukov recalled, "I no longer had such intimate ties as united me with the leaders of the First Duma." In addition everyone seemed to sense that "the Duma was living from day to day." This led to a depressed mood which, Miliukov remembered, "threw a kind of veil over all our work."[89]

There was tension in the Kadet fraction. The first small clash came during the deliberations on how to receive the government's Duma declaration. Miliukov urged against a vote of no confidence. He termed the government declaration "a reef" on which the Duma ship could sink. A vote of no confidence would be pointless and "would not correspond to the Duma's dignity." Some Kadet deputies disapproved of receiving the declaration with complete silence. "But," a participant wrote, "it was the members of the Central Committee and of the dissolved Duma who enjoyed the greatest authority in the fraction; and it was they who decided the issue." Several deputies "obeyed reluctantly, and without enthusiasm, since they were convinced that those who elected them would not understand or approve of their silence."[90]

The premier's declaration breathed a certain amount of liberal spirit. Even Miliukov had to admit that "transmitted to foreign newspapers it showed the cabinet in the best light. No European would have understood how, after such a speech, there could be a vote of no confidence." But, he pointed out in irony, the declaration "seemed the more liberal since it contained only the titles of projects, and not the bills themselves." While the Right benches applauded Stolypin, the rest of the Duma, in accordance with the Kadet plan, sat in studied silence. "The real heroes of the day," thought Miliukov, "were not those who spoke but those who remained silent." He said little about the declaration. He did not even demand a change of cabinets but suggested the weak alternative of "voluntary" individual ministerial resignations.[91]

This mild tone was necessary if, as Miliukov put it, "our first aim is to protect the very existence of the Duma." He knew that the next

[89] VTO, pp. 192, 195; VOSP, I, 423–24.

[90] V. Maklakov, Vtoraia gosudarstvennaia duma (Paris, n.d.), pp. 64–65, 85; VTO, pp. 61–62.

[91] VTO, pp. 69, 75, 197.

dissolution would be followed by a change in the electoral law—a plan which the government had in mind ever since its unhappy experience with the First Duma. It was therefore incumbent upon the Kadets to watch their every step in the Duma. Miliukov urged "not hopeless 'demands,' but a systematic acquisition of the positions occupied by a strong enemy." Yet the illusion had to be maintained that the opposition had not surrendered to the government. Here the slogan of "an orderly siege" came in handy, and Miliukov was pleased when the pro-government *Novoe Vremia* wrote that a siege "is more dangerous than an attack." "How smart you are, Mr. Menshikov," Miliukov addressed the columnist, "and how well and correctly you understood us."[92]

X

Though he had invented the "siege" formula, Miliukov was not eager to apply it. When, in early March, the Kadets planned a bill abolishing Stolypin's field courts-martial, Miliukov demurred "because the bill presented a political risk." Miliukov opposed the courts-martial but wished to wait until the measure, introduced while the Duma was dissolved, lapsed in April. He was overruled, however, and the Kadets raised the issue in the Duma. The Right immediately proposed that, before the bill passed, the Duma should formally condemn political terror. It was, Miliukov pointed out, the old question of who would disarm first, the government or the terrorists. "In any European parliament," Miliukov asserted, "a similar attempt would meet with complete defeat." Duma chairman Golovin skilfully avoided bringing up the Right motion, and an amended Kadet bill passed. It was, however, defeated by the State Council—the first time that the upper chamber had bared its teeth.[93]

Favoring a *modus vivendi* with the government, Miliukov overemphasized any conciliatory gesture by Stolypin. When funds for famine relief became an issue between government and Duma, Miliukov thought he saw a change in the cabinet's attitude toward the Kadets. While the Left proposed having the Duma take care of the starving population directly, the Kadets, through Rodichev, opposed

[92] *Ibid.*, pp. 32, 44, 56, 211, 283.
[93] *Ibid.*, pp. 90, 222, 245; see also Maklakov, V*toraia* . . . , p. 106, and LEV, pp. 261–78.

such actions as resembling the dangerous Left tactics in the First
Duma. Rodichev instead proposed the establishment of a committee
to check the government's handling of relief funds. Stolypin, who
rejected the Left's proposal, declared from the Duma tribune that
"the government fully and completely agrees with deputy Rodichev's
motion." Miliukov immediately seized upon this as "the first concession that the popular legislature has won from the government,"
made, he added, "under the gaze of the entire civilized world." With
exaggeration Miliukov spoke of "a political gesture with which the
chairman of the council of ministers . . . will astound Russia and
Europe. . . . After a liberal declaration a demonstrative concession to
the liberal center—is that not a trump before Europe?" Trying to
capitalize on the new development, Miliukov quoted the London
Times which had wondered how a minister could work with a Duma
in which the chief party was not legalized.[94]

The illusion of collaboration passed quickly, however. As soon as
the Duma committee began gathering data on famine relief, it ran
into trouble. Having invited various outsiders to testify, it found that
they were either forbidden to attend or were not admitted into the
Duma building. Miliukov complained that Stolypin's prohibition to
consult experts "contradicts not only the letter of the Duma rules,
and the needs of the situation, but also the examples of Western
European constitutional practice." Describing these troubles in the
London *Contemporary Review*, Miliukov wrote that

> all relations between the Duma and the Ministry were character-
> ized by a spirit of petty persecution. The Comptroller General
> refused to give the Budget Committee any explanations whatever.
> Other committees connected with the Budget work found it impos-
> sible to get the necessary information from ministerial offices. In
> the Agrarian Committee the Minister, though invited, never put
> in an appearance. The very right of existence was denied to the
> committee on the unemployed question.

Deputies were treated with contempt. Two of them had gone to see
the capital's prefect on business. The gentleman responded by letter
in the official gazette stating that "he finds outside solicitations completely superfluous," instructing the deputies that "sitting in offices
waiting their turn prevents them from carrying out their obligations

[94] VTO, pp. 77–79, 200; see also LEV, pp. 125, 127–29, 131–32.

in the Duma." Miliukov was aghast at such an attitude. "One can just imagine," he wrote, "what an English, French or American deputy would say if the capital's first policeman read him lectures on his 'duties' and made him 'lose time in offices.' . . . No official in the civilized world would permit himself to answer a deputy by such impertinence."[95]

Miliukov's pessimism in regard to the Duma returned with full force. In addition he was worried by attempts on his life sponsored by the reactionary Union of the Russian People, which had engineered the assassination of Gertsenshtein. In March, 1906, the Union also assassinated Grigorii Iollos, an editor of *Russkiia Vedomosti*, and a well-known Kadet publicist. Miliukov escaped two attempts but, for the Duma Easter recess, he went abroad.[96] Henceforth he was to spend much of his vacations in western Europe or the Balkans. This time he visited Paris, where the French translation of *Russia and Its Crisis* was being published with an additional chapter covering the period 1906–7. He invited his French translator to accompany him to Italy and Switzerland and, in a more relaxed frame of mind, returned to St. Petersburg in late April.

On April 30 the Kadets introduced their land bill. All the opposition parties had introduced their own land measures, offering solutions of varying degrees of radicalism. Stolypin's program involved diverting the peasants' interest from the nobles' land to that owned by the communes collectively. His executive decrees now needed legislative sanction but, it seemed clear, would not receive it. His plan of breaking up the commune in favor of individual land ownership smacked too much of a scheme to protect the strong against the weak and involved no confiscation of the nobles' land which, by then, had become an almost sacred formula for all but the conservatives. Miliukov would have liked to postpone the consideration of the explosive land issue. He pointed out, however, that in a Duma in which almost two hundred deputies were peasants "it has proven impossible."[97]

---

[95] VTO, pp. 125–26, 203; CASE, p. 462; LEV, pp. 134–37.

[96] The assassination attempts are described in VOSP, I, 432–33, and GES, p. 238. On Iollos, see P. Miliukov, "Pamiati G. B. Iollosa," VES, 1907, pp. 777–80, and VTO, pp. 177–80. On the trip abroad, see VOSP, I, 433–35, and GES, p. 242.

[97] VTO, p. 97; the text of the Kadet land bill is in VES, 1907, pp. 796–803; LEV, pp. 169–72, has an analysis of it.

The Kadets had spent months perfecting their First Duma land bill. Nikolai Kutler, formerly head of the agricultural department under Witte and now a Kadet deputy, brought all his expertise in the subject into play. Compulsory alienation of certain portions of privately owned nobles' land remained the crux of the measure, but much was done in the bill to protect private property once a redistribution of land had taken place. Miliukov wrote in the London *Contemporary Review* that

> according to the plan proposed by the Kadets the practical details of the reform were to be worked out by local committees on which landowners and peasants were to be equally represented; this done the Duma was to discuss the whole question afresh. Holding this view the Kadets naturally preferred to postpone the consideration of the vast and complex question of agrarian reform as a whole in order to deal with certain equally urgent but less complicated matters. . . .[98]

Though the Socialist fractions disagreed with the Kadets' land bill, the Kadets gained the leadership of the Duma land committee. Kutler was elected its chairman, and a good deal of progress was made toward a bill in the Kadet spirit. Stolypin, however, remained opposed to any solution which would hurt the interests of Russia's landowners. On May 10 he asked for the floor to discuss the various Duma land measures. He criticized the Kadet bill specifically, pointing out that compulsory alienation of land could be used only in a very limited number of cases where no other solution was possible. The government and the Kadets would never agree on how to satisfy the land hunger of the Russian peasant. The Left also remained dissatisfied with what it regarded as the Kadet half-measures in a problem which required a radical solution. What was worse the Socialists continued to treat the Duma as a revolutionary tribune and to endanger its very existence. A series of incidents provoked by the Social Democrats convinced the government that dissolution was the only way out.

Soon a pretext was discovered to destroy either the Social Democrats or the Duma itself. The police found evidence that the former were agitating in the army and that their military organization was planning a conspiracy against the government. Some Social Democratic

[98] VTO, pp. 219–21; CASE, p. 459.

deputies were involved, but Stolypin decided to implicate the whole
fraction. Either the Duma would co-operate, or he would dissolve it.
On June 1 he asked the Duma to surrender fifty-five Social Democratic deputies who, he charged, were implicated in a state crime. The
Duma's last hours had arrived, and all fractions met to decide on their
tactics. Miliukov proposed that, in protest against Stolypin's ultimatum, all Kadet deputies resign. But no one supported him; instead the
Kadets moved that a Duma committee examine the charges against
the Social Democrats, and the Duma accepted their motion. But the
Kadets would be firm with deputies guilty of preparing an armed conspiracy. Miliukov urged that "the guilty ones must be surrendered,"
and a majority (against eight) agreed with him.[99]

The Duma could no longer be saved, but at least it would maintain
its dignity till the bitter end. The Kadets would not issue any statement to the population or utilize the last session for demonstrative
purposes. Miliukov did not want a Duma which would panic at the
last moment. "Such a Duma," he wrote, "would have presented to
Europe the clearest justification of the unavoidability of its dissolution." Few in the West would sympathize with conspirators in the
legislature. "The accusation is not badly thought out," he commented;
"and it might prove convincing to a section of public opinion in
Russia and abroad." The Duma's last session should be devoted to
current business and not to the rejection of the budget and the government's agrarian legislation as the Left proposed. And so, its fate sealed,
the Duma spent its last hours debating a bill on the reorganization of
local courts; a coalition of the Kadets and the Right stopped the
Left from changing the agenda. "By this meeting," Miliukov wrote,
"the Duma proved that there are, in Russia, elements for a genuine
constitutional order."[100]

Four Kadet deputies, still hoping to save the Duma, went to see
Stolypin in the middle of night. Peter Struve, Maklakov, Mikhail
Chelnokov, and Sergei Bulgakov were acting without the authorization of the party. They asked for a compromise, but the Premier told
them that unless all the deputies were surrendered immediately he
would dissolve the Duma. He told his visitors that he was "most sur-

[99] Maklakov, Vtoraia . . . , p. 243. "Razgon II dumy," KA, No. 43 (1930), pp.
67–70.
[100] VTO, pp. 263, 265, 271.

prised that you defend the Duma's position. I thought that you, as Kadets, would meet us halfway because if we remove the Social Democrats from the Duma you will get a Kadet majority, and then you can execute your policies."[101] No Kadet, however, could go as far as the Premier in attacking the Left.

On June 3, the dissolution decree appeared, together with a new restrictive electoral law. The regime was strong enough to take back some of the concessions granted at a moment of weakness. There was no public reaction to the dissolution, not even an ineffective Vyborg Manifesto. Times had changed, and most opposition zeal was gone. It was in fact the end of the Revolution of 1905–7. The old regime had regained confidence in itself and had found means to deal with a divided opposition. Russia would still have a parliament, but it would not be of the type that Miliukov desired. Henceforth it would be even less democratic than the First and Second Dumas. "A new page, perhaps a new chapter, is beginning in the history of our fatherland," wrote Miliukov. "We look on with a heavy heart, in anticipation of new hard efforts, and new sacrifices."[102]

[101] PAD, V, 312. The visit is also described in LEV, pp. 338–39.
[102] VTO, p. 264.

5: THE BARREN YEARS

> The principle of "an autocratic constitution" confused all
> ideas, disappointed all expectations, brought about, in consti-
> tutional Russia, unheard of forms and limits of repressions, in
> a word, it Europeanized Russia in the Asiatic manner.[1]

I

With the new electoral law of June 3, 1907, the character of Russian
political life underwent a drastic change. As Miliukov described it
to an English audience in 1916: "After a few months of meteoric
splendor there followed long years of a very modest existence. I would
call the second age of the Duma's life that of political mimicry."
The Third Duma was, in the witty phrase of Michael Florinsky, "an
illegitimate child of western democratic ideas and of the Russian
autocracy."[2] The suffrage for the First and Second Dumas had been
far from perfect; but now a major step back had been taken. The
law set the clock back in that process of democratization so dear to
Miliukov's heart. It was also a blow at legality; for its promulgation,
without the consent of the legislative institutions, constituted a clear
coup d'état. Miliukov told his English readers that "the new franchise
was introduced by an ordinance which constituted a much more vio-

[1] VTO, p. 246; Miliukov wrote this on May 30, 1907—four days before the
coup of June 3.
[2] REP, p. 27; M. Florinsky, *The End of the Russian Empire* (New York,
1961), p. 96. For a recent study of the coup, see A. Levin, "June 3, 1907: Action
and Reaction," in A. Ferguson and A. Levin (eds.), *Essays in Russian History*
(Hamden, Conn., 1964), pp. 233–73.

lent infringement of the law than the famous ordinances published by Charles X of France under similar circumstances."[3]

The new law gave preponderance to the conservative element in the population. Formerly 31 per cent of the electors had been landowners; this now increased to 50.4 per cent. Forty-three per cent of the electors had been peasants; this dropped to 22 per cent. The number of workmen electors dropped from 229 to 164. The number of city electors increased from 22 per cent to 25.3 per cent of the total, but now 788 electors represented the first city curia, with its high property qualifications, and only 590 electors represented the far larger population of the second city curia. The number of deputies dropped from 524 to 442. Areas which had sent radical deputies had their representation reduced; this affected particularly the non-Russian parts of the Empire and was part of a new Russification policy. Poland now had fourteen instead of thirty-seven seats. Central Asia lost all its twenty-one deputies and the Steppe Region its ten. The Caucasus was reduced from twenty-five to ten deputies. Siberia had sent twenty-one members; renamed Asiatic Russia, it now sent fifteen. Viatka province was reduced from thirteen to eight deputies, Perm from thirteen to nine, Ufa from ten to eight. Only seven instead of twenty-five cities now elected deputies directly. The electorate in the more democratic second city curia was reduced by new property qualifications. Thus the number of voters in the capital dropped from 126,389 to 87,891.[4]

All this was bound to affect Kadet chances in the elections, scheduled for September, 1907, to the Third Duma. The law favored the parties to the right of the Kadets. There were those, like Prince Evgenii Trubetskoi, formerly a Kadet but later a leader of the Party of

---

[3] CASE, p. 466.

[4] Based on S. Harper, *The New Electoral Law for the Russian Duma* (Chicago, 1908), passim; CHER, p. 67, has the following table of curias:

Curia	No. of electors	Percent of total
Landowners	2,594	49.39
First City	788	15.01
Second City	590	11.23
Peasant	1,168	22.24
Worker	112	2.13
	5,252	100.00

See also Miliukov's description of the electoral law in REP, pp. 35–9.

Peaceful Reconstruction, who urged Kadets and Octobrists to join forces. He deplored "a fratricidal conflict between the Right and Left flanks of our political center." In open letters to Guchkov and Miliukov he insisted that the old coalition of moderates and Kadets which had been the glory of the zemstvo congresses be restored, pointing out that "the liberation movement began to suffer defeat when the conservatives left it, and began to work against it." Miliukov did not exclude "technical agreements on local candidates" between the two parties but expressed doubts as to the reforming tendencies of the Octobrists. And besides, he asked Trubetskoi, "where are the guarantees that even this Duma will not be dissolved by those to whom reforms, if indeed they can be effected by such a Duma, will be inconvenient"?[5]

Trubetskoi's aim had been to detach the Kadets finally from any alliance with the Left. Miliukov had, in effect, been moving in that direction ever since 1905, but the old legacy of collaboration died hard. Even in the elections of 1907 he could not bring himself to speak of the socialists as "enemies" though the latter had long treated the Kadets as such. Reviewing the Kadet position toward the Left over the past two years Miliukov wrote: "We had to first place our 'friends on the left' in quotation marks, then to replace the expression by 'neighbors on the left,' and finally by 'rivals on the left.' But, however useful it might be to us, we have not yet learned to speak of 'enemies on the left.'" Nevertheless, the Bolsheviks were ferociously anti-Kadet during the electoral campaign, and only Plekhanov maintained a moderate line toward them. Speaking of him, Miliukov wrote: "Yes, when all these influences win out will we say, decisively and calmly: we have no enemies on the left."[6]

The elections made it clear that, even as enemies, the Left could be no danger in the Duma. The Social Democrats elected only nine-

[5] Riech', June 21, 1907, reprinted Trubetskoi's open letter to Guchkov from Golos Moskvy. See also E. Trubetskoi, "Otkrytoe pis'mo P. N. Miliukovu," Riech', June 28, 1907, and Miliukov's answer in "Posrednichestvo Kniaza Trubetskogo," ibid., June 29, 1907.

[6] P. Miliukov, "U nas net vragov sleva," Riech', September 22, 1907, and "Gde zhe vragi," ibid., September 25, 1907. Alfred Levin has two studies of the September, 1907, elections: "The Russian Voter in the Elections to the Third Duma," Slavic Review, XXI (1962), 660–77, and The Reactionary Tradition in the Election Campaign to the Third Duma ("Oklahoma State University Publications," Vol. LIX [1962]).

teen deputies, the Trudoviks a mere fourteen. The Kadets returned
fifty-three deputies, roughly half of what they had in the Second
Duma and less than a third of their First Duma membership. The
Octobrists, on the other hand, had one hundred and forty-eight members, and the Right camp, divided into three fractions, had one
hundred and forty-four members.[7] To plan a Kadet strategy for such
a parliament was no easy task, and the party met on the eve of the
Duma's session to do so. The fifth congress of the party since its
founding two years earlier, this was the last one for almost a decade.[8]

The accumulated frustrations of the First and Second Dumas were
brought to the congress, and a vocal left minority thrashed them out.
In his opening speech Miliukov referred to rumors of splits in the
party. "Outwardly," he told the delegates, "our party's situation has
never been more difficult than it is now when we leave the election
vanquished. But a formal defeat does not signify a moral defeat," he
said, pointing to the Kadet victory in the second city curia. "The
elections in the large cities," he maintained, "indicate that Kadet
tactics are being preferred to those of the Left parties. With a better
electoral law," he ventured, "this would have occurred everywhere,
and the party would have led the country." His professional optimism
was evident in his assertion that despite its small parliamentary fraction "the Party of Popular Freedom is the country's chief spokesman
in the Duma."[9]

At the second party congress in January, 1906, he had foreseen the
possibility that the Kadets would be in a parliamentary minority. He
had been wrong then, but in the present situation the party was
"forced into the role of a parliamentary opposition." The Kadets, who

---

[7] W. Walsh, "Political Parties in the Russian Dumas," *Journal of Modern
History* XXII (1950), 148, has the following breakdown of the 429 deputies:
    Right 49; Nationalists 26; Moderate Right 69; Octobrists 148; White Russian
7; Polish Kolo 11; Progressives 25; Moslems 8; Kadets 53; Trudoviks 14; Social
Democrats 19.
    For a portrait of the Duma membership, see C. J. Smith, "The Russian Third
State Duma: An Analytical Profile," *Russian Review*, XVII (1958), 201–10.

[8] The congress met on October 23–27, 1907. For its minutes, see "V-yi s"ezd
K. D. partii," VES, 1907, pp. 1981–89, 2041–60, 2088–2100, 2133–63; Miliukov's report is in P. Miliukov, "Doklad ts. kom. V s"ezdu partii Nar. Svob.,"
ibid., 1907, pp. 1833–40; the congress resolutions are in *ibid.*, 1907, pp. 1829–
33 (the last two pages list the forty members of the new Central Committee).

[9] VES, 1907, pp. 1981–84 *passim*.

had been in the center of the first two Dumas, and thus in a position to maneuver, were on the left wing of the new chamber, unable to lead. Furthermore, "the Third Duma," Miliukov admitted, "can no longer serve as a trustworthy instrument for the implementation of broad democratic reforms, nor can it pretend to that popular trust enjoyed by the First and Second Dumas." Even in the Third Duma, however, one could form "what the Germans term *Adwehrmehrheit*— 'a defensive majority' with the aim of protecting the rights of the popular legislature."[10]

This sounded too compromising to more radical delegates. A debate ensued during which the conduct of the Second Duma Kadet fraction and the Central Committee came under fire. A resolution, signed by twenty delegates, criticized the leadership for its "lack of firmness." The attacks concentrated on the visit by four Kadet deputies to Stolypin in an attempt to save the Duma and on the party's refusal to annul Stolypin's legislation, in particular his land decrees. Mikhail Mandel'shtam, who with Nikolai Shchepkin had resigned from the Central Committee in protest over party policies, led the opposition.[11] But Miliukov had the support of the majority. When he mounted the tribune to answer the critics the audience rose and applauded for "several minutes." He admitted that the visit of the four Kadets to Stolypin had been "incorrect, tactless, harmful and naïve." But their motivation was above reproach, and "the Central Committee values these persons too highly to permit their resignation." He warned that "any further blame directed against these persons will be considered to be directed against the Central Committee. Let the congress decide if it wishes to do that."[12] The criticism must have touched a sensitive chord; had not Miliukov visited Stolypin on several occasions, without even divulging the fact to the party?

Miliukov refused to admit that there was any "opposition group" in the party. "We have no bolsheviks or mensheviks," he asserted, "but different nuances. . . . The Party's unity has so far been its advantage." Defending the Kadet record in the Second Duma, he explained that the party could not follow the Left tactics since they proposed solving problems "in a manner not yet employed anywhere in Europe."

[10] *Ibid.*, 1907, pp. 1833–38 *passim*.
[11] The opposition's speeches are in *ibid.*, 1907, pp. 2045 ff.; Mandel'shtam's speech is in *ibid.*, 1907, pp. 2136–38.
[12] *Ibid.*, 1907, pp. 2049–51 *passim*.

Mandel'shtam's hopes, he asserted, were predicated on a new wave
of opposition throughout the country. But, he told his critic, "a
politician cannot gamble on a wave. He must expect the worst." He
promised that in the Duma "the fraction will be oppositional, and
will not start a friendship with the Octobrists." But in the name of
"the party's dignity" he urged the defeat of the opposition's resolution
(which mustered 21 against 60 votes). The Kadets would not adopt
the Left tactics of obstructionism and boycott; the congress resolved
that "unable to play a leading role in the Duma any longer the fraction of Popular Freedom will, nevertheless, participate actively in
legislating."[13]

II

This time Miliukov became a Duma deputy, elected from St.
Petersburg; the Russian European would represent the Empire's most
European city. The government no longer attempted to disqualify
him. "To tell the truth," observed Sergei Kryzhanovskii, the author of
the new electoral law, "Miliukov was considerably more dangerous
outside the Duma than as its member. His chief shortcoming—
tactlessness—often put the party into an embarrassing position in
the Duma."[14] We shall presently have an illustration of this point.
The Duma Kadets naturally elected Miliukov their chairman, and the
fraction became the most disciplined one in the Duma. It decided, on
the first day of the session, not to offer its own version of an address
to the Emperor. Speaking on the Octobrist motion before the house,
Miliukov explained: "We have our own address," he said, "and it is
well known. It is the address of the First Duma. . . . To present such
an address again in the Third Duma is neither necessary nor, evidently,
possible." He regretted that the motion said nothing about "constitutional Russia." "It is said," he continued, "that the word constitution
is not mentioned in the laws. We think that for that reason the Duma
must pronounce that word." It was no argument to allege that the
word was not of Russian origin:

[13] Ibid., 1907, pp. 1830, 2054, 2092–94, 2100, 2133, 2140, 2154–56. There is
poignancy in the fact that, speaking as an emigrant in Paris in 1921, Mandel'shtam admitted: "And I, not having agreed with Miliukov in Helsinki, had
to admit later that he had been right then" (ARKHIV, II, 85).
[14] KRY, p. 97.

They say that the 'constitution' is a foreign word, and some people do not like foreign words. But, gentlemen, 'emperor' is also a foreign word. Monarch, tsar, are also foreign words, and even autocrat is translated from the Greek. . . . The word constitution sounds foreign even in the classical country of the constitution, in England. . . .

The Duma's new masters simply did not wish to admit that anything had changed in Russia; there was a new stress on nationalism, on the superiority of native Russian ways. The address had not mentioned the desires of the non-Russian nationalities of the Empire. What was needed, Miliukov claimed, was "a Russian patriotism, not a Great Russian patriotism."

Look what is happening in Austria [he told the Duma], look what is happening on that small scrap of the earth—the Balkans, where tiny nationalities hold on to the remnants of their past in order to defend their existence. Compare that regime with neighboring Switzerland, compare it with America where in one generation even the most strongly individualistic nationalities flow into a common pool. How do you explain the difference? In one case we have a policy of hate, in the other a policy based on a feeling of solidarity, on common strivings shared by all.

The Kadets disassociated themselves from the feelings of the majority, but the Octobrist motion passed easily.[15]

Stolypin's declaration to the Duma was also cast in nationalistic language. Of a "constitution" he said that "one cannot affix some sort of alien flower to our Russian roots, our Russian stem." He saw his agrarian policies as the only guarantees of peaceful change, in contrast to the Kadet and Left proposals which he termed "revolutionary." Miliukov replied that the government's policy was "more revolutionary" than the Kadet plan of compulsory alienation. "This change," he said of the Stolypin plan of creating a class of small landed proprietors, "this enormous social change which, in the West, took centuries, cannot be accomplished with us in a moment, even by a mighty arm." The Kadets would oppose Stolypin's agrarian reform.

[15] Miliukov's speech is in SO, November 13, 1907, pp. 141–51; the text of the motion is in ibid., 1907, p. 248. There is a list of Miliukov's Duma speeches, arranged chronologically for 1907–16, in "Vystupleniia P.N. Miliukova v gosudarstvennoi dume," PNM, pp. 352–58. The list should be used with caution, being neither accurate nor complete.

"We will never share in this narrow, class legislation," Miliukov concluded, "and we will never divide with you the heavy responsibility before the country and the future which you are taking upon your shoulders by embarking upon this road."[16]

The Premier had warned that the field courts-martial and executions would continue. "The destructive movement created by the parties of the extreme left," he said, "has turned into open brigandage. . . . A phenomenon of this sort can be dealt with only by force. The government considers any weakening in this field to be a crime." Miliukov had not commented on this part of the Premier's speech; it was left to Rodichev to give Stolypin an answer. To dramatize his opposition to the mass death sentences, he coined the word "Stolypin necktie," indicating, by a gesture, the fastening of a noose around the neck of the condemned. The phrase created a sensation; Stolypin, accompanied by the cabinet, left the hall in a huff, while the Right and the Center indicated their solidarity with him by rising. The Kadets remained seated; only Miliukov rose feeling, as he described it, that it was "morally impossible to remain seated." Stolypin challenged Rodichev to a duel. Miliukov suggested that his own rising removed any implication of a personal offense to Stolypin and that Rodichev should apologize to the Premier. This Rodichev did, but the fraction voted that "a mistaken step" had been taken by Miliukov. The latter felt the event to be his "cas de conscience" and told Rodichev in a public speech that his pronouncement "will have enormous influence and will strengthen the idea and feeling of freedom." The editor of the party's Vestnik, A. I. Blokh, was sentenced to one year in jail for printing the phrase "Stolypin necktie."[17] It was the first of those "tactless mistakes" which Kryzhanovsky had indicated Miliukov would commit in the Duma.

It was next the turn of the Minister of Finance to present the budget. Kokovtsov was optimistic, stressing a rise in Russian exports of grain which indicated a modicum of prosperity. Miliukov replied:

[16] The premier's speech is in SO, November 13, 1907, pp. 307–12, Miliukov's reply in ibid., 1907, pp. 357–70.

[17] See ibid., 1907, pp. 396–98 for the incident, and VES, 1907, pp. 1968–70, as well as VOSP, II, 21, for the Kadet reaction. See also A. Tyrkova-Williams, Na putiakh k svobode (New York, 1952), pp. 370–74. The jailing of the Vestnik editor was the beginning of the end; in February, 1908, the weekly ceased publication and reappeared only after February, 1917.

"It has been said many times that our entire export is the result of underconsumption, and that if our Russian peasant consumed as much grain as the German peasant we would have to stop exporting, and start importing grain into Russia." Miliukov reproached the government for limiting the Duma's budget rights to the point where half of the budget could not be affected by the legislature. "In the first place," Miliukov described the situation to an English audience,

> all the expenses which were customary before the granting of the constitution of 1905 were considered sacrosanct and not to be touched. They are specially "protected" from the hasty influence of budget legislation. Doubly protected are the expenses for the Court and Imperial Family, the yearly interest on the State Loans and so on. In the budget of 1908 these protected items amounted to 1,164,000,000 rubles, i.e. they made up forty-seven percent of the whole of the Budget expenses.[18]

Soon after the beginning of the budget sessions, the Duma adjourned for Christmas. Miliukov utilized the vacation for a lightning trip to New York, where he had been invited by the Civic Forum to speak on "Constitutional Government for Russia." The 1907–8 Civic Forum series included such distinguished American figures as Charles Evans Hughes, then governor of the state of New York, and the Honorable William Jennings Bryan. "It was, so to speak, the zenith of my popularity in America," Miliukov recalled.

The Carnegie Hall meeting was held on January 14, 1908 (New Style), and presided over by the Right Reverend Henry C. Potter, Episcopal Bishop of New York. "The hall," an account reports, "was crowded to its utmost capacity by an audience which numbered nearly four thousand persons, representing the most influential elements in the city." In his Chicago lectures Miliukov had proposed the Russian liberals as the mediators in Russia's forthcoming "crisis." Now he reported on the outcome of that crisis, and his party's role in it. "Our position as mediator," he told his audience, "is now very much weakened. Other parties, much more conservative than our own, now play the role of peacemakers. . . . We believe that the political

[18] Miliukov's budget speech is in SO, November 27, 1907, pp. 665–85; Kokovtsov's answer in *ibid.*, 1907, pp. 685–700. See also S. Harper, "The Budget Rights of the Russian Duma," *Journal of Political Economy*, XVI (1908), 152–56, and REP, pp. 40–41.

situation they are going to create will be extremely unstable, being too much of a compromise with the autocracy and the nobility." He had predicted the revolution at Chicago; now he spoke of the future at the revolution's end. It was a somber prophecy:

> If the revolution in Russia has lost something of its external dramatic character, it is not because the movement has been obliterated, but because it now strikes much deeper root in the lower social strata. . . . The social composition of the future Russia is now at stake. The fate of centuries to come is now being determined. And this explains why the masses, silent and mute as they may appear, put all their heart, all their hope, into the issue of the present movement, and why the movement cannot end until, in one way or another, its main problems are settled.

"The address made a profound impression," says our account, "and at its close, on motion of Hon. Elgin R. L. Gould, president of the New Netherland Bank and formerly city chamberlain, a vote of sympathy and appreciation, and of thanks to the speaker was unanimously carried." That "sympathy" was to cost Miliukov some unpleasant moments in the Duma upon his return.[19]

The day after Carnegie Hall Miliukov was to be received at the White House. But an introduction by the Russian Ambassador, Baron Roman Rosen, was needed, and Miliukov the oppositionary refused to ask for it. "Later this appeared ridiculous even to me," he recalled in his old age, "but such were the times then." As a consolation prize Herbert Parsons, member of Congress from New York, gave a dinner in Miliukov's honor in Washington. Present were three members of President Roosevelt's cabinet (William H. Taft, Secretary of War, James Garfield, Secretary of the Interior, and Oscar Strauss, Secretary of Commerce) as well as Joseph Cannon, speaker of the House, and over one hundred members of the Senate and the House. Introducing Miliukov, Congressman Parsons said that "he was certain that this leader of the Constitutional Democratic party of Russia had the complete sympathy of every member of the Government of the United States." "This statement," says our account, "was received with prolonged applause by all present." It must have been wonderful medicine for Miliukov after his recent unpleasant experiences in the Duma; it would have to last him into the less than joyful political future.[20]

[19] The full text of the speech is in CONST; the facts about its reception and Miliukov's activities in the USA are from a "Note" printed there.
[20] "Note" to CONST, and VOSP, II, 23–27.

III

Miliukov's Right opponents fumed at his daring to criticize his government abroad. One writer maintained that Miliukov had gone to America to get funds "for the revolution," promising Siberia to the Jewish bankers who had lent him the money.[21] In the Duma the Nationalist leader Pavel Krupenskii, alluding to Miliukov's ocean voyage, poked fun at "the new Christopher Columbus" who should apologize for Vyborg and New York before being allowed to speak. The Russian people, he said, did not need "the sympathy of American Jews" and did not want "a single kopeck of American money." The Right and the Center walked out twice when Miliukov mounted the tribune; lacking a quorum the session was twice adjourned. Miliukov published his "Undelivered Speech" as a pamphlet, explaining that "an enlightened patriotism" could be critical and still based on love of country.[22]

The attacks had wider implications since the Duma was then constituting its Defense Commission; it was proposed to exclude all Kadets in view of their inability to keep state secrets. The Right leader Vladimir Purishkevich urged Miliukov's exclusion as "a scoundrel and a villain."[23] The Nationalist deputy Count Vladimir Bobrinskii claimed that "Vyborg, Paris and New York are poor thresholds to the Commission on State Defense." Protesting the exclusion, Miliukov deplored the implications of disloyalty suggested by it. Moreover, "the very question of what constitutes a state secret in Russia," he said, "is not at all identical with the question of what constitutes a state secret abroad. We know how limitless are the boundaries of our state secrets, and how hopelessly state secrets are confused with office secrets." But the opposition was excluded, though the pro-government *Novoe Vremia* wrote that it would have been smarter to include the Kadets and make them take an oath of secrecy.[24]

The attacks on Miliukov continued in later months. Count Bobrinskii, during an agrarian debate, charged Miliukov with having wanted to "rouse up the village" at the time of the First Duma. The Kadet leader called this "a lie and a slander" by a man who spoke in the

[21] N. Krivskii, *Vtoroe pravitel'stvo* (St. Petersburg, 1908), *passim*.

[22] SO, January 25, 1908, pp. 1492, 1507–8; P. Miliukov, *Neproiznesennaia Riech'* (St. Petersburg, 1908).

[23] SO, January 22, 1908, pp. 1417–22.

[24] *Ibid.*, 1908, pp. 1579, 1514; *Novoe Vremia* (St. Petersburg), January 30, 1908.

name of his class, and its interests. "The only group represented here which has the right to say that, in the agrarian question, it insisted on the point of view of all classes," he added, "is the Party of Popular Freedom." The Count challenged him to a duel, but Miliukov refused. In common with the Russian intelligentsia, he condemned duels, but in the Duma he admitted that "I expressed myself sharply, and am ready to grant, not in a parliamentary fashion."[25] Another challenge to a duel came from the Octobrist leader Guchkov who took offense at some remark of Miliukov's, but with outside intervention the incident ended peacefully. Only a day later Miliukov was attacked and beaten by men from the reactionary newspaper *Rus* which had been conducting a campaign against him.[26]

Decidedly, the Third Duma was not a pleasant home for Miliukov. But there were some compensations. One was the possibility to debate Russia's foreign policy, which had never occurred in the First and Second Dumas. Some Kadets, led by Andrei Shingarev, argued that the party should avoid the subject since it would have to agree with much of Izvolsky's policy; by thus supporting the government, the party would lose its opposition stamp. But Miliukov's views prevailed —he felt that "in the field of foreign policy we must express opinions, as far as possible, of an all-national significance, we must defend a non-partisan position."[27] The first foreign affairs debate came in February, 1908, when Izvolsky commented on Russian policy in the Far East. His tone was optimistic and conciliatory. Miliukov welcomed this and assured the minister of Kadet co-operation:

> The opposition's disagreements with the views of some ministries very often grow into the dimensions of a sharp contradiction in principle. But I must say there is no such disagreement as regards the representative of our Ministry of Foreign Affairs when he appears on this platform as a messenger of peace, and presents to us views which will protect the Russian people against the repeti-

[25] SO, March 27–28, 1908, pp. 1099–1101, 1205–18; *Riech'*, March 28, 1908.
[26] "Intsident Guchkova-Miliukova," *Riech'*, May 8, 1908, and VOSP, II, 20–21. Also *Riech'*, May 9–13, 1908, *passim*; PNM, pp. 185–86; an interpellation on the matter in the Duma (SO, May 12, 1909, p. 1127) passed the floor but was buried in committee.
[27] BES, pp. 68–69 quoting from unpublished minutes of Kadet Central Committee meetings.

tion of those diplomatic and military adventures which, unfortunately, we witnessed in recent times.

A foreign affairs debate was a welcome beginning, Miliukov conceded, but more was needed to get a well-informed public:

> We consider that one should be consistent, and that if personal appearances are made before the legislature with reports from the Ministry of Foreign Affairs then deputies should be given the possibility of judging the basis of these pronouncements. We think that the Russian people, no less than the other cultured peoples of the world, deserves to be informed about the normal activities of our diplomacy.

Miliukov was pleased with the 1907 Anglo-Russian convention. "It was with great pleasure," he said, "that I heard the announcement about that system of agreements which brings us close to England and finally disposes of the fears, to a considerable extent chimerical, regarding a clash of our interests in Tibet, Afghanistan and Persia." His only fear was that, with peace re-established in the Far and Middle East, Russia would again become aggressive in the Balkans. "We are being told," he concluded, "that we can pass to a more active policy in the Near East. Here is a point of view against which I should like to warn you." If Russia did not act cautiously in the Balkans "we might not avoid some new adventures."[28]

The second debate on foreign affairs came in April, 1908. Izvolsky spoke on the Balkans, particularly on the new solutions proposed for the old Macedonian problem. Miliukov agreed with Izvolsky that the British plan for reform was not acceptable because it pushed Turkey to the wall. The more moderate Russian proposal should be adopted, keeping in mind that Russian policy should be motivated not only by its "moral obligations in the Balkans," but also by a feeling of "healthy egoism." But Miliukov was more interested in the effects of the debate than in its details and quoted with approval the *Times* reaction to the Duma exchange. The London paper had said that such debates "give Russian policy more weight in Europe, since the Russian nation, through its representatives, sanctions imperial policy."[29]

---

[28] Izvolsky's speech is in SO, February 27, 1908, pp. 112–19; Miliukov's reply is in *ibid.*, 1908, pp. 119–24.

[29] The Duma speeches are in *ibid.*, 1908, pp. 1763–77 (Izvolsky) and pp. 1786–98 (Miliukov). See also P. Miliukov, "Otnosheniia inostrannoi pechati," *Riech'*, April 9, 1908.

Miliukov thus began his career as his party's foreign affairs spokes-man in a spirit of caution and moderation. The Kadets did not advo-cate an aggressive foreign policy as is often alleged by Soviet students of the period. In the prewar years, as we shall see, Miliukov opposed any Russian venture which would embroil the country. This was true both of his stand in foreign affairs and of his views on Russian defense. During the Third Duma's first debate on defense, Miliukov opposed the projected increases in naval expenditures. Speaking for the Kadets Miliukov said: "We consider that, in principle, we do not have the right, before our electors, to commit the country for a number of years in advance." But even more important was to avoid entering an unhealthy armaments' race. What had been said "gives rise to fears," Miliukov thought, "that the program will grow too broadly in the direction of a preoccupation with the navy." The Kadets would not vote for any such program.[30]

IV

There was, in addition to foreign affairs and defense, another area which always concerned Miliukov in the Duma—education. One of the Third Duma's genuine contributions was to vote large funds for an expansion of Russia's schools. Russia's universities had prospered after being granted autonomy in August, 1905. But, Miliukov pointed out, "the Ministry of Education is beginning a campaign against the fruits of its own efforts, against the results of the decree of August 27, 1905." As politics moved to the right so did the school administrators. Mili-ukov reminded the Duma of the cost of such retrogressive policies:

> Gentlemen, those of you who passed through this school, who stood close to the activities of the Ministry of Education, through whose hands, as through mine, passed a number of generations both in high school and in the university, will be well aware of why so little that was original, talented and strong passed from this school into life, they will well know how many of the best elements remained by the wayside, were swept aside or squashed, and why this happened.

[30] Stolypin's speech is in SO, May 24, 1908, pp. 1397–1408; Miliukov's reply in ibid., 1908, pp. 1413–14. For a recent Soviet study which speaks of the Kadets as leaders of an "aggressive Russian bourgeoisie," see BES.

It was criminal to interfere again in the universities which, after a period of decline, were thriving as never before. They had never been so full, so busy, lectures never so well attended, students so eager to learn. Was this not a result of the new political conditions? "Is it not a pleasure," he asked, "to find that the only institutions which are doing constructive work as a result of the establishment of political freedom are these very same universities which first, and most energetically, took the path of conquering political freedom"? But the ministry had begun to take back concessions made during the revolution. The old spirit of control and limitation of freedom was coming back. Russia needed a very different kind of educational policy:

> The Russian school must educate the young Russian generation now growing up on the basis of the principles which were created by our fundamental political changeover, it must educate the growing generation in the ideas of political freedom, of civic equality, of justice and law. That is its role. . . . And there lies our hope, the hope that following those events which laid the foundation, even if an imperfect one, of Russian political life, the sufferings of the Russian school will pass away forever.[31]

The meetings on the education budget terminated the first session of the Third Duma in June, 1908. It had been a grey parliamentary year—and more such were to come. Describing the post-1907 Duma to an English audience Miliukov indicated his disillusionment:

> The Duma with its changed composition tried to adapt itself to its political environment. The new majority renounced bold schemes for the general reform of Russia, and devoted themselves to the rather ungrateful task of self-preservation. The Duma was still interesting to observe at close quarters, but it was much more difficult to admire, and indeed was thought negligible as an agent in Russian politics. I suppose that is why the Russian Duma since 1907 has been nearly lost sight of by the world.[32]

Miliukov utilized the summer recess for a trip to the Balkans. Nicholas II and Edward VII of England meeting at Revel had discussed possible joint action there. Miliukov regarded their meeting as a right step in both foreign and domestic politics. "King Edward visited constitutional Russia," he wrote; "in this manner the new

[31] SO, June 9, 1908, pp. 2483–2504.
[32] REP, p. 27.

Russian regime received the stamp of international recognition."[33]
With this cheerful thought Miliukov left for Turkey, his initial stop
on his first tour of the Balkans since 1904. It was a fascinating moment
to visit the Ottoman Empire—the Young Turks had just come to
power. Many years later Miliukov described the atmosphere as follows:

> I was in Constantinople ten days after the revolution of July 23,
> 1908, had begun. I saw the general enthusiasm of the crowds in
> the streets. I sympathized with the initiators of the national move-
> ment; I made acquaintance with some of them one week later in
> Salonica; day by day I was able to follow their first attempts to
> formulate their political programme; it was intended at least as
> much to liberate Turkey from Europe as from the old Sultan. As
> to their relations with Christian nationalities, I saw the chasm
> which existed between their idea of a united Ottoman Empire
> whose members should enjoy equal rights, and the firm decision of
> Christian subjects to preserve their separate national existence,
> their native habits, their inherited traditions.[34]

Though a champion of the Balkan Slavs, Miliukov felt no hostility
toward the Turks, so long as they did not act as oppressors. "I had
occasion to travel in God-forsaken corners of Asia Minor," he wrote,
"in places which are not yet entered on any map . . . I grew to like this
people: simple, honest, sincere, living exclusively on its labor." Now it
seemed this people would live under a progressive regime which might
change the anti-Slav policies of the past. Russia should work with
England in the Balkans to help "create a strong barrier against the
Austrian influence."[35]

On his way from Constantinople to Salonika Miliukov shared a
train compartment with one of the leaders of the Young Turks,
Mehmed Talat Pasha, later deputy chairman of the Turkish parliament, Minister of Interior, and Grand Vizier. Also in the compartment was the Bulgarian Matvei Gerov, editor of the newspaper
Balkanskaia Tribuna, who was returning to Macedonia after twenty
years of exile.[36] Miliukov was again in the midst of the Balkan Slav
movement. Ever since his gymnasium days, when he had volunteered

---

[33] *Riech'*, May 30, 1908.
[34] BALK, pp. 14–15. Miliukov reported his immediate impressions in *Riech'*,
July 27 and 31, 1908.
[35] BAL, XI, 52, 54.
[36] *Ibid.*, XI, 224, and P. Miliukov, "Talaad," PN, March 17, 1921.

on the Slav side in the war of 1877–8, he had been concerned with the fate of these peoples. "All my sympathies were on the side of these aims for liberation," he recalled, "the more so since the leadership in the struggle was already passing from the old 'populists' into the hands of the young generation of the newly-born Slav democratic intelligentsia."[37] This was not the old Pan-Slavism which some were attempting to revive—Count Vladimir Bobrinskii in Russia, and Karel Kramar in Bohemia. The Neo-Slavs, as these men called themselves, were, in July, 1908, meeting in Prague. Miliukov refused to attend and was never associated with the movement.

His aims were of a different sort. First, he wanted to get more reliable information about the area before the Russian public. "So far," he complained, "we do not have a single serious book about the contemporary Slavs. If you wish to read something concrete on this question turn to the French literature on the subject. There everything has been studied and analyzed, including the events of the last days."[38] Second, instead of grandiose Pan-Slav plans he would work for Serbo-Bulgarian co-operation, a modest goal, but one which would bring peace into many a troubled Balkan area. Miliukov was to be accused of partiality to the Bulgarians. But his writing of this period indicates no such bias.[39]

Official Russian policy in the Balkans was, at this moment, groping its way toward new solutions. Miliukov described this phase of Russian diplomacy as follows:

> In August, 1907, a treaty with England had been concluded on Asiatic questions, and in May, 1908, there was an interview between the Tsar and King Edward VII. These two years, 1907–8, represent the period of transition when the Russian Foreign Minister, Izvolsky, after having found new friends in England, was still unwilling to surrender old friends in Austria, and so he is found discussing with them, to our great disadvantage, new schemes conceived under new international conjunctures. The possibility of the final downfall of Turkey, the possibility of the advance of Austria-Hungary

[37] VOSP, II, 27.
[38] BAL, p. 56.
[39] See his "Sofiia i Belgrad: Paralleli," *Riech'*, September 3, 1908, reprinted in BAL, pp. 259–66. The summer trip is described in VOSP, II, 27–38 and 45–7.

to Salonica and of Russia on the Bosphorus, were the subjects of secret discussion on former lines.[40]

The "secret discussions" with Austria led in September, 1908, to the annexation of Bosnia-Herzegovina by Austria without compensation to Russia. It was a diplomatic defeat for Russia; Miliukov called it, with exaggeration, "one of the most humiliating moments of our national existence." Unlike many in Russia, however, he did not blame the reversal on Izvolsky, but rather on "that contradiction between aims and means, between our pretensions to independent policy and our resources, which became the chief cause of our defeat, and which hardly arose only from the personal qualities and views of our diplomat."[41]

Miliukov had been in Sarajevo on the eve of the annexation. He compared the local situation with that during his 1904 visit and noted the progress in political sophistication and the shift from demands for religious autonomy to political questions.[42] Now, as many in Russia where the annexation had made a great stir, he wanted an explanation from Izvolsky. The Foreign Minister proposed to soften the Duma first and wrote his deputy Nikolai Charykov to see Guchkov "and Miliukov who has just been in the Balkan peninsula and, judging by the reports of Sementovskii [the Russian Minister in Sofia] has most healthy opinions on Bulgarian affairs." Charykov followed his instructions; he had known Miliukov when the latter had been a professor in Sofia, and could thus "renew the friendship." He was apparently in sympathy with the Kadet leader who, he wrote later, "fought as well as he could against the reactionary tendencies of the government."[43]

Izvolsky spoke to the Duma on December 12, 1908, when Russia had not yet accepted the annexation (it did so, under German pressure, the following spring). His tone was confident.[44] Then Miliukov took the floor. During his recent tour, he said, he had been appalled at discovering how badly Russian diplomats abroad were informed. He was pleased, however, that Russia was prepared to act in concord with

[40] BALK, pp. 8-9.

[41] See P. Miliukov, "Diplomaticheskaia Tsushima," BAL, pp. 133-58 passim.

[42] Ibid., pp. 267-82.

[43] BES, pp. 104-5; N. Charykov, Glimpses of High Politics (London, 1931), p. 296.

[44] SO, December 12, 1908, pp. 2618-30 passim. Miliukov's speech is in ibid., 1908, pp. 2677-2703.

England. He saw in this "evidence of a change from a period when we had dynastic policies to a time of a genuinely national policy; we warmly welcome this change." It was fine that Russia had not sought compensation at the Straits. "At least we say we do not," he added, and proposed "to leave this idea in peace." It was the first time that he spoke publicly about the Straits, and sounded most moderate indeed. Most needed at the moment was the introduction, in Bosnia-Herzegovina, "of one or another form of constitution." "If free institutions are not granted to this land," he warned prophetically, "then I guarantee decades of struggle." He concluded with a demand for the English solution, "a Balkan Union" as the "chief and decisive step in the interests of Slavdom against the enemies of the Slavs."

V

In the Duma foreign affairs always remained something of an exotic topic. It was the government land bill which was the chief item of business of the 1908–9 Duma session. The bill passed the Duma on May 8, 1909, and, approved by the State Council, was signed into law by the Emperor on June 14, 1910.[45] The Stolypin solution of the land problem would be the law of the land until 1917. The Kadet land project was now buried. In a sense Miliukov was not unhappy about this. Always more interested in political than in economic problems he knew that the land program was the party's most controversial tenet. He told Bernard Pares in June, 1908, that "it did more to wreck us with foreign opinion than anything else." Since 1907 the Kadets had become cautious—Miliukov not the least of them. He had told Pares at an earlier interview: "The whole tendency now is to the right. You know I have always tried to move things that way. Now I seem too left for many Kadets. They want to push farther to the right." He was referring to men such as Maklakov and Izgoev, both on the Central Committee, who defended the Stolypin reform.[46]

[45] See the monumental compilation by A. Ososov, Zemel'nyi vopros v 3-ei gosudarstvennoi dume (St. Petersburg, 1912), and V. Ger'e, Vtoroe raskreposhchenie (Moscow, 1911). An excellent Soviet study is A. Avrekh, "Agrarnyi vopros v III-ei dume," IZ, LXII (1958), 26–83.

[46] PAPERS, "Notebook V, 1908," pp. 10–11; "1908 Bernard Pares Interviews," p. 49. Also RM, 1909, No. 4; 1911, No. 2; 1913, No. 11; A. Izgoev, P. A. Stolypin (Moscow, 1912).

For political reasons Miliukov had to oppose the Stolypin measure in the Duma. He maintained that the government, too, had been
motivated primarily by political, not by economic considerations. The
breakup of the commune had been decreed when the government
decided that the peasantry was not, as Witte had supposed, a conservative force. And so Miliukov took the Duma floor to fight not for the
Kadet bill but *against* the Stolypin bill. The motivation of the bill
was clear, he told the Duma:

> The question regarding which opinion will prevail depends, in
> the last analysis, not at all on agricultural considerations, not on
> considerations which might be suggested by agrarian experts, but
> on the fundamental point of view regarding the political physiog-
> nomy of the peasantry. Is the peasantry, as had been considered
> earlier, "a conservative force"? Or are these "communists" who
> threaten all property in the state?[47]

The nobility had discovered that the peasantry was radical, and it promoted the entire government counteroffensive—the Stolypin land law,
the 1907 electoral law, and the field courts-martial. The nobility hoped
that, by breaking up the commune and encouraging private property
in land a new conservative element would emerge in the village.

Many in the Duma wondered how Miliukov, an individualist to the
core, could defend the collectivist peasant commune. He had predicted
as early as *Russia and Its Crisis* that "to resist the dissolution of the
village community will be a most difficult enterprise."[48] Now he told
the Duma rather cynically: "It is completely immaterial whether I
am an enemy of the commune or not. I am an enemy of the law of
November 9, 1906." He objected to the methods used in putting the
law into effect. Of the three hundred thousand persons who had
already separated from the commune, less than half did so with the
commune's agreement. In the majority of cases the commune was
forced by administrative fiat to let them go. "You are giving freedom
to one million persons," Miliukov charged, "in order to bind the
other one hundred million with the help of policemen and guards."
Why, he continued, had the decree been issued between sessions of

---

[47] SO, October 31, 1908, p. 636. The text of Miliukov's two speeches is in
ibid., 1908, pp. 617–53 and 772–94.
[48] CRI, pp. 349, 352.

the Dumas? Article eighty-seven of the Fundamental Laws, under which the edict had been issued, had not been intended for such measures. "The issuance of the law under this article," Miliukov charged, "appears, from the point of view of a number of European specialists on public law, to be a violation of the constitution."

Miliukov was heckled continuously, particularly when he described how the landowners, through the Councils of the United Nobility, pressed the government into action. His oratory, however, did something for the Kadets' reputation in the country. As he recalled:

> We were listened to by the peasants and clergymen of the Third Duma—a dependent, but democratic element—and through them the news of our fight spread over Russia. A whole stream of peasant deputations from all corners of Russia flowed to us. I particularly remember a delegation of Siberian peasants—tall, mighty, hairy, wrapped up in solid, heavy sheepskin coats. . . . Alas, we could neither give nor promise them anything: but much was done for the opposition's reputation in the Third Duma.[49]

Even Lenin found something to praise in Miliukov's agrarian speech: "In that part of Mr. Miliukov's speech," he wrote "where he appears as a *historian*, and not as a *Kadet*, we have superbly selected facts on the history of the Councils of the United Nobility—facts, the compilation of which does honor to every *democrat*."[50]

Stolypin and his legislation could still, occasionally, unite the Left and the Kadets in opposition. But such joint action was now an accident, and a steady estrangement between the erstwhile partners was in full motion. The Kadets were attempting to adjust to the new political conditions; the Social Democrats refused to do so. Soon Lenin renewed his attacks on Miliukov. The occasion was the publication in the spring of 1909 of the volume entitled *Vekhi* (Signposts), which questioned the major premises of the intelligentsia. Only two of the seven contributors were Kadets (Struve and Izgoev—the same Right Kadet Izgoev who had found much to praise in Stolypin), but Lenin wrote that "*Vekhi* expresses the indubitable essence of present-day Kadetism. The Kadet party is the *Vekhi* party." He refused to make any distinction between Miliukov, who immediately attacked *Vekhi*,

[49] VOSP, II, 60–61.
[50] LEN, XII, 406; italics in the original.

and Struve, who had been drifting away from the Kadet camp.
"Miliukov," wrote Lenin,

> is a practical politician, Struve a doctrinaire of liberalism, yet their
> peaceful coexistence in one party is not an accident but a necessary
> phenomenon because a bourgeois *intelligent, by the nature of
> things,* hesitates between setting his hopes on the masses (who
> will, won't they, help to pull the chestnuts out of the fire), and
> setting his hopes on the Octobrist bourgeoisie.

Lenin was right in making a distinction between Miliukov the politician and Struve the ideologue, but he misrepresented the facts when
he alleged that Miliukov agreed with *Vekhi:*

> Not a single politically thinking person will say that Mr. Miliu-
> kov seriously struggles with the *Vekhi* crowd when he "argues"
> with them, pronounces them "thoughtless," and at the same time
> works with them politically hand in hand. Everyone admits that
> by this Mr. Miliukov proves his hypocrisy without denying the
> fact of his political solidarity with the *Vekhi* crowd.[51]

It was unthinkable, in Lenin's terms, to retain in one party men who
disagreed with the leadership on any vital issue. But the Kadet party,
and its Central Committee, was based on the premise of coalition and
compromise from the outset. Its right wing was simply becoming more
audible than it had been in the revolutionary days. Struve and Izgoev
remained on the Central Committee though Miliukov, the party
leader, subjected their opinions to sharp criticism.

Vekhi questioned some of his dearest beliefs. Mikhail Gershenzon
set the tone of the volume when he rejoiced that "the tyranny of
politics has ended" and that the intelligentsia could return to its
spiritual tasks. *Vekhi* deplored the divisive influence of political parties
on the Russian people. "Nowhere," wrote Sergei Bulgakov, "does
this division penetrate as deeply as in Russia, nowhere does it violate
the spiritual and cultural unity of the nation to a similar degree."
Vekhi questioned Russia's political maturity. "We must at last have
the courage to admit," wrote Izgoev, "that, in our State Dumas, the
vast majority of the deputies, with the exception of thirty to forty
Kadets and Octobrists, did not reveal the knowledge with which it
would be possible to govern and rebuild Russia." Struve wrote that

[51] *Ibid.,* XIV, 237; XV, 61; XVI, 106; italics in the original.

"Russian liberalism considers it its duty to wear the uniform of the intelligentsia, though the sharply renegade nature of the *intelligent* is quite foreign to it." Boris Kistiakovskii alleged that "the Russian intelligentsia consists of persons who are disciplined neither individually nor socially. And this is connected with the fact that the Russian intelligentsia never respected the law, never saw any value in it."[52]

Miliukov accepted only the last allegation with which, he wrote, he "fully agrees." The rest was heresy to be combatted, and so with Petrunkevich, Kovalevskii, and others Miliukov published a reply to *Vekhi* in which his contribution formed more than a third of the total content.[53] He admitted that *Vekhi* had made a contribution in raising fundamental issues. "The positive importance of *Vekhi*," he wrote, "might be insignificant; its practical influence might be harmful and detestable; but this does not stop us from admitting that its critical, provocative value is very great." But the *Vekhi* doctrine had to be opposed, for "the seeds which the authors of *Vekhi* are sowing . . . are poisonous seeds, and the work which they are doing, independently, of course, of their actual intentions, is dangerous and harmful work." *Vekhi* had gone back to that part of the Russian past which Miliukov rejected. "Dostoevsky's *The Possessed*," he alleged, "is the literary prototype of *Vekhi*." The authors claimed that the intelligentsia had no religion and was antistate and cosmopolitan. It must become religious, pro-state, and national minded. But that, Miliukov claimed, was close to the old formula of Orthodoxy, Autocracy, and Nationality. Leaving aside the emphasis on religion which pervaded the *Vekhi* volume, Miliukov criticized the other parts of the triad. Regarding the emphasis on the state, he alleged that "the anarchism of the Slavophils and the anarchism of Tolstoy—here are the two points between which the state philosophy of *Vekhi* places itself." As for demanding national feeling, Miliukov replied that "the question of the positive content on which it would be possible to found Russian

---

[52] N. Berdiaev et al., *Vekhi: Sbornik statei o russkoi intelligentsii* (4th ed.; Moscow, 1909), pp. 65, 92, 123, 126, 164.

[53] P. Miliukov, "Intelligentsia i istoricheskaia traditsiia," in K. Arsen'ev et al., *Intelligentsiia v Rossii* (St. Petersburg, 1910), pp. 89–191. Agreement with Kistiakovskii is expressed on p. 134 of this work. Miliukov wrote two more essays against *Vekhi*: "Natsionalizm protiv natsionalizma," in P. Boborykin et al., *Po vekham* (Moscow, 1909), pp. 37–42, and "Ottalkivanie ili pritiazhenie," *ibid.*, pp. 76–81.

nationalism remains the darkest of all the obscurities of Vekhi."[54]

Leonard Schapiro, who has recently examined the Vekhi controversy, wrote that "Miliukov's essay is witty, a brilliant piece of
advocacy in the sense of scoring debating points against an adversary,
but somewhat devoid of political realism. It was Miliukov's tragedy
that he believed he was a liberal, when he was in reality a radical."
Schapiro agrees with the thesis of the present work that Miliukov was
a Russian European: "It was in all sincerity that Miliukov, a highly
civilized historian, saw himself in 1909 as the equivalent of a Western
European liberal politician." But Schapiro denies that the Kadets
were liberals:

> When the Russian Kadet called himself a liberal, he may have
> believed that he was using this term as meaning, what, say, Glad-
> stone meant by it. But in fact he was in spirit much more the
> liberal of 1848, in other words more a revolutionary, or a radical.
> The great service of Vekhi was to illuminate this fact for the first
> time, even if the illumination came too late, and the message fell
> on deaf ears.[55]

In our view nothing in Miliukov's essay suggests the revolutionary
or the radical. He is, above all, concerned with the anti-political tone
of Vekhi, the very opposite of that public awareness which was
Miliukov's chief concern when he turned from scholarship to politics.
He did not want the Russian intelligent to withdraw into himself.
" 'Politics,' " he complained, "has in effect only just made its first
appearance in Russian life, and that under extremely difficult and
unfavorable circumstances. And yet we have already become disillusioned in politics in a way in which even the countries of classical
election tricks, England and the United States of America, have not
become disillusioned." More, rather than less political consicousness
was needed:

> I am inclined to consider the formation of political parties and
> the first experiment in political conflict as the major, and to the
> highest degree valuable, positive acquisition of that stage of Rus-
> sian political development which we have just left behind. And I

[54] P. Miliukov, "Intelligentsiia i istoricheskaia traditsiia," pp. 113, 145, 146,
162, 187, 188.

[55] L. Schapiro, "The Vekhi Group and the Mystique of Revolution," SEER,
XXXIV (1955–56), 67, 76.

consider it indispensable to oppose most energetically everything which might increase the indifference of our public to this method of "outward arrangements."

He concluded his answer to Vekhi by reminding his opponents of Turgenev's dictum that "the role of the educated class in Russia is to be the transmitter of civilization to the people with the proviso that the people will themselves decide what to reject and what to accept." The Russian intelligentsia could not abdicate this function which had been imposed upon it by the curious path of Russian history, a path which Miliukov had traced in his historical works and which had led him into politics in the first place. "Recall your debt and your discipline," he told the intelligentsia of his day, "recall that you are only a link in that chain of generations bearing the cultural mission of which Turgenev spoke."[56]

VI

Miliukov spent the 1909 Duma summer recess abroad again. This time, however, instead of visiting the Balkans as a private tourist he went to England as a member of a Duma delegation visiting the British parliament. It was an imperfect fulfilment of his 1906 promise to the British public to send to England "representatives of the Russian nation." A Third Duma delegation would not quite fit that definition though the opposition (the only genuine people's representatives in Miliukov's eyes) was represented in it by three Kadets and one representative each of the Moslem and Progressive fractions. The idea for such a visit was the fruit of the 1908 meeting between Edward VII and Nicholas II, which Miliukov had welcomed so heartily. "Constitutional Russia," as he had put it then, would be invited to visit constitutional England. The Opposition would have to be included: the British sense of fair play would demand it. This much was clear to Izvolsky, and to Bernard Pares who arranged the details. It was he who invited Miliukov to come; the latter had to point this out to his Social Democratic critics who accused him of supporting a project organized by the Octobrists for their own glory. The Social Democrats and

[56] P. Miliukov, "Intelligentsiia i istoricheskaia traditsiia, pp. 174–75, 180–81, 184–87, 191.

the Trudoviks, as well as the extreme Right, abstained from the delegation.[57]

After its arrival in London, the delegation became embroiled in an incident. As Miliukov described it, "the presence of a Third Duma delegation was met by sharp criticism and protest from the Left camp where they had not yet forgotten the fate of the First Duma."[58] The Octobrist leadership of the delegation decided to answer the accusations; Miliukov, however, refused to sign such a document. It was the old ambiguity toward the Left which would haunt Miliukov until 1917. Finally, Miliukov suggested a way out: let delegation chairman Khomiakov sign alone. This was done, and everyone was satisfied.[59]

There were other incidents. The most controversial was Miliukov's speech at the London Lord Mayor's banquet. There he said that he belonged "to His Majesty's Opposition, and not to the opposition to His Majesty." There was an immediate Russian reaction. The government-subsidized *Rossiia* wrote: "In England Mr. Miliukov took upon himself a certain responsibility for the Russian opposition. If he fulfils this responsibility he will perform a service to his country for which many of his former sins will be forgiven." The Octobrist *Golos Moskvy* editorialized that the speech "perhaps represents the turning point in Kadet politics, an abandonment of the unsuccessful tactic of opposition for the sake of opposition."[60]

The Left Kadets considered Miliukov's speech a capitulation before the government. His old critic Mandel'shtam recalled that he "led the agitation against such pronouncements, and received a majority in many election districts of Moscow." Miliukov claimed that the phrase had been quoted out of context. He had said:

No one will of course expect me to praise the constitutional establishment in Russia. We, representatives of the Opposition, would like the rights of the Duma greatly enlarged, the electoral law democratized, and the system of political institutions brought into harmony, to make productive legislative work possible. But so long as Russia has a legislative chamber with the right to control

[57] P. Miliukov, "Napadki Sots-Dem. kandidata," *Riech'*, September 10, 1909.
[58] VOSP, II, 44.
[59] *Loc. cit.*
[60] *Rossiia* (St. Petersburg), June 23, 1909; *Golos Moskvy* (Moscow), June 21, 1909.

the budget the Russian Opposition will remain His Majesty's Opposition, and not opposition to His Majesty.[61]

The Left would never let Miliukov forget the incident, but, on balance, he was satisfied with the parliamentary visit. He had participated in the visit because it was "a remarkable manifestation of *constitutional Russia*. It is likely that the defenders of autocracy, as well as our chamber's republicans, did not take part in the delegation for this same reason." The final result was worth the effort: outside its borders "Russia can now appear as a nation, and not only as a government."[62] As in 1906 the visit had been a personal triumph for Miliukov. He met prominent British political figures such as Foreign Secretary Sir Edward Grey, the Minister of War Viscount Richard Haldane, and Winston Churchill, who made the impression, Miliukov recalled, of "an uncorked bottle of champagne." Among those present at a lunch at which Miliukov spoke was Home Secretary Herbert Gladstone, son of William Gladstone. At the University of Liverpool Pares introduced Miliukov as "one of the most outstanding public figures in Europe."[63]

The Russian ambassador in London, Count Benkendorf, had told the delegation that he "continuously urges Petersburg to keep Duma members informed about the course of international affairs, since only the support of the legislature gives diplomacy its force."[64] The next Duma session, however, proved to be quite barren in this respect. Izvolsky spoke to the Duma only once during the year, in March, 1910, and limited himself to budget requests. He said nothing about foreign policy, claiming that "due to various considerations, and in view of the conditions of the moment," he "had not found it possible to ask His Majesty's permission to speak on current foreign policy questions."[65] In reply Miliukov launched into a long foreign policy speech. As soon, however, as he mentioned "the unsuccessful policy of our Minister of Foreign Affairs," Izvolsky and his staff

---

[61] M. Mandel'shtam, *1905 god v politicheskikh protsesakh* (Moscow, 1931), p. 162; P. Miliukov, "Napadki Sots.-Dem. kandidata," loc. cit.

[62] P. Miliukov, "Sleva ili sprava," *Riech'*, September 4, 1909, and "Dym otechestva," *Riech'*, July 30, 1909; italics in the original.

[63] VOSP, II, 45; I. Efremov, *Russkie narodnye predstaviteli v Anglii i Frantsii letom 1909 g.* (St. Petersburg, 1911), p. 84.

[64] *Ibid.*, p. 138.

[65] His speech is in SO, March 2, 1910, pp. 2753–59; for background, see BES, pp. 121–25.

demonstratively left the hall. It was Izvolsky's last appearance before
the Duma; in September, 1910, he was replaced by Sergei Sazonov
and sent as Russian ambassador to Paris.

Returning to Izvolsky's inept handling of the Bosnian crisis, Miliukov charged that the Minister had lost all opportunities of obtaining
some compensation for Russia by ignoring the helping hand of England and France who had offered assistance. Miliukov then turned to
Russian foreign policy in the Far East, to which he devoted the bulk
of his speech.[66] Several Right deputies objected to Miliukov's speech
on the grounds that the Duma, like Izvolsky, should abstain from
foreign policy debates. Purishkevich could not resist addressing the
following venomous remarks to Miliukov:

> The talented leader of the Party of Popular Freedom traveled
> all over the world . . . and touched on everything, so that there is
> nothing for me to say. I am not a specialist, as is deputy Miliukov,
> in international relations and international politics. Listening to
> his speech one thinks of one of the Roman Emperors who, at the
> moment of his death, called out: "What an artist is the world
> losing in me." Nero said that dying. And we can only repeat:
> what an artist, what a specialist in international relations is Russia
> losing, and what does the government think of the fact that Mr.
> Miliukov sits here [pointing to the left benches] instead of speak-
> ing from there [pointing to the government benches].[67]

Despite Miliukov's criticism of the Ministry of Foreign Affairs, the
Kadets voted for its budget along with the majority; only the Social
Democrats and the Trudoviks voted against.

VII

The most dramatic issue of the 1909/10 Duma session was the
legislation on Finland. The Duma's intent, accomplished by its bill,
was to curtail the rights which Finland enjoyed within the Russian
Empire. A recent study shows that "the law tended to make Finland

[66] Miliukov's speech is in SO, March 2, 1910, pp. 2760–90; he quoted from an
article inspired by Izvolsky: Vox Et Praeterea Nihil, "Baron Aehrenthal and M.
Izvolsky," Fortnightly Review (London), September, 1909, pp. 383–401. I leave
out Miliukov's views on the Far East since they played no role in his further
political career.
[67] SO, March 2, 1910, p. 2793.

more a Russian province than an autonomous unit in the Russian Empire."[68] The spirit of militant nationalism, which we observed at the very outset of the Third Duma's existence, was at work here. Miliukov became involved not only as a politician but as a human being. He admired the small Finnish nation and knew the country from personal experience. He had, as we know, lived in Finland before 1905. In the first years of the Third Duma he bought a large plot of land there and built a dacha which remained a place of retreat till 1917; the writer Leonid Andreyev was his neighbor. From the balcony there was a view of the sea—Miliukov's own "window to Europe." The house was equipped for year-round residence, and the two younger Miliukov children, Sergei and Natalia, could ski in the winter, and play tennis in the summer. Miliukov moved his collection of historical works to this new home; from there it found its way, after the revolution, to the University of California library in Berkeley.[69] The rare book room of that library holds an elaborately bound, illuminated scroll presented to Miliukov in November, 1910, by the Finns in gratitude for his opposition to the Duma's chauvinistic aims.

Miliukov's affection for the Finns was construed in rightist circles to be the result of bribery. The reactionary newspaper *Zemshchina* accused *Riech'* of being in Finnish pay; the sum of 250,000 rubles was mentioned. *Riech'* sued for libel, but the outcome was unsatisfactory. Although *Riech'* proved that the monetary transactions involved the purchase of Finnish currency and rotation paper at advantageous rates (a clever business stroke), the editor of *Zemshchina* was declared innocent of libel, and his accusation seems to have lingered.[70] The Nationalist leader Pavel Krupenskii reintroduced the bribery issue when Miliukov spoke of Russia's duty to protect its honor by not violating Finnish freedom. "I fully agree with Miliukov," said Krupenskii, "that we must protect Russia's honor. That is quite correct, and I stress the fact that no 250,000 rubles can make one betray that honor, and sell it for that sum." Miliukov replied as follows:

> I consider it my duty to make some remarks regarding the 250,000 rubles which have lately been mentioned several times in

[68] J. Hodgson, "Finland's Position in the Russian Empire, 1905–1910," JCEA, XX (1960), 158.

[69] VOSP, II, 53–56, 72–76; G. Struve, "K istorii biblioteki P. N. Miliukova v Kalifornii," *Novoe Russkoe Slovo* (New York), February 21, 1960.

[70] *Riech'*, April 19, 1914; GES, pp. 285–86.

connection with my name from this tribune. I would be most grateful to those members of the Duma who mentioned this matter today, and will wish to do so in the future if they, not protecting themselves by the inviolability of members of the State Duma, repeated these accusations in the press. Then I would deal with them as with the original accusers who made it in the newspaper *Zemshchina*, that is, I would sue them for libel, since I do not recognize any other form of reprisal.

Needless to say Miliukov's accusers did not follow his advice. His reward for defending Finnish liberties came in the form of a morning serenade in front of his Finnish dacha, not in gold. The local Finnish youth came to thank him in this picturesque way.[71]

In the eyes of the Right the trouble with Finland was that, after the free days of 1905-6, it could not be subdued as easily as Russia. The Finnish Sejm had too many radical deputies; in 1907 the Social Democrats captured eighty of the two hundred seats; this grew to eighty-six in 1909.[72] Such trends were intolerable to the new masters of the Duma. In the spring of 1908 interpellations were introduced charging that Finland was seething with revolutionary activity. The Octobrists also alleged that the State Secretary for Finland favored Finnish interests to the detriment of imperial Russian interests. Answering the interpellations Stolypin, who had inspired the anti-Finnish measures, charged that the state of affairs in Finland violated Russia's imperial rights.[73] In the spring of 1910 the government Finnish bill was introduced into the Duma. It passed, Miliukov said, "with the speed of an express," clearing both houses in three months (March–June, 1910).[74]

Defending his bill, Stolypin asserted that Russia had too limited a voice in Finnish affairs. "The government is firmly convinced," he said, "that matters which concern the whole Empire, or Finnish laws which concern Russian interests, go beyond the competence of the Finnish Sejm." The proposed Russian supervision over Finnish institutions was necessitated by the Finns' "negative attitude toward Russia and the Russian language."[75] Miliukov began his fight against the bill

[71] SO, March 17, 1910, pp. 958, 970–71; VOSP, II, 73.

[72] Hodgson, op. cit., p. 166.

[73] Stolypin's speech is in SO, May 5, 1908, pp. 2919–41; Miliukov's reply is in SO, May 12, 1908, pp. 417–46.

[74] VOSP, II, 74.

[75] SO, May 21, 1910, pp. 2025–42.

by reminding the Duma that Russia's prestige abroad would decline if the bill passed.

> Gentlemen, *noblesse oblige*. If Russia wishes to play the role of a great world power it must remember that this involves honor, a world moral standard below which one cannot fall. . . . Gentlemen, the world's attention is now focused on the question which you are to decide here. Remember that violence against defenceless nations committed in the name of physical might and the power of a state does not remain without consequences.

His opponents reminded Miliukov that since the Emperor desired the passage of the Finnish bills his will had to be obeyed. "Therefore," said the Octobrist Prince Viacheslav Tenishev,

> it seems to me that deputy Miliukov forgot the words he uttered in his well-known London speech. He forgot that he is a representative of the loyal opposition, His Majesty's Opposition. It seems to me that the opposition which deputy Milukov now advises the Duma to undertake is an illegal opposition. It is an opposition to His Majesty [Miliukov from his seat: "To Stolypin"] and not of His Majesty.[76]

Undaunted, Miliukov proceeded to defend the statutes which had established Finland's special position within the Russian Empire. But the Right only laughed at such insistence on precedents which it wished to sweep away. World legal opinion, he pointed out, was firmly on the side of Finland. An international conference held in London in February 1910 had considered the Russo-Finnish dispute and ruled in favor of Finland, issuing a report signed by a number of European legal authorities. The Octobrist deputy Vasilii Von Anrep urged that the report be ignored.

> I will not say [Miliukov continued] that this point of view is shared by the vast majority of West European jurists who ever studied the Finnish problem, for such a reference will, evidently, not be convincing here. . . . When a question such as Finland is being discussed, according to Von Anrep, no juridical references are needed, and the opinions of European jurists are replaced by a list of Russian professors.

The Duma majority was offended by what it regarded as interference

[76] Miliukov's speech is in *ibid.*, March 17, 1910, pp. 935–48, 970–71; the Octobrist and Right reaction to it is in *ibid.*, 1910, pp. 948–69.

in Russia's internal affairs. "One feels contempt on the part of these unbidden advisors," said Stolypin to the prolonged applause of the Right and the Center. The Duma should ignore recommendations from abroad in the name of Russian patriotism.

> You will be told [he said, solemnly] of the alleged opinion of Europe, they will point to the thousands of signatures collected by the Finns abroad. Here it will be not I who will answer, but all of Russia which will say that under the new regime Russia is not dissolving, not dismembering itself, but growing stronger, and learning to know itself.[77]

When the Duma majority voted the bill urgent and thus curtailed debate, Miliukov remonstrated. "Think only," he said, "that in a number of states there exists a particular method for the passage of constitutional acts. There are special meetings, joint 'great' sessions, etc., in a word the very procedure gives certain guarantees of the seriousness of passing a constitutional act."[78] Nor was he impressed by the majority's allegations that Russia was behaving as all great powers did. It had been said that Russian imperialism was no worse than British imperialism. Miliukov opted for the British variety:

> Does the imperialistic policy of imperialistic England resemble ours? I speak of course of the most recent times. I have before me an issue of the Times from the first days of the new reign [of George V] which reviews all that England agreed to do for the colonies, and describes what the colonies agreed on with England. Why, one is seized with envy when one reads. . . . There, gentlemen, are the fruits of an enlightened imperialistic policy which knows how to bind together the parts through civilized, contemporary means.

Transvaal, he thought, was a good recent example. There the British had "turned an enemy of yesterday into a friend, and granted a constitution. We are taking the constitution away, and turning friends into enemies."[79]

The Kadets convinced the Polish Kolo, the Moslem and the Progressive fractions to boycott the final Duma vote on the measure.

---

[77] Ibid., 1910, pp. 2017, 2042. For the London conference on Finland, see J. Wuorinen, Nationalism in Modern Finland (New York, 1931), p. 276.

[78] SO, 1910, p. 2021.

[79] Ibid., 1910, pp. 2077–78.

"Powerless to prevent the illegality," said their joint resolution, "the Opposition did everything to bring the public's attention to it and to brand its culprits." Miliukov was still optimistic about the future. "We are convinced, gentlemen," he told the Duma, "that the time will come when we shall again strengthen those bonds which you are destroying, and we shall make them more durable than ever before."[80] The March, 1917, revolution would at first confirm Miliukov's prediction, but its consequences separated Finland from Russia altogether.

VIII

The Duma's militant nationalism affected not only Finland but also other minorities. When, in the autumn of 1910, the Duma debated a bill for the introduction of compulsory universal elementary education, the Right wished to make Russian the sole language of instruction. The Octobrists, on the other hand, backed a provision, which Miliukov had helped to draft, stating that "in districts with Polish, Lithuanian, German, Tartar, Estonian, Latvian, Armenian and Georgian populations instruction in the native language is permitted if not less than fifty children of school age belong to any of these nationalities." Miliukov wished to add Jews and Ukrainians to the list. But though the Russian Academy of Sciences had declared Ukrainian a language, the Duma Nationalists spoke only of "an artificial Little Russian dialect" and of "a Jewish jargon," neither of which should qualify as a language of instruction. Despite Miliukov's objection that "the principle of the equality of nationalities is the Alpha and Omega of all good government" his amendment failed. The Duma did pass the original bill only to have the provisions regarding minority languages rejected in the State Council.[81]

Miliukov wanted to increase the zemstvo's role in the projected elementary schools. The government, however, was determined to gain control over them and to share its role only with the church. The Holy Synod was already administering almost half of the country's elementary schools. Miliukov proposed to keep both the Synod and the government out of the elementary school, which traditionally

[80] *Ibid.*, 1910, pp. 2089, 2535.
[81] SO, November 12, 1910, pp. 1238–68 *passim.*

had been supported by the localities. "Thanks to the caprice of history," he pointed out, "our elementary school is our only free school, and has saved itself in some fashion from the watchful supervision of the Petersburg bureaucracy." As between financing church and secular schools, Miliukov's preference was clear. "The choice between the two," he pointed out, "is not difficult for anyone who is convinced that our schools must provide the country with the best and most up-to-date means for victory in the competition of nations." If the government controlled the school, it would use its influence for political ends. The fact that the government insisted on controlling the schools meant, in Miliukov's eyes, that it had no confidence in itself. He quoted Friedrich Paulsen, the German reformer of education, who said that "a government which has a clean conscience, which believes in itself and its own value, also believes in the people. And vice versa, if a government does not really believe in itself it is afraid even of its own subjects."[82]

The education bill, at first quite liberal, was revised at the government's insistence. The Duma retreated on several issues: wide public participation in school administration; simplifying procedures for the opening of new schools; permission to work out details in the localities; and the abolition of all tuition fees in the new schools. These compromises Miliukov blamed on the Octobrists, who retreated before the government. They were beginning to realize that the government no longer needed them. Stolypin had found more reliable allies in the Nationalists.

The Octobrists were beginning to realize their isolation and joined the Kadets in using the budget sessions to attack the government. When the Ministry of Interior budget came up in February, 1911, the Octobrist speeches were sharp, but Miliukov reminded them of their past sins. "You participated," he charged, "in that deception which, for four years, hung over Russia, and which is now exposed—not by your hands. You now admit the exposure of the deception because you can no longer hide it and because it, finally, reached you, and affected your milieu." Even now the Octobrists would not support the Kadet budget tactics of voting against part of the Ministry of Interior budget as a gesture of protest. In 1911 this tactic was supported by the Polish Kolo and the Progressives, though the Octobrists

[82] SO, October 18, 1910, pp. 93–107 passim.

refused to join. It was a minor victory for Miliukov; but then the Third Duma was hardly the arena for major ones. "The government's policy," read the Opposition's resolution, "weakens the state, lessens the country's chances in international competition, threatens new complications at home and abroad, and is therefore anti-state, anti-national, and unpatriotic."

The opposition's resolution spoke of threatening "new complications . . . abroad." The one which worried Miliukov most was the apparent Russo-German *rapprochement* exemplified by the meeting in October, 1910, at Potsdam of William II and Nicholas II. Since little had been said of the meeting officially, Miliukov expected the new Foreign Minister to give the Duma an explanation. But Sazonov failed to appear on the grounds of illness. Miliukov, however, was determined to speak, despite the fact that representatives of the Ministry left the hall when he mounted the tribune.[83] He feared, he said, that, as in the past the direction of Russia's foreign policy was in the hands of a highly placed clique which remained in the background. "In whose hands," he asked, "lies the fate of our country, and on whom does it depend?" The German press had written of the Potsdam meeting in rather ominous terms, as far as Miliukov was concerned. He quoted Theodore Schiemann who, in the influential *Kreutzzeitung*, had dwelt on the friendship between the two emperors, describing "the faithfulness with which Emperor William II supported his friend in the most difficult moments of a none-too-easy reign, when the governments and public opinion of England and France openly took the side of the first revolutionary Duma." Miliukov had warned about the threat of German intervention in the days of the First Duma. He now saw new efforts to wean Russia away from her French and British allies to the German side. He was sure that "that system of our ententes and agreements, of which our former Minister was an assiduous defender, has been seriously shaken in its very foundations." Sazonov was evidently lukewarm toward the entente and under the influence of the Germanophile camp. The

[83] The text of Miliukov's speech is in SO, March 2, 1911, pp. 3300–30; he devoted a good deal of attention to the Far East—a problem I do not discuss here. For background to the Potsdam meeting, see BES, pp. 327–36. See also the first of Miliukov's annual surveys of Russian foreign policy, which appeared in the *Riech'* yearbooks beginning in 1912; P. Miliukov, "Vneshniaia politika Rossii v 1911 g.," EZH, 1912, pp. 1–19.

Potsdam meeting had aroused apprehensions in England and France. "A whole series of forced explanations were made in this regard in European parliaments," Miliukov told the Duma. "It is therefore quite natural that not only Russia, but Europe as well, expects explanations from our Minister; he could give these in this same parliamentary setting." In Russia, however, it was argued that the Emperor made foreign policy and owed no explanation of it to the people. Miliukov rejected this opinion:

> Everywhere [he said] the right of conducting foreign policy belongs to the head of the state. But this has never stopped ministers of foreign affairs from exchanging opinions with parliaments, from seeking support of public opinion and the legislature. This correct procedure was used by our former minister Izvolsky. Mr. Izvolsky went further than merely presenting our foreign policy. He actually discussed it with representatives of the Russian legislative chamber, he answered their questions and criticisms.

In Sazonov's absence one would have to guess the reasons for the new *rapprochement* with Germany. It could mean, Miliukov thought, a repetition of the German advice given Russia at the turn of the century: to turn its attention to the Far East. When followed, this advice had led to the disaster with Japan. Surely Russia did not want to repeat her old mistakes. It would only embitter her present friends, England and Japan.

> This is a development [Miliukov told the Duma] of the old Bismarckian assertion: the role of Russia is in Asia. Go ahead in Asia; there you can freely acquire everything you want if, of course, you know how, and if you are able to, if you are not hindered by China, if England and Japan do not stop you, and if you have enough strength of your own.

But Russia could not afford to leave Europe; she could not trust Germany's promise to check Austria-Hungary's appetite in the Balkans. The past had shown this to be a forlorn hope. The future of the area looked menacing. "There are accumulating in the Balkans," Miliukov warned, "all sorts of national anxieties, all manner of explosive issues are being nurtured. . . . In a word, gentlemen, it is hard to say at the moment what the coming spring will bring." This was said in 1911; the Balkan wars of 1912 were to confirm Miliukov's fears.

IX

Sazonov had not bothered to address the Duma; Stolypin went him one better: he prorogued it for three days in order to pass legislation by executive decree. The government's lack of respect for the legislature could hardly have been demonstrated more brazenly. The incident arose over a bill establishing zemstvos in six western *guberniias* with a heavily non-Russian population. National curias were created to ensure that Russians, even if in a minority, would control a given zemstvo. The nationalistic Duma passed the bill, and the State Council was expected to follow suit. But Stolypin's political enemies in the upper chamber defeated his measure. The Premier then persuaded the Emperor to prorogue the chambers for three days (March, 1911) to allow the measure to pass under Article 87 of the Fundamental Laws, as an executive decree. Stolypin got his zemstvos, but he now had both chambers united in opposition against him. Duma chairman Guchkov, not even consulted about the prorogation, resigned in protest.[84]

The Duma's agitation was such that it passed every interpellation against Stolypin, even the Kadet. "To act in this manner," Miliukov accused the Premier, "is to deprive the will of the legislative bodies of all meaning." Russians might be used to such travesties but, Miliukov hoped, the eyes of Europe would now be opened.

> The measures just taken performed one service for us. Our apparent constitutionalism showed its true colors. Until now, gentlemen, it had been a domestic affair, while abroad our reformed system appeared as something at least resembling a European constitution. . . . Now the whole world will discover the true nature of our legislative institutions.[85]

Stolypin's tactics in proroguing the Duma were deemed unacceptable by a large Duma majority (248:82). His reputation even among his erstwhile supporters suffered an irreparable blow. His last months of office (he was assassinated in September, 1911, not long after his Duma disgrace) were a form of political limbo. Miliukov's estimate of his role in Russian politics was far too negative.[86] The Kadet leader

---

[84] There is a recent article describing the incident: E. Chmielewski, "Stolypin's Last Crisis," *California Slavic Studies*, III (1964), 95–126.

[85] Miliukov's speech is in SO, March 15, 1911, pp. 744–51.

[86] P. Miliukov, "P. A. Stolypin," *Riech'*, September 20, 1911.

maintained that when Stolypin took office in July, 1906, "the revolution was already broken. It was a rare, unique moment in the history of a whole century when a genuine, and not only a fictitious reconciliation could have taken place between the government and the public." Miliukov's memory surely deceived him; had he forgotten the violent language in which the Kadet congress spoke of Stolypin in the autumn of 1906? But, Miliukov continued, instead of supporting the new regime born of the October Manifesto, "it became Stolypin's task to adapt the new institutions to the defense of old interests, and to clothe them in the forms of the old state ideology." The Stolypin regime represented "five years of marking time," five years of "irretrievably lost time." And yet "how much could have been accomplished, how much changed for the better." Even his agrarian reform, which "could have been creative," failed to solve the problem and "cannot but appear as one of the darkest pages in his tragic inheritance."

Stolypin, Miliukov asserted, had believed that the revolution must be smashed before undertaking reforms. But, said Miliukov, only "were one to judge by the number of executions could it be maintained that the real revolution continued into 1907, 1908 and 1909." In the absence of "real revolution," he continued, "there began the struggle with 'revolution' in quotation marks. 'Reforms' were postponed on the pretext of the need for 'a calming down,' and this 'calming down' led to a restoration of the old which threatened to go as far as the public would tolerate it." It was true that not all the disappointments of the "constitutional era" could be blamed on one man. "Despite the importance of the personal element in our political life," wrote Miliukov, "the recent political course was not at all the product of the late premier's personal ideals."[87] Others besides Stolypin had given conservatism, chauvinism, and Russification a new lease on life. Even had Stolypin desired reforms there were forces, Miliukov pointed out, powerful enough to oppose them: the court camarilla, the State Council, and the reactionary nobility.[88]

With Stolypin gone, a rather uncertain interregnum began under the premiership of Kokovtsov, who retained the Ministry of Finance. Miliukov was sure that Kokovtsov "is not the reformer the country is

[87] *Riech'* editorial, September 10, 1911.
[88] "P. A. Stolypin," *Riech'*, March 9, 1911.

waiting for." The old Stolypin course would be continued. "The new course," he concluded, "differs from the old one merely by its lack of the outer splendor of strong power."[89] Nor would the Third Duma, in its last year, satisfy Miliukov's expectations. Its tribune, however, remained useful to him in those days of increasing international tension when he paid particular attention to foreign policy and national defense. These were debated in the spring of 1912, in the last weeks of the Third Duma's existence. Sazonov at last appeared in the Taurida Palace to report on Russian foreign policy. In the Third Duma's five years (1907–12) this was only the third appearance of a Russian foreign minister (Izvolsky had spoken twice in 1908). The Russian legislature was not being spoilt by excessive attention on the part of the makers of Russian foreign policy. This time, however, there was fairly prolonged debate; Miliukov, if not pleased with Sazonov, was surely gratified that the Duma was becoming a factor in the formation of Russian public opinion on foreign affairs.

Sazonov described Russia's situation in rather rosy colors. Miliukov alleged that "the optimism of Minister Sazonov is as baseless as was the optimism of Minister Izvolsky." The Balkans, in particular, were quite agitated; there might be risings in the area even in the current year.[90] The war between Italy and Turkey had led to the temporary closing of the Straits which resulted in substantial losses to Russian shipping: most of Russia's grain exports passed through the Straits. Though Sazonov said nothing of the political aspects of the problem, Miliukov argued, with surprising moderation in view of his future views on the subject, that Russia should be satisfied with the existing situation at the Straits. "It is advantageous to us," he said, "to remain with the *status quo* regardless of the inconvenience of the 'temporary closing' which we face at present." Any alternative policy would

---

[89] Riech' editorials, September 19, 1911 and January 1, 1912.

[90] The text of his speech is in SO, April 13, 1912, pp. 2154–73; Miliukov's reply is in *ibid.*, 1912, pp. 2183–95 and 2218–42. The Balkan wars, in fact, broke out a few months later. I reproduce only Miliukov's remarks on the Near East, although he also discussed the Middle and Far East. He also commented on the termination by the United States of its trade agreement with Russia because of restrictions placed by the latter on American Jews. To the accompaniment of noise on the Right, he said: "As a Russian I am ashamed when Europe and the New World feel entitled to classify us as Asiatics at a time when Asia itself is beginning to accept the basic principles of world culture. Gentlemen, I do not wish us to remain some sort of black sheep of the human race."

entail Russia's entering the Mediterranean. This would be folly in view of the state of Russia's navy.

In the debate on the defense budget, Miliukov took his views a step further: the Kadets voted against appropriating five hundred million rubles for naval construction.[91] As in 1908 the party opposed naval expansion, not wishing to commit the legislature to large defense expenditures in years to come. The proposed fleet was not needed for defense, Miliukov alleged, but for "a definite plan of Weltpolitik." Knowing that the appropriations would pass, Miliukov warned the Duma that "the tone of our diplomacy will become much bolder after your vote." Naval building would lead to the pretensions which led to the 1904–5 catastrophe in the Far East. "Let us not," Miliukov urged, "be possessed by world pretensions and world ambitions, but pursue a policy in accordance with our means." It was fortunate that Russia had not had a larger navy at the time of the crisis in Bosnia-Herzegovina:

> If we had had the fleet you now plan in 1908 we would have had war. We have been careless and arrogant even without a fleet. How much worse would we be with it. . . . Those of you who will vote for the fleet should know that the responsibility for the next war and its results will be on your conscience.

Russia should rely on her agreement with England. It would be better, Miliukov thought, "if we spent money on the army, and let them [the British] build better and cheaper ships." Even with an expanded navy, Russia could not compete with the great naval powers. "Let us be satisfied with being a third class naval power," he concluded.

The 1912 defense debates ended the five-year existence of the Third Duma. Miliukov had few kind words to say about the legislature which had so disappointed his hopes.[92] It had, in his opinion, ignored the urgent tasks which lay before Russia:

> To acquire the sole right of existence this Duma had to become one of the wheels of the bureaucratic machine. It turned out to be powerless not only to enact a broad plan of basic reforms essential for the country's rejuvenation but even to execute the most imme-

[91] The text of his speech is in SO, June 6, 1912, pp. 3789–3810.
[92] P. Miliukov, "Politicheskiia partii v gosudarstvennoi dume za piat' let," EZH, 1912, pp. 77–96 passim.

diate measures without which the country can no longer exist and maintain its place among the Great Powers.

It was too harsh an indictment; but the Russian European was not likely to be charitable toward an institution which compared so unfavorably with the Western models which he wished to emulate. He blamed the Duma for its "chauvinistic nationalism which lowered the Third Duma's reputation in the opinion of the country as well as in the opinion of the entire civilized world." There was, he thought, only one positive result, but it was important. The Duma as such, not the Third Duma, had become a permanent part of Russian politics, "an institution without which Russian life can no longer do."

6: THE WAR AND NEW TACTICS

> The attempt made by the Russian public as represented by our
> party—the attempt to effect a peaceful, painless transition
> from the old, condemned system to a new order—has failed.
>
> The war was the factor which decided the argument between
> the country and the regime.[1]

I

The elections to the Fourth (and last) Duma were held in the
autumn of 1912. The Kadets returned approximately the same number
of deputies as they had in the Third Duma. But the party was a
shadow of its former self—decimated by government persecution and
apathy. There had been no congresses since 1907, and the semi-yearly
conferences called in conjunction with the Duma session registered
only faint echoes of party groups in the land. Politically, it was, outside the Duma, a time of slumber and decay. "No real democratic
party," as Miliukov put it, "could possibly exist in Russia under the
sham constitutional regime of 1907–1917."[2] The Socialist parties,
working largely underground, had kept some touch with the population; but the few open parties, of whom the Kadets were the most
important, had not been able to sink roots in the country. Even the
Kadets partook in some measure of the three characteristics which

[1] The first quotation is from A. Guchkov, "Speech at the Octobrist Conference
on November 21, 1913," *Russian Review* (London), 1914, No. 1, p. 152; the
second is from VOSP, II, 156.
[2] RUS, p. 30; italics in the original.

Miliukov ascribed to Russian political parties: "their transitory nature, artificiality, and powerlessness."[3]

Remaining an unregistered and therefore "illegal" party, the Kadets were harassed by the authorities. This frightened all but the most resolute souls from active political life. Thus, Voronezh officials sued the leaders of the local Kadet branch, charging them with belonging to an illegal organization. The list of accused included the mayor of Voronezh, former members of the First and Second Dumas, a former chairman of the local zemstvo, physicians, lawyers, bank officials, and a rabbi. The trial, involving nineteen persons, was intended to destroy a major Kadet provincial branch. But Russian courts were not hopelessly subservient, and the case was dismissed for lack of evidence. Another suit was initiated before the Ekaterinburg district court, involving the party's district committee of sixteen persons. The defense lawyer was Mandel'shtam, Miliukov's permanent critic from the left wing of the party. He was successful, and this suit too was dismissed. The court's decision was hardly welcomed by the authorities who transferred the judge to a less important post.[4]

On April 30, 1908, the Senate ruled that persons who belonged to "anti-state parties" could not hold public office. The Ministry of Interior tried to extend the rule to Kadets. Thus A. S. Salazkin, mayor of Kasimov and chairman of the Nizhnii Novgorod Fair Committee, was deprived of both of his elective positions. He filed suit against the ministry, but the Senate upheld the bureaucracy.[5] The case indicates that, outside private business concerns, there was virtually no position where the government's long arm could not reach to approve elections or appointments. Thus in Griazovets (Vologda guberniia) the Marshal of Nobility, N. M. Volotskoi, was removed for refusing to stipulate that he did not belong to an anti-state party. Two Ekaterinburg Kadet judges were ordered to resign. The Kostroma zemstvo secretary, the Kadet Preobrazhenskii, was dismissed. Kharkov zemstvo member P. R. Boguslavskii, and chairman of the Starovel'sk zemstvo board N. I. Strukov, both Kadets, were not approved in their elective positions. The Perm zemstvo veterinarian A. P. Khomutov was dismissed from

[3] P. Miliukov, "Russkie Partii," Riech', January 1, 1910.
[4] Riech', November 26, 1908.
  Riech', August 6, 1909, and M. Madel'shtam, 1905 god v politicheskikh protsesakh (Moscow, 1931), pp. 364, 367.
[5] Pravo, 1914, No. 12, p. 3148.

his post for being a Kadet; the authorities then excluded him from Kazan' University where he had gone to study and thwarted his appointment to a position in the Baikal region. I. M. Dobrynin, assistant to the Novocherkassk Ataman, was dismissed for being a Kadet by a personal order of the Emperor. The Emperor also ordered the dismissal of two professors from the Alexander Military—Judicial Academy, D. D. Grimm and M. P. Chubinskii, both Kadets. The Kadets Fedor Rodichev and Georgii Kilevein were not approved as Justices of the Peace in 1911. In 1914 the Kadet Mikhail Chelnokov was not approved as chairman of the Moscow City Duma. In November, 1914, elected mayor of Moscow, he was informed that he could not be approved for the post unless he left the party, which he refused to do.[6]

Since Kadets were not militant, they tended to withdraw from politics as a result of such treatment. Party membership declined rapidly, and in 1908 stood at 25,000, as compared to 100,000 in 1906. A survey of local Kadet groups in 1913 showed only nine organized branches; twenty-seven had been represented at the 1907 congress. The police claimed that even in large cities like Kiev, Smolensk, Tver', Vitebsk, Baku, Revel', and Tiflis, the Kadets gave no sign of life. At a 1913 party meeting, Tyrkova exclaimed: "The Central Committee is a fiction. Who are we? Impostors? Last Mohicans? Kadet diehards?" Miliukov admitted to an interviewer: "In the country the party does not exist." Only the Duma Kadets now spoke for the party and issued accounts of their work. But, as Miliukov admitted, this was insufficient to maintain any party life: "Our connection with the provinces was maintained through our published Duma accounts; but there were few responses to these, and usually they did not reach me."[7]

When the Kadets "infiltrated" existing organizations, they had no success. They had been influential in the Voters Clubs of many Russian cities, but fifteen such clubs in the capital were disbanded by the authorities as "unnecessary." A Kadet Duma interpellation on the matter brought no response. In 1912 the Senate approved the

[6] VES, 1907, p. 2132; 1908, p. 56; Riech', April 1, 1908; A. Polivanov, Iz dnevnikov i vospominanii (Moscow, 1924), pp. 83–100. Also Riech', March 7 and 23, 1914, and Riech', editorial, November 18, 1914.

[7] E. Chermenskii, "Bor'ba klassov i partii v IV gosudarstvennoi dume" (Ph.D. diss., Moscow University, 1947), pp. 220–21, quoting from police archives. Also PAPERS, "Notes 1907–8(2)," interview of April 5, 1908, and VOSP, II, 50.

closing of all such clubs on the rather original grounds that their activity "duplicated the work of the elected city administration, and could lead to undesirable results in case identical questions were solved in a different manner."[8] The organizations of sales personnel (*prikazchiki*) had been another source of Kadet support. For years they were not permitted to form a national organization or to hold a congress; finally one was authorized in 1913. There were plans to discuss Kadet legislation for improving the group's economic situation. But the congress ran into endless official resistance. A detailed agenda of all meetings had to be approved by the Ministry of Interior, which vetoed whatever it found undesirable. Three sessions were closed by the police because speakers mentioned subjects which had been struck from the agenda by the ministry—the right to strike, the economic situation of sales employees, and their representation in the labor inspectorate. When the congress suggested that meetings be held behind closed doors, excluding both press and police, it was ruled that no meetings could be held without the police. The censor mutilated the congress resolutions, excluding phrases such as one referring to "the harm done to the housing situation by land speculation" because it smacked of "socialism." When delegates appeared for the last session they found the doors locked—the police had closed the congress.[9]

It was obvious that the slender liberties gained in 1905–7 were being mercilessly violated by the government. One of the bureaucracy's chief weapons in this campaign were the so-called "exceptional measures," under which much of the Empire was being governed in spite of the Fundamental Laws. An Octobrist newspaper calculated that, in 1912, only five million persons (of the Empire's one hundred and fifty-seven million) did not live under some form of "exceptional measures." This draconian legislation, ranging from a "state of reinforced protection" to a state of siege, gave local authorities practically unlimited powers over the population.[10] As Miliukov noted:

There are countries in which there is no law on exceptional jurisdiction—such as England, and nothing untoward happens

[8] *Riech'*, November 14, 1910; *Riech'* editorial, May 9, 1910; *Riech'*, March 20, 1912.

[9] A full account of the congress appeared in *Riech'*, July 3–5, 1913.

[10] *Utro Rossii* (Moscow), January 1, 1912. See also S. Harper, "Exceptional Measures in Russia," *Russian Review* (London), I, No. 4 (November, 1912), 92–105.

because of it. There are countries where exceptional jurisdiction has its place. But there is no country where exceptional jurisdiction has grown as it has in Russia, and become a normal method of government.[11]

II

Under such conditions and in view of the restricted nature of the suffrage, it was useless to expect that the 1912 Duma elections would yield surprising results. As Miliukov charged, the government had accustomed Russia to "quiet elections" under conditions of "political anesthesia." The bureaucracy was ready for the contest—it had "exceptional measures" and some three million rubles yearly for the preparation of the proper election atmosphere.[12] Guchkov, who since his resignation of the chairmanship of the Third Duma had become an increasingly severe critic of the regime, charged that "the government prepared and carried out a vast plan for falsifying the elections."[13] Every form of chicanery was needed to ensure that the Fourth Duma resemble the Third. Enough Fourth Duma members were shocked by the proceedings to pass a resolution stating: "The Duma finds that the government's defense of clear illegalities proves the existence of a system of illegal interference in the elections by the government." Furthermore, a majority was found to pass a motion stating that "the Duma acknowledges the need for a revision of the electoral law of June 3, 1907, in the direction of widening the suffrage."[14] The regime was beginning to make enemies even among its own creatures.

Unlike 1907, when this would have been politically impossible, the Kadets in 1912 made electoral alliances with parties to their right— the Progressives (formerly the Party of Peaceful Reconstruction) in the two capitals, and even with the Octobrists in areas which had been Right strongholds and where, according to Miliukov, "the constitutional convictions of the Octobrists are beyond doubt."[15]

[11] SO, October 17, 1911, p. 151.
[12] Riech' editorial, August 3, 1912; KRY, p. 104.
[13] Guchkov, op. cit., p. 149.
[14] SO, January 24, 1914, p. 109; March 13, 1913, p. 2223.
[15] Riech', April 17, 1912; CHER, p. 272, quoting from police reports on a Kadet Central Committee meeting.

Although the government did its best to prevent victories by Kadets and parties to their left—by suppressing their literature, closing their meetings, disqualifying their candidates—the Kadets actually managed to increase slightly the number of their deputies; Miliukov, for his part, won a larger percentage of the capital's vote than he had obtained in 1907.[16] Again he would represent the capital of the Russian Empire and lead a Kadet fraction of fifty-nine deputies (as compared to fifty-three in the Third Duma).

The Fourth Duma was a somewhat different body than its predecessor. Three hundred of the four hundred and forty-two deputies were new men. Yet this was new wine poured into old bottles. The proportions of Right, Center, and Left had not changed significantly.[17] Only the position of the Octobrists was altered. The party had lost both a large number of deputies and its old assurance. It could no longer pretend to Duma leadership, and it was no longer allied with the government, which had harassed some of its candidates during the elections. Guchkov was no longer in the Duma; he had been defeated on his home ground in Moscow. There was in the Duma no coalition which could produce legislative results.

The disintegration of the Octobrist fraction was, however, of some

---

[16] For examples of government interference with Kadet candidates, see E. Chermenskii, "Vybory v IV gosudarstvennuiu dumu," *Voprosy Istorii* (Moscow), 1947, No. 4, p. 24, and *Riech,'* October 11 and 13, 1912; figures on elections in St. Petersburg are from *Riech,'* October 27, 1912.

[17] For statistics, see *Riech,'* December 5, 1912; the table below is from REP, p. 32.

		3d Duma	4th Duma
Right	Right	52	65
	Nationalists	93	88
		145	153
Center	Center	0	32
	Octobrists	133	98
		133	130
Left	Poles and Moslems	26	21
	Progressives	39	48
	Kadets	53	59
	Trudoviks	14	9
	Social Democrats	14	15
		146	152

aid to the Kadets. The left and the center of the Octobrists were now more likely to support the Opposition, making possible new voting combinations. This did not signify the possibility of passing reform bills, but it made the Duma more oppositional than at any time since 1907. Thus Sergei Shidlovskii, the leader of the so-called Zemstvo Octobrists, said of the Ministry of Interior's conduct that "it threatened public safety" and that Russia was

> not only not advancing, but going backward. What is taking place now was impossible in the days of Plehve, who once was considered reactionary. The cult of administrative arbitrariness has reached incredible proportions.[18]

Such Kadet language from Octobrist lips was unusual. It was even followed by action when, in 1913, the Octobrists joined the opposition in reducing the ministry's budget. The Octobrist motion, which passed, stated that the ministry's policy "creates general dissatisfaction," because the ministry "refuses to introduce long-overdue reforms." Its nationality policy "serves to weaken Russia's power, and disunites Russian citizens."[19] The Octobrists now paid the price for joining the opposition. They were forbidden to hold a congress, as the Kadets had been for years. At a substitute conference Guchkov delivered a bitter speech, part of which is quoted at the head of this chapter. "Never," he said, "has governmental authority fallen so low. Unable to inspire sympathy or trust, the government is incapable of even provoking fear." His prediction for the future was dark. "Where does the government's course, or rather the lack of any course, lead us?," he asked. "To a sad, unavoidable catastrophe." He urged that the Octobrists start an offensive against the government: "All legal means of parliamentary work must be utilized—freedom of parliamentary expression, the authority of the Duma tribune, the right of interpellation and, above all, the budget right."[20]

Naturally, Miliukov welcomed such unexpected allies. In addition to the Octobrists, there were other moderates who now spoke more belligerently. These were the Progressives, formerly the Party of Peaceful Reconstruction, led by such men as Prince Evgenii Trubetskoi, Maksim Kovalevskii, Miliukov's old teacher, Prince George

[18] SO, November 13, 1912, p. 1106.
[19] SO, May 15, 1913, p. 117.
[20] A. Guchkov, op. cit., passim.

L'vov, and Dmitrii Shipov. These zemstvists and intellectuals were joined by representatives of the industrial and business circles of Moscow, including Aleksandr Konovalov, Pavel and Vladimir Riabushinskii, Sergei Tret'iakov, and Nikolai Morozov. At the Progressive Party's conference in November, 1912, chairman Ivan Efremov made it clear that many members seriously considered supporting the Kadets but "did not find it possible to accept the Kadet program in all its details." Nor could they approve of "all the tactics of that party, and they did not wish to submit to the severe discipline of the Kadet Central Committee." The group's aim, said Efremov, was "the creation of a constitutional monarchy with a ministry responsible before the national assembly." This proved unacceptable to the government, which refused the party legalization on the grounds that its goals "did not correspond to the terminology of the Fundamental Laws."[21]

Miliukov pointed out that the refusal to legalize the Progressives illustrated how the official course had moved to the right since 1905:

> Once [he said] the Kadets had been considered by the government as the sole salvation from the socialists. Then the Party of Peaceful Reconstruction, who now call themselves the Progressives, were to be the salvation from the Kadets. Then the Octobrists were to save the government from the Progressives, and now the Nationalists will have to save it from the Octobrists.[22]

He was pleased that representatives of Russia's business interests had come out into the open political arena, which they now seemed to prefer to their earlier work behind the closed doors of the various ministries. But he stressed the fact that the new party included "those elements of the Russian public which cannot make their peace with the democratically social program of the Kadets." He wished them to admit that they appeared to defend their own interests, and not to pretend to defend the interests of all Russia. "We do not deny," he added, "that the ideology of the entrepreneurs and merchants does, in certain questions, particularly in regard to the new political structure, come close to the views of the Opposition parties. [But] let each

---

[21] S"ezd progressistov 11, 12 i 13 noiabriia 1913 g. (St. Petersburg, 1913), pp. 1–7 passim; Fraktsiia progressistov v IV dume (2d fasc.; St. Petersburg, 1913), p. 17.

[22] Riech' editorial, May 5, 1913.

side remain itself, and let them co-operate not as partisans, but as allies. *Clara pacta, boni amici.*[23]

The Progressives, whose fraction had grown from twenty-five deputies in 1907 to forty-two in 1913,[24] now augmented opposition ranks. The government saw the Duma changing from an obedient tool to a bothersome critic. In the autumn of 1913 Miliukov reported rumors of a plan, promoted by Minister of Interior Nikolai Maklakov, to reduce the Duma's competence. Revelations made after the February Revolution proved the rumors correct. Maklakov had indeed written the Emperor in October, 1913, offering to:

> deliver from the Duma's tribune a calm, clear, but decisive warning to the effect that the path which the Duma is attempting to take is dangerous, and impermissible. . . . If the character of the Duma's work does not change the government will have to ask for Your Majesty's instructions to dissolve this Duma.

The Emperor's reply approved Maklakov's suggestion and went further:

> I desire the immediate consideration in the Council of Ministers of *my old idea* of nullifying that clause of the Duma's statute which provides that if the Duma does not approve changes made in a bill by the State Council, and does not approve the bill, it dies. In the absence of a constitution in our country this is completely senseless.
>
> The submission of majority and minority opinions for the Emperor's decision will be a praiseworthy return to the former peaceful course of legislative work, and will be in the Russian spirit.[25]

Even the very unrepresentative Fourth Duma was much too radical for Nicholas; he desired one in which a vote was of no consequence, a consultative Duma of the Bulygin type. While nothing was done about Maklakov's warning to the Duma, the Emperor did pursue his "old idea" of revising the Fundamental Laws. According to the then Minister of Justice, Ivan Shcheglovitov, a special cabinet meeting

---

[23] *Riech'* editorial, May 18, 1912, and November 14, 1912.

[24] Figures are from W. Walsh, "Political Parties in the Russian Dumas," JMH, XXII (1950), 148.

[25] Miliukov reported the rumors in *Riech'* editorial, September 20, 1913; the letters exchanged between the Emperor and Maklakov are from PAD, V, 194–96, and date from October, 1913. Italics are mine.

was called in June, 1914. "We were asked," Shcheglovitov testified, "to give our judgment on whether to return to the unrealized situation of August 6, 1905, namely whether the State Duma could be changed from a legislative to a consultative institution." According to Shcheglovitov, the cabinet opposed the change, and the matter was dropped.[26] But Nicholas was hardly on good terms with his legislature on the eve of the First World War.

III

The Fourth Duma began its sessions in November, 1912. Premier Kokovtsov presented his program the following month. Commenting on it, Miliukov called it "prosaic and colorless." It was merely a long list of bills which the government planned to introduce. How different, Miliukov regretted, had these occasions been earlier! Goremykin's speech in the First Duma had doubled its opposition. In the Second Duma Stolypin's "You shall not frighten us" had at least been imposing. In the Third Duma he had pleased the majority he had created. But in the Fourth Duma Kokovtsov had left everybody cold; he had merely imitated French cooks by "trying to make a tasty meal from left-overs."[27] Replying to the Premier, Miliukov suggested how the government program should have been formulated:

> How would the matter be handled in any civilized European country with a representative system? Legislative themes would first be discussed by the country's public opinion in the press and at meetings. . . . The population would then elect a legislative majority which would appear in the house in order to defend precisely these themes, these legislative tasks put forward by the people. Finally a cabinet, armed with the support of this majority, would appear here with a clear, practical program realizable within the limits of the next five years.[28]

Instead the Russian government wished "to dictate its will to the country." The Kadets would do nothing to support the government program. They approved, however, of the program of the new Duma chairman, the Octobrist Mikhail Rodzianko, who, in his inauguration

---

[26] PAD, II, 435–37.
[27] *Riech'* editorial, December 8, 1912.
[28] Miliukov's speech is in SO, December 13, 1912, pp. 594–615.

speech, said that "the Duma's first and urgent task must be the implementation of the great Manifesto of October 17" and added: "I will always be a convinced supporter of a representative system based on constitutional principles." The Duma's reply to Kokovtsov suggested that the new Russian legislature agreed with its chairman. The Duma adopted a motion by the Progressives stating that:

> normal legislative activity is possible only through the joint work of the government and the legislative bodies in the direction of a genuine realization of the principles proclaimed by the October Manifesto, and by the establishment of strict legality. The Duma calls upon the government to take this step openly and decisively.

Miliukov stressed that some progress had been made in the Duma's thinking since 1907 when a similar Progressive motion had failed.[29]

The Kokovtsov program for 1912–13 included no bills of any genuine interest to the Kadets. It was to be a dull legislative session, and Miliukov paid more attention to foreign affairs. The Balkan wars of 1912 had broken out in October. Miliukov had spent the previous summer in the area with his American patron Charles Crane. They had visited most of the Balkan states and, after the outbreak of hostilities, had followed the Bulgarian troops moving toward Adrianople. During the Duma 1913 Easter recess, Miliukov returned to the Balkans. He had an audience with Tsar Ferdinand of Bulgaria. Evidently the latter thought that the leader of the opposition was, as in Bulgaria, a potential future premier, for he asked Miliukov to convey to Nicholas II certain territorial demands; needless to say, there was no chance for Miliukov to do so. The Serbs, Bulgaria's chief antagonists, also wooed Miliukov, who was received by the Serbian heir, Prince Alexander, in Salonika. He was then provided with a special Serbian train for an inspection tour of Macedonia, the apple of discord between the two countries. Before returning home Miliukov saw Serbian Foreign Minister Milanovic in Vienna.[30]

Sazonov did not appear before the Duma during its 1912–13 session. In December, 1912, Miliukov urged that more frequent appearances by him before the Duma would be "good both for internal and external consumption." He was, however, in basic agreement with Russian policy in the Balkans because Sazonov, along with France,

[29] *Riech'* editorial, December 15, 1912.
[30] VOSP, II, 125–28.

"guarantees peace to us." The Kadets would always support a peace policy, despite Right allegations that they desired a war which would lead to a new revolution. It was the Right, he charged, which by its patriotic saber rattling could lead the country into danger. How could Russia consider military involvement when eleven *guberniias* had experienced famine the previous spring?[31] Miliukov addressed the Duma on foreign policy again in June, 1913, after the first round of the Balkan wars. Sazonov was ill, this time not diplomatically, and the foreign affairs debate was held in his absence. Miliukov pointed out that, in regard to foreign affairs, the parties' Duma roles were reversed: while the Right attacked the government's Balkan policy as too timid the opposition (without the Social Democrats who condemned all Russian foreign policy as "imperialistic") tended to uphold it.[32] Miliukov was gratified that the great powers had not become involved in the Balkans. Russia's role had been honorable: "Without interfering herself Russia made possible the moves of the Slavs in the peninsula, defending their freedom of action in settling their accounts with Turkey." Serbia and Bulgaria had agreed in February, 1912, to partition Macedonia among themselves. Miliukov opposed this "division of a living organism" and continued to advocate autonomy for all of Macedonia.

Three weeks after Miliukov spoke, the second round of Balkan wars broke out, this time not against Turkey but between the various Christian states. Shortly after the Peace of Bucharest of August, 1913, Miliukov was in the Balkans again, on behalf of the Carnegie Endowment for International Peace, which sent an "International Commission to Inquire Into the Causes and Conduct of the Balkan Wars." Members were appointed from the USA, England, France, Russia, Austria-Hungary, and Germany. Miliukov was chosen as the Russian member not only because of his unquestioned knowledge of

[31] SO, December 13, 1912, pp. 606–15.
[32] The text of Miliukov's speech is in SO, June 6, 1913, pp. 1019–58. Pages 1019–43 are devoted to the Balkans, 1043–53 to Armenia, and 1053–58 to the Far East. The Social Democrat Chkhenkeli attacked Miliukov's position from the Left (*ibid.*, 1913, pp. 1059–79), while Count Bobrinskii dealt it a blow from the Right (*ibid.*, 1913, pp. 1079–92) while also describing it as too Bulgarophile. The text of Miliukov's remarks on Macedonia is also available in German in F. Philipp (ed.), *P. N. Miliukoff uber Macedonien* (Leipzig, 1918), pp. 163–79. For Miliukov's review of Russian foreign policy in 1913, see his "Vneshniaia politika Rossii," EZH, 1914, pp. 1–20.

the area but also because of his adherence to pacifism. His old friend and party colleague, Prince Paul Dolgorukov, had in 1909 organized the Moscow Peace Society, of which the St. Petersburg branch was chaired by Maksim Kovalevskii. The organization never became popular or influential (by 1911 it had only 324 members), it met very rarely, and its officers complained of membership apathy. But this did not dampen Miliukov's enthusiasm. He undertook lectures on behalf of the society, which took him, in addition to the two capitals, to Ekaterinoslav, Taganrog, Astrakhan, Vilno, and Riga. He tried to show his audiences "the realistic foundations of pacifism" and to convince them "how closely the advocacy of peace is connected with the realistic demands of life."[33]

"The contemporary pacifist," Miliukov argued, "is not a fanatic of immediate disarmament and eternal peace." Rather he is an adherent of "revolutionary pacifism" which does not believe that mankind never changes, but that "men always change." They must change their mind about the old belief that war is the best means of solving conflicts between nations. It has yet to be proven that war pays; this is merely "the survival of an outmoded social psychology." Miliukov called his listeners' attention to Norman Angell's *Europe's Optical Illusion* (1909), and his *The Great Illusion* (1910). The author's arguments for peace should be acceptable to Russians, Miliukov hoped, because they "flow logically from the world view of the Russian intelligentsia."

This background made Miliukov eligible for membership in the Carnegie Commission which, in its report, stated that "the Commission only represents pacifist public opinion."[34] Its chairman, Baron d'Estournelles de Constant, was delighted to have secured Miliukov's services. Reviewing the difficulties the commission encountered in the Balkan countries, he said of Miliukov that "his only sin, in the eyes of each country, was his perfect impartiality. He was nobody's man, precisely what we were looking for." In gathering his evidence

[33] The text of his lectures and information about Russian pacifism in 1909–11 comes from P. Miliukov, *Vooruzhennyi mir i ogranichenie vooruzhenii* (Moscow, 1911), from which I am citing. See also VOSP, II, 47–48.

[34] All quotations about the Carnegie Commission are from its *Report of the International Commission to Enquire into the Causes and Conduct of the Balkan Wars* (Washington, D. C., 1914); Miliukov wrote chaps. i, iii, iv, and v of the report.

Miliukov encountered no difficulties in Bulgaria where, in fact, he was received royally. But Belgrade, suspecting his partiality to Bulgaria, asked the commission to leave Serbia. "If, therefore, the work of the commission has miscarried," stated a Serbian government announcement, about Miliukov, "the cause must be sought for in one of its members, the declared enemy not only of Serbia but of Greece."

In Salonika Governor Dragoumis informed the commission that "following the Serbian example" his government "declined to acknowledge Mr. Miliukov." In contrast the Turks made everything easy for Miliukov. His old acquaintance Talaad was now Turkish Minister of Interior and provided all necessary assistance, even putting his personal adjutant and a car at Miliukov's disposal. From Turkey the commission went to Paris for its last sessions and the compilation of its report. Miliukov had seen an endless number of examples of man's unhumanity to man—heartless treatment of prisoners, the bodies of women and children murdered by soldiers, starvation and homelessness, forced conversions and confessions. All the belligerents were equally guilty of these crimes. Miliukov's only consolation was that the "more cultured European countries" would not have behaved in this way.[35] The experience on the commission evidently shook Miliukov's pacifist beliefs. He recalled that:

> the transition from the boiling pot of savage nationalistic passions which had aroused the worst animal instincts into the stale atmosphere of abstract pacifism was too sharp. I do not wish to call this an armchair pacifism, but I must confess that the worm of doubt, which had long since appeared in my mind, received, in this instance, plentiful food for thought. The faith in high ideals seemed blind; the smooth pacifist ideology sounded more like ignorance, the fervor of its preaching more like professional hypocrisy.[36]

Perhaps Miliukov was now less of an idealist; but until August, 1914, he remained a firm advocate of peace and of the limitation of armaments.

IV

The year 1914 opened in an atmosphere of increasing international tension. Russian internal policy, however, seemed calculated to create,

[35] In his article "Voina i mezhdunarodnoe pravo," EZH, 1916, pp. 129–97.
[36] VOSP, II, 139; pp. 128–40 are devoted to Miliukov's recollections of the commission.

rather than to alleviate, the existing friction between government and society.[37] In January, Kokovtsov was replaced as premier by the aged reactionary Goremykin, who himself wondered why he should have been summoned. "I am like an old fur coat," he told Kokovtsov. "For many months I have been packed away in camphor. I am being taken out now merely for the occasion; when it is passed I shall be packed away again till I am wanted next time."[38] Utterly loyal to the Emperor, whom he had served under the old autocracy, Goremykin, in the words of Bernard Pares, "was acceptable to both the sovereigns [the Empress had begun to play a political role] for his attitude of a butler, taking instructions to be communicated to the other servants."[39]

Goremykin adopted an increasingly negative attitude toward the Duma. He refused to answer the Duma's hostile interpellations on the grounds that the chairman of the Council of Ministers was responsible to no one but the Emperor. No previous premier had taken this position.[40] The cabinet also resolved to adopt a new procedure toward Duma bills. If the Duma, unwilling to wait for a government measure (they were often in preparation for years), wished to proceed with its own bill the government would sabotage the effort. No materials or documents would be submitted if the Duma requested them, and no government representative would be permitted to testify or answer questions.[41]

But the issue which most aroused the Duma was the Chkheidze case. During a speech, the Social Democratic deputy Chkheidze, not for the first or last time, advocated a republican form of government for Russia. Though the Duma charter guaranteed deputies freedom of speech, Minister of Interior Maklakov brought suit against Chkheidze. The Kadets and Progressives immediately moved against approving the 1914 budget until the Chkheidze case was dropped. Supporting the motion, Miliukov said that he counted on the votes of all except those "who regard their presence here as paid government service, and themselves as officials." The Duma defeated the motion, but when Goremykin mounted the tribune the Social Democrats and Trudoviks would not let him speak. Twenty-one deputies

[37] SO, April 24, 1914, p. 976.
[38] KOK, p. 439.
[39] B. Pares, The Fall of the Russian Monarchy (New York, 1939), p. 157.
[40] Riech' editorial, March 15, 1914.
[41] Zhurnaly soveta ministrov, 1914–1916 gg. (Petrograd, 1916), March 6, 1914.

were excluded from fifteen Duma sessions; some were led out by
force. The Kadets not only did not join the demonstration, but
voted for the exclusion. Miliukov claimed that any obstruction of the
government in the Duma should be based on its rules of procedure,
which did not include demonstrations. While the St. Petersburg
Kadets approved Miliukov's tactics, the Moscow, Kiev, and Odessa
groups criticized them rather severely.[42]

Another case of what Miliukov called "creating enemies at home"
took place in the Ukraine where, in early 1914, the government
forbade anniversary celebrations honoring the national poet Taras
Shevchenko, claiming these would be used by Ukrainian separatists.
The Kadets sponsored a Duma interpellation on the matter, and
Miliukov spent several days in Kiev with Ukrainian leaders, including
the historian Mikhail Hrushevskii. The latter told Miliukov that
partisans of Ukrainian autonomy and federation for Russia were not
separatists and had no desire to break with Russia. Miliukov refused to
advocate Ukranian political autonomy, but in the Duma he defended
Ukrainian cultural aspirations.[43] Anticipating his stand of 1917, he
told the Duma: "In no way do I share the aims of the autonomists-
federalists, and I would consider the accomplishment of their goal as
harmful and dangerous for Russia." But there was no use opposing
the cultural movement which was "deeply democratic," and "led by
the people itself. This is why this movement cannot be stopped,"
even by the combined forces of the Russian government and the
Russian nationalists. It demanded freedom for the Ukrainian language
and the creation of Ukrainian schools and universities. The Austrians
in Galicia saw the advantage of yielding to Ukrainian demands and
planned a Ukrainian university in Lvov. Miliukov quoted from Henry
Wickham Steed's book, The Habsburg Monarchy, in which the
Englishman urged that instead Russia create a Ukrainian university
in Kiev. "A foreigner," Miliukov told the Duma nationalists, "to
whom our relationships are alien, instinctively adopts the right path
which you do not wish to see." Accusing the Nationalist Savenko,

[42] SO, April 21, 1914, p. 742; P. Miliukov, "Obshchee politicheskoe polozhenie," in Fraktsiia Narodnoi Svobody, Otchety K. D. fraktsii za 1913–14 (St.
Petersburg, 1914), p. 15.
[43] On Miliukov's visit to Kiev, see VOSP, II, 167–68, and E. Borschak, "Mik-
hailo Hrushevsky," LMS, January, 1935, p. 23. Miliukov's Duma speech is in
SO, February 19, 1914, pp. 901–16.

Miliukov concluded that "the real separatists who, in effect, work in Austria's favor, are Messrs. Savenko and his political friends."

While "creating enemies at home," the government was not telling the people enough about the state of the country's defenses. On March 1, 1914, the cabinet met with sixty-five Duma deputies including Miliukov, but not the Social Democrats and Trudoviks, in a consultation about the defense budget. Miliukov accused Goremykin of not keeping the country informed.

> The Opposition demanded, first of all, that in the most important question of armaments, threatening the country with serious difficulties abroad, information which is freely communicated in the parliaments of other countries, including those of our allies; and is also freely discussed in their press, should not be kept from the country.[44]

The Kadets remained excluded from the Duma's Defense Committee and objected to the army contingent bill being discussed behind closed doors. Actually, a good deal of defense information was public; Bernard Pares maintained that "the Duma's budget committee" (of which Miliukov was a member) "gets much more inside information on the military spending departments put before it than ever reaches the private members of the House of Commons."[45] Miliukov, however, considered the information given to the Duma insufficient and moved to postpone Duma consideration of the new army contingents since only a handful of Defense Committee members knew the secret details. "What they want from us here," he argued, "is simply blackmail." His motion, however, was defeated.[46]

The situation abroad, despite Sazonov's reassuring Duma speech, was becoming menacing. The foreign minister addressed the Duma in May, 1914, and, for the last time before the war, Russia had a parliamentary debate on foreign affairs, with speakers ranging from the extreme Left (the Social Democrat Chkhenkeli asserted that "Duma member Miliukov is infected by imperialist germs") to the Right (Count Bobrinskii attacked Miliukov for being anti-Serbian).[47]

[44] P. Miliukov, "Rossiia," EZH, 1915, p. 240; Riech', March 5, 1914.

[45] Riech' editorial, May 10, 1914; B. Pares, "Onlookers at the Duma," Russian Review (London), I (1912), No. 3, 85.

[46] SO, April 24, 1914, p. 974–77, 985.

[47] SO, May 10, 1914; Sazonov's speech is on pp. 336–48, Miliukov's reply on pp. 348–78; Bobrinskii's remarks are on pp. 378–80, Chkhenkeli's on pp. 393–412.

Surveying the scene since June, 1913, Miliukov saw "an enormous change in the situation—and a change not to our advantage, and, at times, not doing honor to our diplomacy." In the Balkans "a liberating war" had become "a war of conquest." The Balkan union no longer existed; Bulgaria had become anti-Russian. Chauvinism and nationalism flourished at home and abroad. Right newspapers were chiefly responsible for this; only "the progressive press—both the Russian, the German, and the English—always rejected the chauvinistic state of mind, the playing on nationalistic passions in which that section of the press is engaged." This campaign was more dangerous in Russia because the Russian government was identified with the rightist press and with super-patriotic demonstrations. "When nationalistic demonstrations take place in London, Paris or Berlin," he said, "nobody considers the government there responsible for them. But everyone knows the status of the press, of meetings, or of street demonstrations in Russia." Only Sazonov's ministry considered the broad spectrum of Russian public opinion.

> The Ministry of Foreign Affairs remains one of the few, and now, I guess, after the smashing up of the Ministry of Finance, the only European department which, in its messages abroad, refers to public opinion, and even to the desires of the State Duma as a ponderable in the field of our foreign policy, while within our country you are being told that you are an imponderable.

But Miliukov worried about the future. "I must state my fear," he concluded, "that the last department which has remained European might be vanquished, as all the others, and might lose the possibility of stopping, in time, that disastrous movement which, it is possible, is leading us to a new catastrophe."

After the Duma adjourned for the summer, Miliukov continued to comment on the gathering clouds in his newspaper. He took a look at the Franco-Russian Entente on the occasion of French President Raymond Poincaré's July, 1914, visit to St. Petersburg. "The Franco-Russian *rapprochement* of love," he wrote, "has long ago turned into a marriage of convenience." Russia could not but regret "the coming heavy sacrifices brought on the altar not of world friendship, but of international militant nationalism." He did not welcome the Poincaré visit since "this time France is bringing us the last word in advanced international enmity." Poincaré was coming to remind Russia of her obligations. But, in Miliukov's view, "the dominant interest in the fulfillment of these obligations is not on our side, but on that of our allies. There is no doubt that the initiative in the formulation of these obligations was theirs." Miliukov regretted that Poincaré could accomplish his task more easily because of the peculiar position of the Russian government vis-à-vis its own people. "Having pushed us into unusually heavy sacrifices," he wrote, "our allies will not be as concerned about Russian public opinion as about their own. And why should they be? In Russia the cabinet is not responsible to the legislature."[48]

This bitter comment was followed by another a week later, after the assassination of Franz Ferdinand in Sarajevo. Miliukov approved of the position of England, which did not wish to become involved in the Balkans. He insisted that the Austro-Serbian conflict be localized, whatever it might cost Serbia. He also criticized the French parliament's attitude toward armaments, sharply condemning French chauvinism. The article ended with a skeptical appraisal of the Franco-Russian Entente which, while desirable politically, might lead Russia into a military abyss: "We must look again at what we give," he wrote, "and what we receive."[49] In the last days of peace, Miliukov pursued his longstanding policy of caution in foreign affairs and firm opposition to all steps leading to a European conflict. This should be remembered in view of his later reputation as the imperialist par excellence, a proponent of war to the bitter end.

V

The war between Russia and the Central Powers broke out on July 19, 1914. For the following two days Riech' was suppressed by the military authorities for its "unpatriotic stand" during the previous weeks. "My position," Miliukov recalled, "was being granted a measure of strength by my enemies."[50] Rodzianko claims in his memoirs that he intervened on Miliukov's behalf with the commander in chief, Grand Duke Nikolai Nikolaievich, urging that the paper be permitted

[48] Riech' editorial, July 6, 1914.
[49] Riech', July 13 and 14, 1914.
[50] Details on the suppression of Riech' are in GES, pp. 325–27; see also P. Miliukov, "Moe otnoshenie k poslednei voine," PN, August 1, 1924, p. 3, and VOSP, II, 181–83, 190.

to reappear. "Miliukov was a fool," he told the Grand Duke, "and is angry at himself. Take his word, and he will change his attitude. We will need newspapers so very much now."[51] The authorities, however, were probably more impressed by the unexpected change in the Kadet attitude toward the government and the war. A new mood of reconciliation and unity descended upon the moderate opposition with the declaration of war. Government and society were to enjoy a brief honeymoon in Russia. The galleys of the suppressed *Riech'* issue contained a proclamation "To Our Partisans" which probably made the authorities reconsider. The proclamation appeared in *Riech'* on July 22. "Whatever our attitudes toward the internal policy of the government," it stated, "our first duty is to preserve the unity of our country. . . . We shall put aside our internal disputes and shall not give our foes the slightest reason to count on the differences which divide us."

Miliukov welcomed the calling of the Duma for a one-day session on July 26, arguing that "the Duma must serve as a means of unifying Emperor and people for the duration of the period during which the terrible trial will continue." The session turned into what Miliukov described as "a grandiose expression of national unity." Only the Social Democrats and the Trudoviks refused to be enthusiastic patriots; but Miliukov argued later that "the agitation of a small group could not have made the slightest impression on the unanimously patriotic mood of the entire nation."[52] The July 26 session impressed Miliukov. For once the government was concerned about public opinion and distributed its *Orange Book* to all Duma members. After brief statements by the ministers it was the turn of party representatives. Several Kadet deputies spoke on behalf of national minorities— I. Goldman for the Latvians, M. Ichas for the Lithuanians, and N. Fridman for the Jews. Speaking on behalf of the Kadet fraction, Miliukov, for the first time in his Duma career, heard himself applauded by the entire body and the cabinet. In 1894 poor Deputy-Governor Chaikovskii had been dismissed for applauding Miliukov's speech; twenty years later His Majesty's entire cabinet gave the Kadet leader practically an ovation.

---

[51] M. Rodzianko, "Krushenie imperii," ARR, XVII (1926), 81.
[52] *Riech'* editorial, July 22, 1914; P. Miliukov, in EZH, 1915, p. 243; also *Riech'* editorial, November 10, 1914.

Speaking after the Social Democrat V. Khaustov and the Trudovik leader Alexander Kerensky, Miliukov, unlike these, refused to dwell on Russia's domestic divisions. "When the time comes," he said, he would "again speak of these problems and again point out the only possible road toward Russia's regeneration. At this moment, however," he continued,

> we have all been deeply impressed by other matters. . . . We fight for the freedom of our native land from foreign invasion, for the freedom of Europe and Slavdom from German domination, and the freedom of the whole world from the unendurable yoke of constantly growing armaments. . . . The leaders of the Faction of Popular Freedom express their firm conviction that their political friends and followers, wherever they may be found and in whatever condition the war may overtake them, will fulfil their duty to the very end as Russian citizens in the impending struggle. . . . Our first duty remains to preserve our country, one and inseparable (Stormy applause in the center, on the right, and left), and to maintain for it that position in the ranks of the world powers which is being contested by our foes.[53]

How did Miliukov come to change his mind about Kadet tactics in both domestic and foreign policy? A year later he described his speech as "not the gesture of a politican, but the firm decision of a citizen."[54] At the time, however, he seemed to have been motivated, as so often in his political career, by the example of Western Europe. Kerensky claims that when he proposed that the Duma ask the Tsar for domestic reforms as a price for its support in the war ("My request," he writes, "was supported by the Progressives, Mensheviks and left-wing Kadets"), Miliukov disagreed. "Citing Britain as an example, he asserted that the Duma must show complete confidence in the government, no matter what its failings, and must make no stipulations."[55]

There were additional reasons for Miliukov's change of heart. He had come to see, as he put it a year later, "that reason does not suf-ficiently rule the world, and that calculations of expediency formed but a thin, superficial cover which burst, and was swept aside by

[53] The English text of Miliukov's speech is in GOL, pp. 35–36.
[54] P. Miliukov, in EZH, 1915, p. 254.
[55] KER, I, 129–30.

the spontaneous force of elementary instincts."[56] He had seen those instincts at work as a member of the Carnegie Commission; now he saw them among the Russian masses as well, as they fell on their knees on Winter Palace Square when the Emperor appeared on the balcony. His idealism, he admitted later, had misled him: "I blame myself," he told an audience in 1917, "for an overly strong pacifism. Closing my eyes, on the very edge of a danger which I did see, I underestimated the importance of this danger. I thought that we would do more through peaceful means."[57] Henceforth he would be increasingly hostile to antiwar sentiments in Russia and abroad; they had betrayed him, and he would now be a realist. Russia, in his eyes, must remain a great power; whatever threatened this goal must be opposed.

Discord and opposition at home would tend to endanger the war effort; this too, therefore, must be subdued. Russia must maintain a united front against the enemy. As Miliukov put it later, the Kadets:

> continued to consider it premature and dangerous to discuss in public the quarrels and disagreements, which had not yet become known to either friend or foe, in the full hearing of the enemy and the entire world, as well as in the hearing of the army, and the nation.[58]

Disagreements did not disappear; they were merely set aside for the duration of the hostilities, or so Miliukov thought at the time. He was impressed by the fact that even Russia's industrial workers, strongly restive on the very eve of the war, had closed ranks after the beginning of hostilities. In early July, 1914, the strike movement had been particularly strong in the capital—some 140,000 workers had walked out and even fought with the police and the army. *Riech'* failed to appear on July 9, 10, and 11 as a result of a printer's strike. Yet Miliukov must have felt assured that his party took the right

[56] P. Miliukov, in EZH, 1915, p. 42.
[57] P. Miliukov, in PAD, VI, 367. Miliukov soon began to reinterpret his past actions in the light of his new convictions. Thus he claimed that his Duma votes against military credits before the war had been motivated by a desire for reform in the War Ministry and as a protest against the limitations imposed upon the Duma's budget rights. "Any attempt to interpret this vote otherwise," he wrote in 1916, "by some kind of anti-militaristic motives, would be incorrect" (TAK, p. 4).
[58] P. Miliukov, in EZH, 1915, p. 254.

stand when he saw "how quickly this mood [of conciliation] spread among the broad masses of the population"; the strike movement died immediately after July 19.[59]

There was one final reason why the war had become acceptable to the Kadet leader: this was Russia's alliance with France and England. "We are marching," he told the Duma in January, 1915, "hand in hand with mankind's most enlightened nations."[60] An enterprise in which England and France supported Russia became noble in Miliukov's eyes. "We acknowledge," Miliukov told the Duma,

> that our country feels the fullest confidence in our allies, and highly values that contribution to our common success which they have already made, and which will continue to grow. . . . We value no less that profound moral meaning which the world war is acquiring thanks to the participation in it of the two most advanced democracies of contemporary mankind. We believe that this participation will guarantee to us the full realization of the liberating goals of this war.

One "liberating goal" had already received official Russian formulation and represented one of the Kadet aims buried since the defeat of the 1905 revolution. This was the official Russian promise, contained in the Commander-in-Chief's Proclamation to the Poles of August, 1, 1914, of Polish autonomy. "Let the Poles," said the Proclamation, "be reunited under the scepter of the Russian Tsar. Under that scepter Poland will be reborn, free in her faith, language, and self-government."[61]

Russia had another "historic task" which the war had put on the agenda of the day. This was the acquisition of the Straits, so intimately connected with Russia's role in the Balkans and with the fate of Turkey. Miliukov, like official Russian diplomacy, had been content to accept the status quo in regard to the Straits. Turkey's behavior in September–October, 1914, however, reopened the question. In September the Turks closed the Straits to all foreign shipping. They followed this, on October 16–17, by bombarding several Russian

[59] *Ibid.*, 1915, p. 242. *Riech'* editorials of July 5 and 12, 1914, discussed the strikes both in the capital and in Baku.

[60] Miliukov's speech is in SO, January 27, 1915, pp. 49–52; Sazonov's speech is in *ibid.*, 1915, pp. 12–22.

[61] The text of the Proclamation is in GOL, pp. 37–38.

Black Sea ports. In answer Russia declared war on October 20; an
Imperial Manifesto stated that Turkey's provocation would "open
to Russia the path towards the settlement of the historic tasks be-
queathed to her by forbears on the shores of the Black Sea."[62] The
important fact for Miliukov was that, this time, far from opposing
Russian ambitions at the Straits, France and England would look
with sympathy upon them. He could not but approve of the words
of the British ambassador at Constantinople to the Grand Vizier
on the eve of Turkey's joining the Central Powers: "To guarantee
the inviolability and independence of Turkey is equivalent to guar-
anteeing the life of a man who has decided to commit suicide."[63]
Henceforth Miliukov, Russia's leading Balkan expert, would become
her chief spokesman on the Straits question.

VI

The war, then, was responsible for a change in Miliukov's attitude
toward the Russian government; but had the latter really changed in
its attitude toward Russian society? Miliukov soon discovered that
it had not. As he put it, "what was meant as a truce was taken to
mean a capitulation."[64] Goremykin's cabinet was no more conciliatory
in late 1914 than it had been before the outbreak of the war. After
the July, 1914, Duma session the legislature was not recalled till
January, 1915, and then for only three days to approve the budget.
"At that moment," Miliukov recalled, "we did not yet demand
lengthy sessions; we began to insist on them later. . . . This was
only the first stage of our differences with the government, and we
were still trying to maintain the outward appearance of peaceful
relations."[65] We saw that, in the open Duma session of January, 1915,
Miliukov supported the government's foreign policy. But in a closed
meeting of deputies with the cabinet at that time he was strongly
critical of policies in Galicia and Bukovina in particular.

It must be understood that the Russian public was not informed
about the true state of affairs at the front and in the newly con-

[62] Russia's declaration of war on Turkey is discussed in SM II, 76–81.

[63] Quoted in P. Miliukov, "Vstuplenie neitral'nykh gosudarstv," EZH, 1915,
pp. 140–41.

[64] TAK, p. 9.

[65] The account of the January, 1915, Duma session is in PAD, VI, 309–11.

quered territories. Little was known about the policies in Galicia
and Bukovina of the new Russian administration. Miliukov wrote
a year after the event:

> Alas, we found out about this sad page of history only afterwards,
> when all of it was already a matter of the past. . . . What is needed
> is an entirely different attitude than that of last year toward the
> language, church, and cultural institutions of the territories under
> question.[66]

Information had not been available in January, 1915. It was only
from deputies, notably the Kadet Igor Demidov and the Right
deputy Purishkevich, who had just returned from the front, that the
Duma learned the sad truth. Purishkevich's patriotism got the better
of his politics: he was as critical of official bungling as his Kadet
colleague. Armed with this information Miliukov and his partisans
went into the meeting with the cabinet. "It was the first meeting
with the government," he recalled,

> under an already changed attitude. Our comrades had arrived from
> the front, and reported that the situation there was unsatisfactory,
> that the army had no munitions. . . . It also became clear that
> Maklakov's internal policy of suspicion toward the population,
> hostility toward the nationalities, and persecution of the press, was
> being continued.

The two villains of the piece were the ministers Maklakov and
Sukhomlinov; Miliukov demanded their resignation. But the Kadets
did not wish to make their accusations public:

> We thought that the time for making such speeches from the
> Duma tribune had not come yet. We considered it essential to
> preserve an outward appearance of peace with the government. . . .
> I criticized the government's position toward the nationalities, the
> Jews, the Poles. . . . I demanded that they submit a bill on Polish
> autonomy, and Goremykin promised this. . . . We said that
> Sukhomlinov had deceived the Duma. . . . Even Purishkevich, who
> had returned from the front, rejected his explanations.

Goremykin failed to keep his promise and said nothing about
Poland in the Duma. The Kadets, nevertheless, voted for the budget,
while the Trudoviks abstained and the Social Democrats voted

[66] *Riech'* editorial, July 29, 1915.

against. The two hated ministers stayed in office. Maklakov continued on his course by closing down the Imperial Free Economic Society for its criticism of government policies. The Duma was prorogued, and no date set for the next session. The government had faced a passive opposition. Miliukov had learned a lesson which bore fruit in the Progressive Bloc, which was organized the following July: without an organized majority to oppose Goremykin, the Duma would remain helpless. Miliukov would have to find the means of uniting the dissatisfied parties, particularly those to the right of the Kadets. The progress of the war would soon help him in this task.

In April the Germans broke through the Russian lines, and an inglorious Russian retreat from Galicia began. By June the earlier Russian territorial gains had been lost and the Germans had gone deeply into Russian Poland. Their artillery barrage overwhelmed the Russians, whose supplies were inadequate: Sukhomlinov at the War Ministry was simply not up to his task. One *guberniia* after another fell into enemy hands. An enormous army of refugees created chaos in the rear. These defeats, coupled with the increasing inflation and sporadic shortages of goods, had an electrifying influence on a public already grumbling about governmental inefficiency. The Zemstvo and Town Unions, in particular, were becoming ever more active in substituting their authority for that of the increasingly isolated bureaucracy. In August, 1914, the Emperor authorized the formation of an All-Russian Union of Zemstvos and an All-Russian Union of Towns for help to the wounded and sick. These organizations had the experience of the Russo-Japanese War, where they had done splendid work. Once again they drew on the men who had been prominent in the Zemstvo and Town Duma movements of 1904–5.

The Kadets played a conspicuous role in this enterprise. The two organizations were headed by Kadets—Chelnokov in the Union of Towns, and Prince George L'vov in the Zemstvo Union.[67] The two had worked together in 1904–5. The Kadets also participated in the War Industries Committees, created in 1914 to organize the production of military supplies. Thus, Kutler represented the Ural industrial district on the Central War Industries Committee headed by

[67] The two organizations usually worked together and became known by their combined initials as the Zemgor.

Guchkov, while Sergei Smirnov, member of the party's central committee, became chairman of the Moscow War Industries Committee. Miliukov praised the work of all these organizations, comparing them with similar undertakings in England and France under Lloyd George and Albert Thomas.[68]

But soon conflicts arose over the jurisdiction of these organizations. Miliukov expressed indignation at the increasing government interference with their work. The government excused all interference on the grounds that the Zemgor was using government funds. "But," asked Miliukov, "do not all funds ultimately come from the population?"[69] Minister of the Interior Maklakov wrote the Emperor on April 27, 1915:

> Prince L'vov and others are going to their goal systematically. What is this goal? To darken the light of your fame, Your Majesty, and to weaken the power and significance of the ever holy and always salutary Russian idea of autocracy. . . . I hear and feel painfully all this unflinching, though carefully masked, tendency among our militant intelligentsia.[70]

The situation in the spring of 1915 was reminiscent of that in 1905, when the Russian public had clamored for change during an unsuccessful war. Many of the same organizations were again on the scene, but there was also the Duma, which had not existed then. The demand now rose for the calling of the legislature. This time, Miliukov insisted, there must be a lengthy session.

To prepare for the Duma session the Kadets called, in early June, 1915, their first conference since the war. It was relatively well attended, with some one hundred delegates representing thirty-seven local groups. To meet the accusations of several provincial delegates that the Kadets had been too conciliatory toward the government, Miliukov complained that the government had not respected the union sacrée:

> Everywhere abroad . . . where the common danger led to a rapprochement of the most varied public forces, and to the temporary postponement of internal struggle, the agreement and unity reached in this manner were understood as the product of a cer-

[68] Riech' editorial, June 11, 1915.
[69] Riech' editorial, March 14, 1915.
[70] PAD, V. 204.

tain silent compact about an internal truce. This truce was kept, with more or less good faith, by both sides. In our country, unfortunately, it was kept by only one side.[71]

The time had come, Miliukov admitted, to speak out publicly against the government. But the January tactic of silence had borne fruit: the odious Minister of Interior was finally gone. The day before the conference Maklakov was replaced by Prince Nikolai Shcherbatov, not a popular figure but at least not a militant reactionary.

Miliukov had no real answer to the allegations by several delegates that the party had no contact with the masses. Lev Krol' of Ekaterinburg was worried about the workers who seemed passive in their attitude to the war. Miliukov could only agree, stressing that "in England the ministers continuously court the workers, become acquainted with their mood, try to take action in regard to it both directly, and in parliament, and this gives results. With us the matter is handled quite differently." Some delegates reported that many in the provinces wanted to end the war, which was going so badly. Miliukov found the materials brought together by the conference "too accidental, fragmentary, and incomplete to base any definite directives to the fraction on it."

Actually, as always in party gatherings, he wished to steer a middle course and maintain party unity. There was a group at the conference, represented by Maklakov, A. F. Babianskii, and A. V. Vasil'ev, who would not sanction any opposition in wartime. Miliukov, for his part, would not go so far but put his hope in a reorganized government working in unanimity with a Duma in more or less permanent session. It was his view that

> with all its deficiencies the Duma is, nevertheless, the sole organized center of national opinion and will, and the only body which can be placed against the bureaucracy. . . . The Duma has placed itself higher in the nation's estimation than it has ever stood before. All hopes are pinned to it. This has its drawbacks. As in 1905 the nation again expects too much from the Duma.

But even some Kadets expected too much from the Duma, demand-

[71] An incomplete account of the Kadet conference in Petrograd of June 6–8, 1915, is in N. Lapin (ed.), "Kadety v dni galiitsiiskogo razgroma," KA, LIX (1933), 110–44. Half of the account is devoted to Miliukov's report to the conference and his answer to speeches from the floor.

ing a government responsible to the legislature in the parliamentary sense. Parliamentary responsibility was not practicable under the circumstances, Miliukov told the conference:

> Our party's old goal [parliamentary government], proclaimed by us in the First and Second Dumas, has, at present, been accepted by the broad masses of the population, and in part by the army. But a "ministry responsible to the Duma," without a change in the electoral law and the State Council, would be useless, considering the Right majority in the Fourth Duma.

Instead of this unrealistic goal, Miliukov asked for "a ministry enjoying the confidence of the public," a public more liberal than the Duma.

As so often in the past, Miliukov's middle-of-the-road program won the day at the conference. Its resolutions provided simply for the immediate calling of the Duma and for a reconstruction of the cabinet "to ensure the proper organization of the rear, the preservation of internal peace in the country, and a close collaboration between the government and the public." Miliukov would now set about trying to implement this modest program.

VII

Since the outbreak of war Miliukov had adopted new tactics; they were about to bear fruit. He began to loom as a leader of a new coalition aimed, not to the left, but to the right of his party. The Duma Trudoviks and Social Democrats had, both in July, 1914, and January, 1915, used the old Left tactics which Miliukov rejected. His choice could only lead him into the arms of men more conservative than even the Right Kadets. Having posited the Duma as the center of Russian wartime life, he had to abandon all radicalism in order to win support for his patriotic stand. He wished to profit from the new respectability that the Kadets had acquired. The loose prewar coalition of Kadets, Octobrists, and Progressives would now be cemented into a more permanent alliance, the Progressive Bloc. Miliukov would be its leader because he had dissociated himself from the Left.

Already in October, 1914, the Octobrists offered their hand to the Kadets in a new way. As their newspaper wrote:

> Those Russian parties which, till now, had been considered anti-

governmental, and, therefore, illegal, have proven in practice their respect for the state, and their readiness to sacrifice their blood and life for the fatherland. . . . It must be admitted that there were mistakes on both sides which resulted in mutual misunderstanding. . . . The heart of every Russian would be filled with joy if he could say with pride that Russia had no political criminals, that the old mistakes and crimes had been forgiven.[72]

The war had created a new political solidarity extending from the Kadets to the Right; the Left was not included and, for the time being, Miliukov saw nothing wrong in this. He had been doubtful of the Left ever since the Second Duma. The war, he thought, had created a new "unanimity," which the Kadets had brought about. As in the days of the First Duma the Kadets somehow, in Miliukov's eyes, represented the whole nation. This was a misconception now, as it had been then, but only the future would make this clear. For the moment all looked promising, and Miliukov exalted in the Kadets' new role. "The party," he wrote,

> which played the decisive role in the establishment of "unanimity" of the Duma and of public opinion by this fact at one stroke destroyed the barriers of partisan prejudices, of old reproaches and slanders which stood in its way. The party was *understood* more fully and widely than it had ever been understood before. Perhaps many only *discovered* the party for the first time in the circumstances of this national struggle.[73]

The Kadets had once been mistrusted by both the Left and the Right. The latter had now begun to change their mind. Miliukov could hardly be blamed for rejoicing that the number of his foes had been reduced. The Left, he thought, would also come around when they saw results.

And the new tactics did seem to produce results. On June 17 an Imperial Rescript summoned the Duma "not later than August." The wording of the rescript was promising:

> From all corners of our Fatherland we receive messages testifying to the eager desire of the Russian people to join in the work of provisioning the army. . . . We consider it essential to hasten the

---

[72] *Golos Moskvy*, quoted in *Riech'* editorial, October 7, 1914.
[73] TAK, p. 9; italics in the original.

calling of the legislative bodies in order to hear the voice of the Russian land.[74]

But the Duma did not wish to wait till August. A group of party leaders visited Goremykin to persuade him to advance the date. Miliukov spoke for the delegation. It was the first time in Duma history that he fulfilled such a role. Goremykin promised to reconsider and to inform the Duma.[75]

On July 8 an Imperial Rescript summoned the legislature for July 19, the first anniversary of the war's outbreak. Addressing the cabinet on July 16, the new Minister of War, General Aleksei Polivanov, said with emotion: "I consider it my civic and official duty to state to the Council of Ministers that the fatherland is in danger."[76] It was in this critical military situation that the Fourth Duma reassembled for its most significant session. It faced a cabinet which had been purged of its most detested members: perhaps Miliukov's restraining tactics could bring results after all. Sukhomlinov was gone, as was Minister of Justice Shcheglovitov, and Procurator of the Holy Synod Sabler—those most distrusted by the public. Only the aged Premier had not been replaced, but, opening the session, he promised to work "in full unanimity with the legislative chambers." Unfortunately, as in the First Duma, he presented no program: "We are convinced," he observed, "that the present is no time for program speeches." Faced with Russia's difficult hour, the government did not know which way to move. Even the Nationalists now asked for a new government. Their motion, which won a majority composed of themselves, the Center, the Zemstvo Octobrists, and the Kadets, stated that a speedy victory in the war could be achieved "only through the country's close union with a government enjoying its full confidence."[77]

The new formula had now been sounded from the Duma tribune, significantly enough by one of the most conservative factions. It resembled the resolution passed earlier by the Kadet conference. Miliukov, therefore, opposed a motion by the Progressives which stated that the Duma would support only a government which "openly acknowl-

[74] Riech', June 17, 1915.
[75] Riech' editorial, July 4, 1915.
[76] Iakhontov, p. 15.
[77] SO, July 19, 1915, pp. 9, 72.

edges the Duma's authority, announces its readiness to submit to its control and leadership, and realizes its responsibility to the nation's representative body."[78] Arguing against, Miliukov stated: "We consider it impossible to introduce this party goal of ours [a government responsible to the Duma] into a non-party formula which is to represent our unity before the threatening danger." He then outlined the tasks which faced the Duma session. He praised Goremykin for having alluded to future Polish autonomy. "Finally," he said, "we heard that cherished word autonomy, a word which, ten years ago, we wrote into our program, for which we earned unjust accusations and unfounded reproaches." He then urged the passage of the old *volost'* zemstvo bill, passed by the Third Duma, but buried in the State Council. Village self-government he asserted, would guarantee a more efficient supply of food. He warned that the government must stop persecuting labor leaders, since this was causing economic disturbances. What was needed was not "cruel methods of police repression" but "those methods of peaceful mediation which are being successfully implemented by our allies."[79]

Answering Sazonov, who had spoken on foreign policy, Miliukov urged, to the loud applause of all sections of the Duma, "the final solution of our centuries old national task: access to the open sea, without which the building of a great state organism cannot be completed." The alternative, as he saw it, was a domination by the Central Powers "from the Danube to the Persian Gulf, which will push us finally into that bewitched continental prison from which the strong hand of the great founder of Petersburg first liberated us." Despite the enormous sacrifices necessary, the war was essential to Russia's greatness. "Gentlemen," he concluded, "all our past, and all our future are in this war. Everything, I think, is said by this."[80]

His speech, as it dealt with domestic issues, contained most of the Progressive Bloc program as announced five weeks later. He had succeeded in grouping around it most of the Duma, except for its "two extremes," whom he condemned. On the extreme Right the speech of Nikolai Markov had been full of "party polemics" and had "aroused bewilderment." As for the Left "the speeches of Kerensky and Chkheidze went completely beyond the limits of the general

[78] *Ibid.*, 1915, pp. 90–91.
[79] The text of Miliukov's speech is in *ibid.*, 1915, pp. 92–109.
[80] Sazonov's speech is in *ibid.*, 1915, pp. 20–27.

mood and took the side of the well-known position of international socialism." Miliukov wished to profit from "the general mood" which, as he interpreted it, was one of concerned patriotism and anger at the government's ineptitude, but not of radicalism. He would not compromise his chances of success by demanding more than would be acceptable to his moderate allies. When Chkheidze asked whether the Kadets planned to introduce their bills on political freedom, Miliukov answered in the negative. First preference should belong to bills which "aimed at organizing the country for victory," and "could unite all." He clearly meant "all the moderates." The Social Democrats and the Trudoviks were to remain outside the future bloc. In a prophetic vein Kerensky said of the Kadets and their new coalition: "We do not judge you, we do not wish to fight with you, and we will calmly wait until you are disillusioned . . . and come to us for help."[81]

VIII

The war, which had already claimed so many Russian victims, now delivered a cruel blow to Miliukov. His younger son Sergei was killed on the Austrian front. It was a tragic hour for the Kadet leader, and his sorrow was respected. His memoirs show that his personal sorrow was deep. He had advised his son, who could have joined the army in the safe Far East, to volunteer for the Austrian front. He never ceased blaming himself for his son's death.[82]

The political news, however, continued to be encouraging. On July 21 the Kadet Shingarev was elected chairman of the Duma's Army-Navy Commission, the former Defense Committee which had been closed to the Kadets since 1907. Nothing could better have illustrated the new respect the party enjoyed. Only the Trudoviks and Social Democrats maintained that it was a mistake to accept responsibility for a body in which the opposition did not have a majority. But the Kadets were already pushing for a bill providing

[81] *Riech'* editorials, July 20 and 22 and August 31, 1915.

[82] *Riech'*, July 25, 1915; VOSP, II, 197–98. The twenty-year old boy, Miliukov discovered from some correspondence with a relative, "worshipped me—and at the same time suffered from a lack of intimacy between us." He had been living in Moscow with the family of Miliukov's brother Aleksei (who died in 1913). Miliukov's older son Nikolai was still serving in the artillery in 1917. (G. Vernadsky, *Pavel Nikolaevich Miliukov* [Petrograd, 1917], p. 25).

for the creation of a chief administration of army supply based on the English model of a ministry of supply. It would be advised by a Council representing the public and have powers to take over plants, fix prices, and so on.[83]

The government had other plans. It proposed creating four special councils to deal with, respectively, defense, food provisioning, fuel, and transport. Each council was to include four Duma members appointed by the Emperor. The Duma amended the last provision, stipulating the election of its representatives. It was to have nine (not four) members in the Council on Defense, and seven in each of the other councils. When the Special Council on Defense met for the first time under the Emperor's chairmanship on August 26—the day on which the Progressive Bloc announced its program—it included Shingarev among its members.[84]

We must now return to the political situation at the Duma's opening. It had become Miliukov's task to transform a more or less accidental majority of one day into a permanent coalition. The Progressives had to be convinced to support the formula of "a government enjoying the country's confidence" rather than their demand for a government responsible to the Duma; this Miliukov accomplished. He then had to persuade the Octobrists that a prolonged Duma session was needed. The Duma presidium, consisting mostly of Octobrists, was permitting deputies to leave the capital on the slightest pretext.[85] He had to find allies against Goremykin inside the cabinet. There were members of the government who favored co-operation with the Duma and concessions to its emergent program. The leader of this small group was Minister of Agriculture Aleksandr Krivoshein. In later years Miliukov suggested that one of the inspirations for the new Duma coalition might have resulted from Krivoshein's ambition to replace Goremykin. "It must be said," he testified in 1917,

> that perhaps the first thought about it [the Bloc] originated in ministerial circles. Krivoshein was constantly on the lookout and

[83] Riech' editorial, July 22, 1915. A. Sidorov, "Bor'ba s krizisom vooruzheniia russkoi armii v 1915–16 gg.," Istoricheskii Zhurnal (Moscow), 1944, No. 10–11, p. 49.
[84] P. Gronsky, The War and the Russian Government (New Haven, Conn., 1929). pp. 34 ff.
[85] Riech' editorial, August 3, 1915.

thought that his time would come after all, that he would become Premier, and he considered it necessary to rely on a majority in the chambers. . . . So that, perhaps, the very attempt of the initial negotiations was called forth by this.[86]

It was Krivoshein who had written the eloquent Imperial Rescript summoning the Duma. But in the opinion of War Minister Polivanov, Krivoshein had little chance of becoming premier since he was "the son of a baptized Jew, and a Catholic Polish mother," an origin highly suspect to the Emperor.[87]

The plan, in any case, did not meet with Miliukov's approval. "The basic disadvantage of all bureaucratic candidatures," he wrote, "is their belatedness, which, in itself, proves how this milieu is cut off from real life, and how incapable it is of understanding what is happening."[88] He was doubtless more impressed by the list of the shadow cabinet published by the Progressives in their newspaper.[89] The Kadets' allies proposed a cabinet headed by Duma chairman Rodzianko in which Miliukov would take the Foreign Ministry and the Kadets would get the ministries of finance, communications, and justice.

The government, meanwhile, was groping to solve the political crisis. The Procurator of the Holy Synod Aleksandr Samarin told the cabinet that "the Duma speeches have made a terrible impres-

---

[86] PAD, VI, 316.

[87] A. Polivanov, op. cit., p. 65.

[88] Riech' editorial, August 25, 1915.

[89] Utro Rossii (Moscow) August 13, 1915, printed the following list:

Post	1915 Shadow Cabinet
Premier	Rodzianko (Octobrist)
Interior	Guchkov (Octobrist)
Foreign .	Miliukov (Kadet)
Finance	Shingarev (Kadet)
Communications	Nekrasov (Kadet)
Trade	Konovalov (Progressive)
Agriculture	Krivoshein (bureaucrat)
War	Polivanov (bureaucrat)
Navy	Savich (Octobrist)
Comptroller	Efremov (Progressive)
Holy Synod	V. N. L'vov (Center)
Education	Count Ignat'ev (bureaucrat)
Justice	Maklakov (Kadet)

sion on all classes of the population and have deeply influenced the attitude toward the government." Sazonov admitted that "the government hangs in the air, having no support either from below or from above." Shcherbatov argued that a report be sent to the Emperor explaining that "a government which has the confidence of neither the Emperor, the army, the towns, the zemstvos, the nobility, the merchants, nor the workers not only cannot work, but cannot even exist. Sitting here we seem a group of Don Quixotes."[90] A new issue now divided the cabinet—the Emperor's determination to take over the supreme military command from his uncle, Grand Duke Nicholas.

The Emperor's decision was supported by Goremykin but was regarded by the majority of the cabinet as disastrous. In the eyes of the nation, the Emperor would now become responsible for the army's defeats and would thus endanger the very existence of the monarchy. Ten of the twelve ministers planned to resign unless Nicholas reconsidered his decision. But he remained adamant.[91] Meanwhile every kind of organization which had a voice demanded changes in the government. The first All-Russian Congress of War Industries Committees urged that Russia follow the French and English example and include a "few strong persons" in the government. The Moscow Town Duma passed a unanimous resolution demanding a government enjoying the country's full confidence and empowering Moscow's mayor to inform the Emperor of its recommendation. Some forty Town Dumas from all corners of Russia telegraphed the Moscow Duma expressing approval. The Petrograd Town Duma sent an identical resolution to the Emperor.[92]

The majority of the cabinet now opposed Goremykin, and eight ministers sent the following letter to the Emperor: "A basic difference of opinion has arisen between the Chairman of the Council of Ministers and ourselves in estimating the actions to be taken by the government. Such a situation is fatal at a time like the present. We are losing faith in the possibility of serving you." Yet while the cabinet majority wanted to make concessions to the public, it did not wish to surrender to the Duma. The entire cabinet was agreed that the Duma should be prorogued as soon as possible, though not till after the Bloc's pro-

[90] Iakhontov, pp. 60, 91.
[91] Ibid., p. 91.
[92] Prigovor moskovskoi dumy 18-go avgusta 1915 g. (Moscow, 1915), passim; Petrogradskaia gorodskaia duma v 1913–15 gg. (Petrograd, 1915), p. 214.

gram had been examined. Some ministers feared trouble from the Duma. "I am told," said Minister of Justice Aleksandr Khvostov, "that Mr. Miliukov boasts openly that all the threads are in his hands . . . and that he need only push the button to start disorders all over Russia." Sazonov was more cynical; "Miliukov is the biggest bourgeois," he said, "and is more afraid of a social revolution than of anything else. And the majority of the Kadets tremble for their wealth." It was decided to delay the prorogation till the Bloc's program had been considered.[93] That document finally appeared on August 26.

It was a most moderate statement. After urging the formation of a new government, it went on to demand: a partial political amnesty, the cessation of religious persecution, a bill on Polish autonomy, better treatment for Jews and Finns, the restoration of the Ukrainian and labor press and of the labor unions, and bills dealing with the zemstvos, co-operative societies, and the working conditions of employees of various categories. When the cabinet came to examine the program, Sazonov exclaimed: "There is no question of accepting the whole program. I am convinced that even the magician and wizard Pavel Nikolaevich Miliukov thinks the same." But on the whole the ministers found little in the document to reject outright. It was agreed that four of the ministers should meet with the Bloc's representatives "for purposes of information only."[94]

State Comptroller Peter Kharitonov, speaking for the ministers, explained they were not empowered to agree to a cabinet "enjoying the country's confidence"; that depended entirely on the Emperor. Miliukov, speaking for the Bloc, explained that the coalition would be satisfied with the appointment of a new premier enjoying the country's confidence, who could then choose his own cabinet. Characterizing the Bloc, Miliukov told the ministers that "it unites, for the first time in Russian life, all elements of society who uphold legality." The discussion of the Polish and Jewish problems also reas-

---

[93] Iakhontov, pp. 98, 104, 114.

[94] The text of the Bloc's program is in GOL, pp. 134–36. Complaining of the censorship, Miliukov told the Duma: "Gentlemen, in the countries allied to us the governments did everything to acquaint the public with the military danger and showed it what was needed for victory. I must say that in our country you will find the opposite" (SO, August 25, 1915, pp. 1055–74, for the text of Miliukov's speech on the censorship). Also Iakhontov, pp. 106, 111, 121.

sured the ministers; it revealed that the Bloc included both anti-
Semites and Polonophobes. Only Miliukov insisted that a bill on
Polish autonomy be introduced into the Duma at once, to preclude
an international solution for the Polish problem.[95]

Miliukov concluded that "the ministers were particularly struck
by the fact that the Bloc's representatives showed complete solidarity
in all their demands." In fact, Kharitonov thought that no major
trouble need be expected from the Bloc. It was "founded on compromise" and was "temporary in nature."[96] The danger of this coalition
would soon pass. "The agreement on which it is based," he said, "is
not one of principle, but is dictated by temporary considerations."
Only Sazonov was pleased that here was "an organization which
represents all of the anti-revolutionary Duma." Shcherbatov was convinced, quite correctly as it happened, that the Bloc had been "called
forth by fears of a social revolution if the present indeterminate situation should continue." He did not wish to offend the Bloc for "this
would place the government face to face with the Left elements." "If
we succeed in getting at least two hundred Duma members against the
Kerenskys," he asserted, "we shall gain much in political terms."[97]

Feeling rather calm about the Bloc, the cabinet returned to the
question of the Duma's prorogation. Only Goremykin wished to
dismiss the legislature without further ado. The majority demanded
that the country first be assured that a new cabinet was being formed.
A declaration to that effect should be read in the Duma before the
prorogation. The meeting ended without Goremykin committing
himself on this point. When he returned from a visit to the Emperor,
he announced to his astounded colleagues that the Duma would be
prorogued on September 3. No government speech would be made
before the prorogation. The Emperor would consider the question
of a new cabinet when the military situation permitted.

Goremykin's news was greeted with amazement. Arkadii Iakhontov,
deputy secretary of the Council of Ministers, noted that he had
"never seen the cabinet in such an uproar."[98] The Duma heard out

---

[95] An account of the meeting is in KA, L–LI (1932), 145–50.

[96] TAK, p. 36; Iakhontov, pp. 119–25.

[97] In fact the Bloc controlled 241 votes, or more than half of the total. Miliukov calculated that the Bloc had 89 votes against a majority of 99 in the State
Council (P. Miliukov, in EZH, 1915, p. 286).

[98] Iakhontov, pp. 128–29.

the prorogation decree in silence. A meeting of deputies was held afterward and instructed Rodzianko to ask for an audience with the Emperor, but the latter refused to receive him.[99] The public reaction to the prorogation was mild. There were political strikes on the Duma's behalf in the two capitals, but they lasted only three days and did not involve large masses of workers. The Putilov workers did demand "a responsible ministry," but the agitation soon died down.[100] The Zemstvo and Town Unions held their congresses in Moscow immediately after the prorogation. They tried to interfere on the Duma's behalf but without effect; their delegation was not received by the Emperor, and only their resolution remained on record. "As a lighthouse in the dark labyrinth of events," said congress chairman Prince L'vov, "the Duma kept indicating the correct path. We cannot but conclude that its prorogation pushes us back into the darkness."[101]

Miliukov himself advocated no drastic measures. Commenting on the Duma's adjournment till November 1, he wrote: "We can only appeal to the greatest caution." In regard to the Bloc he added, borrowing Prince L'vov's terminology: "The Bloc's program will continue to serve as a lighthouse by which various public aspirations will set their course."[102] The only measure of protest he advocated was a Duma boycott of the Special Councils. While the Progressives agreed, the rest of the coalition was opposed, and the Bloc decided against the move. According to Miliukov, the step had been abandoned because "the walk-out of the Opposition parties alone would have deprived the act of its larger political significance and would have bared disagreements within the Bloc, which is what its enemies most desire."[103] But the French ambassador in Petrograd might have also played a certain role in dissuading Miliukov. Maurice Paléologue recorded that he had dinner with Miliukov, Maksim Kovalevskii of the State Council, and several other Kadets, on the eve of the Duma's prorogation. "In other countries," he commented, "this dinner would have been the most natural thing. Here the separation between the official world and the progressive elements is so profound, that I expect to be strongly criticized." To protect himself

[99] P. Miliukov, in EZH, 1915, p. 282.
[100] M. Balabanov, Tsarskaia Rossiia XX veka (Moscow, 1927), pp. 164–65.
[101] P. Miliukov, in EZH, 1915, pp. 282–83.
[102] Riech' editorial, September 3 and 4, 1915.
[103] TAK, p. 40.

Paléologue met the men in a private house. When the Russians told the ambassador that their parties would withdraw from the Special Councils, he protested their decision:

> I cannot claim to understand your motives, and your political calculations. But as Ambassador of your Ally France, of France which entered the war for the sake of Russia's defense, I have the right to remind you that you are *face to face with the enemy*, and that you must abstain from any act or expression which might bring about a lessening of your military effort.[104]

Since, by this time, the Russian armies had evacuated Warsaw, Brest-Litovsk, and Vilno, and the German navy was in the Bay of Riga, the ambassador's words must have struck home. At any rate the Russians, he recalled, "promised to reconsider."

The Bloc now remained in suspense. At the time it appeared to Miliukov that there was much hope for the future. The situation was not revolutionary, and no one, even among the Left, advocated radical steps. The population might complain of high prices and a bungling government, but it was not ready for any overt action. Rasputin's evil work had not yet destroyed Russia's faith in the dynasty. Miliukov was not a coward, but experience had taught him that the nation was slow to move in the Duma's defense. Besides he remained a parliamentarian, determined that the Duma, and not the mob, should bring Russia out of her difficulties. And he was too much of a patriot to desire internal trouble in the midst of a dangerous war. He would bide his time, convinced that another opportunity would come.

It was only in retrospect that he changed his mind about the significance of the events of September, 1915. "Revolution became unavoidable in Russia after the autumn of 1915," he was to write later, "when the Tsar ignored the last attempt of the Duma majority to bridge the chasm between him and public opinion by working out a moderately progressive program and nominating a ministry 'enjoying the country's confidence.'" Similarly, it was only in exile that he came to regard his role in the Progressive Bloc as "the culmi-

[104] PAL, II, 72–3; italics in the original.

nating point of my political career."[105] In the autumn of 1915 he could not have foreseen the supreme irony that was in store for the Bloc. Not until February 28, 1917, did the Emperor order Rodzianko to form a new cabinet from among the Duma. The Bloc was to achieve its victory too late. The days of the monarchy were then numbered, and the war could not be won. The Bloc failed in 1915; it had no chance in 1917. The old regime had refused the sole helping hand that was offered. The monarchy's last real chance for survival had been missed in 1915, when discussion was still possible. Once the people began to make their demands in the streets, it was too late to rely on the Bloc, which had been the tool of evolution, not of revolution.

[105] BOLSH, p. 68; VOSP, II, 207. For an estimate of Miliukov's role in the Bloc, see T. Riha, "Miliukov and the Progressive Bloc in 1915: A study in Last Chance Politics," JMH, XXXII (1960), 16–24.

7: THE ROAD TO REVOLUTION

> In those months [late 1916] I was, it so happened, rereading
> Taine—in a different frame of mind than that of my student
> days, when I used to contrast him with Michelet. Our Rus-
> sian experience had been sufficient to remove from "the revo-
> lution" as such its halo, and to destroy its mystique in my
> eyes. I knew that my place was not there.[1]

I

The Russian government, far from reforming itself as a result of the
pressure by the Progressive Bloc, became in the autumn of 1915 more
reactionary than ever. The ministers who had dared to suggest change
were replaced, one by one, by men who had more than conservative
reputations. In late September, Samarin was replaced at the Holy
Synod by Aleksandr Volzhin, a nonentity. At the Ministry of Interior,
Shcherbatov was replaced by Aleksandr Khvostov, once a dreaded
governor of Nizhnii Novgorod and now leader of the Duma reactionaries. "The fact that he is the chairman of the Duma's Right," wrote
Miliukov, "is sufficient explanation for his attitude toward the Bloc."
It was the first appointment engineered by Rasputin and the Empress
while the Emperor was at General Headquarters. As for Samarin's
removal, Miliukov recorded that "it led to expressions of sympathy
from all strata of the Moscow population which took on the character
of a political demonstration. At the end of it Moscow was put under
martial law."[2]

[1] VOSP, II, 208.
[2] *Riech'* editorials, September 27 and October 5, 1915. Samarin, however, was
hardly a friend of Miliukov. "No matter what disguise he will assume," the Proc-

There was no hope for a *rapprochement* with the new master at the Interior. The appointment was a slap in the Bloc's face. In an interview with the press, Khvostov described the Bloc's program as "lifeless, foreign, and one which cannot be understood by the masses." He charged that "the demand for a ministry enjoying public confidence is tantamount to interference in the monarch's prerogatives." He threatened the appointed members of the upper chamber who had joined the Bloc. "If I were the chairman of the State Council," he said, "I would take pains to make it clear that persons bearing high court titles have no business belonging to any Bloc." The Right camp now had a determined and demagogic leader in the cabinet: the days of Maklakov were back with a vengeance.[3]

Krivoshein was now out of place in the cabinet and resigned in October, 1915. Miliukov regarded the move as a dismissal in disguise and wrote that "Krivoshein's dismissal is a step from unrealized conservatism to open reaction." Though he had not wanted Krivoshein as premier he had respect for the man.

> He was not a person enjoying "the confidence of the public." But neither was he a pure bureaucrat. If there were in Russia a party of intelligent conservatives, he would doubtless have all the chances of becoming its accepted leader. But his tragedy lay in the fact, which he himself admitted, that in Russia the conservatives were not intelligent, and political minds were not conservative.[4]

In November an Imperial Ukase postponed the calling of the Duma until its budget committee had finished its work. The press published the Emperor's comment on the Petrograd Town Duma's resolution demanding a government "enjoying the country's confidence." "I am confident," wrote the Emperor, "that the Petrograd Town Duma

---

urator of the Holy Synod said in the cabinet, "Miliukov will remain a revolutionary in my eyes until he justifies his pronouncements abroad" (Iakhontov, p. 104).

[3] Khvostov's interview with the press is reported in *Riech'* editorial, December 14, 1915.

[4] *Riech'* editorial, October 28, 1915. Three years later in December, 1918, when Miliukov and Krivoshein were both leaving Russia in the midst of the civil war, Krivoshein told Miliukov that "had he known me better two to three years ago he would have accepted the Premiership, and events might have taken another course." (*Dnevnik*, p. 410).

will apply all its efforts to serve Me and the country and will not be carried away by questions of state policy."[5]

It was a strange time to celebrate the tenth anniversary of the October Manifesto and of the founding of the Kadet party. The government did nothing to acknowledge the anniversary of the Manifesto. Miliukov, however, devoted a good deal of that day's *Riech'* to it. Symbolically for the times, the newspaper was full of white spaces showing the zeal of the censor. Yet Miliukov was optimistic about the future. "The Manifesto," he wrote, "pulled out the ground from under the feet of the old regime. The ten years have not been in vain." There were Kadet meetings to celebrate the party anniversary. Speaking at the Moscow banquet Miliukov was hopeful. "We have before us," he said, "a straight and open path to a brighter future, and it is possible that this future will come soon."[6]

Many in the party, however, did not share the leader's views. We have, unfortunately, only the secret police report to throw light on the party's mood. The report specifies that Miliukov's position was attacked by Mandel'shtam, Kizevetter, and Viktor Obninskii, who claimed the party was compromised by remaining in the Bloc. The real forces of the country, Miliukov's critics alleged, were outside the Bloc. The Petrograd Okhrana's report saw the Kadets divided into three groups. The right wing, led by Miliukov, wanted "to achieve a peaceful revolution behind the back, and with the sanction of, the government." It included most of the party's old leaders. There was a center wing, composed particularly of the Moscow intelligentsia, which protested against the Bloc's inclusion of the Moderate Right and demanded a ministry responsible to the Duma. Finally, a left wing, strong in the provinces, wanted the Bloc to include the socialists and stressed party activity among the masses, particularly in the rapidly growing co-operative movement.[7]

It is difficult to estimate the real state of affairs among the Kadets. There was a slight revival of party activity in connection with the anniversary, and at least one regional party conference was held in Saratov.[8] It was true that the Kadets were involved in the co-operative

---

[5] *Riech'* editorial, November 30, 1915.

[6] *Riech'*, October 17 and 19, 1915.

[7] GRABUR, pp., 65–67.

[8] *S"ezd saratovskoi oblastnoi partii K.D. 10–11 okt. 1915 g.* (Saratov, 1915); see also S. Shtern, *Desiatiletie kadetskoi partii v Odessa,* 1915).

movement, one of the few ways in which they penetrated the countryside. Already in 1912 Aleksandr Manuilov, Kadet elected member
of the State Council, had become chairman of the board of the Moscow People's Bank which financed the co-operatives. In May, 1915,
he was replaced in that position by Fedor Golovin, former Kadet
chairman of the Second Duma. Prince Shakhovskoi, an old Kadet,
was also active in the co-operatives. As for Miliukov's position in
the party, it is true that he had veered to the right, but he remained
the supreme conciliator of wings and dissensions. Under the political
conditions of 1915 he could hardly know where the mass of the party
stood. Besides, as in 1905, so again in 1915, he was the head of a
coalition and felt bound to respect his partners. This time, unlike
1905, these were all to the right of him.

II

While the Duma remained in adjournment, the Bloc continued
to meet. It elected the Octobrist Sergei Shidlovskii as chairman,
and the Centrist Pavel Krupenskii, secretary. Miliukov remained
the unofficial leader but, through these elections, gave the Octobrists
and the Center additional reasons for remaining in the fragile coalition. The Bloc's bureau met periodically in the home of V. V. Meller-
Zakomel'skii, a State Council representative. About a dozen men
were usually present; on occasion outsiders were invited for consultation. The first meeting was called for the end of October, 1915, on
the initiative of the Zemgor group, who wished to discuss future
tactics vis-à-vis the government. The guests included the Kadets
L'vov for the Zemstvo Union, Chelnokov and Nikolai Astrov for
the Union of Towns, and the Octobrist Guchkov for the Central
War Industries Committee.

Everyone present agreed that the military situation had improved;
demands for a new government seemed less urgent now. Chelnokov
and Astrov thought that "the country is in a passive mood." The Bloc
would have to "arm itself with patience, and wait." The more bellig-
erent Guchkov urged that the Duma, when recalled, should refuse
to pass the budget. Miliukov, now more cautious than the Octobrist
leader, objected that the public would not support such tactics.
Unlike his colleagues he was not worried about those who remained

outside the Bloc. "Let us not be afraid of the Left," he said. "They will respect us as long as we remain active."[9]

The work of the Duma's budget committee terminated in January, 1916; there was no further excuse not to call the legislature. Goremykin wanted to summon it for only five days. But there seemed to have been some fear of protest over such a brief session. The old Premier had finally outlived his usefulness. On January 19, 1916, he was replaced by Boris Sturmer. The Bloc had finally achieved its goal—the removal of Goremykin. But it was a false victory. Sturmer was no improvement on his predecessor. He was an insignificant and reactionary bureaucrat whom his former colleague in the Ministry of Interior, Vladimir Gurko, remembered as "a little cheat." Even the Emperor wrote of him after a few months: "He is an excellent and honest man but, it seems to me, unable to make up his mind to do what is needed."[10]

Before setting the date for the Duma session, Minister of the Interior Khvostov invited Miliukov to a meeting to inquire whether the Duma would speak about Rasputin. The intriguing monk had become the notorious hero of the hour. "I was much surprised by such a formulation of the problem," recalled Miliukov. He told Khvostov that the deputies had far weightier problems on their minds.[11] An Imperial Rescript finally summoned the Duma for February 9. At a Bloc meeting, Miliukov was hopeful about several of the Bloc's bills in the Duma, but feared their rejection by the State Council, which was not controlled by the Bloc. Only one of the Bloc's bills had become law so far, ironically enough by executive decree, namely increased pay for postal and telegraph employees. The bills on the equalization of peasant rights with those of other citizens and the bill on co-operatives remained in committee. The bills on the *volost'* zemstvo and on vacations for trade employees had

[9] BLOK, KA, LII (1932), 144–56, 163–65.

[10] For Gurko's remarks, see *ibid.*, LII, 185. This was the same Gurko whom in 1906 the Kadets had exposed as a shady dealer in government grain procurement. Now he was Miliukov's respected Bloc colleague, as a representative of the State Council. For the Emperor's remark, see his letter to the Empress of June 11, 1916, in M. Pokrovskii (ed.), *Perepiska Nikolaia i Aleksandry Romanovykh* (Moscow, 1923–27), IV, 306.

[11] PAD, VI, 323.

been rejected by the State Council. For the future Miliukov proposed
that the Duma should adopt the tactics of "a parallelism without
obligations." This meant the Duma should work in total disregard
of the incompetent government. The time had come, he thought,
for a policy of contemptuous silence, not of aggressive actions toward
the government.[12]

On February 2, a week before the Duma opening, the Bloc met
with the Zemgor leadership. The Zemgor was eager for some action
and sure that military victory could never be achieved under the
existing government. The Kadet Nikolai Kishkin, speaking for the
Union of Towns, urged that the Zemgor take over the management
of the means of communication, supply, and the relief of refugees.
He thought many army commanders, particularly generals Mikhail
Alekseev (the chief of staff under the Emperor), Nikolai Ivanov,
and Mikhail Ditrikhs would welcome this. It was the beginning of
those tactics of winning over the army command to the point of view
of the moderate opposition which would bear fruit in the February
revolution. But the meeting dispersed without agreeing on how to
put the move into effect.[13]

The Duma's opening session on February 9 held a pleasant surprise. For the first time in the history of the Russian legislature, the
Emperor made a personal appearance in the Taurida Palace. He was
acclaimed with great enthusiasm, but his speech was very brief and
quite colorless. He then shook hands with the individual party leaders:
it was the only time that he and Miliukov ever met, and not a
word passed between them. Miliukov read much more into the visit
than was evidently intended, though the Emperor's motives, and
his sudden decision to come to Petrograd, were not clear to anyone.
The reactionaries had always been pleased that the autocrat had never
deigned to visit the Duma. Now, Miliukov hoped, the Emperor would
come to value his legislature. Commenting on the visit, Miliukov
wrote: "Yesterday the defenders of the old absolutism were deprived
of one of their arguments which had seemed particularly strong."[14]

Sturmer read the Duma a weak government declaration: the points
of the Bloc's program which he mentioned were the reform of the
town administration, the introduction of zemstvos to Siberia, and

[12] BLOK, KA, LII (1932), 184–87.

[13] Ibid., LII, 187–94.

[14] Riech' editorial, February 10, 1916; see also GOL, pp. 106–7.

the volost' zemstvo bill. Speaking for the Bloc, Shidlovskii restated its entire program, ending with the now more than familiar demand for a new cabinet. It seemed that nothing had changed since July, 1915. The following day Miliukov took the floor to accuse the government of lacking patriotism.[15] The country, he said, "had come to the terrible conclusion that what is decisive for the government is not love of country but the instinct of self-preservation, a cold estimate of personal advantage." The Bloc's chief demand had been utterly perverted. "We do have a ministry enjoying confidence," he quipped, "only it is the confidence of the Union of the Russian People," the notorious reactionary organization which had come into new prominence.

The government, he alleged, continued to sow national hatred and religious intolerance. The suppressed Jewish press had not been restored, and there was a recurrence of pogroms. Nothing had been done in regard to Poland; once the area was regained by Russian troops, surely the government did not intend to reinstate its officials there? The economic situation, too, was growing more serious, with inflation ever more acute. The only forces keeping Russia out of chaos were the Zemstvo and Town Unions, which the government did its best to hinder. As in the sixteenth century, Miliukov charged, Russia was still divided into an *oprichnina* and a *zemshchina*.

> Look how in the lands of our allies, where there is no such division, they easily reached the stage of a full utilization of national energies though they too experienced a period of disorganization. But there the country's will is transformed, without hindrance, into governmental action because there the government and its agencies are an expression of the popular will. In our country the government's jealous wardship, motivated by the fear of losing power, fetters all popular energies and hinders their development.

There was no doubt in his mind that the situation was growing more somber every day. "Yesterday's visit of His Majesty," he said, "the first in the history of our constitutional institutions, should have reminded us of the seriousness of the present moment." Miliukov concluded his speech in an unusually pessimistic tone:

> I know the way out, but I do not know how to reach it. We have

[15] The Sturmer and Shidlovskii speeches are in SO, February 9, 1916, pp. 1224 and 1250 ff. Miliukov's speech is in SO, February 10, 1916, pp. 1304–23.

no means of solving this question through our own efforts, and we
are no longer willing to turn to the government. This is why I, on
the eve of what may be decisive events, am more alarmed than
ever before, and leave this platform without an answer, and
without the hope of getting one from the present cabinet.

It was a new tone for this professional optimist. His new tactics had
brought no more results than the old ones. It was a devilishly frustrating task to be a parliamentarian in a backward country fighting
an unbearably heavy war.

III

Miliukov had come to the point of admitting that only a non-
parliamentary solution of the crisis seemed possible. But, as always
since 1905, he shrank from the consequences of such an admission.
The Left Kadets were bolder; his old critic Mandel'shtam had in
October, 1915, urged the abandonment of caution and conciliation.
"Let us be frank," he had said to a Kadet gathering in Moscow,

> there are many among us who are frightened by the specter of the
> revolution . . . but these very fears should dictate to us tactics
> diametrically opposed to Miliukov's. If we do not want the forth-
> coming popular day of judgment against the criminal government
> to become disorganized, chaotic and senseless, we cannot stand
> aside from the popular movement, we cannot but try to play the
> leading role in it.[16]

A demand must have been made for a discussion of the issues, for
in February, 1916, the Kadets called a party congress in Petrograd,
to which representatives of twenty-eight party organizations came.
This first Kadet congress since 1907 was to give the leadership an
approximate estimate of party feelings about Miliukov's wartime
tactics.[17]

Mandel'shtam led the attack against the leader. "The tactics of
the right wing Kadets, led by Miliukov," he was reported as saying,

> threaten to hopelessly compromise the party not only in the broad
> democratic circles of the population, but also in the eyes of the

[16] His speech was reported by the Okhrana; see GRAKLAS, p. 310.

[17] No printed account of the congress appeared. We must, therefore, use the
Okhrana reports printed in GRAKLAS, pp. 310–13, and GRABUR, pp. 73–75.

liberal intelligentsia. . . . It is said of Miliukov that his tactics are leading the party to a dead end, into a swamp, transforming it into something close to the Octobrists. Miliukov's cardinal error consists in the fact that he is absolutely ignorant of, and unwilling to get acquainted with and take into account the mood of his party's broad circles. He sees only the Duma Kadet fraction, persons completely immersed in the Petrograd atmosphere, and he judges all Russia by them.[18]

It was, unfortunately, quite true that Miliukov breathed only the Petrograd Duma atmosphere and was not in touch with the country at large. What was worse, he was now about to go abroad again and would spend several months in Western Europe. He was sure, as we shall see presently, that he already knew Russia's convictions about the war, and he continued to be blinded by this preconception.

There were a large number of men at the congress who agreed with Mandel'shtam. Of the eighty-seven delegates forty-six voted for his *rapprochement* with the Left, with twenty-seven opposed and fourteen abstentions. The opposition forced the adoption of two resolutions incorporating its demands. The first stated that "even in the temporary coalition of the Progressive Bloc the party must ceaselessly defend the interests of the popular masses and the equality of nationalities and, as far as possible, must keep in contact with the other democratic parties." Another resolution urged that "the Central Committee be instructed to work out a plan organizing party branches throughout the country and put it into immediate effect."[19]

We lack the text of Miliukov's answer to his critics, but we do have Okhrana reports on his views in February, 1916. The tenor of his urgings was always the same: let us not rock the boat while we are at war. Once we win it we shall be masters of the situation, for the government will be able to do nothing without us at the peace conference and the negotiations with our allies. To try arousing the country now would only help the government. "For God's sake," Miliukov told the Kadet fraction,

> do not get caught in the government's provocation; working with all its power for a separate peace with Germany the government is trying to provoke troubles in the country. Such troubles would give

[18] GRAKLAS, p. 311.
[19] *Riech'*, February 23, 1916.

it a free hand. Blaming the growth of the revolutionary movement
in Russia the government would have an excuse before the Allies
for terminating the war, and it would blame the defeat on the
revolutionary and opposition circles. . . . . All we can do now is to
patiently tolerate everything, swallow the most horrible pills, not
sharpen but, on the contrary, hold back the boiling mood, all this
because with the imminent day of reckoning the government's
position will be hopeless, and Russian liberalism's victory complete
and unquestioned.[20]

Miliukov seemed to believe the rumors that the government con-
templated taking Russia out of the war.[21] It was a widely held belief
at that time, and Miliukov was to exploit it in his Duma speeches
henceforth. For his part he never doubted a Russian victory as part
of an Allied triumph. This, in turn, would put control in the Duma's
hands. Never again, Miliukov believed, would Europe lend money
to a Russian government without certain conditions:

> A reactionary government, not responsible to the Duma and not
> enjoying the country's confidence will get no money after the war
> from either France or England. . . . The liquidation of the war will
> demand colossal sums which may be obtained only through foreign
> loans. And it is thus, through the State Duma, that Russian liber-
> alism will reach its goals, and that our victory is assured. Without
> the State Duma and while in conflict with it the government will
> not get a kopeck abroad.[22]

Evidently, Miliukov's calm reasoning convinced the aroused delegates, for the great majority (seventy-three of the eighty-seven delegates) voted for further participation in the Bloc. The published
statement of the congress to the country was couched in optimistic
tones:

> The sixth congress of the Party of Popular Freedom . . . renews
> that appeal to unity, cheerfulness and faith in victory which the
> Party's Central Committee addressed to the country in the very
> beginning of the war. . . . And, together with national victory over

[20] GRAKLAS, p. 301.
[21] I cannot go into detail on this theme; Sergei Mel'gunov's *Legenda o separatnom mire* (Paris, 1957) is a careful study of it.
[22] GRABUR, p. 80; italics in the original.

the enemy, let there come an hour of internal renewal, an hour of a general triumph of freedom and law.[23]

The congress happened to coincide with the tenth anniversary of *Riech'*—another cause for optimism in the bleak conditions of war and reaction. Miliukov used the occasion to strike another note of hope:

> Ten years in the life of a Russian progressive newspaper [he wrote] is not a common feature of our public life. . . . We are now entering a period resembling, to a certain degree, the time which gave birth to our newspaper. . . . Our sole desire consists in this: that we should be able to serve our old cause even on the eve of our new reconstruction, hopefully with even greater practical success.[24]

Miliukov then took his "moderation till victory" tactics to Moscow, where the Zemgor were holding their national congresses in early March. The two Unions, like the Kadet party, had left wings which urged more radical tactics vis-à-vis the government.[25] The Union of Towns was about to pass certain radical resolutions which Miliukov opposed since they might serve as "a spark which will ignite a great conflagration." At a Zemgor banquet Miliukov made some positive commitments for the postwar period. Turning to the representative of Finland, he pledged that Russian society would return to Finland all that the Russian government had taken away. Then speaking to his old Polish friend Lednitskii he said, to the loud applause of the hall: "The Russian public will know how to keep its promises. These promises represent not bits of paper as they do for the government, not empty words, but a sacred debt of honor."[26] It sounded like the banquets of 1904-5.

In the Zemgor, at banquets, and at his party's congress, Miliukov was out of touch with the real Left for whom his tactics were not

[23] *Riech'*, February 24, 1916. *Riech'* also reported the election of a new Central Committee with representatives from the South, the Volga Region, the Baltic, and the Caucasus—a broader spectrum than the old committee which was almost entirely of persons from the two capitals. The paper, unfortunately, did not list the members of the new committee.

[24] *Riech'* editorial, February 23, 1916.

[25] GRABUR, pp. 94-95.

[26] *Ibid.*, pp. 90, 93.

merely a mistake but proof that "the bourgeoisie" was "counter-revolutionary." In the Duma the Social Democrats left no doubt of that; their spokesman, Chkhenkeli, spoke more brutally than Mandel'shtam. "He was the first," said Chkhenkeli of Miliukov, "of the Opposition ranks to make a speech of a clearly counterrevolutionary hue when the country had not yet pronounced the word revolution. Never, perhaps, did a political leader descend to such blindness for the sake of a temporary parliamentary combination." It was a note to be sounded more and more often against Miliukov from the Left, until it would travel from the Duma tribune to the streets in 1917. And the Kadet leader justified this growing reputation by answering Chkhenkeli in the most conservative terms he had yet used in the Duma. "Gentlemen," he told the deputies,

> I cannot be sure that the government will lead us to defeat. We are afraid of it and wish to prevent it. But I know that a revolution in Russia will, without fail, lead us to defeat, and no wonder our enemy so desires it. Were I told that organizing Russia for victory meant organizing it for revolution I would say: better leave her, for the duration of the war, as she was, unorganized.[27]

It was a speech that the Left would never let him forget; they would taunt him with it all through 1917.

Speaking about strikes in the Duma three days later, Miliukov admitted that, for him, the workers and their world were a mystery. "We know each other too little," he conceded, "and speak too rarely to each other, and when we must communicate we discover that we speak in different languages." But the workers' economic demands could still be met, he was sure, "if labor mediation were organized as it is in any civilized country, that is with the help of conciliation boards." The government needed more power to deal with industry and with obstinate employers. "The ministers of our allies," he said, "have more systematic and wider rights. Lloyd George can sequestrate a plant, and can also fix wages and limit profits." But even more important was to make the workers realize what an important part they played in the country's defense. The antiwar agitation beginning

---

[27] Chkhenkeli's speech is in SO, March 4, 1916, pp. 2737–48, Miliukov's in ibid., 1916, pp. 2795–2814.

to sound in Russia's factories would die down if matters were properly explained:

> Tell the workers, tell them as Lloyd George does in England. Speak as did this English minister when he was convincing the workers that shells are needed to reduce the loss of human lives. . . . These, gentlemen, are the arguments which will reach the minds and hearts of those who hold the so-called defensist views.[28]

Miliukov was impatient with the Left accusations that Russia's continued war effort was being made only in the name of imperialism, for the annexationist goal of the Straits. In his view, expressed in a Kadet brochure, Russia was not guilty of the imperialist sin:

> For a contemporary state, called upon to live and develop in an epoch when the old "continentalism" has finally passed away, the possession of the open sea is the most vital and organic need. The acquisition of the Straits represents the completion of the state's organic growth, and not the initiation of "imperialism"; it is the end of a centuries-old historical process, not the beginning of anything new.[29]

The allies' "sympathetic attitude" had in fact already produced the secret Straits Agreement between Russia, France, and England of March, 1915, granting the Straits as a war prize to Russia.[30] It fell to Miliukov to make the first Russian public announcement of it in a Duma speech of March 11, 1916. The secret treaty had first been mentioned by the English journalist, Emile Dillon, in a *Fortnightly Review* article of February, 1916. Miliukov wished to put the Duma on record as a participant in the pressure for the agreement, even if only by its expression of Russian "public opinion." He reminded the Duma of the speech in January, 1915, in which he had first discussed the Straits. As he made his references, Miliukov must have, at least in a small way and for the first time, felt himself the maker of, rather than a mere commentator on, foreign policy:

> What constitutes our Russian interest in the war? The Duma . . . announced it to the world in its January session, and its voice was heard—we need an outlet to the open sea. We did not begin

[28] SO, March 7, 1916, pp. 2859–70.
[29] TAK, pp. 7–8.
[30] For an analysis of the Straits Agreement of March, 1915, see SM II, 185–272.

the war for that. But we began it, and without this we cannot end it. Our Russian interest in this war requires the annexation of the Straits. . . . The beginning of April 1915 New Style is the date which deserves to be known to our broad masses, so that they might know what they are fighting for. That is the date of a definite agreement on the Straits between us and our allies. A not inconsiderable share of the success of this agreement belongs to you, gentlemen.[31]

Miliukov's speech did not pass unnoticed in England. Sir Edward Grey was asked about it in the House of Commons and gave, according to the Russian ambassador in London, "an evasive reply." Before something would be said publicly of the agreement, the ambassador wrote Sazonov, the French would have to consent and the Italians would have to be informed—they had not signed the agreement. The allies would also have to consider what impression the announcement might make on neutral Rumania.[32]

It was Miliukov's conviction that, once Russia's chief war aim was publicly announced, all Russians would support the war to its victorious conclusion. He told the Duma that the enemy was close to exhaustion: "The highest development of his potential has already been reached—ours, and that of our allies, is still in the future." Therefore, he warned amidst the loud applause of all benches, there must be no talk of a separate peace. "Gentlemen," he added, "your expression of agreement indicates that, in formulating my thoughts, I was expressing those which unite all of us." It was, as the near future was to show, a false unanimity. And Miliukov knew that there were many, even among the allies, who had yet to agree to granting Russia the Straits. He told the Duma, therefore, that the planned Russian parliamentary delegation to Western Europe was a necessary step toward "consultations in regard to joint policies." The delegation was to leave in April, 1916, and visit England, France, and Italy.[33]

IV

It was Miliukov's second participation in a Duma delegation to Western Europe. As in 1909 his action was attacked by the Left as

[31] The text of this speech is in SO, March 11, 1916, pp. 3237–61.

[32] Benkendorf to Sazonov about his conversation with Grey of March 24, 1916, KONST, I, 412–14. The Agreement was announced publicly only in November, 1916.

[33] SO, March 11, 1916, loc. cit.

giving aid and comfort to the enemy—the government; the conservatives welcomed his presence as proof of the opposition's basic loyalty to Russia. The Trudoviks and Social Democrats, though asked to participate (they had been ignored in 1909), declined to go along. The delegation included six members of the State Council and ten Duma deputies. Of these sixteen, four were Kadets, and a total of nine belonged to the Progressive Bloc. The delegation's chairman was Aleksandr Protopopov, an Octobrist deputy chairman of the Duma. This strange figure, soon to become the Empire's last Minister of Interior, enjoyed a dubious reputation. The Russian ambassador in London said of him, "C'est un imbecile." "On the other hand," the Russian chargé d'affaires in London, Konstantin Nabokov, recalled that "such men as Miliukov, Shingarev, and other prominent leaders of the Duma gave the Delegation the necessary weight and dignity."[34]

For Miliukov it was, undoubtedly, his most glamorous appearance in Western Europe, a splendid dress rehearsal for the future Russian foreign minister. During his two months abroad he was received by the kings of Norway, England, and Italy, and the president of the French Republic. He spoke with the premiers of England, France, and Italy, with their foreign ministers, and with numerous cabinet ministers. He was the guest of the parliaments in each respective country. He talked to the leaders of the Russian emigration and to the socialists of Western Europe. It was a chance to renew that first-hand contact with Europe to which he had been accustomed before the war.

It was the British who, as in 1909, had taken the initiative in inviting the delegation. They hoped to reassure their public that the Russian ally would remain faithful to the common cause. Nabokov asserted that:

> the object of the deputation was to reaffirm to the governments and the public opinion in the Allied countries that in the matter of pursuing the war to a successful conclusion all parties were at one in Russia. . . . The Delegation undoubtedly served the useful purpose of fostering the faith of Great Britain in Russia's will to win.

Baron Roman Rosen, a member of the delegation representing the State Council, thought there was another reason for the invitation:

[34] K. Nabokov, *Ordeal of a Diplomat* (London, 1921), pp. 53–54.

I also believe that the object of the invitations extended to the delegates from our Legislative Chambers was to impress them with the colossal extent of the preparations being made in Allied countries for the effective continuation of the war, in the hope that by their reports and influence they would counteract the suspected pacifist tendencies of the Government, and encourage it to increasing efforts and activity in the conduct of the war.[35]

The delegation was picked up by the British cruiser "Donegal" in Norway and escorted by a convoy to Scotland. The trip took place at the height of the German submarine campaign, and "the Lords," as Miliukov called the members of the State Council, were frightened by the secrecy and the precautions. But there were no incidents, and the Russians even caught a glimpse of the British fleet at Scapa Flow. A royal train took them to London, where the visit began. It was, wrote Nabokov, a favorable moment to arrive:

Russia, as I have already mentioned, was at the zenith of her popularity in England. The Delegation, therefore, was accorded a very warm welcome. It fell to my lot to accompany the Delegation in its journeys in Great Britain, and to witness the exceptional kindness with which it was surrounded, and the interest it evoked.[36]

At a government dinner for the delegation Premier Herbert Asquith made, according to the Times, "a pointed reference" to the "complete agreement which has been established between the British and the Russian Governments in regard to Eastern affairs." The Times added editorially that "few statements of more significance have been made since the war began. . . . The visit of the eminent representatives of the Council of the Russian Empire and of the Duma could hardly have been more auspiciously inaugurated."[37]

Miliukov spoke at a reception of the Lord Mayor of London where he limited himself to more general sentiments. "They came to England," he said of the delegation,[38]

representing divergent political views and parties, but they were now united by the sacred bond of national safety, and by the

---

[35] Ibid., pp. 47–48; R. Rosen, Forty Years of Diplomacy (London, 1922) II, 217–18.

[36] Nabokov, op. cit., p. 53.

[37] Times editorial, May 11, 1916, p. 9.

[38] Ibid., May 10, 1916, p. 5.

necessities of national defense. . . . They were more than ever convinced that they were in the right when they found Great Britain
on their side. (Cheers.) . . . We Russians are ready to endure and,
together with you, our Allies, we look forward to a victorious con-
summation which will mark a decisive stage in the advance of
civilized humanity. (Loud cheers.)

During the following days, he saw Lloyd George, who arranged a
visit to a munitions plant and impressed Miliukov as "the coming
man." Miliukov the historian had a chance to address the Russia
Company, a trading corporation dating back to Richard Chancellor's
discovery of Archangel. The old port had, once again, become important for shipping. "The work of the Russia Company," Miliukov told
the traders,

> far from being lost, now brought new fruit. English merchantmen
> once more opened Europe to them [the Russians] by the only out-
> let left free. This concatenation of events was most significant and
> almost symbolical. But I want Englishmen of trade and commerce
> to do more than establish their ancient predominance on the
> northern route to Europe. We want them to win in this great
> battle of trade and commerce against German supremacy. . . . You
> must begin now, without waiting for the end of the war.[39]

After a country weekend and a little excursion into history Miliukov
had a taste of high diplomacy in his long interview with British
Foreign Secretary Sir Edward Grey:

> Sir Edward Grey, particularly, impressed me by the extraordinary
> care with which he handled the sphere of Russian interests. In
> reply to any question Grey always told me: this is Russia's affair,
> let Russia tell me about this, and all Russia's interests will be taken
> into consideration; we shall never conclude an agreement which
> would contradict Russia's interests.[40]

Whether the subject touched upon the Straits, Armenia, Poland,
Bulgaria, Rumania, or the dismemberment of Austria-Hungary, Grey
proved to be most understanding.

In Paris the French turned out to be less co-operative in regard

[39] *Times*, May 15, 1916, p. 5.
[40] "Russkaia parliamentskaia delegatsiia zagranitsei v 1916 g.," KA, LVIII
(1933), 8; cited below as "Russkaia Delegatsiia." Miliukov's account of the interview is in "Dnevnik Londòn," pp. 43–48, and VOSP, II, 243–48.

to the Straits. Many French Socialists were opposed to the issue, which smacked of imperialism and would unnecessarily prolong the war. Since Italy had not officially been informed of the Straits Agreement nothing should be said in public about it. As Russian Ambassador to Paris Izvolsky telegraphed Sazonov:

> They were somewhat embarrassed at the Quai d'Orsay that Miliukov, in an interview with *l'Oeuvre*, gave the exact date of the agreement on the Straits. The newspaper was confiscated in view of the difficulties with Italy. On the other hand our parliamentarians' declaration on the attitude of all layers of the Russian people to the question of Constantinople and the Straits can have the most beneficial influence on public opinion here.

Tsarist diplomacy now found Miliukov useful, quite unlike his performance in Europe at the time of the First Duma. Another Izvolsky dispatch said that the visit "made a strong and very useful impression on the local extremist circles."[41]

After a few days in neutral Switzerland the delegation arrived in Italy. Miliukov, the only delegate who spoke Italian, obviously enjoyed himself hugely. It was a very different visit from that of his student days when he had come, almost penniless, to visit the great museums. Now he was feted with banner headlines, addressed the Italian chamber of deputies, sat next to the King at a lunch on the front, and, finally, addressed the Roman populace from a balcony on the Capitol. The glow of that memory was still warm in his old age.[42]

> Italy is the country of inspiration, and I was inspired again, and improvised a speech. I was most proud of my Russian associations: on the same spot where, thirty-five years earlier I, an unknown student, had been held by museum guards on the suspicion of possible theft, I now spoke, as a representative of my country, from the Capitol to the people of Rome—only a step from the statue of Marcus Aurelius, and next to that same museum.

Speaking to the press after his return to Petrograd, Miliukov described three features of allied public opinion he had observed. First, there was "a unanimous determination to bring the war to a victorious end." Second, "the ideology of the war" was shared by

[41] KONST, I, 344; dispatch of May 12, 1916.
Ibid., I, 304; dispatch of December 16, 1916.
[42] VOSP, II, 255.

all. Third, all in the West were "ready to support Russia's national aspirations in the war."[43] It was a misrepresentation of the actual state of affairs. He gave a closed session of the Duma's Defense Committee a more realistic picture, though his conclusions remained too rosy. He recounted how the delegation had failed to have the Straits Agreement published. He admitted that "some French circles" opposed the Agreement "since it might prolong the war, and was not one of the reasons for it, or one of its aims."[44] The delegation, he thought, had succeeded in proving that all Russians wanted the Straits:

> We considered it essential to use all our efforts during our visit to the allied countries to show particularly the left-oriented public that all of Russian public opinion, with few exceptions, holds the point of view of a national solution of the chief and most important question for Russia. It is my impression that our efforts produced a certain effect.

The "few exceptions" in Russia had their counterpart abroad where, in Miliukov's opinion, the antiwar sentiment was equally negligible:

> I had occasion to speak with the most left and extreme circles in the allied parliaments, and it is my general impression that, at present, they themselves admit that they are completely powerless, and deprived of any possibility of influencing the general popular mood which is fully unanimous, and decisive. But of course one cannot close one's eyes to the possibility that the mood, now weak, may, in the future, become strengthened.

In less than a year that "weak mood" was to grow to unprecedented proportions, as Miliukov would find out to his own peril. But, for the time being, he assured the Duma that its delegation had accomplished its task:

> Gentlemen, I must say—perhaps some of you will be surprised by this—but I must say that they trust the Progressive Bloc abroad. (Voices from the left: "Unfortunately." Laughter.) There they not only understand the importance of the Progressive Bloc . . . but also invest it with some of those hopes that had earlier been bestowed on the Russian Opposition. By its defense of this par-

[43] Riech', June 18, 1916.
[44] Miliukov's speech to a closed session of the Duma's Defense Committee of June 19, 1916, is in "Russkaia Delegatsiia," pp. 3–23.

liamentary combination the Opposition lent its credit to those parts of the parliamentary bloc which had not enjoyed this credit earlier.

Hoping that the Left might be persuaded to join the Bloc, he told his audience that some of the leaders of the Russian emigration would approve:

> In Rome I spoke with a prominent representative of our emigration, Plekhanov, and I must state that the Progressive Bloc's policy has the full support of this leading Social Democrat. I heard the same from Kropotkin whom I visited in the South of England. I was also visited by representatives of former Socialist Revolutionaries now working in the newspaper *Prizyv* who also support the policy and tactics of the Duma's majority.

All this gave Miliukov the false hope that "we may build friendly relations with the dissenters in our own midst."

Dining with the French ambassador a few days later, Miliukov was, in private, more realistic about the Left's attitude toward the Bloc. He told Paléologue of the risk his tactics presented:

> As for a strike against the Duma I do not doubt that Stürmer and his band think of it. But we will not give him the opportunity, or even a pretext. We are resolved to respond to no provocation, and to oppose him only with wisdom and patience. We shall see after the war. But these tactics have one great disadvantage for us: because of them we are accused of timidity by the liberal circles, and they may lose us, bit by bit, all contact with the masses, who will follow the violent men.

Paléologue "congratulated my guests on such patriotic behavior" but recorded Miliukov's fear in regard to economic conditions in Russia: "We would have to expect serious trouble if there should be a famine," Miliukov told the ambassador. "On this point I am not without apprehension in regard to next winter." The near future would show that Miliukov's fears were only too justified.[45]

For the time being, however, the Duma was in summer recess, and

---

[45] Miliukov's comments to Paléologue are in PAL, III, 310–11. The ambassador added that Miliukov and his colleagues, when in Paris, had "added a reproach in my regard—a reproach that I did not frequent liberal circles sufficiently, that I did not show them my sympathy openly enough, finally that I did not exploit my friendly relations with the Emperor to convert him to parliamentarism" (*ibid.*, III, p. 25). Miliukov, however, said nothing of this to Paléologue directly, nor

Miliukov went abroad again. The indefatigable Pares had arranged that Miliukov, Struve, Roman Dmowski, A. S. Lappo-Danilevskii, and Harold Williams should speak at a Cambridge summer session. Miliukov had once observed a Cambridge summer session as a young *Privatdocent* in the 1890's; this time he was to be one of its chief attractions. He was to speak about Russian parliamentarism, and about the Balkans. All the causes dear to his heart—university and public education, Russian politics, the Balkans, Anglo-Russian co-operation, were here united. He even received a Cambridge doctorate. An honorary degree, it was, nevertheless, that doctorate which his Moscow alma mater had never bestowed upon him. At a banquet in his honor the chief speaker was his former teacher, now Sir Paul Vinogradoff. It was a moving and encouraging experience.[46]

In his lecture on the Balkans Miliukov naturally touched upon the Russian demand for the Straits and Constantinople. He had a new argument against the Turks. Quoting from Edward Freeman's *The Ottoman Power in Europe* he implied that Russia was better qualified to hold Constantinople than the non-European Turks: "The presence of the Turk in Europe," Freeman had written, "is incidental. They remain at the end of five hundred years as much strangers as they were at the beginning. European ideas and words, like 'nation,' 'government,' 'law,' 'sovereign,' 'subject,' do not apply to them."[47] The Russians, Miliukov implied, knew what these terms meant. And yet he was forced to complain to his English listeners about the shortcomings, in Russia, of the one European institution he knew best— the Russian parliament. "It is no use," he said,

carrying through the Duma sweeping orders of the day expressing

---

does he mention it anywhere in his writings. Paléologue's assertion is seconded by George Louis, French ambassador to Russia in 1909–13, in the second volume of his *Carnets* (Paris, 1926, pp. 242–44), where he records that several unnamed Duma members asked for Paléologue's recall in 1916. Paléologue doubtless knew the fate of another predecessor of his, Maurice Bompard, recalled at Russia's insistence in 1908 because a police report submitted to the Emperor stated that he had dined with Miliukov in a St. Petersburg restaurant. Bompard denied this to Izvolsky, and the Russian Foreign Minister believed him, but Bompard was recalled nevertheless. See his *Mon Ambassade en Russia, 1903–1908* (Paris, 1937), p. 286. In a review of the book, Miliukov corroborated Bompard's denial; see *Russkiia Zapiski* (Paris), October, 1938, pp. 205–7.

[46] Miliukov's account is in VOSP, II, 267–71.

[47] BALK, pp. 12–13.

strong disapproval perhaps of the whole administration. The Cabinet is not responsible to the elected Chamber. The question of ministerial responsibility is, I might say, the most delicate, and the most burning question of the present day in Russia.[48]

But Russia would overcome these difficulties, of this he was sure, and he predicted this victory a mere six months before it was to occur:

Lord Robert Cecil told you in his inaugural address at this Summer Meeting that British political conceptions of freedom and justice appealed to Russian ideas. Well, I am here to witness that they do appeal to the Russian representative assembly. . . . Permit me again to quote the words of Lord Robert Cecil: "It may be truly said that freedom is as much admired in Russia as in England." Yes, ladies and gentlemen, it may be truly said that we worship freedom, we are worthy of freedom, we shall have freedom.[49]

Miliukov saw many political figures in Western Europe. On the way to England he stopped in Christiania, where he was received by King Haakon. He asked Haakon why the other crowned heads of Europe did not warn the Russian Emperor of the dangers inherent in his domestic policies. The King replied that such attempts had been made, and that another exchange of views was to take place in the future. In London Miliukov found Ambassador Benkendorf most concerned about Russia's foreign relations. The British no longer trusted him with political secrets since they suspected Sturmer, who had become the new Russian foreign minister. Sazonov had been removed from office in early July. Regretting the move, Miliukov had written:

The actions of Russian diplomacy, led by him [Sazonov] did not, by any means, meet with our approval on all occasions. But of one thing there is no doubt: Sazonov correctly conducted the chief line of policy which was needed for the securing of our international interests, the line of a *rapprochement* with the Entente.[50]

Thus disappeared from the cabinet the man whom the Empress, in a letter to the Emperor, described quite incorrectly as "Miliukov's bosom friend."[51]

[48] REP, p. 42.
[49] Ibid., 46.
[50] *Riech'* editorial, July 10, 1916.
[51] Aleksandra Feodorovna, *Letters of the Tsaritsa to the Tsar* (London, 1923), p. 460.

While abroad Miliukov observed the impact of this change of Russian foreign ministers on Allied opinion. He was collecting evidence for his famous "Stupidity or Treason?" speech which he would make at the opening of the Duma's autumn session. Izvolsky told him in Paris of the attempt by Sturmer's assistant Ivan Manasevich-Manuilov to bribe *Novoe Vremia* with German money. Russian émigrés in Lausanne gave Miliukov information purporting to prove that the Russian government was negotiating for a separate peace with Germany.[52] Having gathered all the "incriminating" data, Miliukov returned to Russia just before the appointment of one of the last grave diggers of the old regime, the new Minister of the Interior Protopopov, who took office in September, 1916.

VI

Protopopov's appointment as the old regime's last Minister of the Interior was full of irony. A naïve observer might have interpreted it as a concession to the Bloc. Was not the Octobrist Protopopov a member of the Bloc, and had he not been the leader of the Duma's delegation to the allies? These surface appearances turned out to be quite misleading. Miliukov pointed out that:

> Protopopov did not consider it necessary to ascertain the Bloc's opinion prior to his appointment. He has evidently not yet thought about his attitude toward the Bloc's program. Under these conditions it is self-evident that the Bloc too cannot consider itself bound by the decision of its member.

The new minister had no program. "He announced," Miliukov commented, "that a program depended on the entire cabinet, and that to the extent that it was a program of his ministry he had not yet received instructions to direct him." The government's procedures never ceased to amaze Miliukov. "It is strange," he added, "that a program is being determined not before the acceptance of a post, but *after*. One would have thought that the opposite would have been the normal procedure."[53] The new minister's actions spoke louder than words. Immediately after his appointment he ordered the police to attend all closed meetings of the Zemgor. Miliukov described the move as an obvious worsening of the political situation and a sign

[52] VOSP, II, 270.
[53] *Riech'* editorial, September 19, 1916; italics in the original.

of the government's increasing distrust of the public.[54] A meeting
between Protopopov and members of the Bloc made it clear that
only the worst could be expected in the future. When Protopopov
complained that he had expected friendly treatment from Miliukov
after their joint trip abroad, the latter exclaimed: "A man who works
with Sturmer, who freed Sukhomlinov, and who persecutes the press
and the public organizations cannot be our friend. They say your appointment was brought about by Rasputin." For his part Protopopov
informed the group that as deputy chairman of the Duma "I consider
myself non-party, and thus do not count myself as a member of the
Bloc." Miliukov replied that he was only too pleased to hear this.
Though Protopopov offered to legalize the Kadet party (to which
Miliukov made no reply), the meeting ended on a totally negative
note. Miliukov told the Minister: "You are leading Russia to ruin";
the latter stated that the meeting had been his "last attempt at a
compromise with the Bloc."[55]

The government, it was clear, was only getting worse, and so were
economic conditions. Food was becoming scarce, and prices rose. The
provisioning crisis which Miliukov had feared in his discussion with
Paléologue was approaching. "The coming autumn and winter,"
wrote Riech' in September, "will be more difficult than all that we
have lived through so far."[56] The Kadets had proposed several measures to deal with the crisis. They suggested the use of ration cards
for the large cities months before the system was adopted. They
demanded fixed prices for food, shoes and clothes, soap, and kerosene.
They proposed strict measures against speculators, and the transfer
of provisioning to the Zemgor organizations.[57] But the authorities
stalled, and the public mood grew uglier by the week. During a visit
to Moscow, Miliukov was shocked to notice the changes that had
come over the city. He told his Duma colleagues on his return to
Petrograd:

> I have known Moscow for several decades, but if someone had
> told me twenty years ago that Moscow's mood would undergo such
> a metamorphosis I would have taken it for a silly joke. The most

[54] PAD, VI, 342.
[55] An account of the meeting is in A. Shliapnikov, Kanun semnadtsatogo goda (Moscow, 1920), II, 89–91.
[56] Riech' editorial, September 11, 1916.
[57] See Riech' for May 14, August 31, October 18 and 19, 1916, for details.

inert and ignorant circles have begun to speak in the language of irreconcilable revolutionaries. . . . One begins to fear for tomorrow, since we well remember what the Moscow lower depths are capable of when driven to despair and fury.[58]

Miliukov was still under the impact of his Moscow experience when he attended the regular autumn Kadet conference in Petrograd, October 22–24, 1916. Riech' published only a slight account of the proceedings, but the Okhrana reported that Miliukov faced strong opposition.[59] "There is no question," Miliukov was reported as having said,

> that after the war we must expect a terrible popular upheaval. . . . In its struggle with this upheaval the government will find itself in a vacuum—it will have no one to lean on. . . . In the ultimate moment, frightened, it will grasp for us, and it will then be our task not to destroy the government, which would only aid anarchy, but to instill a completely different content into it, that is to build a genuine constitutional order. That is why, in our struggle with the government, despite everything, we must retain a sense of proportion. The popular mind is anyhow close to anarchism. . . . To support anarchy in the name of the struggle with the government would mean to risk all the political conquests which we have made since 1905.

Miliukov foresaw that, as in 1905, the Kadets would be the natural successors to a reactionary government. But they must remain constitutionalists at all costs and wait for the end of the war.

The population, however, could not be counted on to display similar patience. Delegates from the provinces reported that people of all strata were tired of the war, exasperated with the food shortages and high prices, and critical of any further passivity toward the government. The party's left wing demanded radical measures. Prince Paul Dolgorukov described the outcome of the conference as follows:

> Finally, as always, Miliukov succeeded in defeating his opponents, and made them follow him. But this was accomplished only after a prolonged and heated struggle. The conference showed that

[58] GRABUR, pp. 142–43.
[59] See the Okhrana report on the conference in ibid., pp. 145–48. There is also material on the Kadets in "Politicheskoe polozhenie Rossii nakanune fevral'skoi revoliutsii v zhandarmskom osveshchenii," KA, IV (1926), 3–35 passim.

the party's left wing is growing constantly stronger. . . . The provincial delegates accused Miliukov that, while continuing to travel abroad, he is badly informed about the mood of the Russian public. . . . Miliukov sees the center of attention in the parliamentary struggle with the government, the "provincials" insist on shifting the center of attention to the organization of the masses, to a *rapprochement* with political groups to the left.

Miliukov, "as always," won out in the end among his own, but the accusations leveled against him were revealing. His astonishment at Moscow's mood could only be the result of insufficient acquaintance with Russian public opinion. His trips to Western Europe had only made worse a situation which was probably inherent in Miliukov's approach to Russian politics.

Still he must have been pleased with delegates' reports that the army was behind the Duma and that the officers' corps sympathized with its struggle against the government. It was a factor which would prove vitally important in the February revolution. In their slim published resolutions the Kadets spoke of the need for "maintaining contact with the broad masses of the population, and the organization of the country's democratic elements in order to resist the common danger." The left wing had quite clearly something to do with this resolution. It called for "joint discussion by all interested circles, that is the zemstvos, town unions, co-operatives, workers' groups, industrial and business organizations, with the full and active participation of party figures." Provisioning was to be the chief issue of these discussions. In a foreign policy gesture the conference sent a telegram to the British ambassador asking him to "transmit to our English allies the most profound respect of the Kadet party conference." "I am deeply touched," answered Buchanan, "I consider the Anglo-Russian alliance as the surest guarantee of world peace."[60]

All attention now turned to the forthcoming Duma session which was to open November 1, 1916. The Bloc Bureau met to plan strategy. Miliukov proposed to concentrate the attack on Sturmer. The Bloc discussed a declaration for the Duma's opening. Miliukov's text was watered down by his colleagues. Instead of accusing Sturmer of treason, as Miliukov was to do, they said of his foreign policy (he was rumored to be negotiating for a separate peace with Germany):

---

[60] *Riech'*, October 27, 1916.

"The country is deprived of judging whether this is happening because of ignorance and inability, or is based on a secret intrigue." The Bloc also deleted Miliukov's conclusion, which read: "Only having taken all the measures at its command will the Duma feel free to disclaim responsibility for a national catastrophe which it foresaw, and against which it warned." Miliukov regarded the declaration as "an overture to general action," whatever that might mean.[61] If it accomplished nothing the Bloc should disperse.

Though the declaration was to remain secret until the Duma opening, it became known to the government through Pavel Krupenskii, leader of the Center, who was found to have been a government agent in the Bloc. It was a measure of the compromises being made by Miliukov during these years that he collaborated with a man whom he had called, as early as 1912, "the well-known government agent in the Third Duma, P. N. Krupenskii."[62]

The Bloc suffered another blow: the Progressives withdrew from it. As they put it: "The Progressive fraction considers that if, in response to the experiences that Russia underwent in these last years, it has moved to the left, it is not its fault if the Kadet fraction has found itself on its right." Miliukov remained unconvinced: "The withdrawal of the Progressives from the Bloc," he wrote, "would be understandable if it became clear that the Duma's right wing, and its center, were incapable of rising to the level of thinking and attitude of the country." But, he observed, even such conservative organizations as the Council of the United Nobility were now highly critical of the regime and demanded a new government.[63]

In preparation for the Duma's reopening, Sturmer informed the Emperor of the Bloc's critical declaration and suggested that the Duma might have to be dissolved. Rodzianko, too, was concerned when he heard of Miliukov's planned attack on the government and warned him not to mention "certain persons." Miliukov was to disregard this suggestion in unprecedented fashion. He had decided on

[61] Miliukov's notes on the Bloc's meetings in October, 1916, are in BLOK, KA, LVI (1933), 82–117. Miliukov's entries are in the nature of abbreviated statements and summaries and are not a full stenographic account.

[62] PAD, VI, 91–92; Riech' editorial, November 1, 1916; Riech', November 5, 1912.

[63] Zapiska fraktsii progressistov ob vozniknovnenii progressivnogo bloka (mimeographed; Petrograd, 1915), p. 14; Riech' editorial, November 1, 1916; Riech', October 31, 1916.

his "stupidity or treason" formula as the keynote of his accusations. These "winged words" were to fly all over Russia.[64]

VII

The Duma was in an ugly mood on November 1, 1916. As Sturmer testified after the revolution, "the anger [in the chamber] was such that I could not even think of taking the floor." The cabinet attended only the State Council opening, thus avoiding having to listen to the Duma's accusations. The usual decorum was no longer preserved. Kerensky was deprived of the floor for pointing to the empty government benches and calling the ministers "traitors to the interests of the country." Shidlovskii read the Bloc declaration which said that "the ministers arouse open distrust in the country" and that while allied confidence in Russia was breaking down, "the country does not know whether this is happening from a lack of understanding of the situation, or whether the Minister of Foreign Affairs [Sturmer] is doing it consciously."[65]

Then Miliukov mounted the tribune to deliver his historic speech, observed by overflowing galleries. He contrasted "the present government, which has sunk even beneath the level on which it stood under normal Russian conditions," with the allied governments which had "summoned to their support the best men of all parties."[66] Rodzianko was not in the chair during Miliukov's speech; the deputy chairman, it appeared later, did not know German. This enabled Miliukov to read some crucial passages from the Swiss newspaper *Neue Freie Presse*, passages which he would not have been permitted to deliver in Russian. He quoted the paper's comments on the appointments of Sturmer and Protopopov: "Das ist der Sieg der Hofpartei, die sich um die junge Zarin gruppiert." Although Rodzianko censored the stenographic report and struck out the sentence, the audience had heard and understood. It was the first time that the Empress and her influence on Russian politics had been mentioned in the Duma.

---

[64] PAD, VI, 347–48; BLOK, KA, LVI (1933), 113.

[65] PAD, I, 228; SO, November 1, 1916, pp. 9–12.

[66] The stenographic account of the speech was heavily censored. I have used the full text published in 1917: *Riech' P. N. Miliukova 1 noiabria 1916 g.* (Petrograd, 1917). An incomplete English text is in GOL, p. 154–66.

Miliukov referred to pro-German propaganda in Russia and appealed to the evidence of the British ambassador in Petrograd.

> To uncover the ways and means of that propaganda of which Sir George Buchanan told us openly not so long ago, we need a judicial investigation such as was undertaken in Sukhomlinov's case. At the time when we accused Sukhomlinov, as now, we did not possess the facts which were brought to life by the investigation. We had only what we have today—the instinctive voice of the entire country, and its subjective certainty.[67]

Miliukov told the Duma how Sturmer's appointment as Sazonov's successor had been received in western Europe:

> Of course, it is true, gentlemen, that relationships built up in the course of decades are not destroyed at the caprice of a single individual. . . . But in the delicate affairs of diplomacy there are nuances. There is fine lace work, as there is rough sewing, and lace work is possible only under special conditions and under favorable circumstances. Gentlemen, I witnessed the destruction of these most slender, most delicate threads of the international fabric; I saw this destruction. It was going on before my very eyes in London and Paris. That is what Mr. Sturmer has accomplished.

After his every accusation Miliukov asked the rhetorical question: "Is this stupidity, or is this treason?" Answering it he said:

> Does it matter, practically speaking, whether we are dealing with stupidity or treason? While the Duma everlastingly insists that the rear must be organized for a successful struggle against the enemy the government persists in claiming that organizing the country means organizing a revolution . . . and deliberately prefers chaos and disorganization. Is this stupidity, or is this treason? Choose either one, the consequences are the same.

Miliukov left little doubt as to his conviction on the matter. When the reactionary deputy Nikolai Markov shouted at him: "And your speech is what—stupidity or treason?," Miliukov answered: "My speech is a service to the country which you will not make. No,

---

[67] Miliukov was referring to Buchanan's speech the previous month to the Anglo-Russian Society in which the ambassador complained of German propaganda in Russia aimed particularly at England. See Buchanan, II, 29–31.

gentlemen, by your leave, there is a little too much stupidity. It seems hard to explain all this merely by stupidity."[68]

Several weeks passed before an incomplete text of Miliukov's speech became available to the public through the legal press. But it had meanwhile circulated in hundreds of thousands of illegally printed, hectographed, and even typed and handwritten copies, apparently with a substantially more inflammatory text than that of the original. It was reported that, as long as Miliukov's speech had been available illegally, with various textual substitutions, it had a huge success. When printed legally, "it aroused disappointment."[69]

For a few days Miliukov was the hero of the hour. *Riech'* printed messages of support for his Duma stand from various town Dumas, zemstvos, industrial groups, and merchants' associations throughout Russia. On November 10 he spoke at a public meeting, sharing the platform with Sir Paul Vinogradoff and Shingarev. The huge Alexander Hall of the Petrograd Town Duma was packed. When Miliukov appeared the audience rose to give him an ovation lasting several minutes. His Duma speech had also been well received by at least one Russian diplomat abroad, Count Benkendorf in London. "The Ambassador's spirits rose," wrote his chargé d'affaires, "when Miliukov made his famous speech in the Duma which resulted in Sturmer's resignation."[70]

The government's reaction to the speech was halfhearted. Sturmer asked the cabinet for authority to prosecute Miliukov as a political criminal, but his colleagues urged him to sue Miliukov for libel. Sturmer did this, but the February Revolution put an end to the suit.[71] The fact remained that November 1 brought about Sturmer's downfall. Miliukov pointed out that, "for the first time in the history of our representative institutions the relationship between the opinion of the Duma's majority about the cabinet, and the existence of the latter, was established in . . . clear and definite form." But Sturmer's

[68] Writing his history of the revolution two years later, Miliukov reinterpreted his stand, claiming that "though the speaker inclined rather to the first alternative [stupidity] the audience, by its approval, supported the second [treason]." See *Istoriia*, I, 33.

[69] RV, December 8, 1916.

[70] *Riech'*, November 11, 1916; Nabokov, *op. cit.*, p. 56.

[71] A thorough investigation of the facts and legends connected with Miliukov's speech is in Mel'gunov, *op. cit.*, pp. 279–318, which shows that Miliukov was wrong on most counts.

successor Alexander Trepov, the former Minister of Communications
and a brother of that Trepov with whom Miliukov had negotiated
in 1906, was not a great improvement. As Miliukov put it, it was
"a reseating of the musicians." Commenting on the Trepov appointment, he wrote: "The difference between that which occurred, and
that which was desirable, is great indeed." He had few illusions about
what the Duma meeting had accomplished:

> The result is great only in comparison with the usual routine of
> our public life. But in comparison with that which was demanded
> by the Duma majority . . . the result is still very small. . . . It is
> even less than appeared at first glance. The impulse given by the
> Duma has already been considerably weakened by not having
> brought about the results which had been anticipated.[72]

Opinion about the consequences of Miliukov's most famous Duma
pronouncement varies. The conservative deputy Vitalii Shul'gin, who
had become the regime's bitter critic, thought that Miliukov had
expressed the feelings of the vast majority of the population. "If,"
he wrote, "by some miracle all of Russia could be admitted into this
white hall of the Taurida Palace, and Miliukov were to repeat his
speech before this sea of millions, the applause would deafen us as
a hurricane." Others thought the speech was the signal toward the
revolution which its author wanted to avoid. One of these was Iosif
Gessen, the co-editor of Riech'. After the speech he had said to Miliukov: "Do you realize that this is the beginning of the revolution?"
To this the latter replied: "Only in your pessimistic imagination. It
is still far to that."[73]

Writing the history of the revolution two years later, Miliukov
saw the matter differently. He now alleged that "public opinion unanimously acknowledged November 1, 1916, as the beginning of the
revolution." It was not so much public opinion as Kadet opinion
which was to make November 1, 1916, a sacred date. Thus thought
Petrunkevich and Kizevetter who wrote of Miliukov's pronouncement that it was "the first truly revolutionary speech in the Taurida
Palace," and that "the first initiator of the revolution which over-

[72] Riech' editorials, November 11 and 19, 1916.
[73] V. Shul'gin, Dni (Belgrade, 1925), p. 86; GES, p. 347.

threw the old regime was none other than P. N. Miliukov." Kornilov
agreed, and wrote:

> I think that without Miliukov's speech of November 1, 1916,
> without that manly and daring act, it would not have been possible
> to arouse the proletariat and the army so unanimously. . . . The
> extent of the influence that our leaders' speeches had on the atti-
> tude of the army and of the government is no secret to anyone.[74]

Even Miliukov's perennial rival Mandel'shtam called the speech
"the beginning of the Russian revolution," to the loud applause of
the March, 1917, Kadet congress. The Socialist Ekaterina Kuskova
wrote that "in the circumstances of those days that speech had a
revolutionary character and increased the revolutionary mood of the
Russian public far more than all the underground manipulations
of the Bolsheviks."[75]

In December, 1916, Miliukov evaluated his speech the following
way:

> The active patriotism of the broad masses of the public—here
> is the new phenomenon which appeared on the political scene after
> November 1, evidently in connection with that historic day. And
> no matter how dangerous the forthcoming jump into the unknown
> might be for us, we shall be accompanied into the darkness by this
> fact of vast public importance. The country has awakened: here is
> the brief and very meaningful formula of this fact.[76]

What he saw ahead was "a dangerous . . . jump into the unknown."
What had made him take what was, for him, a radical step? There was
no question that the effect of the speech would be felt particularly
in the army. The testimony of officers by no means sympathetic to
the Kadets indicates that the speech was in great demand among the
soldiers. V. B. Stankevich recalled that the soldiers of his company often asked him to read them Miliukov's speech. General Peter
Krasnov forbade the reading of the speech to the troops and, when
it was brought to his sector in large packets, ordered the contents

---

[74] *Istoriia*, I, 34; PETR, p. 355; A. Kizevetter, *P. N. Miliukov* (Petrograd,
1917), p. 28.
[75] *Riech'*, March 28, 1917; PN, December 5, 1925. For a similar analysis from
the Right camp, see A. Rezanov, *Shturmovoi signal' P. N. Miliukova* (Paris, 1924),
and I. Nazhivin, *Glupost' ili izmena?* (Brussels, 1930).
[76] *Riech'* editorial, December 17, 1916.

destroyed. He did, however, read the speech to his officers and in a two-hour harangue argued against it point by point. The old officers agreed that the speech was treasonous, but the young ones considered it an act of bravery. When Krasnov made inquiries at other sectors of the front, he found that almost everyone agreed with the speech. The reactionary Markov had been right when he told the Duma that he was glad the government had forbidden the printing of the speech. Once it got to the soldiers, he said, "even its authors, no matter how Red they are, will be astounded by the results." The Okhrana reported that "the speeches had great agitational significance, and were in large part responsible for the revolutionizing of all groups of the population."[77]

Miliukov took the risk he did because he clearly feared that the alternatives were even more dangerous. He had lost faith in those who, like Rodzianko, argued that pressure should be put on the Emperor in a private audience. When the Duma chairman asked in October, 1916, that Bloc representatives go with him to the Emperor, Miliukov refused to participate in what he termed "an unconstitutional act." He insisted that everything should be said publicly from the Duma tribune.[78] The Duma, Miliukov felt, must do something to regain the full confidence of the population which it seemed to have lost by its passive tactics. The Duma, Miliukov was convinced, must again become the spokesman for the people. To do that it would have to use more outspoken language—to match the popular mood. As the Okhrana reported: "We have not yet seen the masses so angry. In comparison with the mood of the present moment [October, 1916] the mood of 1905-6 was, without question, more favorable to the government." As Miliukov warned Paléologue on the eve of the Duma session: "Certain things will have to be said from the tribune. Otherwise we shall lose all authority over our constituents, and they will turn to the extreme parties."[79]

[77] V. Stankevich, Vospominaniia, 1914–1919 (Berlin, 1920), p. 64; P. Krasnov, "Pamiati imperatorskoi russkoi armii," Russkaia Letopis (Paris), V (1923), 56. For Markov's remark, see SO, November 4, 1916, p. 202; the Okhrana report is in "V ianvare i fevrale 1917 g. Iz donesenii sekretnykh agentov A. D. Protopopova," Byloe (Petrograd), 1918, No. 13, p. 109.

[78] M. Rodzianko, "Gosudarstvennaia duma i fevral'skaia revoliutsiia," ARR, VI (1922), 51.

[79] The Okhrana reports are in GRAKLAS, pp. 173–74, 183; see also PAL, III, 84.

Finally, Miliukov worried about the rumors of separate peace negotiations between Russia and Germany which threatened his Dardanelles dream. The belief in the possibility of such a peace was widespread at the time; even Lenin thought it a distinct possibility. He was only contemptuous of Miliukov's guesses ("The Miliukovs and Guchkovs chatter the more the less they know"). By January, 1917, Lenin was ready to believe that a separate peace had been concluded, but secretly, since, as Lenin saw it, Nicholas II warned William II: "If I sign a separate peace openly then, tomorrow, my august cosigner, Thou will have to deal with a government of Miliukov and Guchkov, if not Miliukov and Kerensky."[80]

VIII

The memorable Duma session resulted in Sturmer's dismissal. Miliukov testified after the revolution that "this gave the impression of a full victory of the Duma, after its attack on Sturmer. It seemed, that, formally, this was the first step toward a government responsible to the Duma. . . . Of course this was only a first impression."[81] Still the Duma received proof that at least two of the important ministers were eager for its co-operation. The Minister of War, General Dmitrii Shuvaev, and Naval Minister Nikolai Grigorovich asked for the floor on November 4 and made short speeches promising that they would do everything to work with the Duma for victory. To loud and prolonged applause, Shuvaev asserted that "the enemy is broken, he will not recover. I repeat once again—every day brings us closer to victory." He based his facile optimism on the fact that Russian armaments had reached proportions unheard of at the beginning of the war. Using January 1, 1915, as his base he told the Duma that Russia now produced four times more rifles, thirteen times more artillery shells, nineteen times more explosives, and twenty times more heavy artillery. It must have sounded like heavenly music to Miliukov, who congratulated Shuvaev on his speech and demonstratively shook his hand to the great disgust of the Empress who wrote the Emperor: "Shuvaev did the worst thing—he shook hands with Miliukov, who

[80] V. Lenin, "O separatnom mire," Sotsial-Demokrat, November 6, 1916, and "Povorot v mirovoi politike," ibid., January 31, 1917, reprinted in LEN, XIX, 284, 380–81. I refer the reader again to Mel'gunov, op. cit.
[81] PAD, VI, 348.

only just launched forth things against us." Miliukov commented that "the Ministers of War and the Navy took their stand on the side of the Duma, and the nation." These were valuable allies, as the February days would soon show.[82]

On November 19 Trepov addressed the Duma as the new head of the old cabinet. The hated Protopopov remained at his post. The Social Democrats and the Trudoviks boycotted Trepov, provoking loud demonstrations on the Duma floor. Trepov was forced to leave the tribune three times. Only when several Left deputies were forcibly excluded could he speak. His only surprise was the public announcement of the Straits Agreement, calculated to give him prestige. But the Duma's reaction was most disappointing. There was only scattered applause, while Miliukov remarked: "Bravo to Sazonov." Not even the Duma cared any longer about the issue on which Miliukov was to stake so much.[83]

In Riech' he expressed pleasure at the announcement. The fact that it had finally been made would, in his opinion, "put an end to all rumors and questions." As for the Left's boycott of Trepov he condemned it. The Kadets and the Progressives had voted for the exclusion of the Left deputies because the boycott had been undertaken without consulting them. It was Miliukov's view that:

> boycott tactics are seldom successful but, in any case, a cardinal condition of their success would seem to be, first, a unanimity arising from the concentration of the general will in one direction and, second, a calculation based on a brief, but strong action, and on immediate success.

Since neither of these conditions had been met Miliukov could only deplore the incident. Neither the Social Democrats nor the Trudoviks would let the Kadets forget their "betrayal."[84]

In his Duma reply to Trepov Miliukov congratulated the deputies

[82] Shuvaev's speech is in SO, November 4, 1916, 203–5; the Empress' letter is in Aleksandra Feodorovna, op. cit., p. 437; Miliukov's comment is in Riech' editorial, November 6, 1916.

[83] The Trepov speech and the Left boycott is in SO, November 19, 1916, pp. 240–59.

[84] Riech' editorial, November 20, 1916. During the Duma obstruction, Chkhenkeli had called the Bloc leaders "pharisees," and the Trudovik Sukhanov had said to Miliukov: "Why do you permit the existence of a government of fools and traitors?"

on Sturmer's dismissal: "It is your victory, gentlemen, the first victory of this kind."[85] The Duma had re-established its popularity: "Gentlemen, the country has found you again after November 1, and is ready to accept you as its leaders, whom it will follow." The myth of the Duma as the creator of the February Revolution was in the making. Its radical speeches had made the Duma friends in the army, Miliukov said: "Gentlemen, our speeches are being read by the army as well, and I dare say the army has approved of them. It has understood the aims which motivated them, and has acknowledged our aims to be its own." As to the Straits Agreement he alleged its announcement had been received coldly only because it was made by Trepov, not by Sazonov.

The new premier, he said, was not the man the Duma had been waiting for. He was only a bureaucrat who had "to put up with Protopopov by higher order. He has no right to form his own cabinet. He can only speak for himself, since Protopopov has his own policy." But Miliukov proposed no drastic measures: "We are not announcing any boycott or obstruction of this government. Only we cannot guarantee that we can bring Russia to victory with such a government." It was, in any case, not in the Duma's competence to act: "The Duma is not the executive power and cannot replace the executive power."

Miliukov then turned to the problem which was to agitate Russia's urban centers until the February Revolution—food provisioning. The Kadets, he said, had long ago demanded a ministry of provisioning. Instead Protopopov had assumed its management and, with him, Miliukov said, "any undertaking is bound to be paralyzed." The Minister of Interior had introduced politics into provisioning, which was "dangerous, and impermissible." So far trade had been based on fixed prices. Protopopov now proposed a return to free trade in grain. Even England had realized that provisioning had to be strictly controlled.

The provisioning crisis now alarmed the most conservative circles. Even the State Council, that stubborn oasis of the status quo, voted (105:23) for "the decisive removal from governmental affairs of hidden, irresponsible forces." A smaller majority (94:34) voted for "the formation of a government . . . based on the public's confidence." Miliukov commented that "from Karpov to Grimm in the upper

[85] SO, November 22, 1916, pp. 323–47.

chamber, from Purishkevich to Miliukov in the lower—this is such
a wide sweep, such an unusual concentration of public opinion in
one focus, as has never before taken place in the history of our
representative institutions."[86]

The desirable government of the hour had assumed new form in
Miliukov's mind. He now thought what was needed was a dictatorship enjoying the public's confidence. The Allies could provide
an example of this:

> The French parliament is the initiator and creator of Briand's
> dictatorship; in England parliament remains the ultimate and sov-
> ereign judge of Lloyd George's dictatorship. The English and
> French "dictatorship" is popular and responsible. . . . Its leaders
> have been advanced by parliamentary majorities, not by some dark
> forces. . . . In the full meaning of the word this is a dictatorship
> enjoying the confidence of the public. . . . Only such a dictatorship
> can organize all the living forces of a country for the struggle
> ahead.[87]

Trepov's government was clearly no such dictatorship. Miliukov
pointed out that it was doing nothing—it was "simply gaining time
before the Christmas recess" which would save it from having to
give the Duma any explanations.[88] Protopopov forbade a series of
gatherings—a congress of War Industries Committees, a Zemgor
congress, and one of the Periodical Press Society. The Zemgor congress
had been barred because Trepov claimed that zemstvo leaders should
remain in their localities, where they were needed. "What helpless
thinking," exclaimed Miliukov, "what hypocrisy!"

> What would you say if the commanders of the Allied armies,
> who meet from time to time for joint deliberations in order to plan
> a common front and a joint plan of military operations, were to
> adopt this argument, and announce that they should rather remain
> at their posts?

The political situation, Miliukov told the Duma, resembled that
of 1905:

> Russian political life has once again achieved that united front
> which it maintained up to October 17, 1905. . . . We want to lead

[86] *Riech'* editorial, November 24, 1916.
[87] *Ibid.*, November 27, 1916.
[88] SO, December 16, 1916, pp. 1171–79.

this mighty stream into legal channels. Gentlemen, I repeat again, it can still be done. . . . The air is full of an approaching storm. But in order that the thunder not take the form that we do not desire . . . we must prevent this stroke of lightning. . . . We must show that we are not satisfied with the half measures we have been getting.

Some of his expressions sounded enigmatic. He said: "The atmosphere is saturated with electricity. No one knows when and where the lightning will strike." It soon became clear that he spoke of the projected assassination of Rasputin of which he was informed by Maklakov, a participant in the plot.[89]

Everyone, it seemed, was aware of the approaching storm, except the Imperial couple. Former Minister of the Interior Maklakov testified later that, in the last months before the revolution, it was clear to all that "a thorough job of repair was necessary. But we saw that . . . the sovereign's heart was not disposed toward it." The Empress was continuously urging her husband to take drastic measures of repression. She wrote him in December:

> I should have quietly, and with a clear conscience before the whole of Russia, sent Lvov to Siberia (one did so for far less grave acts), take Samarin's rank away (he signed that paper from Moscow), Miliukov, Guchkov and Polivanov also to Siberia. It is war, and at such a time interior war is treason, why you don't look at it that way I really cannot understand.[90]

IX

Thus came the end of 1916. On December 27 Trepov was replaced by Prince Nikolai Golitsyn, a harmless nonentity, who was to be the last premier of the old regime. The Duma was prorogued until February 14, 1917. Miliukov had written in early December: "Let the public demands, which, so far, have been directed exclusively to the Duma, turn also to other factors which might influence the course of political events."[91] Was he hinting at the secret plans for a palace coup, designed to remove the Imperial couple and establish

---

[89] V. Maklakov, "On the Fall of Tsardom," SEER, XVIII (1939), 79.
[90] PAD, V, 288; Aleksandra Feodorovna, op. cit., p. 456.
[91] Riech' editorial, December 12, 1916.

a regency for the young heir to the throne? Among the conspirators were Guchkov, Mikhail Tereshchenko, and several army commanders. Their aim, according to Guchkov, was "to get a constitution without letting the mob into the streets." Miliukov later testified that he was included in some of the planning, but the project was only in its initial stages; the date proposed was March, 1917. The Emperor was to be forced to abdicate in favor of his son, under the regency of Grand Duke Michael. General Anton Denikin claimed that generals Aleksandr Krymov, Nikolai Ruzskii, and Aleksei Brusilov favored the plan, but the chief of staff, General Mikhail Alekseev, opposed it. Miliukov did nothing to promote it, but he recalled that, when asked why the Duma did not act, he replied: "Bring two regiments to the Taurida Palace, and we shall take power." He preferred a Duma coup to a palace coup.[92]

There was one other possible avenue of influencing the Emperor toward making concessions—the forthcoming Allied Conference, scheduled for February, 1917, in Petrograd. The regime might be frightened into improving relations with the Duma under the threat of receiving no more foreign aid. Miliukov and his colleagues tried to enlist the help of the Allied leaders coming to Petrograd who included Lord Milner, Sir Henry Wilson, and the French Minister for the Colonies Gaston Doumergue. Paléologue took Doumergue to see Miliukov, Maklakov, Shingarev, and General Polivanov. After listening to the Russians, Doumergue thought them to be, Paléologue recorded,

a bit too excited, a bit too ardent to engage in a fight against tsarism, and he preached patience to them. At the word "patience" Miliukov and Maklakov flew into a temper: "Enough of patience. . . . We have exhausted all our patience. . . . Anyhow, if we do not

[92] E. Martynov, *Tsarkaia armiia v fevral'skom perevorote* (Leningrad, 1927), p. 55; PAD, VI, 350; Denikin, I, 37–39; VOSP, II, 282. The planned palace coup remains one of the most obscure episodes of the February Revolution; for a study of the evidence, see S. Mel'gunov, *Na putiakh k dvortsovomu perevorotu* (Paris, 1931). Kerensky has written that Miliukov did not favor a palace coup: "He foresaw two possible results: either the supreme authority would come to its senses in time, and ask the Bloc to form a government; or the revolution would be victorious, and the victors, being unskilled in governing, would ask the Bloc to form a government on its behalf. In support of his argument he cited the French Revolution of 1848" (KER, I, 149).

act soon the masses will no longer listen to us." . . . Doumergue answers, very calmly: "I spoke of patience, not of resignation. . . . I understand your disquietude, your annoyance, and the extreme difficulties of your situation. But, above all, think of the war."[93]

As if Miliukov was not already thinking of the war far too much for his own political good!

The Allied diplomats did not stay for the Duma opening on February 14. New groups of the population were now coming onto the political stage. The Workers' Group of the Central War Industries Committee was becoming active. It represented 219,000 workers, just over half of the capital's total. In January the group issued a proclamation advocating "the removal of the autocracy" and "the full democratization of the country." It demanded "a Provisional Government" and summoned a workers' demonstration before the Taurida Palace on February 14.

Not surprisingly most of its members were arrested. On January 29 a protest meeting was held. The Okhrana reported that Miliukov's speech at the meeting provoked disbelief. He said that he "failed to understand the policy of the working class," which meddled in affairs outside its jurisdiction. "Only the State Duma," he maintained, "can dictate the conditions of the struggle with the government." Chkheidze attacked Miliukov's passive stand. "This is a blow against the working class," he said, "but remember that if the workers perish it will be your turn next." The meeting came to no conclusion, but Miliukov decided to warn the workers not to march on the Duma.[94]

On February 9 a letter of his appeared in the newspapers, printed next to a warning to the workers by the Commander of the Petrograd Military District, General Sergei Khabalov. In the eyes of many this was hardly good company for the leader of the Party of Popular Freedom. Miliukov admonished the workers not to be provoked into senseless sacrifices:

> It has been brought to my attention that a person whom I do not know, and who represents himself as Duma deputy Miliukov,

[93] PAL, III, 188. The Allied Conference in Petrograd is described in SM II, 460–66. Miliukov also attempted to influence the British delegation: "My friends," he recalled, "put me at Lord Milner's side on purpose. . . . I told him that the storm was approaching, that if at the last hour the dynasty would not consent to compromise its fall was inevitable" (RUS, p. 295).

[94] The Okhrana report is in GRABUR, pp. 180–84.

has, during the past few days, been carrying on propaganda in the factories, calling upon the workers to go out on the streets of Petrograd on February 14, the day when the State Duma resumes its session, to demand, in a more determined manner, action by the State Duma, and protest against the war. . . . I hasten to warn those who believed such declarations that they have been the victims of the most brazen fraud. To listen to such counsels means playing into the hands of the enemy. I, therefore, earnestly request all persons who have heard such counsels to refrain from any demonstration on February 14, and to remain calm on that day. Their calm will frustrate the plans of their enemies, and most effectively help their friends. The intelligent attitude of labor toward the difficulties we are experiencing makes me hopeful that my warning will be heard and that the treacherous design will fail.[95]

Miliukov testified after the revolution that he had written the letter fearing that, as in 1905, the government wanted to provoke an uprising in order to drown it in blood. The testimony of a former director of the Police Department indicates that some police provocation was taking place in early February.[96] At any rate there was some room for legitimate doubt. The Left, however, attacked Miliukov for his stand, and the Bolsheviks distributed a leaflet entitled "The Provocation and Demagogy of the Miliukovs," written by Aleksandr Shliapnikov. "The Miliukovs," it said, "whose servility knows no bounds, must meet with the most decisive opposition not only of the Social Democratic organizations, but of every honest democrat." In a letter to Lenin of February 11 Shliapnikov wrote: "The liberals, and particularly Miliukov, behave as scoundrels toward the revolutionary movement. Brand him before the democrats of the entire world."[97] It was not a very promising tone to adopt only a few days before Miliukov was to become a major figure of a new government.

February 14 passed without incidents. Speaking in the Duma the following day, Miliukov noted that the police had been ready for the proposed demonstration.[98] He blasted the government for arming the police with machine guns "while there are not enough of them

[95] The text of the letter is in GOL, pp. 185–86.
[96] For Miliukov's testimony, see PAD, VI, 350–52; Evgenii Klimovich testified that the Okhrana had a hundred agents among the Petrograd workers: ibid., I, 121–22.
[97] A. Shliapnikov, Semnadtsatyi god (Moscow, 1923), I, 51, 65.
[98] SO, February 15, 1917, pp. 1328–45.

at the front. Yesterday you could see these 'military operations' in the rear of the Duma building." He asserted that "the last two months have deeply changed our internal situation for the worse." A new premier had appeared: "But that is nothing new. . . . Almost every session begins with a new premier." The government, he continued, "has returned to what we had not seen since October 17, 1905—to a struggle against the entire country for an indefensible position lost beforehand." The situation was fast reaching a point of no return.

Miliukov concluded with a plea for a renewed war effort. "We believe," he said, and one wonders how many there were who believed this with him, "that the nation will not allow any diminution of national energies in those decisive moments which we have now approached. . . . When you compare what our nation could give for victory with what our government is giving us, does not the heart of each of you bleed?" One of those whose heart was not bleeding was Kerensky, who followed Miliukov on the tribune.[99] The relations between the two men were already not of the best. Kerensky accused the Bloc of being too timid: "Did you dare," he asked, "to take any personal risks in the fight with the old system which is destroying the country?" Miliukov answered from his seat: "We have done more than you."

In *Riech'* Miliukov commented on Kerensky's ambivalent position toward the war:

> Kerensky was defending the point of view if not of peace at any price, or a war without victory, then still something fairly close to these positions. . . . He did not cover himself with laurels in the Duma. . . . But let us not hide from ourselves the fact that this point of view is fairly widely held among the public. If even Kerensky could not speak in the name of the nation he is, nevertheless, backed by a certain group of the intelligentsia.[100]

If only Miliukov could have known and admitted that Kerensky spoke more "in the name of the nation" than he did.

The Bloc and its leaders was to celebrate one small victory over the government before the end. The Duma discussed, on February 23 and 24 when the streets were already full of angry marchers, the critical supply situation in Petrograd. The entire chamber (with only

[99] *Ibid.*, 1917, pp. 1345–59.
[100] *Riech'* editorial, February 16, 1917.

two dissenting voices) accepted the Bloc's plan of turning over Petrograd's supply machinery to the Town Duma. On February 24 Prince Golitsyn complied with the Duma vote.[101] The cabinet even initiated discussions with the Duma, sending ministers Nikolai Pokrovskii and Aleksandr Rittikh to negotiate. But no agreement was reached, since the Duma demanded a new cabinet. The street demonstrations, begun on February 23 because of food shortages, were becoming daily more violent. Political strikes spread through the capital like wildfire. Troops, called out to quell the disorder, refused to fire on the crowds and in fact opened fire on the police. The cabinet, completely helpless and paralyzed, decided at least to rid itself of the obnoxious Duma. On February 26 it was prorogued till April, and the following day it met for the last time, to hear out the prorogation decree in silence. It would never meet again in its full complement.[102]

When the first insurgent troops and crowds began to arrive at the Taurida Palace, Rodzianko called an unofficial meeting of the deputies. It was reported that the entire cabinet had resigned and, as Miliukov put it later, "there was then, in Russia's capital, neither Emperor, Duma, nor Council of Ministers. The 'disorders' had taken the form of a genuine 'revolution.' "[103] The excited deputies were proposing the most unexpected solutions to the alarming situation. Miliukov's contribution to the discussion must have disillusioned many:

> We have here three proposals with regard to the Government: (1) A committee of ten persons, but I cannot agree that such a committee could possess dictatorial powers over everybody, including ourselves; (2) that of Nekrasov I also consider inappropriate; (3) the proposal of Chkheidze and of Dziubinskii to create a new Government is impracticable, the moment has not yet come for this. Personally, I have no concrete suggestion. So what can we do? To go, as suggested by Kerensky, and appease the troops, but this would hardly appease them; we must look for something more tangible.[104]

After more desultory discussion it was agreed to appoint a Temporary Committee to Restore Order and Make Contact with Public Organi-

[101] N. Avdeev, *Revoliutsiia 1917 g.* (Moscow, 1923), I, 23–25.

[102] VOSP, II, 289. An account of these turbulent days, compiled from the most varied sources, is in BROWKER, I, 26–45.

[103] VOSP, II, 290.

[104] An account of the meeting is in BROWKER, I, 45–47.

zations in Petrograd. The very name suggested reluctance to act.

In another wing of the Taurida Palace a much more determined organization was forming—the Soviet of Workers' and Soldiers' Deputies was being resurrected. One of its leaders and historians, the Menshevik Nikolai Sukhanov, has left us a memorable picture of Miliukov in the Taurida Palace on February 27, lost in thought, and undecided:

> Up and down the Catherine Hall, all alone, walked P. N. Miliukov, the central figure of bourgeois Russia, the leader of what was, at that moment, the only official organ of power in Petersburg, the actual head of the first revolutionary government. . . . His whole appearance suggested that he did not know what to do. Various people went up to him, spoke to him, reported to him. He gave them answers, unwillingly and vaguely. His interlocutors left him, and again he walked alone.[105]

When Sukhanov, on that same fateful day, approached Miliukov, quite officially, in the name of the Petrograd Soviet, to ask the Duma leader about his plans for forming a government, he got the following revealing reply:

> First of all I belong to a party which, in its decisions, is bound by a more general collective, the Progressive Bloc. Without it our party can do nothing, decide nothing, since it is part of it. . . . And then we, as a responsible Opposition did, without question, aim for power, and marched on the road to it—but we aspired for power not by way of revolution. We rejected this road, it was not our method.[106]

[105] Sukhanov, I, 104–6.
[106] Ibid., I, 119.

8: MINISTER OF FOREIGN AFFAIRS

> My fundamental idea was that there are no such things as the
> "Tsar's diplomacy" and the "Provisional Government's diplo-
> macy," that what we have is a joint Allied diplomacy, a di-
> plomacy which we share . . . with the leading democracies who
> came to an agreement with us about the common task.[1]

I

While on February 27 the Duma Temporary Committee met in
prolonged session, a telephone call for Miliukov came from the Preobrazhenskii Regiment barracks. The regiment, said the message,
"waits for the orders of the Temporary Committee." Miliukov informed the callers that Duma member Colonel Boris Engel'gardt was
on his way "to take over the Regimental command." "With a solemn
air" Miliukov then said to Sukhanov: "A decision has been made, we
are taking over the power."[2] Miliukov's doubts were resolved; events
had finally taken the course for which he had always hoped. The army
was offering itself to the Duma. Henceforth he would always maintain
that the Duma had been the crucial factor in the February Revolution. "It was clear to all," he wrote in his history of the revolution,

> that the success or failure of the movement depended on the par-
> ticipation or non-participation of the Duma in its leadership. . . .
> The intervention of the State Duma gave the street and the mili-
> tary movement a center, gave it a banner and a slogan, and thus

[1] Miliukov at a conference of Duma deputies, May 4, 1917, cited in BROW-
KER, III, 1271–72.
[2] Sukhanov, I, 141–43.

transformed an uprising into a revolution which ended by the
overthrow of the old regime and of the dynasty.[3]

The Duma was vital not only to the Preobrazhenskii Regiment and
the Petrograd garrison, but also to the commanding staff of the
armies, to the Chief of Staff General Mikhail Alekseev and the commander of the Northern Front located close to the capital. "If there
had been no Duma," Miliukov told an American audience in 1921,
"the responsible leaders of the army, such as General Alekseev or
Ruzskii, would never have taken sides with the revolutionaries. The
Tsar would not have been induced to abdicate so soon and so easily."[4]

The Duma had decided to take the side of the revolution. But
the old regime had not yet been defeated, and, in the very Duma
building, a rival contender for power—the Petrograd Soviet—was
making its claims. In his first speeches to the soldiers, on February
28, Miliukov urged them to follow only the Duma. He told the
Lifeguard Grenadiers:

> We must first of all be organized, united, and subordinated to
> one authority. This authority is the Temporary Committee of the
> State Duma. You must submit to it and to no other authority, for
> dual authority is dangerous and threatens to split and divide our
> forces. . . . Remember that the enemy does not sleep and is pre-
> paring to wipe us off the face of the earth. (Cries: This will not
> happen.) Then this will not be.[5]

Already on the second day of the revolution Miliukov foresaw the
cause of all future problems, that "dual authority," which was soon
to wreck all his plans. He spoke in the same vein in the barracks to
which he was summoned by the officers. He seemed to take quite
easily to this unexpected role of popular tribune before the army.
"I was astounded," recalled Prince Paul Dolgorukov, who observed
Miliukov among the soldiers, "by the confidence and aplomb with
which he greeted the men, walking through the ranks, and chatting
with the officers and men."[6]

By March 1, however, it was clear that dual authority was an

[3] Istoriia, I, 39, 43.
[4] RUS, pp. 23–24.
[5] The text of the speech is in BROWKER, I, 51–52.
[6] P. Dolgorukov, Velikaia razrukha (Madrid, 1964), pp. 12–13; see also VOSP,
II, 297.

established fact. Though the Soviet voted not to participate in any new government, it regarded itself as a sovereign authority in no way subject to the Temporary Committee or to the new government then being formed. Its famous Order Number One, addressed to the Petrograd garrison on March 1, was put into effect independently of all other authorities.[7] The Soviet proposed a set of conditions under which it would tolerate the Provisional Government. A leading member of the Soviet, Iurii Steklov, thus described the constellation of forces between the Duma and the Soviet:

> The Duma Committee was also the product of the revolution, but it was a pale and weak creation which emerged from the privileged strata, whereas our Soviet emerged from the healthy, broad masses of hundreds of thousands of people who revolted and established their authority.[8]

The negotiations between the Duma Committee and the Soviet lasted through March 1 and 2. As Sukhanov recalled, Prince L'vov, the head of the future cabinet "did not utter a single word all night." It was Miliukov who "spoke for the entire Duma Committee; everyone considered this a matter of course. It was clear that Miliukov here was not only a leader, but the *boss*." He made no objections to the Soviet demand for an amnesty or for the proclamation of political liberties. This had been his program since 1905. But he objected to the third point: "The Provisional Government must not take any steps to predetermine the future form of government." He had made up his mind that the monarchy should be kept under Nicholas' son Aleksei, with Grand Duke Mikhail as Regent. Defending his candidates for the throne, he said that "one is a sick child, and the other a thoroughly stupid man." It was a strange recommendation, but on this point he refused to budge. He did accept the abolition of the police and the calling of a Constituent Assembly.

Such were the Soviet's conditions. Speaking for the Duma Committee, Sukhanov recalled, "Miliukov demanded from us a declaration which would point out that *whereas* the Government was being

---

[7] For the text, see BROWKER, II, 848–49. Miliukov reprints (*Istoriia*, I, 79) the text of the Kadet Central Committee resolution of March 7 urging the immediate anullment of Order Number One in the name of the war effort.

[8] Speech at the All-Russian Conference of Soviets on March 30, reprinted in BROWKER, III, 1225.

formed by agreement with the Soviet of Workers' Deputies, this Government should be recognized as legitimate by the masses of the people and enjoy their confidence." The Soviet was willing to issue such a declaration. But there was still the thorny question. of the monarchy. Sukhanov recalled the final debate on the subject:

> "You can scarcely be hoping," I said at last as a final argument," that a Constituent Assembly will leave a monarchy in Russia? So all your efforts will be fruitless after all. . . ." In reply to this, Miliukov . . . said, emphatically and with evident sincerity: "The Constituent Assembly may decide as it pleases. If it pronounces against the monarchy, then I shall be able to go. But now I cannot. Now, if I am not here, there is no Government at all. And if there is no Government, then . . . you yourselves can understand. . . ."[9]

The Soviet yielded and agreed to let the government deal with the Romanov question. For its part, the Soviet would "engage without delay in a broad struggle for a democratic republic." On this basis the long negotiations came to an end. It seemed that the government had won a victory, but this was pure illusion. Even the printing of the joint proclamation had to be attended to by the Soviet because, as Miliukov put it, "the printing presses are more under your control." Dual authority was a fact of Russian political life.

It was now possible to announce the membership of the new government. The honor fell to Miliukov, and on March 2 he told an immense crowd in the Taurida Palace:

> We are present at a great, historical moment; only three days ago we were but a modest opposition, while the Russian government seemed omnipotent. Now this government has toppled into the mire from whence it came, while we and our friends of the left wing have been brought forward by the revolution, the army, and the people to take the place of honor as members of the first Russian government to represent the public. (Loud, prolonged applause.)[10]

To the question from the audience as to "who elected you," he answered triumphantly: "We were elected by the Russian revolution."

[9] The account of the Soviet-Duma negotiations as reported by Sukhanov is from *ibid.*, I, 117–24; Miliukov's account is in *Istoriia*, I, 46–49, and VOSP, II, 305–8.

[10] The text of his speech is in BROWKER, I, 129–33.

To the cries of "Who are the ministers," Miliukov gave interesting replies. L'vov's name, he said, "symbolizes organized Russian society which was so ruthlessly persecuted by the old regime." To the objections from the floor that L'vov represented "privileged society," Miliukov answered that " 'nonprivileged' society is also represented in our ministry": Kerensky, he said to a storm of applause, would, as Minister of Justice, "administer just retribution to the obsequious servants of the old regime." To the shouting "How about you," he answered as follows:

> My comrades have entrusted me with the reins of Russia's foreign policy. (Stormy and prolonged applause, growing into an ovation to the speaker, who bows in all directions.) It may be that I will turn out to be a weak minister in this post, but I can promise you that while I am in office the confidential matters of the Russian people will not fall into the hands of our enemies. (Stormy and prolonged applause.)

He was surely not making any excessive promises for his ministry.

Of the Minister of War and Navy, Guchkov, he said that he had been "my political enemy (cries: 'Friend') during the course of the entire life of the State Duma. But, ladies and gentlemen, we are now political friends, and then one should be just even to the enemy—after all, it was Guchkov, who, in the Third Duma, undertook the reorganization of the Russian army." Recommending Aleksandr Konovalov as Minister of Trade and Mikhail Tereshchenko as Minister of Finance, he said only that they were "representatives of that liberal group of the Russian bourgeoisie who were the first in Russia to attempt to organize the representatives of the working class." His two party colleagues, Shingarev and Nikolai Nekrasov, would be ministers of Agriculture and Transport, respectively. The latter, he said, "is especially liked by our left-wing comrades." He said nothing about the new Procurator of the Holy Synod, Vladimir L'vov, and the State Comptroller Ivan Godnev, both relics of the Progressive Bloc, and the crowd did not ask about them.

But many wanted to know about the Romanovs, and here Miliukov came upon his thorniest problem. "You ask about the dynasty," he said. "I know beforehand that my answer will not satisfy all of you." It was an understatement, for when he announced that "the power will be transferred to the regent, Grand Duke Mikhail Aleksandrovich," there were prolonged outbursts of indignation. When he added that "the heir will be Aleksei," there were cries, "This is the old dynasty." Miliukov was forced to give an explanation:

> Yes, ladies and gentlemen, this is the old dynasty, which perhaps you don't like and which perhaps I do not like either. But . . . we cannot leave unanswered and undecided the question concerning the form of government. We can visualize it as a [form of] parliamentary, constitutional monarchy. Perhaps others visualize it differently, but if we start arguing about this now instead of reaching an immediate decision, then Russia will find herself in a state of civil war. . . . The freely elected representatives of the people will decide [the question as to] who more faithfully expresses the public opinion in Russia: we, or our opponents.

And he prudently decided to close his speech: "My voice is becoming hoarse; it is difficult for me to continue speaking. . . . (Tempestuous applause. Commotion in the hall. The speaker is lifted several times, swung, and finally carried out of the Ekaterinskii Hall.)"

It was a triumph in many ways. But he had stirred the hornet's nest of the monarchy, and the question would not be allowed to rest. Too many Russians wanted no more of the Romanov dynasty, and they lost no time in saying so. Later that day many officers came to the Taurida Palace and said that they could not return to their units unless Miliukov took back his words about the Romanovs. After some discussion Miliukov agreed to tell the press "that the portion of his speech which dealt with the temporary regency of the Grand Duke Mikhail Aleksandrovich and the succession of Aleksei was an expression of his personal opinion." In his history of the period Miliukov pointed out that

> that was, of course, incorrect, because in all previous discussions this question had been considered as settled precisely in the sense in which P. N. Miliukov outlined it. But frightened by the growing wave of excitement the Temporary Committee quietly gave up its previous opinion.[11]

Miliukov was not to give up as quietly.

[11] *Istoriia*, I, 52.

II

He did not know, while he was making his speech, that the Emperor had abdicated in favor of his brother, not in favor of his son; Mikhail Aleksandrovich was thus transformed from regent into emperor. "Such a change," Miliukov wrote in his history, "made the defense of constitutional monarchy still more difficult, because the calculation on the minority of the new emperor, which would constitute a genuine transition to the strength of a firmly constitutional regime, disappeared."[12] The new cabinet wished to dissuade Mikhail from accepting the throne. But Miliukov insisted that he be permitted to argue for acceptance, and a conference of the government with Mikhail took place on March 3.

Entering the apartment where the meeting took place, Miliukov was met by Mikhail, who quipped: "Well, it's a fine thing to be in the position of an English King. Very simple and comfortable, isn't it?" Miliukov's answer could not have been more typical: "Yes, Your Highness, it is very peaceful to rule observing the constitution."[13] But there was neither peace nor constitution in Russia at that moment. No one knew this better than Miliukov. Yet he decided to take a stand on principle, hoping that he would convince Mikhail by his rational arguments. Even Guchkov admired the old opponent whom he had always accused of republicanism: "I give great credit to P. N. Miliukov that, at that moment, he knew how to put aside his political sympathies and take an exclusively patriotic point of view."[14]

Both Rodzianko and Kerensky argued for abdication. Miliukov recorded his argument against as follows:

> P. N. Miliukov developed his idea that a strong authority, which was essential for the consolidation of the new order, required the support of a symbol of power to which the masses were accustomed. He said that the Provisional Government alone, without a monarch, represented "an unseaworthy craft" which might sink in an ocean of popular unrest; in this case, the country would be in danger of completely losing its national consciousness and of falling into complete anarchy, before the convention of the Constituent

[12] *Ibid.*, I, 52–53.
[13] VOSP, II, 316.
[14] A. Guchkov, "Iz vospominanii," PN, September 20, 1936, p. 2.

Assembly; [if left] alone, the Provisional Government would not live long enough to see it.[15]

Only Guchkov supported Miliukov. Then others spoke against the two men, arguing that there were no reliable military units to protect Mikhail. Miliukov objected, claiming that outside of Petrograd "there was ample possibility of gathering the military force required for the protection of the Grand Duke." He had just spoken to Colonel A. E. Gruzinov, the new commander of the Moscow Military District, who had kept the Moscow garrison under discipline. "I suggested," Miliukov recalled, "that one should immediately drive to Moscow by car; there an organized force will be found, essential to support the positive decision of the Grand Duke. I was convinced that this was a comparatively safe solution."[16]

Mikhail, however, preferred not to take risks and decided to refuse the throne. At the crucial moment no one but Miliukov wanted to test the monarchy's chances. Writing about the event in his history, Miliukov asserted that "all could have gone differently if the degree of self-assurance and determination of the leaders had been different." In his eyes a grave mistake had been committed; it was "the first capitulation of the Russian revolution. The government had created a situation defective in the very source, a situation from which all subsequent mistakes of the revolution had to develop."[17]

It was the end of an era. The Romanov dynasty, which had ruled

---

[15] *Istoriia*, I, 53–55, translated in BROWKER, I, 115–16. Another dramatic account, factually identical, is in V. Shul'gin, *Dni* (Leningrad, 1926), pp. 179–83. The British ambassador used arguments similar to Miliukov: "The Russian people are very religious," he wrote, "but their religion is one of symbols and ceremonies, and in their political life they look for symbols also. They must have as chief of state some figurehead whom they can look up to with feelings of reverence as the personification of their national ideals" (Buchanan, II, 114).

[16] VOSP, II, 317; for Gruzinov's popularity in Moscow in those days, see BROWKER, I, 172, 174.

[17] *Istoriia*, I, 55–56. Discussing the military chances of the monarchy, General Anton Denikin wrote: "Considering the entire situation of March, 1917, I conclude that . . . the support of the regency of Mikhail Aleksandrovich would have been carried out with some struggle but without shocks and with unquestionable success. The confirmation of Mikhail Aleksandrovich on the throne appeared somewhat more difficult but still possible on condition of his granting a broad constitution." See A. Denikin, *Ocherki russkoi smuty* (Paris, 1921), I, Part I, 56.

Russia for over three centuries, was no more. The first of its line had been a Mikhail, as was the last. Miliukov refused to remain in the cabinet under the new conditions. As Trotsky put it picturesquely: "After the desertion of Mikhail, Miliukov had not even a straw to grab." Guchkov, too, decided to resign. Premier L'vov told the new head of the chancellery of the Provisional Government, Vladimir Nabokov, a party colleague of Miliukov's, that "Miliukov absolutely must be persuaded to remain. You and your friends must help us." Nabokov agreed, since he was sure that "Miliukov was the strongest figure in the first Provisional Government—mentally and politically." We have already noted that this was also the opinion of Sukhanov. Trotsky, too, agreed, writing that "the axis of the Provisional Government, although not formally its head, was Miliukov."[18] A delegation of the Kadet Central Committee persuaded their leader to remain in the government. Guchkov reconsidered his own decision. For the time being the first Provisional Government remained intact.

Announcing the final formation of the government in the press, the Temporary Committee said of the ministers that "their past political and public activities assure them the confidence of the country."[19] Their program recapitulated the agreement concluded between the Temporary Committee and the Soviet, including a provision that "those military units which took part in the revolutionary movement shall be neither disarmed nor withdrawn from Petrograd." Here was the seed of future trouble which Miliukov would taste to the full: the Petrograd garrison was to defy him in only a few weeks. He could not oppose this provision, he wrote, because "we did not know, at that moment, whether or not they [the insurgent troops] would have to engage in further combat with the 'loyal' units that would be sent to the capital."

The Soviet statement, printed alongside the government's announcement, described the new cabinet as one "created from socially moderate elements of society." The reforms promised, it said, "should be welcomed by wide democratic circles." Its continued support of the government, however, was promised only conditionally. "We

[18] L. Trotsky, *The History of the Russian Revolution* (New York, 1932), I, 179, 186; for Nabokov's remarks, see Nabokov, "Vremennoe pravitel'stvo," pp. 17, 52.

[19] The government program and the Soviet proclamation are from *BROWKER*, I, 135–36; Miliukov's comment is in VOSP, II, 307.

believe," the Soviet said, "that, in so far as the emergent government acts in the direction of realizing these obligations and of struggling resolutely against the old regime, the democracy must lend it its support." This was the famous "in so far as" formula which would hang like a sword of Damocles over the Provisional Government. But major friction was still ahead, and the present was filled with hopes. The Kadet Central Committee's first appeal after the revolution stressed unanimity. "Let all the differences of party, class, estate, and nationality," it said, "be forgotten within the country. Let the united Russian people rise in a burst of enthusiasm. . . . And let hope kindle in the hearts of all that this time we will succeed in avoiding fatal disunity." Only Lenin, from his Swiss exile, openly rejected such delusions. "A week of workers' bloody battles," he wrote to Alexandra Kollontai on March 3, "and Miliukov plus Guchkov plus Kerenskii in power. True to the 'old' European pattern." He would break that pattern in a few months.[20]

III

For the moment, however, Miliukov was "in power" in the Foreign Ministry and so informed Russian diplomatic representatives abroad. In his March 4 telegram to them, he stressed the continuity of Russian foreign policy and the positive effect of the revolution, in his eyes, on the war effort. "In the sphere of foreign policy," he wired,

> the cabinet, in which I accepted the portfolio of the Minister of Foreign Affairs, faithful to the promises given by Russia, will strictly observe the international obligations contracted by the fallen regime. . . . Faithful to the treaty that binds her by indissoluble ties to her glorious Allies, Russia . . . shall fight our common foe to the end, unswervingly and indefatigably. The Government, of which I am a member, will devote all its energy to the achievement of victory. . . . The Government is firmly convinced that the great exaltation which now animates the whole nation will multiply its forces and bring nearer the hour of the final triumph of regenerated Russia and of her glorious Allies.[21]

On the same day Miliukov received Paléologue, who found him

[20] The Kadet statement is from BROWKER, III, 1199; Lenin's letter is in *Leninskii sbornik*, II (Moscow, 1924), 289.
[21] The text is in BROWKER, II, 1042–43.

"much changed, very tired, aged by ten years." It had been a traumatic week for the new Foreign Minister. Paléologue offered him congratulations and best wishes but was most concerned about the effect of the revolution on the war. "You shall receive all guarantees in this respect," Miliukov assured him. In his telegram to Paris, however, the French ambassador remained skeptical, reporting "disorganization and anarchy." He did not share the optimism of *Riech'*, which, in its first editorial after the revolution, described it as "this eighth wonder of the world, for history shall forever visualize the present revolution as such."[22]

Buchanan, like his French colleague, made it clear to Miliukov that the new government would not be recognized until Britain had guarantees in regard to the war. "I told him," Buchanan recorded,

> that before acting on the authorization already given me I must have an assurance that the new Government was prepared to fight the war out to a finish, and to restore discipline in the army. Miliukov gave me this assurance, but said that they were obliged to proceed cautiously an account of the extremists, and that his own position was a very difficult one. He was regarded with suspicion for having supported the Grand Duke Michael's claim to the throne, and he must either make some concessions or resign. Which course, he asked, would I prefer him to take? The former, I unhesitatingly replied.[23]

The ambassadors expected a declaration more formal than the one Miliukov wired abroad. Such a statement was included in the first declaration of the Provisional Government made on March 6. "The Government," the declaration stated, "will sacredly observe the alliances which bind us to other powers and will unswervingly carry out the agreements entered into with the Allies." Even this was not enough to satisfy Paléologue, who protested to Miliukov that no mention had been made of Germany, of Prussian militarism, of the war aims. "France too had made a revolution with the enemy at the gate," he said; "but Danton in 1792 and Gambetta in 1870 had used quite a different language." No wonder Miliukov listened "quite pale, and most discomfited." He objected that the declaration was intended only for the Russian people and that "a more temperate

---

[22] PAL, III, 243–48; *Riech'* editorial, March 5, 1917.
[23] Buchanan, II, 90–91.

vocabulary" was now in use in contrast to 1792 and 1870.[24]

It was only the American ambassador, David Francis, who made no trouble for Miliukov and was, in fact, only too eager to extend recognition to the new regime and to be the first one to do so. He achieved his aim, and on March 9 he was received by the Provisional Government in a formal ceremony. Miliukov addressed him in the following words:

> Mr. Ambassador, I know America sufficiently to say that these new ideas of free Russia are your ideas also, and that our takeover will give a strong push toward the spiritual upsurge of our two democracies. I am happy to say that I have received, in these last days, a veritable stream of telegrams from my American friends, and their content indicates to me that the broad circles of your public opinion are with us.[25]

Among these was a New York Times editorial which must have pleased Miliukov's historical sense. "If the present revolution in Russia has an analogue," the Times wrote on March 18 (New Style), "it is not the French Revolution, but the creation of the French republic out of the ruins of the Empire some eighty years later. . . . Theirs was the leading spirit of France then, as Miliukov is in Russia of the present moment." When Francis suggested that American labor send a message, too, Miliukov asked that it go to the Soviet; doubtless he thought they needed moderate advice more than he did. Samuel Gompers and the council of the American Federation of Labor then sent a telegram to Chkheidze, president of the Petrograd Soviet, which must have amused that body. "May we not urge you to build practically and constructively," Gompers telegraphed, concluding with the wise dictum: "It is impossible to achieve the ideal state immediately."[26]

On March 11 France, England, and Italy followed the United States in formally recognizing the Provisional Government. The old imperial pomp had disappeared, and there was no one to receive the ambassadors and their numerous retinue at the ministry; finally, Miliukov appeared and personally fumbled with the lights in various

---

[24] The declaration is in BROWKER, I, 157–58; see also PAL, III, 256–57.

[25] The text is in VOSR, p. 432.

[26] D. Francis, Russia from the American Embassy (New York, 1921), pp. 97–98.

MINISTER OF FOREIGN AFFAIRS

rooms, till one was found which was large enough. But the speeches made up for the lack of ceremony. A participant recorded the occasion with a touch of humor:

> While the diplomats spoke, the ministers stood looking at the ground, bowing at the conclusion of each speech. I could not think of it as a ministry of victory. I did not like to look at their faces, when they were all looking at the ground . . . so I looked at the ground too, and then I saw their boots. What an extraordinary collection of boots they were!

Much was being said about continuing the war to victory and, our participant recalled, "Miliukov replied with a declaration that Russia would fight till her last drop of blood. I have no doubt that Miliukov would, but can he answer for Russia?" Paléologue, too, remained skeptical and had telegraphed to Paris the previous day: "In the present stage of the revolution Russia can make neither peace nor war." He found that the cabinet, in their fear of the Soviet, would not even attend a dinner which he wished to give in their honor; it might, they feared, "be misinterpreted in the extremist circles."[27]

A graver matter than the cancelled banquet was the fate of the former Emperor and his family, a more serious bone of contention between the government and "the extremist circles." The government wished to send the former Emperor to England for the duration of the war, and Miliukov approached Buchanan for help. The ambassador received authorization on March 10th and informed Miliukov that "the King and His Majesty's Government were happy to accede to the request of the Provisional Government." Miliukov was delighted but "begged that the fact that the Provisional Government had taken the initiative in the matter should not be published." The Soviet had already learned of the government's plan and declared its opposition to it. On March 9 it had voted "to inform the Provisional Government at once of the unswerving determination of the Executive Committee not to permit the departure of Nicholas Romanov for England and to arrest him." Nevertheless, arrangements continued to be made for the former Emperor's departure. Miliukov wished to get the "unconstitutional" Russian monarch safely to constitutional Britain. But the British changed their minds, and, toward the

[27] A. Knox, With the Russian Army, 1914–1917 (London, 1921), II, 584–85; PAL, III, 265, 269–70, 272–73.

end of March, withdrew their offer of asylum. The further fate of
Nicholas II and his family was no longer in Miliukov's hands.[28]

IV

A word must now be said about Miliukov's management of his
ministry. He had taken possession of the establishment on Palace
Square on March 4. His predecessor, Nikolai Pokrovskii, had requested
permission to remain in the ministerial residence until he found an
apartment, and Miliukov readily agreed—he had no plans of moving
into the luxurious suite. He recalled that, if forced to remain in the
building overnight, he slept in a small room for servants, off the
corridor. The new minister was known for his simplicity and was
not about to change his modest way of life. A friend recalled that,
waiting in one of the ministry's elegant reception rooms, he observed
Miliukov's wife Anna Sergeevna, who had brought her husband a
lunch wrapped in newspapers. The American ambassador commented
on the fact that there were no banquets or receptions. "There is no
official social life here," he reported to Washington. "The Ministers
meet daily, remaining in session after midnight, working assiduously,
having refused all social invitations including from myself [sic] to
whom they profess to feel very close."[29]

We have seen that Miliukov did not contemplate any changes in
foreign policy. Nor did he plan to conduct any purge of the establishment he inherited. Already in 1906, when there was a chance that
he might join the cabinet, he had told a British journalist:

> We are not a political party in the sense in which you under-
> stand political parties in England and America. We have not got

[28] The ambassador's account is in Buchanan, II, 103–5. See also the franker
account of his daughter: M. Buchanan, *The Dissolution of an Empire* (London,
1932), pp. 192–99. On the Soviet's action, see BROWKER, I, 181. There is
some fresh information in H. Nicolson, *King George V* (London, 1952), pp.
299–302. Miliukov's recollections of the events are in several articles: "O vyezde
iz Rossii Nikolaia II," PN, September 8, 1921, p. 2; "Memuary Buchanana ob
ot'ezde Nikolaia II," Zveno (Paris), April 9, 1923, No. 10; "Ekaterinburgskaia
tragediia," PN, June 12, 1932, p. 2, which is a comment on Muriel Buchanan's
book, and "Kto vinovat," PN, January 26, 1936, p. 3, which is a comment on
Vladimir Kokovtsov's account of the tragedy.

[29] Francis to Lansing, April 15, 1917, in *Papers Relating to the Foreign Relations of the United States, Russia, 1918* (Washington, D.C., 1931–32), I, 154.
See also VOSP, II, 302, 337, and Dolgorukov, *op. cit.*, p. 16.

an army of candidates for offices hungry for the spoils. The majority of the Chinovniks are quite ready to worship the rising sun. There would, of course, have to be a few dismissals, but very few. . . . Besides, a very great number of the officials are themselves in our ranks.[30]

The intervening decade had not changed Miliukov's opinion of the matter. There would be continuity in personnel, as well as in policy. As he recalled the situation:

I valued the operating machine from the point of view of technique and tradition. I knew that there were, among the officials, men who did not share my views on the current tasks of foreign policy, but I did not fear their influence on me and relied on their professional conscientiousness.[31]

He retained one of the two deputy ministers of the old regime, Anatolii Neratov; the other, A. A. Polovtsev, retired on March 14 and was replaced by Boris Nol'de, who had long been a legal advisor to Sazonov and was an old friend and party colleague of Miliukov. Another Kadet and former associate, Petr Struve, became the director of the ministry's new Economic Department. But this was hardly a party appointment, since Struve was only in "coldly correct" relations with Miliukov at that time.[32] Another old associate was Prince Grigorii Trubetskoi, who had long been head of the ministry's Near Eastern Department and, briefly, minister to Serbia.

A commission was formed to revise the official ministry regulations dating from 1828, but evidently few substantive changes were made. A participant recalled only one concrete innovation: women were henceforth to be admitted to the lower ranks of the officialdom. But Miliukov did do something about the financial situation of his subordinates. On March 9 he persuaded the government to increase salaries and pay bonuses and travel allowances in his department. Heretofore, salaries had been very low, and many worked without any compensation whatever.[33]

The diplomatic personnel abroad was little affected by the change

[30] Paul Miliukov Papers, Russian Archives, Columbia University, Box 8142, File 20A: "The Outlook in Russia. An interview with Professor Miliukov [1906]."
[31] VOSP, II, 336.
[32] See S. Frank, Biografia P. B. Struve (New York, 1956), pp. 112–13.
[33] V. Korostovets, Seed and Harvest (London, 1931), pp. 205, 307; the author was Miliukov's secretary in the ministry. Unfortunately, his work is almost totally devoid of revealing information about his superior or the ministry.

of regime. Most Russian envoys kept their positions. On March 5
Izvol'skii telegraphed Miliukov from Paris that if he decided to
keep him at his post "you may utterly trust in my most devoted
co-operation in the fulfillment of your most difficult task." Coming
from a former Russian foreign minister, this message must have
pleased Miliukov.[34] Izvol'skii was asked to stay and was replaced by
the Kadet Vasilii Maklakov only shortly before the October Revolution. No new ambassador arrived in London, and the chargé d'affaires
Nabokov remained at his post throughout 1917. At least he could
say of himself, "I personally rejoiced at the change of regime."[35] The
same was not true of the Russian ambassador in Washington, Georgii
Bakhmet'ev, a bitter monarchist, who resigned only in April. Only
a few minor diplomats were dismissed, and the Paris Okhrana headquarters, which had spied on thousands of Russians, including Miliukov, were closed. Yet Miliukov had evidently not been overly tolerant
of his subordinates. An investigator, appointed by Kerensky, hardly
Miliukov's friend, gave him a clean bill of health on this score. The
investigator was a Socialist Revolutionary and not inclined to
whitewash the Kadet minister, who was by then out of office.[36]

Miliukov fared less well when he had to handle the touchy problem
of repatriating thousands of Russian political émigrés, some of whom
were of the "defeatist" persuasion. After the amnesty granted by the
Provisional Government, Miliukov instructed Russian diplomats
abroad to help all émigrés who wished to return to Russia. He urged
the formation of advisory committees composed of émigrés to establish "the identity of the political émigrés desiring to return to Russia"
and assist consuls "in any doubts on this question."[37] The matter
had rich political implications; aside from Miliukov's views about

[34] V. Storozhev, "Diplomatiia i revoliutsiia," *Vestnik Narodnogo Kommissariata Innostranykh Del* (Moscow), 1920, No. 4–5, p. 88.
[35] K. Nabokov, *The Ordeal of a Diplomat* (London, 1921), p. 76. Sazonov had actually been appointed to the post but was detained in Petrograd by ill health.
[36] He was Sergei Svatikov, appointed by the Minister of Justice (Kerensky). His report is in Ministerstvo Inostranykh Del, *Sbornik Sekretnykh Dokumentov iz Arkhiva Byvshego Ministerstva Inostranykh Del* (Petrograd, 1917–18) No. 5, pp. 183–95. See also A. Popov (ed.), "Diplomatiia vremennogo pravitel'stva v bor'be s revoliutsiei," KA, XX (1927), 3–38, on the Okhrana.
[37] *Ibid.*, XX, 4–5; see also "Vozvrashchenie emigrantov," *Riech'*, March 30, 1917, p. 4.

political exile, the Allies believed that "defeatists" should not be assisted in repatriation. Besides there was not enough space to accommodate all the returnees. As Nabokov in London put it bluntly: "The task of repatriating Russian citizens was akin to the dragging not merely of a camel, but of whole caravans, through a needle's eye."[38]

Soon an outcry arose against the handling of the delicate operation. Lenin, with his customary ferocity, blamed everyone concerned. "It is clear," he wrote to a member of the Bolshevik Central Committee in Stockholm on March 17, "that the agent of Anglo-French imperialist capital and the Russian imperialist Miliukov (and Co.) are capable of all, of deception, of betrayal, of all, of all, to prevent the return of the internationalists to Russia."[39] Miliukov, it is true, was not anxious to assist men who were bitterly opposed to the war, yet he did not wish to create unnecessary difficulties with the Soviet. Thus he transferred the Russian ambassador in Stockholm to another post when it became clear that he was the cause of friction. As the ambassador recalled:

> I have reason to believe that, in appointing me to Madrid, Miliukov was actuated by the wish to remove me from a country . . . too much overrun by the most extreme Russian elements; he was aware of my irreconcilability on certain principles, and he feared a clash of opinions which might create difficulties for the Foreign Office.[40]

Officially, Miliukov's conscience was clear, for he telegraphed to Paris and London: "Earnestly request, for internal political reasons, not to distinguish between political émigrés who are pacifists and non-pacifists." But he must have agreed with the feeling of Nabokov in London who wrote: "Something must be done to stop the influx of Bolsheviks into Russia. If you will continue to allow this immigration without any discrimination whatsoever, you will cut the branch upon which you are sitting." Thus when Trotsky was arrested by the British, Miliukov asked that they detain him and his comrades "until further information about them had been obtained."[41]

---

[38] Nabokov, The Ordeal, p. 95.
[39] LEN, XX, 52, letter to I. S. Ganetskii; italics in the original.
[40] NEK, pp. 492–93.
[41] Popov, op. cit., p. 9; Nabokov, The Ordeal, p. 103; Buchanan, II, 120–21.

The Soviet, not sure of Miliukov's stand, blamed the British.
"British authorities," it said,

> are permitting some emigrants to leave for Russia and are detaining
> others, depending on their convictions. . . . The Executive Com-
> mittee of the Soviet of Workers' and Soldiers' Deputies protests
> against such conduct on the part of the British Government. . . . It
> requests the Minister of Foreign Affairs to adopt urgent measures
> assuring the return of all political emigrants, without exceptions,
> to Russia.

Buchanan would not have his government blamed and threatened
to disclose the facts unless Miliukov cleared the British. Miliukov,
therefore, told the Soviet:

> The British Government has never refused to endorse the pass-
> ports of any Russian political emigrants on whose behalf a Russian
> Embassy or Consulate has requested permission for the return to
> Russia. Not a single Russian emigrant was denied a visa on grounds
> of his political beliefs. . . . Cases of denials of visas were not induced
> by political considerations, but by difficulties in transportation by
> sea owing to German submarine warfare.

Trotsky was released, though he did not arrive in Petrograd till after
Miliukov's fall. The episode did much to arouse Left hostility toward
the foreign minister.[42]

The most famous returning émigré was, of course, Lenin. When
the group's planned trip in a German "sealed car" became known,
Miliukov asked his colleagues: "Gentlemen, are we going to let
them in under such conditions?" The ministers agreed that no legal
obstacle could be put in Lenin's way and that the public would
condemn Lenin and his comrades. "It must be said," recalled a participant, "that, in relation to these passengers [of the sealed car], the
Provisional Government entertained the deepest illusions. It was
thought that the very fact of the 'export' of Lenin and Co. by the
Germans will absolutely discredit them in the eyes of public opinion."
But, more important, any other course of action was then unthinkable. The editorial in Riech' on Lenin's arrival illustrates this. "It
is not only natural," wrote the paper,

> but most desirable that the leaders of our leftist parties, who were
> forced for such a long time to languish in foreign lands, should

[42] For the above, see ibid., II, 120–21, and BROWKER, II, 1088–89.

hasten home in order to take part in the great struggle. Such universally recognized leaders of our socialist parties as Plekhanov and Lenin should now be present in the arena of contest, and irrespective of the opinion one has of their views, their arrival in Russia may be welcomed.

Miliukov would soon regret such sentiments. Abroad, according to one witness, the government's toleration aroused disapproval. The Russian chargé in London wrote of Lenin's return: "The fact that the Provisional Government allowed him to cross the Russo-German border and to live in Petrograd unmolested contributed more to the loss of prestige in London of the Russian government than any other of their errors."[43] As for the Germans, they clearly saw the advantages of shipping further "defeatists." A message of the German minister in Bern to Berlin indicates this. "Lenin," wrote the minister,

> received a splendid welcome from his followers. . . . It is not clear yet which course the revolution will take. Perhaps it will be enough to substitute several members of the Provisional Government, like Miliukov and Guchkov, by socialists. In any case it would be absolutely necessary to increase the number of the partisans of peace by an influx from abroad. It is therefore recommended that those émigrés who are prepared to leave should receive the same facilities as Lenin and his comrades. . . . The émigrés lack the means for the conduct of their propaganda. . . . I would be grateful for telegraphic information about whether the revolutionaries are being supported in any other way.[44]

V

Lenin was the foreign minister's most implacable enemy. But an increasing number of voices disagreed with Miliukov's foreign policy

[43] The above is from *ibid.*, II, 1093; Nabokov, *The Ordeal*, p. 102; and Nabokov, "Vremennoe pravitel'stvo," pp. 61, 75.

[44] Count von Romberg to the Chancellor, G. Michaelis, April 30, 1917; marginal note by Count von Pourtales: "I have spoken to Romberg. With that, the last sentence of his dispatch was settled." See Z. Zeman (ed.), *Germany and the Revolution in Russia, 1915–1918* (London, 1958), pp. 52–53. See also the telegram of the German minister in Copenhagen to the Foreign Minister in Berlin of March 21, 1917: "Dr. Helphand [Parvus] believes that as soon as the amnesty for political offenders comes into force there will be an opportunity to work effectively against Miliukov and Guchkov through direct contact with the Socialists" (*ibid.*, p. 25).

stand. The revolution revealed how isolated his point of view had become. The Soviet was clamoring for a new foreign policy, and even the government was by no means unanimous in its support of Miliukov. Kerensky soon revealed this publicly. The two men had never been fond of each other. An observer of cabinet meetings recorded that "Miliukov was his *bête noire* in the full sense of the word. He did not miss an opportunity to speak of him with ill will, irony, sometimes with genuine hatred." Kerensky himself, in recalling the past, merely accused Miliukov of lacking political realism:

> Because of his natural bent as a historian [Kerensky wrote,] Miliukov tended to look at political events in rather too much perspective, as one looks at them through books or historical documents. Such a lack of real political insight would not have mattered much under more stable conditions, but at the critical moment of the nation's history through which we were then living, it was little short of disastrous.[45]

In a press interview on March 7, Kerensky argued that Russia did not need Constantinople. A British general present recorded: "He says Miliukov has no tact, and we are not to believe him when he says that Russia wants Constantinople." The interview had immediate repercussions abroad. Nabokov wired from London that the statement "may give rise to agitation in a certain part of the British press and parliamentary circles." Since the French press also responded, Miliukov wired London, Paris, and Rome to explain that there was no truth in "our allegedly renouncing the 1915 agreement regarding Constantinople and the Straits." Only "the extreme social-democratic organs," Miliukov claimed, thought otherwise; "the serious press and all the broad public circles of Russia share our aforementioned point of view, which also finds a sympathetic response in the army."[46]

Miliukov evidently excluded the Soviet from the "broad public circles," for that body went further than Kerensky in rejecting Miliukov's claims. On March 14 the Soviet unanimously passed its famous "Appeal to the Peoples of All the World," which stated that "the time has come to begin a decisive struggle against the acquisitive ambitions of the governments of all countries. . . . The Russian democ-

---

[45] Nabokov, "Vremennoe pravitel'stvo," p. 35; A. Kerensky, *Russia and History's Turning Point* (New York, 1965), p. 242.
[46] See Knox, *op. cit.*, II, 576–77, and BROWKER, II, 1057–58.

racy announces that it will oppose the policy of conquest of its ruling classes by every means." The Soviet newspaper *Izvestiia* commented that "the attitude toward the war as expressed in the Appeal differs radically from that of the bourgeois parties and that part of the democracy that allies itself with them." And the paper continued:

> Russia has made known her desire for Constantinople, the Dardanelles, Galicia, Armenia, and the recovery of liberated Poland. . . . And all these aggressive aspirations Messrs. the Chauvinists refer to as "decisive victory" over the enemy. The Soviet of Workers' and Soldiers' Deputies took another position with regard to the war. This is the position of the Zimmerwald and Kienthal conferences. . . . We do not aspire to conquer foreign lands.

The time had come, the paper editorialized, to abandon "secret diplomacy":

> You cannot pour new wine into old bottles. The new power, created by the revolution, must also make a decisive break with the traditions of the Izvol'skiis and the Sturmers in the realm of foreign policy. . . . Only on the foundations of a new foreign policy can a new diplomatic system be built, answering to the principles of freedom, and worthy of such a people. Clean dealings require clean hearts.[47]

In response to the Soviet Appeal, Miliukov decided to issue a statement explaining his ministry's policies. In an interview with the press printed on March 23, he decisively rejected the demand for "peace without annexations," which he labeled "a German formula that they endeavor to pass off as an international socialist one."

> As to the question of Constantinople and the Straits, he continued, it cannot be considered as involving the interests of the Turkish nation because the Turkish nation, in spite of five hundred years' domination, has not spread its roots deeply there. Up to the present day Turks remain an alien element there, resting exclusively on the right of the conqueror, the right of the strongest. The transfer of the Straits to us would in no way contradict the principles advanced by Woodrow Wilson when he spoke of the possibility of transferring their ownership. The possession of the Straits is the protection of "the doors to our home," and it is understandable that this protection should belong to us, while a neutralization of

[47] For the above, see *ibid.*, II, 1077–82.

the Straits, especially a complete neutralization providing for a free passage into the Black Sea of men-of-war of all nations, would be even less acceptable to us than their remaining in the hands of the Turks.[48]

It was a restatement of Miliukov's old Duma position. The cabinet preferred to hide behind much vaguer phrases. Premier L'vov suggested a discussion of the "secret treaties." When Miliukov acquainted the government with their text, Vladimir L'vov expressed "sincere, utter, and naïve indignation," calling them "plunderous and knavish" and urging their immediate disavowal. Miliukov found little support even among the Kadet ministers. Only Shingarev stood behind him without qualifications. Manuilov, recalled a participant, "supported Miliukov very inertly—I would even say that there was in fact no actual support." The Premier preferred not to take any position and was, in the words of one eyewitness, "the incarnation of passivity." Even Guchkov, on whose help Miliukov had counted most, proved to be a passive spectator. He had his hands full with the restless army and wished to forget the Straits. "At this moment," he wrote in his memoirs, "I did not consider this question important enough to give battle over it to my colleagues, and therefore I did not support Miliukov in his steadfast position."[49]

The Soviet, however, wished to give battle to Miliukov, and

[48] *Ibid.*, II, 1044–45. Miliukov called Constantinople "a Cosmopolis, not a Turkish city." Of the 1.2 million inhabitants, he said, only half a million were Turks, while there were 220,000 Greeks, 200,000 Armenians, 60,000 Bulgarians, and 60,000 Jews. "In occupying Constantinople," he asserted, "we are violating no national interest." As for Wilson, Miliukov had the following argument: "The arrangement which I consider normal for a unique sea passage such as the Dardanelles and the Bosporus must, in my opinion, resemble the Panama Canal arrangement in two directions: in respect to Russia's sovereignty over the shores, and her right to build fortifications in the canal, and on the islands near its entry." See P. Miliukov, "Konstantinopl' i prolivy," *Vestnik Evropy* (Petrograd), April–June, 1917, pp. 530–35. As for neutralization, Miliukov opposed it, because "it would bring about great dangers for peace"; Russia would be obliged to maintain a powerful navy in the Black Sea. See an interview with Miliukov which appeared in *Le Temps* (Paris), April 9, 1917.

[49] The above is quoted from a brilliant portrait gallery of the cabinet in Nabokov, "Vremennoe pravitel'stvo," pp. 34–65; for Miliukov's comments on the individual ministers, see VOSP, II, 326–33, and *Istoriia*, I, 85. For Guchkov's memoirs, see A. Guchkov, "Iz vospominanii," PN, September 20 and 30, 1936.

a delegation of its Executive Committee, known as the Liaison Commission (it maintained permanent contact with the Provisional Government) arrived for a meeting with the cabinet. It demanded a declaration on foreign policy more in keeping with its own "internationalist" position. Miliukov maintained that such a declaration "might be interpreted by the Allies as the beginning of a separatist action in preparation for a break with them." Ministers Nekrasov, Tereshchenko, and Vladimir L'vov took issue with him. Nekrasov, though a Kadet, seemed never to follow his party leader, while Tereshchenko was fast becoming Kerensky's chief cabinet ally. Miliukov was left to fight his battle with the Soviet representatives alone. "In vain," as he described the scene,

> did Miliukov try to convince them that the very bases of their calculation—the possibility of an agreement with the socialists of all countries on the basis of the Zimmerwald formula—did not exist, because the vast majority of the socialists of both warring camps upheld the national point of view, and would not give it up.

The Liaison Commission remained unconvinced, and one of its Menshevik members, Matvei Skobelev, teased Miliukov with a reference to his 1916 European trip with the Duma delegation:

> Was it not you who told us, after your return from your trip abroad, what difficulty you had . . . to make England recognize Russia's claims on Constantinople? But precisely because you then so clearly showed us what immense efforts it took to convince England to accept your point of view we now find it difficult to believe that England will feel offended if Russia gives up the Straits.

The comment was hardly designed to make Miliukov feel comfortable.[50]

The Soviet demanded that, in place of Miliukov's interview, the government issue an official declaration on foreign policy. The cabinet was forced to agree, and the Liaison Commission returned for a second meeting with the cabinet. It insisted on a phrase stipulating that Russia would abstain from any "seizures of foreign territories." The cabinet declined to use such wording, and the Soviet voted the declaration "unacceptable." Late at night, however, Premier L'vov informed the Soviet that the cabinet had a compromise formula

---

[50] The meeting is described in I. Tsereteli, Vospominaniia o fevral'skoi revoliutsii (Paris, 1963), I, 66–67, and Istoriia, I, 85.

which would be included. No wonder that a leader of the Liaison Commission, Iraklii Tseretelli, told the Conference of Soviets that "there has not been a case yet when the Provisional Government has turned against us on any important question to which we have given the character of an ultimatum."[51]

On March 27 the government issued its Declaration on War Aims. Miliukov had convinced his colleagues that it should be published as a domestic statement and not as a diplomatic note. This was a victory of sorts, but he could hardly like the wording. The Declaration made substantial concessions to the Soviet point of view:

> Leaving to the will of the people [it said], in close union with our Allies, the final solution of all problems connected with the World War and its conclusion, the Provisional Government considers it to be its right and duty to declare at this time that the aim of free Russia is not domination over other nations, or seizure of their national possessions, or forcible occupation of foreign territories. . . . But the Russian people will not permit their fatherland to emerge from this great struggle humiliated and sapped in its vital forces.

Only the last sentence was ambiguous enough to suit Miliukov. He regarded the Declaration as a compromise which he could utilize as he saw fit. He reserved the right, he wrote, "to interpret it in his sense and to use the ambiguous expressions in the direction of his earlier policy, consonant with the policy of the Allies and with Russia's national interests." The Allies, for their part, were quick to react to the Declaration. Nabokov telegraphed from London that "the Government and the press discern in this statement an abandonment of our rights to Constantinople and other territorial acquisitions."[52]

VI

It was a frustrating task to administer Russian foreign policy under the watchful gaze of the Soviet. There were, however, policy decisions which must have given Miliukov genuine satisfaction. Among these

[51] Tseretelli's statement is in BROWKER, III, 1228; on the meeting see his Vospominaniia, I, 70–72.

[52] The text of the Declaration is in BROWKER, II, 1045–46; Miliukov's comment is in Istoriia, I, 87; Nabokov's telegram is in BROWKER, II, 1050, n. 6.

were the government's declarations on Finland and Poland. They embodied some of the Kadets' old dreams and did not involve tussles with the Soviet. Finland was the simpler of the two problems, or at least so it seemed in March, 1917. Immediately following the revolution, the government arrested the reactionary governor general of Finland and appointed the liberal Mikhail Stakhovich in his place. The odious Stolypin legislation on Finland, which Miliukov had so stubbornly fought, was repealed, and the government issued a Manifesto confirming the constitution of Finland, and all its previous privileges. "By this act," the Manifesto proclaimed,

> we solemnly affirm to the Finnish people, on the basis of its Constitution, the steadfast preservation of their internal independence and their rights to their national culture and languages. We wish to express our firm conviction that Russia and Finland will henceforth be bound together by their respect for law, for the sake of mutual friendship and the prosperity of both free peoples.[53]

It was language that Miliukov had always used in regard to Finland. Neither he nor anyone else could have foreseen that the days of Finland's existence as part of the Russian state were numbered.

Poland also deserved new treatment, but the government's moves were largely academic. Russian Poland was occupied by enemy troops. As Miliukov wrote in his history, in which he always referred to himself in the third person:

> At the initiative of P. N. Miliukov, the Provisional Government immediately took a definite stand in favor of the complete independence of Poland and the unification of her three ethnographic parts. Obviously, in view of the German-Austrian occupation of Russian Poland, the revolutionary government could not realize its intentions immediately. Instead of a manifesto regarding the independence of Poland, we had to issue a proclamation to the Poles which did not speak in the precise juridical language of the Finnish document but in the words of an inspired and ardent appeal— to fight for the common cause. . . . The Provisional Government made a reservation only with regard to the rights of the Russian Constituent Assembly.[54]

[53] The text is in *ibid.*, I, 334–35.
[54] *Istoriia*, I, 64–65, translated in BROWKER, I, 321–22; the Proclamation to the Poles is in *ibid.*, I, 322–23.

The only tie that the new Poland would maintain with Russia was
to be "a free military alliance."

The proposed settlement far outstripped all the Kadet Polish
projects of the past. Miliukov had at first been unwilling to go as
far as the Poles desired. His old friend Aleksandr Lednitskii, who had
taken the lead in the matter in March, 1917, and became chairman
of the Liquidation Commission on Matters Pertaining to the Kingdom of Poland had to pressure Miliukov. Lednitskii, described by
a friend as "not a 'Muscovite,' but a cultured 'European,'" perhaps
reminded Miliukov of his statements after the parliamentary visit of
1916, when the latter had written: "We would reassure Allied public
opinion if, in our solution of the Polish problem, we would give
proof of our desire to keep abreast of the leading democracies."[55] As
Lednitskii recalled: "Pavel Nikolaevich gave up his position on the
autonomy of the Polish Kingdom not at once, and with difficulty."
Miliukov proposed that Russia restore the office of State Secretary
for Polish Affairs, vacant since 1831. It was he who proposed a military union between the two countries, which the Poles amended
to "a free military alliance." But through the efforts of Lednitskii, a
compromise version was formulated and approved by the government.
Here, too, Miliukov could not have known that the settlement
would never be put into effect.

There was another event which cheered Miliukov in March, 1917,
when his foreign policy efforts were bringing him little satisfaction.
This was the seventh Kadet Party Congress, which assembled for
a three-day session in Petrograd on March 25. The Kadets were the
first party to meet after the revolution. There was something symbolic
for Miliukov in the fact that they gathered in the elegant hall of
the Mikhailovskii Theater which, since the 1870's, had been used

[55] The Statutes of the Liquidation Commission are in *ibid.*, I, 327–28; for
Miliukov's thought on Poland in March, 1917, see A. Lednitskii, "P. N. Miliukov
i pol'skii vopros," PNM, pp. 214–17. The most advanced Kadet project on Poland
is summarized by Miliukov in EZH, 1916, pp. 66–67, and in KA, LIV–LV
(1932), 19–20.

On Lednitskii, see V. Maklakov, "F. I. Rodichev i A. R. Lednitskii," *Novyi
Zhurnal* (New York), XVI (1947), 245; Miliukov's statement is from *Riech'*
editorial, July 9, 1916. See also L. Kozlovskii, *Russkaia revoliutsiia i nezavisimost'
Pol'shi* (Paris, 1922), and P. Miliukov, "Aleksander Lednicki," *Przeglad Wspolczesny* (Warsaw), XVIII (1939), Series LXVIII (January–March), 25–71, as
well as P. Miliukov, "Alexander Lednicki," SEER, XIII (1934–35), 677–80.

exclusively by a French troupe for the performance of a French repertoire. There was hardly a more "European" setting in Petrograd.

The Kadets could well feel satisfied with the changes which had occurred since their last congress in February, 1916. They had been transformed from a persecuted opposition group to the most important party in the new government, in which they had four ministers. Kadets now headed many important government institutions. Kokoshkin was chairman of the Special Council for the Constituent Assembly. Golovin was Commissar of the former Ministry of the Imperial Court which administered the large properties of that institution. Mitrofan Voronkov was Commissar for the Don Region, Vasilii Kharlamov was chairman of the Special Transcaucasian Committee, and Nikolai Shchepkin chaired the Turkestan Committee. Whole regions of Russia were now being administered by Kadets. The party had cause to feel triumphant.

The chief item of business for the 323 delegates representing 52 guberniias and regions was a programmatic statement in regard to Russia's form of government. The Kadets had upheld a constitutional monarchy. Now they wanted to declare themselves for a republic. "The formula about the democratic republic is on everyone's lips," said Kokoshkin, who reported on the subject. "Monarchy," he said, had been, for the Kadets, "not a question of principle but of political expediency." It was now expedient to be republicans. He used Miliukov's kind of language when he said that since 1906 "the political development of Russia proceeded much faster than the development which took place under analogous circumstances in other states." It was at this very moment that Miliukov entered the hall and was met by prolonged applause. The congress voted the following resolution unanimously:

> Russia must be a democratic parliamentary republic. Legislative power must belong to the national representatives. At the head of the executive power must be a president of the republic elected for a definite period of time by the national representatives and governing with the aid of a ministry responsible to the people.[56]

---

[56] A stenographic account of the first day of the congress is in *Stenograficheskii protokol' zasedanii VII s"ezda Partii Narodnoi Svobody. I-ii den' s"ezda.* (Petrograd, n.d.); excerpts of Kokoshkin's speech and the resolution on the republic are in BROWKER, III, 1200–1201.

Explaining the mood of that moment to an American audience
later, Miliukov specified that "all parties—even conservative ones—
which were working in the limelight of politics, became formally republican." Miliukov himself was surely the most "formal"
of republicans—three weeks earlier he had made a determined effort
to save the monarchy. But he remained the party's great conciliator,
the man whom all Kadets could continue to call their leader. Republicanism was a gesture toward the left wing. But now there were new
right wingers in the party, and they too must be made happy. Thus
it was that Miliukov was introduced to the congress, not by one of
his old colleagues, but by Prince Evgenii Trubetskoi, who had left
the party in 1907 because it had become too radical for him and who
had then urged Miliukov to collaborate with the Octobrists. He was
now, it appeared, the spokesman for those Kadets who entered the
party after the revolution because it was the only non-socialist party
with any chance of success. These men, appalled at the new outburst
of class feeling which they saw all around, regarded Miliukov as a
man of the golden mean. It was thus that Trubetskoi introduced
Miliukov: "Our dear unifier," he called him, a comforter after the
"heavy impressions of discord and struggle."

Receiving a long standing ovation, Miliukov endorsed the congress
decision on republicanism.[57] "With all my heart," he said, surely with
a dose of hypocrisy, "I adhere to the decision which is not accidental,
but which followed from the position our party occupied since its
foundation. We never considered the question of the old monarchy
as a question of principle." Having paid lip service to the mood of
the moment, he then went on to reaffirm his old belief that the Kadet
party remained Russia's only non-class party, the only guarantor of
class peace and national progress.

> Only a party such as ours, he said, a party which stands above
> classes, can act as an arbiter among class aspirations. . . . This
> party guarantees that the new principles of freedom and truth will
> become established without unnecessary shocks, and the party will
> know how to combine the ideas of freedom and order.

The loud applause that accompanied the statement must have

[57] Miliukov's statement above is in RUS, pp. 27–28; his speech at the congress,
as well as the remarks of Trubetskoi and Mandel'shtam which follow, are from
Riech', March 28, 1917, p. 5.

expressed the fervent Kadet hopes that revolutionary Russia would somehow live up to this miracle.

To emphasize Miliukov's role as the party's "unifier," he was followed on the platform by Mandel'shtam, his old critic from the left who had so often deplored Miliukov's tactics as too moderate. Now he delivered a paean of praise to the leader approving, post facto, Miliukov's wartime strategy which, he said, had helped to unify the Duma, the army, and the nation, and had thus made the revolution possible. Developments since the revolution had apparently cooled Mandel'shtam's ardor, for he declared himself no friend of the Soviet. To prolonged applause, he said that "all power must belong to the Provisional Government; at present no dual power is permissible." He had always urged that the Kadets turn to the Left. Now that the Soviet had shown its mettle, he warned that "in no democratic country is it possible that some organization should have power without bearing responsibility for it."

The left and right wings of the party seemed to be unified for the moment. The congress also basked in the illusion, though not for very long, that the Kadets retained the allegiance of Russia's national minorities. Thus Sadrii Maksudov, a delegate from Orenburg and a member of the Temporary Central Bureau of Russian Moslems, told the congress that "the thirty million Moslem population of Russia marched with the Party of Popular Freedom in the past and will march with it in the future." He was, however, not speaking for all the Moslems; a day later a statement appeared, signed by fifteen members of the Moslem Bureau, alleging that "the credit of the Kadet Party with the Moslems of Russia is permanently undermined." Miliukov, it appeared, was to blame for this. "P. N. Miliukov's statements," the fifteen critics charged, "clearly indicated that the Kadet party applies one criterion to the nations of Europe, another to the nations of Asia, in particular to the Turks." Miliukov's stand on Constantinople and the Straits offended more than just Russia's "internationalists."

The congress did little business aside from declaring itself for a republic. Its resolutions provided for the earliest calling of the Constituent Assembly, but little was said in respect to that body. In regard to the war, the congress announced that it was in favor of "not interfering with the freedom of other nations, but also would not permit any detriment to the vital interests and rights of Russia." A commission was appointed to revise the party's agrarian program in time for the next congress in May (how many such commissions there had been in the past!), and it was ruled that a new Central Committee would be elected at the next congress.[58] The meetings must have done much for party morale, but they achieved little else.

VII

Though the front was calm, the war remained the ever-present issue of Russian life. It could not but be the central problem for Miliukov. He had greeted the revolution as a guarantee that the nation would now fight with more unanimity than ever before. It had been a false assumption. Miliukov was hardly ignorant of the actual situation in the army. "I personally," he recalled, "as a member of the Duma, received many letters from soldiers at the front which proved that the demoralization of the army had already begun before the Revolution of March, 1917." But though Order Number One had done much to break down discipline, the situation was far from hopeless. "Relatively speaking," Miliukov wrote, "the army remained battleworthy (as did the Southern Fleet) until the penetration of agitators, sent by the Soviets." The officer corps could still oppose the breakdown of discipline. The officers of the Third Siberian Artillery Division, for example, wrote to Defense Minister Guchkov in March in regard to the military meddling of the Soviets: "We ask the question that Duma member P. N. Miliukov once asked of the old government: 'What is this? Stupidity or treason?' "[59]

Along with many army leaders, Miliukov was convinced that soon all would be well again at the front and the army would launch a new offensive. Victory, in his eyes, was that common goal which could unite all Russians, irrespective of class or political persuasion. His friend Nabokov recalled that Miliukov expressed his conviction in the following terms:

> In one of my many automobile trips with Miliukov I expressed my opinion . . . that one of the fundamental causes of the revolu-

[58] The full text of the two statements is in VOSR, pp. 739–40. The congress resolutions are in *Rezoliutsii delegatskogo s"ezda Partii Narodnoi Svobody 25–28 marta 1917 g. v Petrograde* (Petrograd, 1917), *passim*.

[59] BOLSH, p. 68; P. Miliukov, "Dlia vsiakoi istorii," PN, January 23, 1925, p. 2; the officers' letter is cited in Tseretelli, *op cit.*, I, 19–20.

tion was war fatigue. Miliukov disagreed decidedly: "Who knows, perhaps it is thanks to the war that everything still hangs together somehow, and without the war it would have broken down more quickly."[60]

Observing the disintegration of the Russian social fabric, Miliukov put all his hope in the cement of patriotism. He refused to see that others were far less sure of it than he.

Only a few days after the revolution, he said in an interview with the press: "The war is in decline, and is approaching a denouement. . . . If we strengthen discipline the situation will improve even more. . . . Toward the middle of the summer we shall be able to speak of the war's end more concretely." America's entry into the war in late March provided extraordinary cheer. "Miliukov and I," Paléologue recalled, "congratulated ourselves in respect to this event which deprived the Germanic powers of their last chance of survival." When several ministers, including Miliukov, visited the Army General Head-quarters, they were met by enthusiastic crowds, orchestras, and a pleased General Alekseev. Miliukov was evidently inspired and was in the midst of a speech when his train started on its journey back:

> The train is picking up speed, the wheels clang louder and louder. The Minister of Foreign Affairs is making a farewell speech from the car platform. Because of the noise neither his words nor his voice, grown hoarse from the speeches, can be heard. The groups of listeners change, and the Minister, still on the platform, speaks, and speaks.

The government communiqué, published after the ministers' visit, was full of optimism. "The army's attitude improves daily," it said, "discipline is being strengthened, and no threatening symptoms are visible in the armies. . . . The revolutionary crisis, both at the front and in the rear, has passed."[61]

General Alekseev planned an offensive for the first days of May. This was sure to revive the soldiers' lagging spirits and take their minds off political issues. In the meantime army delegations kept

---

[60] Nabokov, "Vremennoe pravitel'stvo," p. 41.

[61] M. Dal'nyi, "Beseda s Min. Inost. Del," Riech', March 10, 1917, p. 2; PAL, III, 290; the description is from S. Mel'gunov, Martovskie dni 1917 goda (Paris, 1961), p. 278. The communiqué is from Vestnik Vremennago Pravitel'stva (Petrograd), April 1, 1917.

arriving in Petrograd with greetings for the Provisional Government. Some declared that they would not permit the Soviet to dominate the cabinet. Thus at the end of March a delegation of the 265th Infantry Regiment told Miliukov that the Soviet's interference "aimed merely for personal gain" and was "provoking disharmony." "All your statements are just," Miliukov answered. But time was needed, he said, to iron out the difficulties, since "the present government will not resort to the force of the fist." The deputations always carried banners calling for "War to the End," but, a Soviet observer noted, they preferred Soviet to government speakers and would have been taken aback if told that their slogans did not agree with the Soviet's position. As Sukhanov put it to Miliukov: "The army, as a weapon of politics, is not joining your camp."

> Miliukov interrupted me. His face expressed sincere indignation, and even sadness. "But what are you saying? How is it possible to put it that way? The army is not joining our camp! *The army must fight at the front.* That is the only way to put the question, and that is how we are putting it. That is all there is to our policy in regard to the army."[62]

Miliukov knew exactly where the army should "fight at the front." He urged an expedition to seize the Straits and Constantinople, planned originally for the spring of 1917. The commander of the Black Sea Fleet, Admiral Aleksandr Kolchak, was convinced that it would succeed. When Miliukov visited General Headquarters on March 17–18 he had been briefed on the subject by Nikolai Bazili, director of the diplomatic chancery at headquarters, and Captain Aleksandr Bubnov, deputy head of the naval division there. The three men urged that the expedition be undertaken, but General Alekseev was unwilling to commit the necessary troops. Nevertheless, plans continued to be made for the campaign, particularly since Bazili and Bubnov thought that Alekseev's successor, General Anton Denikin, "realizes perfectly well the importance of the Bosporus operation; a most co-operative attitude toward this plan may be expected from him, much more so than from General Alekseev."[63]

---

[62] *Riech'*, March 30, 1917, p. 3; Tseretelli, *op. cit.*, I, 40; Sukhanov, III, 124; italics in the original.

[63] Bazili letter to Miliukov of April 8, 1917, in BROWKER, II, 1059–60; for Bubnov's optimistic views on the chances of a Straits expedition, see A. Bubnov, *V tsarskoi stavke* (New York, 1955); several chapters are devoted to his analysis of the problem from the naval point of view.

This was a misunderstanding, for Denikin wrote rather contemptuously of the "young, ardent sailors" around Miliukov and said of the expedition that "General Headquarters treated this venture completely negatively as not corresponding to the situation of our armies." He understood Miliukov's hope that the seizure of the Straits "would confront the revolutionary democracy, full of protest against annexations, with an accomplished fact." But he knew, better than Miliukov, that the army's spirit was simply not up to the task. The bulk of the "Constantinople Division" were aged reservists, tired of the war, and not battle ready. Their spokesmen informed the divisional commander that "our comrades declare categorically they will not go into any landing parties nor board any ships."[64]

Though Kolchak continued to press for the expedition, he could not undertake the venture with naval forces alone. Only the Black Sea fleet remained eager for the undertaking, and even Kerensky, who visited the area in May, 1917, admitted that "the sailors were in a patriotic frame of mind and anxious to come to grips with the enemy, and when I arrived in Sebastopol both officers and men were hoping for landing operations in the Bosporus." Only a day before Miliukov's resignation, Riech' printed a telegram to the Provisional Government from the officers and sailors of the cruiser "Ochakov" proclaiming: "We must have a free exit from the Black Sea." The Socialist parties, however, were at work even on the sailors, and practically no one to the left of Miliukov dared to support his stand. When the old revolutionary Nikolai Chaikovskii spoke in the Soviet in favor of seizing the Straits, he was supported by no one, and his declaration was met "with derisive laughter." Plekhanov, too, told Admiral Kolchak that "to renounce the Bosporus and the Dardanelles means to live with one's throat held by foreign hands. I think that Russia will never be able to live without them as she would like to." But his voice no longer had any real influence in his party.[65]

---

[64] For Denikin's views, see Denikin, op. cit., I, Part I, 182–83; the description of the "Constantinople Division" is from N. Krishevskii, "V Krymu (1916–1918 gg.)," ARR, XIII (1924), 75–84. The author was an officer assigned to the expedition in Sevastopol.

[65] The "Ochakov" telegram is in Riech', May 2, 1917, p. 5; for Kerensky's recollections, see Kerensky, op. cit., p. 280. Chaikovskii's appearance is described in Tseretelli, op. cit., I, 52. Kolchak spoke to Plekhanov on April 21, 1917: see "Protokoly doprosa Admirala Kolchaka," ARR, X (1923), 221.

VIII

The Allies, for their part, decided to calm the anti-imperialist zeal
of the Soviet. France and England sent delegations of their own
Socialists to make the Soviet more reasonable. France dispatched
Ernest Lafont, Marius Moutet, and Marcel Cachin, all members of
the Chamber of Deputies; England sent John O'Grady and Will
Thorne, union leaders, and William S. Sanders, Secretary of the
Fabian Society. The men appeared before the Soviet in early April.
They were subjected to hostile examination there and in the process
resorted to verbal compromises which could hardly please Miliukov.
"How do you expect me to resist the pretensions of our maximalists,"
he asked Paléologue, "when the French socialists themselves give up
the fight?" He would not change his tone to suit the visitors and
spoke to them, on behalf of the cabinet, in his usual language:

> Only a short time has elapsed since we saw you in England and
> in France. . . . We felt that your trust in us was clouded by your
> distrust of the dark forces of tsarism. Now everything has changed.
> . . . When you return to your country please say that free Russia
> has doubled its strength, that in spite of the revolution we have
> preserved the main purpose and the meaning of this war.

Kerensky's speech to the visitors was of a very different order. "Up
to now," he told them,

> you have not heard the voice of the Russian democracy, because
> you were addressed, on behalf of the Russian people, by the repre-
> sentatives of the ruling classes. We were not among those who
> went to see you in England and in France and who spoke to you
> in the name of the Russian people. At that time the Russian
> democracy, the Russian people, were compelled to remain silent.
> . . . Comrades, you should know that at the present time the Rus-
> sian democracy is the master of the Russian land. . . . We expect
> that you will exert on the other classes of your countries' popula-
> tions the same decisive influence as the one we have exerted here,
> inside Russia, on our bourgeois classes, which have now declared
> their repudiation of imperialistic aspirations.

Not only did Miliukov have to listen to such notions, he even had
to act as Kerensky's interpreter! "The most curious—and the most
humiliating for me," he recalled, "was the fact that I was forced to

translate Kerensky's speech into English for the English deputies."[66]

There was worse to come. On April 9 there arrived in Petrograd another prominent Frenchman—Albert Thomas, Socialist member of the cabinet and replacement for Paléologue, whom the French planned to recall from Petrograd. Originally, Miliukov had expressed pleasure at the visit. On March 20 he wired Izvol'skii instructing him to express "the warm gratitude of the Provisional Government for this attention and for the choice of M. Thomas whose mission we welcome with the liveliest sympathy." After the event Miliukov was to write that "it was M. Albert Thomas, in particular, who dealt the final blow to the First Provisional Government, while energetically working to bring about the first Coalition."[67]

Immediately upon arrival Thomas met with the Allied ambassadors to decide upon his attitude toward the Soviet and the Provisional Government. In a last attempt to save Miliukov, Paléologue argued:

> With Miliukov and the moderates of the Provisional Government, we still have a chance of stopping the progress of anarchy and keeping Russia in the war. Kerensky implies the assured triumph of the Soviet, which means the unleashing of popular passions, the destruction of the army, the rupture of national ties, and the end of the Russian State.

Thomas however, supported by Buchanan, "declared himself categorically for Kerensky." He believed that "all the power of the Russian democracy is in his revolutionary élan. Only Kerensky is capable of forming, with the Soviet, a government worthy of our confidence."[68]

Buchanan had also abandoned Miliukov. He noted in his diary in the middle of April:

> I should not be surprised if Miliukov has to go. He would be a loss in many ways, as he represents the moderate elements in the Cabinet and is quite sound on the subject of the war, but he has so little influence with his colleagues that one never knows whether he will be able to give effect to what he says.

The British ambassador had begun to see more of Tereshchenko, the

---

[66] For the above, see PAL, III, 303; the Miliukov and Kerensky speeches are in BROWKER, II, 1051–52; Miliukov's last remark is from VOSP, II, 354.

[67] The Miliukov telegram to Izvol'skii is in V. Storozhev, op. cit., p. 95; Miliukov's later comment is in BOLSH, p. 77.

[68] PAL, III, 312–13.

Minister of Finance, who seemed qualified to succeed Miliukov.
Miliukov admitted that Tereshchenko would do as Foreign Minister.
"At least he is not altogether illiterate in these questions," he told
a friend, "and will be in a position to talk with the ambassadors."
From Buchanan's point of view, Tereshchenko held more realistic
views on the subject of Russia's war aims. "I had some conversations
with him about Constantinople," Buchanan noted:

> He had [he said] never been a partisan of its permanent occu-
> pation by Russia, as it would prove a white elephant and have to
> be held by a large garrison. He would like to see it made an open
> port over which Russia should be given some controlling power. He
> told me that I was wrong in supposing that Prince Lvov, like
> Miliukov, favored annexation.

A few days later Tereshchenko saw Buchanan again, and this time
went further:

> He was [he said] most anxious to see peace negotiations opened
> with Turkey, and, if Constantinople was the only bar to such a
> peace, he thought that His Majesty's Government might approach
> the Russian Government with a proposal for its neutralization. I
> said that were we to do so we should lay ourselves open to the
> charge of ill-faith, and under present conditions it would be diffi-
> cult for either Russia or the Allies to propose a revision of their
> respective agreements. He admitted this, but contended that, with
> the exercise of a little tact, an exchange of views on the subject of
> Constantinople might be invited.[69]

Miliukov was being sabotaged not only by his natural enemies
on the left but even by those whom he had always considered his
friends and allies. The Russian European was being abandoned by
Western Europe and by representatives of the Russian middle class.
Abroad, Russia was being disregarded at Allied conferences. The
British, French, and Italians had met twice, at Folkestone and at
St. Jean de Maurienne, in discussions over Asia Minor. No Russian
representative had been invited to these meetings. Miliukov protested
these insults to Russia's honor in telegrams dispatched to Russian
diplomats in the Allied capitals:

---

[69]Buchanan, II, 117–19, 125; Miliukov's remark about Tereshchenko is in
Nabokov, "Vremennoe pravitel'stvo," p. 62.

In my conversations with the ambassadors concerning the recent meetings of the statesmen of France, Great Britain, and Italy in Folkestone and at St. Jean, I have expressed to them my great surprise that the Russian government was not notified beforehand of either the forthcoming conference or its subject, and was advised only afterwards of the decisions that took place. . . . The fact that we are not participating in these negotiations and are even uninformed with regard to the subject of the forthcoming conferences may produce a very unfavorable impression on our public opinion and even occasion undesirable rumors of frictions and disagreements between the Allies.[70]

From the other side of the Atlantic there came warnings of another kind. Secretary of State Robert Lansing telegraphed Petrograd as follows:

The Congress has passed $7 billion war loan, of which $3 billion are to be assigned to Russia and the Allied governments. The political reforms of the Russian state have been met here with great enthusiasm. However, the latest reports, widely disseminated by the press, of the Government being under the influence of extreme socialist parties that aim at a separate peace for which Germany yearns so intensely, are doing much damage to the Russian interests here; if these communications do not cease, they might prevent Russia from obtaining her share of the loan assigned to the Allies.

Miliukov was between two fires. On the one hand, the Allies were ceasing to consider Russia as a great power and a respectable partner. On the other, the Soviet made the Allies doubt Russia's further value as a participant in the war. The Russian Foreign Minister was obviously caught in this dilemma. It would soon become clear that he was unable to solve it. The Left pressure on Miliukov was increasing, particularly from Lenin and the Socialist Revolutionary leader Victor Chernov. Miliukov considered Lenin "an honest but harmful fanatic." He warned against any measures of violence against him and urged that the Leninist movement be fought "by word and persuasion." It was impossible, he told his followers, to fight one's enemies by the methods of the old regime. In private conversation he was less tolerant. Buchanan recorded the following conversation with Miliukov:

Miliukov . . . said that popular feeling against Lenin was grow-

[70] The Miliukov telegram of April 13 is in BROWKER, II, 1063; Lansing's telegram of April 8 is in *ibid.*, II, 1053.

ing, that the troops were ready to arrest him whenever the government gave the word, but that the latter did not wish to precipitate
matters for fear of provoking civil strife. . . . The Government were
but waiting for the psychological moment, which was not, he
thought, far distant.

The coming weeks were to show that the government could not
count on the troops. As for the police, it had been disbanded and
replaced by an ineffectual militia. Lenin saw clearly that the police
was needed, even if the Provisional Government did not. As he wrote
in March, 1917: "The Guchkov-Miliukov government will be unable
to restore the monarchy or to stay in power at all if it does not *restore
the police*. . . . That is clear, as clear as God's bright day."[71]

Chernov was, for the moment, more dangerous than Lenin because
he was less of an extremist and had, from the moment of his return
from foreign exile, an assured place in the Soviet. In the opinion of
a recent student of the Russian revolution, "the man who led the
concerted assault upon Miliukov's foreign policy and who more than
any other was responsible for the minister's resignation was the SR
generalissimo, V. M. Chernov." He invented the nickname "Miliukov-
Dardanel'skii" which was making the rounds in those days and called
Miliukov "that reincarnation of Guizot who will persevere in his
doctrinaire stand until history shows him the door." In Chernov,
Miliukov met his most determined opponent:

> In the twenty years or so of his political activity there are some
> equivocations and many deviations, but in one particular he never
> wavered: he was invincibly determined that Russia should not have
> the Straits. Not even the land question could strike such fire from
> the SR leader.[72]

IX

The presence of the Allied Socialists and of Albert Thomas
gave Kerensky new ammunition. He determined to push for a re-
examination of Russian foreign policy. On April 13 the newspapers

[71] "Miting Partii Narodnoi Svobody," *Riech'*, April 17, 1917, p. 5; Buchanan,
II, 119; *Leninskii sbornik* (Moscow), II (1924), 350; italics in the original.
[72] O. Radkey, *The Agrarian Foes of Bolshevism* (New York, 1958), pp. 104,
155–56, 158; see also the editorial in *Delo Naroda* (Petrograd), April 15, 1917.

carried an announcement, inspired by him, that "the Provisional Government is at present preparing a note which it will submit to the Allied Powers." This was false, and Miliukov demanded that the statement be withdrawn. The next day the announcement was officially disavowed. But the damage had been done, and the Soviet aroused. As Miliukov informed Izvol'skii on April 17, it meant:

> the resumption by the Soviet of Workers' Deputies of their insistent requests to the Government for the transformation of the Declaration to the citizens on the aims of the war, issued by the Government, into a diplomatic document, which would serve as a motive for re-examining the views of the Allies on war aims. . . . Thomas suggested a few days ago that I should communicate the Declaration of the Government to the Allied Powers. I told him that I would agree to do it only provided I were certain that the contents of the Declaration would not cause misunderstandings, particularly with regard to our alleged willingness to renounce the Straits.[73]

Miliukov preferred to send no note, but the Soviet issued an ultimatum: it refused to approve the Liberty Loan, the government's bond issue for vitally needed funds, until a note was sent. The government capitulated, and on April 18 Miliukov sent the note, the wording of which was approved by Albert Thomas. It contained a typical Miliukov flourish, stating that "liberated Russia can at the present time use a language understandable to the advanced democracies of contemporary mankind." But the Foreign Minister continued to play his own game and not that of his critics. Instead of declaring against "annexations and indemnities," he concluded his note by affirming that "the leading democracies will find a way to establish those guarantees and sanctions which are required to prevent new bloody encounters in the future." It was an innocuous statement, but *Riech'* clarified it:

> It is obvious that the system of pacts and agreements which binds us to our Allies . . . cannot become subject to sharp alterations without provoking stresses in Allied relations themselves. It is especially important to maintain the stability of these relations precisely at the present moment when . . . we are nearing the time

[73] The announcement and counter-announcement are in BROWKER, II, 1096–97; Miliukov's telegram to Izvol'skii is in *ibid.*, 1097.

to reckon the totals. Russia's share in these totals is large enough and should not be weakened nor reduced during the remaining period of the struggle.[74]

In the aroused atmosphere of the moment, Miliukov's note had the impact of a bombshell. The Menshevik newspaper wrote: "Mr. Miliukov's note played the role of a match tossed into a keg of dynamite." Maksim Gorky's daily demanded Miliukov's resignation:

> A champion of the interests of international capital has no place in the ranks of the government of democratic Russia! We have no doubt that the Soviet of Workers' and Soldiers' Deputies will not delay in taking the most energetic measures to make Mr. Miliukov harmless immediately.

Before the Soviet could take "energetic measures," there were spontaneous outbursts of indignation in Petrograd. On April 20 two regiments besieged the government in the Marinskii Palace and asked for Miliukov's resignation. Hostile demonstrators displaying placards "Down With Miliukov" marched from the workers' districts. "Everywhere," Izvestiia reported, "the streets are filled with crowds of people. They are speaking in agitated tones and discussing the startling issues." The demonstrations continued to grow in size, and by evening the city was filled with them. The famous "April Days" had begun. It was the first time that Miliukov had provoked mass demonstrations; it was also the last time that he was at the center of public attention. His supporters organized counter-demonstrations expressing confidence in him. By evening an estimated twenty-five thousand persons waited at the Marinskii Palace to hear him. The Kadet Central Committee, in a public message, asked how a government which had granted independence to Poland could be accused of imperialism. "Neither the Provisional Government in its entirety," it said, "nor the Minister of Foreign Affairs in particular are, or can be, conducting an aggressive policy, based on a desire to dominate other nations." Evidently trying to strengthen Miliukov's hand, the American ambassador also intervened. "In the midst of these hostile demonstrations," he wrote,

> I called upon Miliukov . . . and told him . . . that having risked

[74] The text of the note is in ibid., II, 1098; see also Riech', April 20, 1917, p. 2. Miliukov states (in VOSP, II, 360) that Thomas approved the wording of the note.

my judgment in asking my Government to recognize the Provisional Government . . . I felt considerable official and personal responsibility concerning a stable government in Russia, and that if more satisfactory evidence was not given of such a government, I should feel compelled to advise my Government not to extend the aid which I have been continuously recommending.

Guchkov, who was present at the interview, "seemed very much pleased at the statement and asked if I would make it public, but before I could answer Miliukov remarked that he trusted there would be no occasion for me to do so." Miliukov was pleased with the results of the demonstrations which seemed to be going his way.[75]

Late on April 20 the government met with the Soviet in an attempt to arrive at a compromise. This, however, seemed impossible, since the Soviet pronounced the note "unacceptable," and Miliukov refused to send a new one. During the meeting he was called to the balcony of the Marinskii Palace, from which he addressed the huge crowd of his supporters. Speaking of the "Down With Miliukov" banners, he said: "I feared not for Miliukov, but for Russia." He came back to the meeting in triumph. But his opponents were in no mood for concessions. The Soviet demanded Miliukov's resignation:

> Chernov criticized severely the entire activity of the Minister of Foreign Affairs. While acknowledging the ability of his political opponent, Miliukov, he concluded that the latter might be very useful, for example, as Minister of Education; as Minister of Foreign Affairs he would remain a source of weakness and discord in the government and the country, for by his public recognition of the Tsarist war aims he had become absolutely unacceptable to the democracy of the toilers.

The suggestion that Miliukov become Minister of Education prompted the acid comment of Trotsky: "Constantinople as a topic in geography would at any rate be less dangerous than as a topic in diplomacy." For the time being, however, Miliukov's colleagues

---

[75] Editorial in *Rabochaia Gazeta* (Petrograd), April 23, 1917; *Novaia Zhizn'* (Petrograd), April 20, 1917, p. 1; *Izvestiia* (Petrograd), April 21, 1917, p. 1. For a description of the pro-Miliukov demonstrations, see D. Zaslavskii, and V. Kantorovich, (eds.), *Khronika fevral'skoi revoliutsii* (Petrograd, 1924), p. 225; "Vozvanie ts. kom. partii nar. svob.," *Riech'*, April 21, 1917, p. 2; Francis, op. cit., pp. 110–11.

refused to give him up, and the meeting ended inconclusively.[76]

The day's most foreboding lesson had been the behavior of the troops. They were loyal to the Soviet, not to the government, which in any case did not wish to use force. When the Petrograd commander General Lavr Kornilov asked for authority to suppress the disturbances, Premier L'vov and Kerensky refused to act. "Our strength," said the Premier, "lies in moral influence; to resort to armed power would mean a return to the former violence which I consider impossible." Tereshchenko threatened to resign if any blood were shed. "Only Miliukov," recalled Guchkov, "was ready to defend himself." He was impatient with the passivity of his colleagues. "Here we can talk and discuss anything we want," he said, "but it is quite possible that in a short while we shall all, in a body, sit in the Kresty Prison, or in the Peter and Paul Fortress." Kornilov reported that of the 125,000-man garrison he could count on only 3,500. But, since these were disciplined troops, "we could defend the Provisional Government in case of an attempt to overthrow it." The War Minister could only comment: "This scene stunned me."[77]

The crisis was clearly not over. Neither side had yet spoken its last, and the Left was by no means satisfied with the results achieved. "To swallow the pill presented by Guchkov and Miliukov," wrote Lenin, "would mean to give up forever an independent political role—tomorrow Miliukov will 'put his feet on the table' and reduce the Soviet to a bare zero."[78]

X

It was not likely that Miliukov would "put his feet on the table," but the demonstrations and counter-demonstrations continued the following day, April 21. "Immense throngs," Kerensky wrote, "appeared in the streets in a great demonstration in honor of the

[76] An account of Miliukov's appearance on the balcony of the Marinskii Palace is in Riech', April 21, 1917, p. 3; V. Chernov, The Great Russian Revolution (New York, 1936), p. 201, contains his remarks. See also Trotsky, op. cit., I, 344. There are accounts of the meeting in Tseretelli, op. cit., I, 98–106, and Sukhanov, III, 279–89.

[77] The above is based on A. Guchkov, "Iz vospominanii," PN, September 23, 1936, p. 2, and "Protokoly doprosa Admirala Kolchaka," op. cit., p. 222; Kolchak was present at the meeting between Kornilov and the cabinet.

[78] Lenin in Pravda, April 21, 1917, reprinted in LEN, XX, 208.

Provisional Government and, particularly, of Miliukov." Lenin wrote in *Pravda*: "The bourgeoisie occupies the Nevsky—in the expression of one paper, the Miliukovsky Prospect—and the adjacent sections of prosperous, bureaucratic and capitalistic Petrograd." There were banners proclaiming "Long Live Miliukov," and "Miliukov's Resignation Means the Resignation of the Provisional Government." The support thus demonstrated misled Miliukov. Describing the events to a Kadet congress in early May, he spoke of a trend which:

> stands for the preservation and the consolidation of the colossal achievements, both political and social, which the revolution has achieved. With regard to these achievements, this trend is conservative because it stands for their preservation. . . . One can be certain that the huge majority of the reasonably inclined population of the country also stands for it. But this majority is not organized. It manifests itself only in moments of extreme danger to public order and authority, as happened during the events of April 21–22.

Miliukov was doubtless right in asserting that the majority of the "reasonably inclined" were with him. But did the "reasonably inclined" form the majority of the population? Quite evidently not, since the anti-Miliukov demonstrations showed no signs of abating, and several persons were killed and many wounded during April 21. Nevertheless, as Ambassador Francis reported to Secretary of State Lansing on April 22: "The Minister of Foreign Affairs, who had lunch with me today, is much elated over the situation." He must also have been elated over the editorial which appeared in *Le Temps*. "The circular note of the Minister of Foreign Affairs P. N. Miliukov," it said, "proves that the new Russia has a healthy understanding of the liberating character of this war; this fact indicates that Russia has become mature enough to transform itself into a great democracy."[79]

[79] A. Kerensky, *The Catastrophe* (New York, 1927), p. 136; *Pravda* April 23, 1917, quoted in BROWKER, III, 1247; the pro-Miliukov demonstrations are described in *Riech'*, April 22, 1917, pp. 5–6, and *Vestnik*, 1917, No. 1, pp. 20–21. Miliukov's speech of May 9 to the Kadet congress is in BROWKER, III, 1291. The results of a judicial investigation of the April Days are printed in V. Rakhmetov (ed.), "Aprel'skie dni 1917 g. v Petrograde," KA, XXXIII (1929), 34–82. The Francis telegram to Lansing is in *Papers Relating to the Foreign Relations of the United States*, loc. cit., p. 41. The editorial of *Le Temps* (Paris), April 21, 1917, is from "Inostrannia Pechat,'" *Vestnik Vremennago Pravitel'stva*, April 23, 1917, p. 3.

While demonstrations filled the streets, negotiations continued. Since the Soviet refused to accept Miliukov's note, the government agreed to send an "explanation" which was to remove all ambiguity. "By 'guarantees and sanctions' for a lasting peace, mentioned in the note," the explanation stated, "the Provisional Government has in mind the limitations of armaments, international tribunals, etc." To protect Miliukov the explanation specified that "the note of the Minister of Foreign Affairs was the subject of careful and extended discussion by the Provisional Government and its text was approved unanimously." Appearances were preserved, but the essence of the matter was clear: the Soviet had won once again. "This explanation," the Soviet stated in its acceptance of the government's move,

> puts an end to the possibility of interpreting the note of April 18 in a spirit foreign to the demand and interests of the revolutionary democracy. The fact that the question of renunciation of forcible annexation has brought forward for international consideration should be regarded as a great victory for democracy.

The Soviet Executive Committee was now ready to draw practical consequences from its victory. The stand it adopted made a mockery of Miliukov's position as Russia's Foreign Minister. "The following principles were accepted for guidance," said the Soviet resolution:

> 1. The Executive Committee considers it necessary to adopt resolute measures at once for increasing its control over the activities of the Provisional Government and, primarily, over the activities of the Minister of Foreign Affairs; 2. no major political act must be published without first notifying the Executive Committee; 3. the personnel of the Russian diplomatic corps abroad must undergo a radical change.[80]

It would have been below Miliukov's dignity to remain in office under such conditions.

It was a sad finale to what had promised to be a brilliant term of office. The future looked bleak not only to Miliukov but to the Provisional Government as well. In a declaration issued on April 26 it warned that:

---

[80] The text of the explanation and the Soviet's acceptance of it is in BROWKER, II, 1100–1101. The Soviet resolution on supervising Miliukov is in *ibid.*, III, 1242.

the difficulties of the tasks which have fallen to the lot of the Provisional Government threaten to become insurmountable. . . . Before Russia rises the terrible apparition of civil war and anarchy, carrying destruction to freedom. There is a somber and grievous course of peoples, a course well known in history, leading from freedom through civil war and anarchy to reaction and the return of despotism. This course must not be the course of the Russian people.

On April 27, on the eleventh anniversary of the summoning of the First Duma, the deputies of all four Dumas met to celebrate the occasion. Many of the speeches sounded a tragic note. Guchkov concluded by warning: "Our Fatherland is on the verge of ruin." The conservative Shul'gin asserted that "our people are not yet fully ripe for politics." The Duma sounded like a voice from the grave, and Izvestiia pronounced the death sentence over it: "The Duma has died forever. This is the lesson to be derived from the meeting of April 27." Miliukov, who did not speak at the meeting, had his own explanation of the dilemma facing Russia. "Never," he told an immense Kadet meeting held on the same day, "in any country did such vast problems have to be solved in wartime." His habitual optimism seemed to be exhausted. Paléologue, who had him for dinner on April 28, noted the change:

> For the first time Miliukov appears to me to be deprived of his courageous optimism, his confidence, and his fighting spirit. In his speech he affects the same assurance as before; but the hollow sound of his voice and his ravaged appearance clearly reveal his internal distress. We are all struck by it.[81]

On May 1 Guchkov resigned as Minister of War. The April Days had shown him that the crisis in the Russian army was deepening. He spoke of "conditions which I am powerless to alter and which threaten the defense, freedom, and even the existence of Russia with fatal consequences." The first Provisional Government was beginning to fall apart. Against Miliukov's objections the cabinet proposed the formation of a coalition government, with the participation of

---

[81] The text of the government declaration is in ibid., III, 1249–51; the speeches of April 27 are in ibid., III, 1261–62; Izvestiia's comment is in ibid., III, 1266. Miliukov's speech is from "Mitingy 27 aprel'ia," Riech', April 29, 1917, p. 6. See also PAL, III, 341.

representatives of the Soviet. After long debates the Soviet voted
to enter the government. "I objected to this," Miliukov said later,
"believing that a mixed government would be not stronger but
weaker than the government that emerged from the revolution." It
was still hoped that Miliukov would remain as Minister of Education.
But, he maintained,

> it was perfectly plain to me that changing the portfolio of Minister
> of Foreign Affairs for the portfolio of the Minister of Education
> would not free me from responsibility for those foreign policies
> which I have followed during the entire war and which are well
> known to the whole world. I cannot accept such a responsibility.
> That is why I resigned.[82]

As a last gesture before vacating the foreign ministry building
which he had occupied so modestly, Miliukov gave a banquet in
honor of the departing Paléologue, his most faithful European friend
of recent days:

> I decided, for the first and last time during my tenure of office,
> to give him a farewell dinner in style. . . . The footmen were in
> full ceremonial dress, as required by old tradition. Solemn speeches
> were made. Thomas also was invited and said to me, in an aside:
> "Ah, ces cochons les tovarisch!" Paléologue praised me, in another
> aside: I was a minister "of the right kind." But the general mood
> was funereal.

At the Finland Station Paléologue was to meet Sazonov, who was
to travel with him to England as the new Russian ambassador in
London. But that, too, was not to be. A letter from Premier L'vov
delivered at the station informed Sazonov that his appointment was
canceled due to Miliukov's resignation.[83] A new spirit was to rule in
the Russian Foreign Office. It remained to be seen whether Miliukov's
successor would be more successful.

[82] Guchkov's letter of resignation is in BROWKER, III, 1267–8. Miliukov's
objection to the coalition is from ibid., III, 1494. His refusal to become Minister
of Education is in ibid., III, 1274.

[83] Miliukov's description of the banquet is in VOSP, II, 371; the scene at the
Finland Station is from PAL, III, 344–45.

9: CONCLUSION

> Let us give this type a name as complex as he is himself. He is
> a Russian who has grown up in the conviction that though he
> was not born a European, he is duty-bound to become one.
> For two hundred years already this type dominates over all
> others both in its influence on our society, and in its interest
> for the historian. . . . Around him there concentrate, and
> sometimes from him there originate, the most important intel-
> lectual, and sometimes even political movements.[1]

I

In 1927, on the tenth anniversary of the revolution, living as an
émigré in Paris, Miliukov wrote that

> he who has studied the history of the great revolutions of the past
> will know how to distinguish the generic traits common to all revo-
> lutions. . . . One of the common phenomena of these revolutions
> is the successive passage of power from the hands of the moderate
> factions to those of others, with more extreme ideas.[2]

After April, 1917, Miliukov was fated to observe this process at first
hand in his native country. Following his resignation, he observed
the scene more or less passively, from the sidelines, without much
hope of influencing events in the direction in which he believed.

Already in April, during one of the meetings between the cabinet
and the Soviet, Sukhanov had boasted to Miliukov that socialism
was about to win in Russia.

The revolution, said Sukhanov, has developed as broadly as we

---

[1] V. Kliuchevskii, *Sochineniia*, VII (Moscow, 1959), 148.
[2] P. Miliukov, "Le Dixième Anniversaire de la Revolution Russe," LMS, 1927,
No. 11–12, p. 190.

wanted, and as you did not want. You did not succeed in turning
the new Russia into a plutocratic England or France by consoli-
dating the political dictatorship of capital here. The outcome of
our struggle is clear. It has become apparent that you do not, and
cannot, possess any real force against the democracy.

Miliukov disagreed with this formulation of the problem. In his eyes
the situation was at once simpler and less promising.

> Surely you do not think, he replied to Sukhanov, that we are
> actually conducting some sort of our own class, bourgeois policy,
> that we have a definite line of our own. . . . There is nothing of
> the kind. We are merely forced to see to it that everything should
> not disintegrate completely. All one sees around are gaping holes,
> and so one jumps first here, then there, to help even a little bit, to
> adjust, to mend.[3]

Miliukov would never admit to being a bourgeois and saw his policy
as that of the entire nation, not of any class. The times, it appeared
to him, demanded only one program: continuing the war and leading
Russia to the Constituent Assembly which would decide all issues
by democratic vote. Until the meeting of the Assembly, only the
Provisional Government spoke for the country. He did not recognize
the Soviet as a legitimate expression of popular will. It had not been
elected by methods which could be described as European. It was
an institution without precedent in European political practice, and,
one suspects, this was sufficient to disqualify it in Miliukov's eyes.
It represented another Russia, which Miliukov had never inhabited.
In his Chicago lectures of 1903 he had spoken of the existence of
two Russias and had told his listeners that only one was real—that
of the people and the intellectuals who led it. The other, official
Russia, had no claim to anyone's attention and was condemned to
disappear. In 1917 there were again two Russias, but, this time,
Miliukov seemed to find himself in the very camp which he had
once condemned, in that official Russia which might enjoy the
trappings of power and the recognition of Europe but which was
destined to be swept away by the revolutionary process.

He refused to admit this sad reality. When the first elections after
February, those for the Petrograd district dumas in May, 1917, failed
to give the Kadets more than a third of the vote and exposed them

---

[3] The Sukhanov-Miliukov exchange is in Sukhanov, III, 124–25.

to electoral abuse and even violence, Miliukov reminded Russians that they were only beginning to learn the meaning of political freedom. "We must remember," he wrote, "that our freedom is a young, newborn babe; it is from the Allies that we must learn the ways in which mankind gained freedom for itself."[4] The population, however, refused to be tutored by Miliukov's party. From February on the Kadets were identified with the status quo, with privilege, and with property. Once popular freedom had been won, the Party of Popular Freedom seemed to be of no further use. Though its program remained radical when seen through European eyes, it was too moderate to suit the Russians of 1917. As one participant put it:

> Now behind the Constitutional Democratic party were organized all the political and social forces of the country representing the interests of the propertied classes, of the high command, the remnants of the old bureaucracy, and even fragments of the aristocracy. . . . The Constitutional Democratic Party had retained its entire ideology. Only the human material filling its ranks had changed radically.[5]

The Kadets found themselves on the Right where, they were persuaded, they did not belong and where they certainly did not wish to be. The revolutionary process gradually deposited them there and Miliukov, involuntarily, helped to bring this about. As Chernov remarked:

> His chief weakness was a complete lack of feeling for popular, mass psychology. He was too much a man of the study, hence, a doctrinaire. The studious side of his nature had been moderated by the long schooling of parliamentary life and struggle . . . that peculiar little world which, in Russia more than elsewhere, was isolated, protected against the pressure of the street.[6]

Once deprived of his "peculiar little world," the parliament which, for a decade, had served him as a substitute for popular opinion, Miliukov seemed lost. Though a member of the two appointive assemblies of August and October, 1917, his voice there belonged

[4] See "Napadenie na biuro Partii Narodnoi Svobody," *Riech'*, May 30, 1917, p. 6, and "Soiuzniki i voina," *Riech'*, May 31, 1917, p. 4.
[5] A. Kerensky, *The Catastrophe* (New York, 1927), p. 250; for a similar analysis by a Kadet, see G. Vernadsky, "O litse partii," *Vestnik*, 1917, No. 6–7, p. 5.
[6] V. Chernov, *The Great Russian Revolution* (New York, 1936), p. 172.

to the opposition from the Right, not from the Left. At the Moscow State Conference in August, Miliukov's speech seemed to echo the oration of the commander in chief, General Lavr Kornilov, who had become the most outspoken critic of the Soviets. Miliukov spoke as the civilian leader of those circles which saw their military leader in Kornilov. "It is true," he said at the State Conference, "that, at the present time the unorganized masses have submitted to the party slogans which sound most promising; but it is not true that the parties, which advance these slogans, have a monopoly on democracy, for Russia does not consist of socialists alone."[7] It was true that Russia did not consist only of socialists, but the others, now led by Kornilov and Miliukov, were made to appear as reactionaries, and counter-revolutionaries.

During the Kornilov affair, Miliukov played a rather ambiguous role. He attempted to mediate between Kerensky and Kornilov but only succeeded in finally convincing most socialists that he would go to all lengths to set the clock back. Armed Red Guards tried to arrest him, and even Kerensky insisted that he leave Petrograd for several weeks as a condition of keeping Kadet ministers in the Provisional Government. Miliukov returned to Petrograd in early October to lead the Kadet delegation in the Council of the Republic. It was Kerensky's last attempt to gather Russian public opinion around his government. The Council, with a strong Socialist majority, could hardly have been a comfort to Miliukov. He was forced to listen to plans for increasingly radical solutions of Russia's dilemma. For his part he could only laugh at those who thought that the Russian revolution had created a system superior to that of the West. "We should not," he told the Council one week before the Bolshevik coup,

> boast before them [the Allies] of our democratic superiority. It is not for us to give them lessons they do not need. . . . Ending my speech I would like to say: Long live the flower of humanity, the advanced democracies of the West, which have long ago covered a considerable part of the journey on which we have just embarked with halting steps! Long live our gallant Allies![8]

[7] His speech is in BROWKER, III, 1494.
[8] The documents used to label Miliukov a Kornilovite were the unprinted *Riech'* editorial of August 30, 1917, welcoming Kornilov (the galley had been withdrawn at the last moment but fell into Bolshevik hands) and the letter to Miliukov of General Alekseev soliciting financial aid for the defeated Kornilovites

Then came the Bolshevik revolution. Miliukov's prediction to
Mikhail Romanov that the Provisional Government would not live
long enough to see the Constituent Assembly had been accurate. The
Bolsheviks declared the Kadets "Enemies of the People" and ordered
Miliukov's arrest. Miliukov went to Rostov on the Don, where he
joined generals Alekseev and Kornilov who were building up an
armed force against the Bolsheviks. He was elected to the Constituent
Assembly, but neither he nor any of the seventeen Kadet deputies
attended the first and only meeting in January, 1918. The elections
must have been a huge disappointment to him. Only 1.9 million
Russians (of 41 million) cast their votes for his party. At the ninth
Kadet Congress in July, 1917 he had said: "We should not be upset
if, possibly, the first experience of universal elections will not give
us complete victory." The actual outcome was immeasurably worse,
but it made little practical difference; the great issues of the day
had not waited for the Assembly. It was only later that Miliukov
admitted that:

> it meant expecting too much from the degree of civic education of
> the Russian peasant to ask him first to fight on to the bitter end,
> with the risk of being killed, and then to await the decision of a
> Constituent Assembly on that momentous question of land.[9]

All Miliukov's thoughts now turned to plans for a forcible overthrow of the Bolsheviks. When Alekseev's Volunteer Army proved
unequal to the task, Miliukov turned to the Germans occupying
the Ukraine. In June and July, 1918, he soiled his reputation by
visiting German generals and diplomats in Kiev in an attempt to
gain allies against the Bolsheviks. The plan failed and earned him

---

in September, 1917. The first document is printed in V. Vladimirova, *Kontr-
Revoliutsiia v 1917 g.* (Moscow, 1924), pp. 181–82; the second is in BROW-
KER, III, 1603–6. The text of his speech of October 18, 1917, is in BROWKER,
II, 1150–51.

   [9] The Bolshevik decree of December 11, 1917, outlawing the Kadet party is
in J. Meisel and E. Kozera (eds.), *Materials for the Study of the Soviet System*
(Ann Arbor, Mich., 1953), p. 31. Election figures are from O. Radkey, *The
Elections to the Russian Constituent Assembly of 1917* (Cambridge, Mass.,
1950), pp. 16–17, 21. Miliukov's speech at the ninth Kadet congress is in
Riech', July 29, 1917, p. 5; his remark on the Constituent Assembly is from
RUS, pp. 32–33.

only the hostility of many Kadets and the suspicion of the Allies, who were still at war with Germany and too distant to help rid Russia of her new masters. After the armistice of November, 1918, he turned to the Allies hoping that they would become Russia's saviors. He attended a conference of Russians and Allied diplomats at Jassy, Rumania, in November, 1918, which discussed the ways and means of Allied intervention in Russia. Along with several others he was commissioned by the conference to go to the Allied capitals in search of aid and political recognition. It would be a very different delegation than the one which took him to the same capitals in 1916. He was to be ignored and humiliated, expelled from Paris by a Clemenceau indignant at his "pro-German stand" and forced to resign from the delegation. He would never see Russia again.[10]

On the boat which was taking him to Constantinople, Miliukov wrote a letter to Petrunkevich, then in the Crimea, which might serve as his political testament. It was a summing up in regard to Russia, addressed to the founder and patriarch of the Kadet party. "Who can help it," wrote Miliukov on December 4, 1918, "if our historical chronology does not coincide with the Western one, and if our revolution showed us that some groups of our population live not in the twentieth, not even in the eighteenth, but in the thirteenth and fourteenth centuries." The epilogue came on the very day that the Jassy delegation was received by Admiral Amet, commander of the French forces in Constantinople. In the city which Miliukov had hoped to win for Russia, the French dignitary, having heard Miliukov's plea for Allied help, answered him rather harshly: "You are imagining us in the role of some sort of *providence créatrice*, expect everything from us, and do nothing to help yourselves."[11]

[10] For Miliukov's negotiations with the Germans, see "Dnevnik P. N. Miliukova," *Novyi Zhurnal* (New York), LXVI (1961), 173–203, and LXVII (1962), 180–218. On the Jassy Conference, see the excellent summary of R. Mc Neal, "The Conference of Jassy," in J. Curtiss (ed.), *Essays in Russian and Soviet History* (Leyden, 1963), pp. 221–36. For Miliukov's reception in the West in December, 1918, see *Pall Mall Gazette* (London), January 15, 1919: "M. Miliukov's Statements Translated from *Le Temps* of December 26, 1918 by Mrs. Lucy Edwards."

[11] Miliukov's letter to Petrunkevich of December 4, 1918, is in the Miliukov Collection of the Russian Archives, Columbia University, as is his diary for 1918–1920, from which comes Amet's remark, dated December 4, 1918, p. 414 of the manuscript.

II

In casting a retrospective glance at Miliukov's political career, which had now come to an end, one can divide it into three stages: the revolution of 1905–7, the decade following, and the year 1917. During the first stage Miliukov's ideas seemed, for a brief moment, to offer the most promising solution to Russia's political dilemma. The country would be reformed through the co-operation of a constitutional monarch and a legislative assembly elected under a restricted suffrage, but ready to fulfil many age-old desires of the Russian people. The existing state structure would provide the element of continuity needed for a peaceful transition toward new forms. The Kadets would be the monarch's indispensable helpers, would serve him as constitutional ministers and officials, would guide his legislature, and lead Russia along the path which the West had traveled earlier.

The first stage, however, turned out differently. The old regime proved strong enough to do without the Kadets, who were not wanted by the radical parties either; these were clearly more powerful in the political sense. The Emperor refused to make all the concessions which Miliukov considered necessary and opposed the pressure of the radicals by force. The product of the first stage of Miliukov's career turned out to be a mere parody, or so he thought, of that political structure he wished to build. He became a leader of His Majesty's Opposition, but in a parliament unworthy of that name. Unable to bring about domestic reforms, Miliukov turned to issues of foreign policy and adopted principles which would prove politically fatal to him in 1917. He had been a pacifist, but when war came he welcomed it as a means of accomplishing his ends. He did not know that he had made an alliance with forces beyong his control. He led a Duma coalition which, he made himself believe, represented all Russia and could both prevent the revolution and reform the country. But the revolution came unbidden and released passions which could be controlled only by means unacceptable to Miliukov. In the last stage of his career the man seemingly triumphed, only to be eliminated from the Russian political scene. He had made some major errors, to be sure, but it is difficult to escape the conclusion that he and his party could not have succeeded in 1917 under any circumstances. Once the traditional state structure disappeared, they could not even survive.

An examination of the three stages of Miliukov's political career will show that his chances were best in the first stage, only moderately promising in the second, and largely nonexistent in the third. The politics which he embraced required the presence of certain institutions which were viable in 1905–7, weakened but still not negligible in the following decade, but decomposed by 1917. Though occasionally he spoke of a jump from autocracy to republic, his schemes required a far slower transition, with prolonged periods of consolidation. The first of these periods opened with the October Manifesto and presented the Kadets with a golden opportunity. This chance, Miliukov's critics asserted, was destroyed by his intransigence and doctrinairism. His most eloquent critic was Vasilii Maklakov; his books, written in emigration, contained a scheme of Kadet "revisionism." Briefly summarized, the scheme charged Miliukov with being a radical when he should have been a liberal. Already in his Osvobozhdenie articles, Miliukov had maintained, said Maklakov, that there were no intermediate positions between autocracy and consistent constitutionalism. In 1906, Maklakov charged, Miliukov insisted on his doctrinal stand when a compromise might have meant victory. During the first revolution, said Maklakov, Miliukov had been as impatient with the autocracy as the masses were to be with the Provisional Government in 1917. He should have collaborated with the monarchy and the bureaucracy, for they alone guaranteed the legal order essential for the existence of liberty. Working against the state structure could only bring chaos and dictatorship, as 1917 was to show. Miliukov should have led the right wing of his party in a moderate direction, even at the risk of a split in the Kadet ranks. In co-operation with the Octobrists, he could have built a middle camp which, with the liberal bureaucracy, would have represented a force sufficient to oppose both the reactionaries and the Left. A coalition of Miliukov, Guchkov, and Stolypin, Maklakov maintained, could have led the Emperor into a brighter future.[12]

The Maklakov thesis is seductive only at first sight. It rests on a number of assumptions which dissolve into wishful thinking once examined against the evidence. It presupposes, as a recent student

---

[12] Maklakov's thesis is developed in his "Iz proshlago," SZ, 1929–31, 1934–36; Pervaia gosudarstvennaia duma (Paris, 1939); Vlast' i obshchestvennost' Na zakate staroi Rossii (Paris, 1936); and Vtoraia gosudarstvennaia duma (Paris, n.d.).

of Russian liberalism has pointed out, a knowledge of the future which was not available to Miliukov or anyone else in 1906. It also grants the Emperor and the bureaucracy far more credit than they deserve. "In view of Russian conditions," writes Marc Raeff,

> it seems to me, the more radically-minded liberals were also the more realistic politicians. They could not have foreseen the dangers of totalitarian democracy as inherent in revolutionary radicalism. The pessimistic and hazy forebodings of Struve, Maklakov and Trubetskoi could not impress a generation that had not known the First World War or 1917. Correctly, I feel, they believed that the first obstacle to be removed was the autocracy. But could this be done without radicalism? . . . Nothing but the strongest pressure could have changed the imperial regime.[13]

Miliukov rejected Maklakov's thesis outright. "I think," he wrote, "that history justified me and not Maklakov with his foggy conception of the possibility of collaboration with Tsardom. The Maklakov solution, incidentally, was tried several times—unsuccessfully. It in fact brought Russia to the revolution of 1917." We have seen that Guchkov in 1913 agreed with Miliukov's formulation of the problem.

Though one is forced to agree with Miliukov against Maklakov, there is no question that the first revolution revealed a number of things which should have served as warnings to Miliukov. It was, first of all, the power at the command of the Emperor and his servants. This force was indispensable in any attempt to rebuild Russia in Miliukov's sense. Any attempt to destroy it would create a vacuum which the Kadets would be unable to fill. They relied too much on a legislature which even Miliukov recognized to be "a hothouse plant on a Russian street." He had to admit that the First Duma was popular primarily because of its Trudovik deputies. They alone represented the Russian peasants, for whom the Kadets would always remain an alien party. Like the Social Democrats of the Second Duma, they showed a singular lack of respect for the constitutional niceties so dear to Miliukov. They had no basic respect for the legislative process, an attitude shared by the Emperor and the bureaucracy. Only the Kadets made a fetish of it, and because they had done

[13] M. Raeff, "Some Reflections on Russian Liberalism," RR, July, 1959, p. 226. Miliukov's statement is from P. Miliukov, "Liberalizm, radikalizm, i revoliutsiia," SZ, LVII (1935), 313. See also his "V. A. Maklakov mezhdu 'obshchestvenost'iu' i 'vlastiu,' " PN, May 28, 1937, p. 2.

so well in the elections to the First Duma Miliukov believed that Russia thirsted for a parliament.

In fact, neither a parliament nor the law were of any inherent value to most Russians. Even Miliukov's party was swept along by this current of brute force, and by their ambiguity on the question of terror the Kadets soiled their reputation with the moderates. The Vyborg Manifesto was the price the Kadets paid for being Russians and operating under Russian political conditions. But Miliukov rationalized by claiming that the Manifesto was based on European precedent. Answering an English journalist who, in 1906, had asked: "Why did the Constitutional Democratic Party, which takes its stand upon the law, advocate the violation of the law in the Vyborg Manifesto?" he said:

> The right to advocate refusal to pay taxes or furnish recruits for the Army is not a breach of the law, it is an English expedient practiced centuries ago by the Whigs, and practiced quite recently by your passive resisters. We took the idea of passive resistance from the English nonconformists.[14]

Most Russians did not have to resort to such elaborate explanations. They believed in force and did not need to justify it by English procedure.

They also believed in radical solutions of Russia's economic problems. If they needed land they would take it from those who held it, without bothering about the consequences. The elaborate compensation schemes worked out by the Kadets did not interest them. Miliukov's party did not have a program acceptable to more than a minority of Russians. Petrunkevich had admitted in 1906 that the West offered no lessons to the Kadets in economic questions. Miliukov, who based himself on the British model, could hardly learn from Britain when it came to economic problems. Britain's economy was quite different from Russia's and could offer no precedent designed for the immediate present.

British and American politics even misled Miliukov. Russian political parties, unlike those in the Anglo-Saxon world, were based on the class principle. The Socialist Revolutionaries were a peasant

[14] The unpublished interview is in the Miliukov Collection of the Russian Archives, Columbia University, Box 8142, File 20A: "The Outlook in Russia. Interview with Prof. Miliukov."

party, while the Social Democrats represented the workers. The landowners and merchants, too, had their parties, even if miniscule. Only the Kadets claimed to represent no party and to advocate the interests of all, or rather to put principle above narrow privilege. This might have represented real strength had they found principles upon which all Russians were agreed. But this they failed to do, and they enjoyed their brief heyday only so long as they were better organized than the other parties. Miliukov misrepresented this accidental situation because it seemed to justify his hopes. It gave him the impression that only the Kadet party could save Russia.

It was true that the Kadets were not a class party in any Marxist sense. Even Lenin recognized this when he said of them: "It is a party not exclusively connected with any one class of bourgeois society but it is, nevertheless, bourgeois through and through."[15] Had there been a powerful bourgeoisie in Russia, the Kadets might have had a more impressive power base. As it was, their vote (and it never was a mass vote) came from a scattering of groups. It was what the British call a "floating vote." Its basic ingredient would always be too small to weigh against the socialist parties. Thus the Kadets could stand alone but had to find allies to the left or to the right. In 1905–7 it was the former, after 1912 it was the latter coalition which they chose. The Left and the Right, however, could really manage without them, as the two revolutions proved. Caught in the middle the Kadets could at best mediate; they could never lead.

III

These were the lessons the Kadets should have learned in 1905–7. Here was a revolution which could not be called "bourgeois," for its most significant gains were achieved primarily through the pressure of mass violence. The bourgeoisie was successful only so long as it could lead the nation. In Russia such leadership was of very short duration, as both 1905 and 1917 were to illustrate. A party like the Kadets, which, in the popular mind, was identified with the bourgeoisie, could never stand at the helm in a prolonged revolution-ary situation. Its best chance came at a time of social peace when

[15] V. Lenin, V. I. Lenin ob otnosheniiakh revolutsionnogo proletariata k bur-zhuaznym i melkoburzhuaznym partiiam (Moscow, 1958), pp. 164–65.

the state reasserted its authority and guaranteed the party a place in the sun by virtue of its oppositionary character.

This, of course, presupposed a state more tolerant and enlightened in political matters than was Russia in the decade after 1907. The government was not interested in the political maturation of its citizens. It knew that such maturation would spell the end of its rule and would sweep away what remained of the old order. The electoral law of 1907 deprived too many Russians of the vote. It slowed down the educational process essential for the existence of the democracy on which Miliukov depended. He recognized this when he wrote in the emigration:

> All requisites for organizing the masses were lacking. Autocracy is thus greatly responsible for the absence of good political guidance, and, as a result, for the chaotic and elemental development of the revolutionary process. *All* political parties, either bourgeois or socialistic, were equally handicapped in their attempts to reach and to instruct the popular masses.[16]

Though all parties paid a price for the political anesthesia of 1907–17, the Kadets paid the heaviest. They could least afford the prolonged semi-illegality and the absence of grass-roots democracy. Their socialist rivals were used to training cadres underground and could come back to life on a moment's notice. Not so a party which represented only an educated minority and which lacked a creed capable of swaying the masses. This was why Miliukov so strongly condemned the electoral law of 1907. "This electoral law," he wrote in 1924, "was the beginning of the second revolution. If the Fourth Duma could not take the revolution in hand it was because it was the Duma of June 3."[17]

And still the Duma, as the sole fruit of so many hopes, became valuable to Miliukov despite its shortcomings. It was a nursery for the future democratic Russia. "The Duma," Miliukov wrote in 1920,

> which existed only ten years, had not contributed in any appreciable degree toward the growth of political consciousness among the masses. And yet we note that among the leaders of nearly all political movements during the revolutionary period and the

[16] RUS, p. 30; italics in the original.
[17] P. Miliukov, "Respublikansko-Demokraticheskoe ob "edinenie," PN, September 13, 1924, p. 3.

"counter-revolution," from the Right to the Left, with the exception of the extremists, no new names are to be traced. All these leaders are former members of the Duma. . . . What if the Duma had been a good one, and not a bad one—a truly representative Assembly—and had been in existence not for ten years, with forced interruptions and changes in the system of elections, but for a longer term of years, and had been composed of elements representing the nation and its spirit at least as fully as did the First Duma, forcibly dissolved?[18]

The institution was not at fault; it was the regime which misused it for its own purposes.

Though Miliukov believed the Third and Fourth Dumas to be impure vessels, he was, perhaps unbeknownst to himself, corrupted by them. His parliamentary decade affected him more deeply than the brief revolutionary upsurge. While the socialist leaders regarded the Duma as a necessary evil, he came to look upon it as sacred, and an end in itself. It offered satisfactions which his publicistic career had never provided. Unlike most Third and Fourth Duma deputies, he was elected by a mass and direct vote and basked in the illusion that this gave his party a special mandate. He put all his political eggs into one basket—the Duma. For a political leader it was a rather narrow choice, but such were Russian political conditions at the time. His oppositionary tone became a sufficient guarantee of mass support. He rather fancied his role as the leader of His Majesty's Opposition. Perhaps he was made primarily for that role, and not for that of a leader of a nation constructing a new order without European precedent. There was, after all, something sterile about his program, based on Western example and unrealistic for Russian conditions. He admitted that "opposition" suited his temperament. In an interview with Samuel Harper in July, 1907, when it was clear that the Kadets would no longer control the Duma, he admitted that he looked forward to his new role as a critic from the sidelines. It was wonderful that the Kadets would no longer be responsible "for making everything go right. But this," he warned his American friend, "must not be said in public."[19]

The Duma's existence had one further consequence for Miliukov.

[18] P. Miliukov, "The Third Anniversary of Soviet Rule," *The New Russia* (London), III (1920), No. 41, 328; italics in the original.
[19] PAPERS, "Notes 1907–8," interview with Miliukov of July 18, 1907.

It turned his attention from domestic to foreign policy. As he told his American audience:

> The activity of the Duma—even in its chastened form—far from removing the danger of a new revolution, rather contributed to increase this danger. Any constructive work which might satisfy public needs and thus help to mitigate popular disaffection was made impossible by the government majority and by the Upper House.[20]

Powerless to reform Russia, Miliukov tried to strengthen her international position by cementing her alliance with the advanced democracies. As in domestic so in foreign policy he thought he was defending a nonpartisan position in the name of national and not class interests. Because of his unusually thorough background on foreign policy issues, he won himself new recognition, based on a different political constellation, in place of the old one. Being a pacifist meant having a clear conscience; he could brush aside all accusations of imperialism, and his Duma votes against defense appropriations gave concrete meaning to his stand. He did not take the criticism of his speeches seriously; if it came from the Right it was merely pro-German and conservative, if it came from the Left it represented a stand which Miliukov, now in the grip of power politics, considered unrealistic. As far as he was concerned, his views were never challenged in a meaningful way. This conviction was to bear evil fruit in 1917.

By 1914 Miliukov was almost fully preoccupied with foreign affairs. When war came he could justify it to himself because Russia fought on the side of England and France. The first stage of his political career had helped to bring to Russia the beginnings of a parliamentary regime. In the second stage he would help win Russia new standing as a Great Power. To prove her standing, Russia had to acquire the Straits and Constantinople. It was a worthy goal, not only because of its tactical importance, but as a Russian national task posed already by Peter the Great. Miliukov the historian came to the aid of Miliukov the politician. As he pointed out in his memoirs: "Acting as a politician, I remained faithful to my historian's calling."[21] If he helped Russia acquire this glittering prize, he would be remembered as an

[20] RUS, p. 6.
[21] VOSP, II, 155.

architect of Russia's greatness at home and abroad. "If this favorable moment is now allowed to pass," he wrote in 1917, "it will, most likely, never reoccur, and our centuries-old task will remain unfulfilled through the fault of our generation."[22]

The wartime Duma proved to be a fitting tribune for Miliukov. As in 1905–6 so again in 1914–15 he detected that national unity irrespective of class and party which was his goal. In 1905–6 he had tried to lead the nation against the old order, relying mainly on the power of the Left. This time he led a coalition more easily controlled, for it depended not on the volatile popular mood but on the more manageable Fourth Duma. At last he was a true parliamentary leader, the chief of a majority with a largely political rather than economic, program, capable of uniting all moderates. Had the government then been more sensible, he would always allege, the disasters of 1917 could have been avoided. Had the Emperor yielded to the Progressive Bloc, he would have saved his throne and with it a chance to build an order based on the English model. No wonder that Miliukov saw his role in the Progressive Bloc as the culmination of his political career. After 1906 it was his second and last chance. Of course, all historical determinists will disagree, since they believe, with Trotsky, that "if Nicholas had gone to meet liberalism and replaced Sturmer with Miliukov, the development of events would have differed a little in form, but not in substance." Miliukov would never accept such fatalism. It was his credo that "a politician, like a doctor, must swear an oath not to lose hope until the last minute."[23]

IV

The Progressive Bloc, for all the satisfaction it gave Miliukov, was, however, too one-sided an achievement. As in 1906 Miliukov was misled into believing that if he led the Duma he led the nation. He disregarded the fact that, without the Left, the Bloc could not be a potent force. But since neither he (nor anyone else) expected a revolution quite so soon he thought he could ignore his Left rivals and concentrate on the ancient enemy, the old regime. His trips abroad had shown him that England and France managed their war-

[22] P. Miliukov, "Konstantinopl' i prolivy," VE, 1917, April–June, p. 526.
[23] L. Trotsky, *The History of the Russian Revolution* (New York, 1936), I, 100; VTO, p. 235.

time affairs through a "parliamentary dictatorship." This, he was
sure, would work in Russia as well. His foreign trips misled him in
another respect as well. In the Allied countries only a minority was
anti-imperialist; Miliukov thought the same situation obtained in
Russia. Because his interest was now largely confined to foreign policy
issues, he tended to ignore the domestic situation. Traveling between
Petrograd, the Allied capitals, and his Finnish dacha, he saw nothing
of Russia and the front. His speeches of 1916 showed how little he
knew of the workers who would soon be making policy in Russia.
All his calculations for the future depended on two factors: the Duma
and a monarchy forced into concessions by a nation determined to
win the war.

The February Revolution upset this scheme completely. The
Duma and the monarchy disappeared, and the nation showed itself
more interested in peace than in the Straits and victory. Miliukov
entered the third stage of his political career more burdened by the
past than most Russians. He had hoped to come to power through
the invitation of the monarch. Instead he was put there by a revolution which proved itself to be an even more exacting master than
Nicholas II. While the Left created its substitute for the Duma in
the Soviet, Miliukov was deprived of his tribune and support. The
alpha and omega of his dreams had disappeared. The Left leaders,
with their old traditions of maximalism, had no trouble adjusting
to the fast political pace after February. Miliukov remained in his
old frame of mind and could not keep in step.

He had never known a Russia in which there was no institution
to lean on, in which the state structure was overturned so completely
that a vacuum existed. The Kadets, with all their opposition to it,
depended on the state far more than any party to their left. Miliukov
recognized this in his dogged fight for the preservation of the
monarchy and was ready to give up the game when he lost that battle.
But he remained on the scene because of his interest in diplomacy.
As in the previous stage of his career, he would again overlook the
domestic scene and concentrate on foreign affairs. This time, however,
no one was minding the house, as the bureaucracy had done in the
past. Miliukov played his diplomatic fiddle while Russia burned. He
forgot that Russian life was not European life, and his ambitions far
outran the possibilities of the moment. He had once said of Peter
the Great that he had Europeanized Russia in the Asiatic manner.
He was about to witness a repetition of the process.

In his *Ocherki* Miliukov showed that, in Russia, the state was the principal agent of Western ideas. It was to remain so after 1917, but a different set of ideas would now be introduced. They were to be forced upon the Russian people in the same brutal manner in which Peter the Great had once acted. They would be put into practice by leaders quite different from those whom Miliukov would have chosen. He had paid too much attention to figures like Plekhanov and Kropotkin who, in the clever phrase of Sukhanov, had ceased being leaders and had become " 'icons' of the Russian revolution." A Russian socialist who did not adopt the most extremist solution in 1917 was likely to fail. Miliukov recognized this later when he admitted that "the socialists collapsed in 1917 because, in essence, they talked in Kadet language, not excluding Kerensky, and even Chernov." He had once ridiculed the Slavophiles who pretended that Russia had something new to offer to the West. "Lenin," he said in 1917, "repeats Kireevskii and Khomiakov when he asserts that from Russia will come the new work which will resuscitate the aged West." For years Miliukov had maintained that "the idea of the dictatorship of the proletariat is a childish one, and not a single serious person in Europe can seriously support it."[24] He forgot that Russians were not serious Europeans.

Miliukov knew that he was beaten quite early in 1917. But there was never to be any bitterness in the man. "I regard the past not as a mistake, but as an experience," he was to say later.[25] Even his political enemies acknowledged his admirable resilience. "He had," wrote Chernov, "another quality of special value for a political leader: he was not discouraged by failure, he accepted defeat philosophically, and like a true sportsman he bore from each defeat unshaken faith in the possibility of *revanche*, and zest in preparing for it."[26] In his debate with *Vekhi*, Miliukov had quoted Turgenev's dictum that the role of the Russian educated class was merely to transmit civilization to the people, permitting the people itself to decide what to accept and what to reject. If the Russian people opted for socialism in its more extreme forms, it was not for Miliukov to regret the fact but to explain it.

This he did in various ways. One way was to compare the fate of

[24] V. Sukhanov, 171; ARKHIV, II, 37. Also BROWKER, II, 1148, and *Riech'*, September 15, 1912.

[25] ARKHIV, II, 941.

[26] Chernov, *op. cit.*, p. 172.

liberal Russia with that of Czechoslovakia, which, led by another
scholar-statesman, had succeeded where Russia had failed. "Masaryk,"
wrote Miliukov,

> led his country to freedom and reached his goal for the accom-
> plishment of which the country was prepared by the work of the
> entire nation, and by an especially favorable international situation.
> In contrast the efforts of the Russian "liberation movement" met
> with the blind opposition of the government, and the unprepared-
> ness of the popular masses. The international situation created by
> the prolonged war which tired and exhausted the country proved
> to be unusually unfavorable to us. The support of democratic
> Europe which helped Masaryk to create a new free state did not
> extend to those who could not stand on their own feet in the diffi-
> cult moments. To speak of someone's *guilt* would be out of place
> here; it was our *misfortune*. But neither should the sad meaning
> of the parallel be hidden if anyone found it necessary to seek it.[27]

His other, most interesting attempt to explain the puzzle of his
own career is contained in the introduction to his history of the
Revolution of 1917. Though written soon after the events, it is based
not on political passion but on sound historical analysis. There is
still optimism, but it is tempered by all the experience of the failed
politician. In *Russia and Its Crisis* he had tried to fathom Russia's
political future by examining her past. In his work on "the second
Russian revolution," to which he came chastened by defeat, he took
another look at the evidence. It was not surprising that it acquired
a more somber aspect. In October, 1905, the Kadets had unlimited
faith in the Russian people and its political wisdom. "The Russian
people," the first Kadet Congress had said, "is sufficiently rich in
mature political forces to be able to manage its own fate."[28] The years
which followed showed that this had been an overly sanguine view
of the situation.

Writing after the second Russian revolution, Miliukov spoke of:

> the lack of political consciousness and darkness of the Russian
> popular masses which, in fact, made utopian the application to
> our realities even of such ideas as are completely timely and even

[27] P. Miliukov, "Moi vstrechi s Masarykom," PN, September 21, 1937, p. 2;
italics in the original.

[28] From the resolutions of the first Kadet Congress: Konstitutsionno-Demokraticheskaia Partiia, S"ezd 12–18 oktiabria 1905 g. (St. Petersburg, 1905), p. 22.

already partly realized among peoples more prepared for immediate participation in state activity. . . . These masses preserved the outlook of centuries other than our own; but, in the last period of the old regime, they were deliberately held back in darkness and ignorance by the partisans of this regime.

Russia was far behind Europe in the twentieth century because it had adopted Western ways much later than the rest of the civilized world:

> Our entire new cultural tradition [from Peter on] was created by a mere *eight generations* of our predecessors; it was sharply and irretrievably separated from the *popular* cultural tradition, itself a product of a long period lacking national consciousness which, among other peoples, forms their *prehistoric* past. Standing on the shoulders of a mere eight generations we succeeded in assimilating the cultural acquisitions of the West. . . . But one thing we did not succeed in doing: we were as yet unable to work out anything resembling a stable Western cultural type.[29]

This type required factors which were largely undeveloped in Russia. Among these was the presence of a strong middle class. Miliukov now spoke of "the almost complete absence of the 'bourgeoisie' in the true sense of that word, its political impotence despite the widely-spread application of the revolutionary sobriquet 'bourgeois' to anyone wearing a starched collar and a derby hat." He also stressed the lack of respect for law and order which he had always seen as characteristic of Russians at their particular stage of development. "The fundamental trait manifested by the revolutionary process," he wrote, "which accounted for its unhappy outcome, was the weakness of Russian statehood and the predominance in the country of elements of anarchism." He thought that this trait also was "the inevitable consequence of a historical process in which the imported statehood, whether under Riurik or Peter the Great, or in our 'imperialism' of the nineteenth and twentieth centuries, outran the internal organic growth of the state." He pointed out once again, as he had in *Russia and Its Crisis*, that Russia suffered because her political revolution had come too late. He spoke of:

> the profound difference between us and the European West in the history of the long struggle for political freedom, the vast chronological distance between the beginning of this struggle there and

---

[29] *Istoriia*, I, 14–15. *Ibid.*, I, 13; italics in the original.

here, and the unavoidable consequences of this difference: the merging, with us, of the political overthrow with the social one.

Finally, he spoke of the Russian tendency to utopianism, the lack of political moderation, characteristic of a people which had been suppressed too long. Alluding to his predictions in *Russia and Its Crisis*, he wrote in his later work:

> Many of the utopias which I had thought buried rose again; and the political circles which, according to my calculations, should have fought against these utopias, proved sympathetic to them and incapable of firm resistance. Russia paid for this incomplete adjustment of Russian political parties to the demands of Russian reality by the failure of two of her revolutions.[30]

V

Even a failure, however, must be used toward a positive end. The Russian Revolution did not create the order for which Miliukov had worked throughout his political career. Nevertheless, he saw it, not as a disaster, but as a necessary prerequisite of what, he continued to hope, would be a process of growth which would lead to the desired end at a later date. "It might be," he wrote,

> that this catastrophe will serve as that jolt by which the prehistoric, subconscious, so to speak ethnographic stage of the people's existence will end, and a historical period of coherent self-awareness and unbroken social memory will begin. In that case we will, with great delay, move along the path long ago trodden by the cultured nations.[31]

Though he rejected the Bolshevik regime, he did not lose faith in the future of Russia. "We are witnessing," he told an American audience in 1921, "the birth of the Russian democracy, in the midst of the ruins of the past, which will never return. One must not be impatient with the great and complicated revolutionary process which

---

[30] *Ibid.*, I, 12, 14.

[31] *Ibid.*, I, 16. The Introduction to Miliukov's *Istoriia vtoroi russkoi revoliutsii*, from which I have quoted here, is translated, with a slight abridgment, in A. Adams (ed.), *The Russian Revolution and Bolshevik Victory* (Boston, 1960), pp. 1–7.

in other countries took decades, if not centuries, for its completion."[32]

As an émigré he returned to his first love, history, that study of the Russian past which he had never really abandoned. It continued to confirm his conviction that, sooner or later, Russia would come to resemble the West, not only in its technology, but also in its social and political order. "We believe," he told a conference of English historians several years after the revolution, "that Russia is a part of the civilised world: and so long as there is a civilised humanity, the leading principles of English and Anglo-Saxon political life cannot be extinguished. They are immortal."[33]

[32] RUS, p. viii.
[33] P. Miliukov, "The Influence of English Political Thought in Russia," SEER V (1926), 270.

BIBLIOGRAPHY

UNPUBLISHED MATERIALS

CHERMENSKI, E. "Bor'ba klassov i partii v IV gosudarstvennoi dume, 1912–1917 gg." Unpublished Ph.D. dissertation, Moscow University, 1947.

"The Samuel N. Harper Russian Papers," Harper Library, University of Chicago.

Konstitutsionno-Demokraticheskaia Partiia. "Arkhiv 1920–1924." 2 vols. Hoover Library, Palo Alto, California.

Paris Okhrana Archive "P.N. Miliukov" (File XVII), Hoover Library, Palo Alto, California.

"The Paul N. Miliukov Papers," Archive of Russian and East European History and Culture, Columbia University, New York.

SMITH, N. "The Constitutional-Democratic Movement in Russia, 1902–1906." Unpublished Ph.D. dissertation, University of Illinois, 1958.

PUBLISHED MATERIALS

ADAMOV, E. (ed.) Konstantinopl' i prolivy po sekretnym dokumentam byvshego ministerstva inostranykh del 2 vols. Moscow, 1925–26.

Agrarnyi vopros: Sbornik statei. 2 vols. Moscow, 1905–7.

ALEKSANDRA FEODOROVNA, Empress of Russia. *Letters of the Tsaritsa to the Tsar*. London, 1923.

AVREKH, A. "Agrarnyi vopros v III-ei dume," *Istoricheskiia Zapiski* (Moscow), LXII(1958), 26–83.

BELOKONSKII, I. "K istorii zemskogo dvizheniia v Rossii," *Istorischeskii Sbornik* (St. Petersburg), 1907, pp. 25–125.

_____. *Zemsvo i konstitutsiia*. Moscow, 1910.

BELYI, A. *Na rubezhe dvukh stoletii*. Moscow, 1930.

BERDIAEV, N., et al. *Vekhi*. 4th ed. Moscow, 1909.

BERZIN, I. (ed.). "Dnevnik P.N. Miliukova," *Krasnyi Arkhiv* (Moscow), LIV–LV (1932), 3–48.

BESTUZHEV, I. *Bor'ba v Rossii po voprosam vneshnei politiki, 1906–1910*. Moscow, 1961.

BING, J. (ed.). *The Secret Letters of the Last Tsar*. New York, 1938.

BLACK, C. *The Establishment of Constitutional Government in Bulgaria*. Princeton, N. J., 1943.

BOMPARD, M. *Mon Ambassade en Russie, 1903–1908*. Paris, 1937.

BROWDER, R., and KERENSKY, A. (eds.). *The Russian Provisional Government: 1917*. 3 vols. Stanford, Calif., 1961.

BUCHANAN, G. *My Mission to Russia*. 2 vols. Boston, 1923.

CHARYKOV, N. *Glimpses of High Politics*. London, 1931.

CHERMENSKII, E. *Burzhuaziia i tsarizm v revoliutsii 1905–1907 gg.* Moscow, 1939.

CHERNOV, V. *The Great Russian Revolution*. New Haven, Conn., 1936.

CHMIELEWSKI, E. "Stolypin's Last Crisis," *California Slavic Studies*, III (1964), 95–126.

CHURCHILL, R. "Paul N. Miliukov," in B. SCHMITT, (ed.). *Some Historians of Modern Europe*. Chicago, 1942, Pp. 324–48.

CRISP, O. "The Russian Liberals and the 1906 Anglo-French Loan to Russia," *Slavonic and East European Review* (London), June, 1961, pp. 497–511.

DENIKIN, A. *Ocherki russkoi smuty*. 5 vols. Paris-Berlin, 1922–26.

"Doklad Rataeva," in MENSHIKOV, L. (ed.). *Russkii politcheskii sysk za granitsei*. Paris, 1914. Pp. 182–95.

DOLGORUKOV, P. *Velikaia razrukha*. Madrid, 1964.

DOSTOEVSKII, F. *Pis'ma*. Moscow, 1959. Vol. IV.

DRUZHININ, N. "Recollections and Thoughts of a Historian," *The Soviet Review* (New York), IV(1963), No. 1, 22–46.

DUBROVSKII, S. *Krest'ianskoe dvizhenie v revoliutsii 1905–1907 gg.* Moscow, 1956.

EVREINOV, B. "Bibliografiia pechatnykh trudov P. N. Miliukova, 1886–1930," in S. SMIRNOV, et al. (eds.). *P. N. Miliukov: Sbornik materialov po chestvovaniiu ego semidesiatiletiia, 1859–1929.* Paris, 1929. Pp. 313–51.

————. "Vystupleniia P. N. Miliukova v gosudarsvennoi dume," *ibid.,* pp. 352–58.

FISCHER, G. *Russian Liberalism.* Cambridge, Mass., 1958.

FRANCIS, D. *Russia from the American Embassy.* New York, 1921.

FRANK, S. *Biografiia P. B. Struve.* New York, 1956.

GESSEN, I. *V dvukh vekakh.* Berlin, 1937.

GOLDER, F. (ed.). *Documents of Russian History, 1914–1917.* New York, 1927.

GRAVE, B. (ed.). *Burzhuaziia nakanune fevral'skoi revoliutsii* Moscow, 1927.

————. "Kadety v 1905–1906 gg.," *Krasnyi Arkhiv* XLVI (1931), 38–68; XLVII–XLVIII (1931), 112–39.

————. *K istorii klassovoi bor'by v gody imperialisticheskoi voiny.* Moscow, 1926.

GRUZENBERG, O. *Vchera.* Paris, 1938.

GUCHKOV, A. "Iz vospominanii," *Posledniia Novosti* (Paris), (1936), August 9, 12, 16, 19, 23, 26, 30; September 2, 6, 9, 13, 16, 20, 23, 27, 30.

————. "Speech at the Octobrist Conference on November 21, 1913," *Russian Review* (London), 1914, No. 1, pp. 141–58.

GURKO, V. *Features and Figures of the Past.* Stanford, Calif., 1939.

HARCAVE, S. *First Blood.* New York, 1964.

HARPER, S. "Exceptional Measures in Russia," *Russian Review* (London), 1912, No. 4, pp. 92–105.

————. "The Budget Rights of the Russian Duma," *Journal of Political Economy* (Chicago), XVI(1908), 152–56.

————. *The New Electoral Law for the Russian Duma.* Chicago, 1908.

HODGSON, J. "Finland's Position in the Russian Empire, 1905–1910," *Journal of Central European Affairs,* XX (1960), 158–73.

IAKHONTOV, I. "Tiazhelyie dni: Sekretnyia zasedaniia soveta ministrov 16 iuliia–2 sentiabria 1915 g.," *Arkhiv Russkoi Revoliutsii* (Berlin), XVIII(1926), 5–136.

IZVOL'SKII, A. Au Service de la Russie. 2 vols. Paris, 1937.
————. Recollections of A Foreign Minister. Garden City, N. Y.,
1921.
KALINYCHEV, F. (ed.). Gosudarstvennaia duma v Rossii v dokumen-
takh i materialakh. Moscow, 1957.
KERENSKY, A. Russia and History's Turning Point. New York, 1965.
————. The Catastrophe. New York, 1927.
KIRIUKHINA, E. "Vserossiiskii krestianskii soiuz v 1905 g.," Istoriches-
kiia Zapiski (Moscow), L (1955), 95–141.
KIZEVETTER, A. Na rubezhe dvukh stoletii. Prague, 1929.
KLIUCHEVSKII, V. "Otzy v o issledovanii P. N. Miliukova, 'Gosudar-
stvennoe khoziastvo Rossii v pervoi chetverti XVIII v. i reforma
Petra Velikogo,'" Sochineniia. Moscow, Vol. VIII(1959), pp.
177–83.
————. "Riech', proiznesennaia v torzhestvennom sobranii Mos-
kovskogo Universiteta 6 iuniia 1880 g., v den' otkrytiia pamiatnika
Pushkinu," ibid., Vol. VII(1959), pp. 145–52.
KNOX, A. With the Russian Army, 1914–1917. 2 vols. London, 1921.
KOKOVTSOV, V. Out of My Past. Stanford, California, 1935.
"Kommissiia po organizatsii domashnego chteniia v Moskve," Mir
Bozhii (St. Petersburg), May, 1894, pp. 231–36.
KORNILOV, A. "P. N. Miliukov," in Novyi Entsiklopedicheskii Slovar'
Brokgauz-Efrona. St. Petersburg, n.d. Vol. XXVI, pp. 543–46.
KOROSTOVETS, V. Seed and Harvest. London, 1931.
KOVALEVSKY, M. "American Impressions," Russian Review (Hanover,
N.H.), X(1951), 37–45, 106–117, 176–84.
KOZLOWSKI, L. Russkaia revoliutsiia i nezavisimost' Pol'shi. Paris,
1922.
KRASNOV, P. "Pamiati imperatorskoi russkoi armii," Russkaia Letopis
(Paris), V(1923), 5–64.
KRISHEVSKII, N. "V Krymu. (1916–1918 gg.)," Arkhiv Russkoi Revo-
liutsii (Berlin), XIII(1924), 71–124.
KRYZHANOVSKII, S. Vospominaniia. Berlin, n.d.
LAPIN, N. (ed.). "Kadety v dni galitsiiskogo razgroma," Krasnyi
Arkhiv (Moscow), LIX(1933), 117–22.
————. "Progressivnyi blok v 1915–1917 gg.," ibid., L–LI(1932),
117–60; LII(1932), 143–96; LVI(1933), 80–135.
LEDNITSKII, A. "P. N. Miliukov i pol'skii vopros," in S. SMIRNOV, et
al., P. N. Miliukov: Sbornik materialov po chestvovaniiu ego semi-
desiatiletiia, 1859–1929. Paris, 1929. Pp. 212–17.

LENIN, V. Sochineniia. 3d ed. Moscow, 1935–37.

———. V. I. Lenin ob otnosheniiakh revoliutsionnogo proletariata k burzhuaznym i melkoburzhuaznym partiiam. Moscow, 1958.

Leninskii sbornik. Moscow, 1924–59.

LEVIN, A. "June 3, 1907: Action and Reaction," in A. FERGUSON and A. LEVIN, (eds.). Essays in Russian History. Hamden, Conn., 1964. Pp. 233–73.

———. The Reactionary Tradition in the Electoral Campaign to the Third Duma. ("Oklahoma State University Publications," Vol. LIX[1962].)

———. "The Russian Voter in the Elections to the Third Duma," Slavic Review (Seattle), XXI(1962), 660–77.

———. The Second Duma. New Haven, Conn., 1940.

LOUIS, G. Les Carnets. 2 vols. Paris, 1926.

McNEAL, R. "The Conference of Jassy," in J. CURTISS, (ed.). Essays in Russian and Soviet History. Leyden, 1963. Pp. 221–36.

MAKLAKOV, V. Pervaia gosudarstvennaia duma. Paris, 1939. In translation: The First State Duma. Bloomington, Ind., 1964.

———. "Vlast' i obshchestvennost' na zakate staroi Rossii. Paris, 1936.

———. Vtoraia gosudarstvennaia duma. Paris, n.d.

MANDEL'SHTAM, M. 1905 god v politicheskikh protsessakh. Moscow, 1931.

MARTYNOV, A. "Istoriia konstitutsionno-demokraticheskoi partii," in L. MARTOV, et al. Obshchestvennoe dvizhenie v Rossii v nachale XX v. St. Petersburg, 1914. Vol. III, pp. 1–85.

MEISEL, J. and KOZERA, E. Materials for the Study of the Soviet System. Ann Arbor, Mich. 1953.

MEL'GUNOV, S. Legenda o separatnom mire. Paris, 1957.

———. Martovskie dni 1917 goda. Paris, 1961.

———. Na putiakh k dvortsovomu perevorotu. Paris, 1931.

MILIUKOV, P. "Aleksander Lednicki," Przeglad Wspolczesny (Warsaw), XVIII(1939), Series LXVIII, 25–71.

———. Balkanskii krizis i politika A. P. Izvol'skago. St. Petersburg, 1910.

———. "Bolgarskaia konstitutsiia," Russkoe Bogatstvo (St. Petersburg), 1904, No. 8, pp. 193–216; No. 9, pp. 26–69; No. 10, pp. 28–59.

———. Bolshevism: An International Danger. London, 1920.

———. Constitutional Government for Russia. New York, 1907.

————. "Demokratizm i vtoraia palata," *Russkoe Bogatstvo* (St. Petersburg), 1905, No. 7, pp, 193–210.

————. "Deux Historiens Russes, Platonov et Kizevetter," *Le Monde Slave* (Paris), March, 1933, pp. 454–64.

————. "Dnevnik," *Novyi Zhurnal* (New York), LXVI(1961), 173–203; LXVII(1962), 180–218.

————. "Doklad ts. kom. V s"ezdu partii Nar. Svob.," *Vestnik Partii Narodnoi Svobody* (St. Petersburg), 1907, pp. 1833–40.

————. "Finliandiia," in *Ezhegodnik gazety Riech' 1913*. St. Petersburg, 1913. Pp. 302–11.

————. *Glavnyia techeniia russkoi istoricheskoi mysli*. Moscow, 1897.

————. *God bor'by*. St. Petersburg, 1907.

————. *Gosudarstvennoe khoziaistvo Rossii pervoi chetverti XVIII veka i reforma Petra Velikogo*. St. Petersburg, 1892.

————. "Intelligentsiia i istoricheskaia traditsiia," in K. ARSEN'EV et al. *Intelligentsiia v Rossii*. St. Petersburg, 1910. Pp. 89–191.

————. *Istoriia vtoroi russkoi revoliutsii*. 3 vols. Sofia, 1921–24.

————. *Iz istorii russkoi intelligentsii*. St. Petersburg, 1902.

————. "Konstantinopl' i prolivy." *Vestnik Evropy* (Petrograd), (1917) January, pp. 354–81; February, pp. 227–59; April–June, pp. 525–47.

————. "K redaktoru 'Russkikh Vedomostei,'" *Russkiia Vedomosti* (Moscow), September 17, 1905.

————. "Le Dixiéme Anniversaire de la Revolution Russe," *Le Monde Slave* (Paris), November–December, 1927, pp. 188–246.

————. "Letnii universitet v Anglii: Iz poezdki v Kembridzh," *Mir Bozhii* (St. Petersburg), May, 1894, pp. 194–206.

————. "Liberalizm, radikalizm, i revoliutsiia," *Sovremennyia Zapiski* (Paris), LVII(1935), 285–315.

————. "M. M. Vinaver, kak politik," in *M. M. Vinaver i russkaia obshchestvennost' nachala XX v.* Paris, 1937. Pp. 19–52.

————. *Neproiznesennaia Rech'*. St. Petersburg, 1908.

————. "Obshchee politicheskoe polozhenie," in *Otchet K.D. fraktsii*, 1909–10, pp. 6–22; 1910–11, pp. 1–9; 1911–12, pp. 3–7; 1912–13, pp. 5–11; 1913–14, pp. 5–16. St. Petersburg: Fraktsiia Narodnoi Svobody, 1910, 1911, 1912, 1913, 1914.

————. "Obshchestvennoe mnenie, parlamenty, i pravitel' stva soiuznikov: Rossiia," *Ezhegodnik gazety Riech' 1915*. St. Petersburg, 1915. Pp. 235–90.

_____. *Ocherki po istorii russkoi kul'tury*. 3 vols. St. Petersburg, 1897–1909. Jubilee ed. Paris, 1930–1937.

_____. "Petr Velikii I ego reforma," *Na chuzhoi storone*. Paris, 1925. Book X, pp 5–28.

_____. *Piat' etnograficheskikh kart Makedonii, s tektsom P. N. Miliukova*. St. Petersburg, 1900.

_____. "Pierre le Grand et sa Réforme," *Le Monde Slave* (Paris), February, 1925, pp. 157–85.

_____. "Pis'ma iz Makedonii," *Russkiia Vedomosti* (Moscow), 1898, Nos. 159, 168, 181, 183, 277.

_____. "Pis'mo v redaktsiiu," *ibid.*, No. 356.

_____. "Pokazaniia P. N. Miliukova," in P. Shchegolev (ed.). *Padenie tsarskogo rezhima*. Moscow. Vol. VI(1926), pp. 295–372.

_____. "Politicheskiia partii v gosudarstvennoi dume za piat' let," in *Ezhegodnik gazety Riech'* 1912. St. Petersburg, 1912. Pp. 77–96.

_____. "Poslednii den' v Peterburge," *Illiustrirovannaya Rossiia* (Paris), October 29, 1927, pp. 1–4.

_____. *P. N. Miliukoff über Makedonien*. Leipzig, 1918.

_____. "Present Tendencies of Russian Liberalism," *Atlantic Monthly* (Boston), March, 1905, pp. 404–14.

_____. "Rasprostranenie universitetskogo obrazovaniia v Anglii, Amerike i Rossii," *Russkoe Bogatstvo* (St. Petersburg), March, 1896, pp. 79–121.

_____. *Riech' P. N. Miliukova, proiznesennaia v zasedanii gosudarstvennoi dumy 1-go noiabriia 1916 g*. Moscow, 1917.

_____. "Rokovye Gody," *Russkiia Zapiski* (Paris), IV (1938), 109–18; V, 109–19; VI, 115–31; VII, 126–36; VIII–IX, 108–24; X, 128–38; XI, 135–49; XII, 116–25; XIII(1939), 117–28; XIV, 120–34; XV, 101–12; XVI, 127–39; XVII, 106–20; XVIII, 111–21; XIX, 104–20; XX–XXI, 96–111.

_____. "Russia," *Athenaeum* (London), July 6, 1889, pp. 26–28; July 5, 1890, pp. 25–27; July 4, 1891, pp. 29–32; July 2, 1892, pp. 25–27; July 1, 1893, pp. 27–30; July 7, 1894; pp. 22–25; July 6, 1895, pp. 24–26; July 4, 1896, pp. 25–27.

_____. *Russia and Its Crisis*. Chicago, 1905.

_____. *Russia Today and Tomorrow*. New York, 1922.

_____. "S. D. Sazonov," *Posledniia Novosti* (Paris), December 29, 1927, pp. 2–3; January 5, 1928, pp. 2–3.

_____. "Sergei Muromtsev: Biograficheskii ocherk," in *Sergei A. Muromtsev: Sbornik statei*. Moscow, 1911. Pp. 1–53.

————. "S makedonskoi granitsi," *Russkiia Vedomosti* (Moscow), October 10, 1903.

————. *Taktika partii Narodnoi Svobody vo vremia voiny.* Petrograd, 1916.

————. "Talaad," *Posledniia Novosti* (Paris), March 17, 1921.

————. "The Case of the Second Duma," *Contemporary Review* (London), XCII (October, 1907), 457–67.

————. "The Influence of English Political Thought in Russia," *Slavonic and East European Review* (London), V(1926), 258–70.

————. "The Representative System in Russia," in J. DUFF, (ed.). *Russian Realities and Problems.* Cambridge, 1917. Pp. 25–46.

————. "The Third Anniversary of Soviet Rule," *The New Russia* (London), III, No. 41 (November 11, 1920), 327–31.

————. "The War and Balkan Politics," *ibid.* Pp. 1–24.

————. *Tri popytki.* Paris, 1921.

————. "Tseli voiny," in *Ezhegodnik gazety Riech'* 1916. St. Petersburg, 1916. Pp. 32–128.

————. "U nas net vragov sleva," *Riech'* (St. Petersburg), September 22, 1907.

————. "University Extension," in *Entsiklopedicheskii Slovar' Brokgauz-Efron.* St. Petersburg, LXVIII (1902), 803–9.

————. "Universitety v Rossii," *ibid.*, 788–800.

————. "V. A. Maklakov mezhdu 'Obshchestvennostiu' i 'Vlastiiu,'" *Posledniia Novosti* (Paris), May 28, 1937, p. 2.

————. "Vneshniaia politika Rossii," in *Ezhegodnik gazety Riech'* 1912. St. Petersburg, 1912. Pp. 1–20. 1913. (1913.) Pp. 1–17. 1914. (1914.) Pp. 1–20.

————. "V. O. Kliuchevskii," in V. O. *Kliuchevskii: Kharakteristiki i vospominaniia.* Moscow, 1912. Pp. 183–217.

————. "V. O. Kliuchevskii, kak lichnost'," *Posledniia Novosti* (Paris), January 24 and 26, 1932.

————. *Vooruzhennyi mir i ogranichenie vooruzhenii.* Moscow, 1911.

————. *Vospominaniia* (1859–1917). 2 vols. New York, 1955.

————. "Vstuplenie Turtsii," in *Ezhegodnik gazety Riech'* 1915. St. Petersburg, 1915. Pp. 122–41.

————. *Vtoraia duma.* St. Petersburg, 1908.

————. "Vvedenie," in K. ARSEN'EV et al. *Nuzhdy derevni po rabotam komitetov o nuzhdakh sel'sko-khoziaistvennoi promyshlennosti.* St. Petersburg, 1904. Vol. I, pp. 1–40.

————. "Sergei I. Witte," in Entsiklopedicheskii slovar' Granat. 7th ed. Vol. X (Moscow, 1911), pp. 342–72.

MITSKEVICH, S. Revoliutsionnaia Moskva, 1888–1905. Moscow, 1940.

NABOKOV, K. The Ordeal of a Diplomat. London, 1921.

NABOKOV, V. "Vremennoe pravitel'stvo," Arkhiv Russkoi Revoliutsii (Berlin), I (1921), 9–96.

NEKLUDOFF, A. Diplomatic Reminiscences before and during the World War, 1911–1917. London, 1920.

NICOLSON, H. King George V. London, 1952.

OBOLENSKII, V. "Miliukov kak politik," in S. SMIRNOV, et al. P. N. Miliukov: Sbornik materialov po chestvovaniiu ego semidesiatiletiia, 1859–1929. Paris, 1929. Pp. 99–111.

Osvobozhdenie. Stuttgart-Paris.

PALÉOLOGUE, M. La Russie des Tsars Pendant la Grande Guerre. 3 vols. Paris, 1921.

Papers Relating to the Foreign Relations of the United States. 1918. Russia. 3 vols. Washington, D.C.: U. S. Department of State, 1931–32.

PARES, B. My Russian Memoirs. London, 1931.

————. The Fall of the Russian Monarchy. New York, 1961.

————. "The Peterhof Conference of 1905," Russian Review (London), II(1913), No. 4, 87–120.

PARRY, A. "Charles R. Crane, Friend of Russia," Russian Review (Hanover, N.H.), V(1945), 20–36.

Partiia Narodnoi Svobody, Otchet Tsentral'nogo Komiteta Konsti-tutsiono-Demokraticheskoi partii za dva goda, s 18 oktiabria 1905 g. po oktiabr' 1907 g. St. Petersburg, 1907.

————. Rezoliutsii delegatskogo s"ezda partii Narodnoi Svobody (25–28 marta 1917 g. v Petrograde). Petrograd, n.d.

————. Stenograficheskii protokol' zasedanii VII s"ezda partii Na-rodnoi Svobody. 1-ii den' s"ezda. Petrograd, n.d.

P. B. "Neskol'ko zamechanii ob 'Ocherkakh po istorii russkoi kul-'tury' g. Miliukova," Russkoe Bogatstvo (St. Petersburg), 1898, No. 8, pp. 1–21.

Petrogradskaia gorodskaia duma v 1913–1915 gg. Petrograd, 1915.

PETRUNKEVICH, I. Iz zapiskok obshchestvennogo deiatelia. Berlin, 1934.

"Piatyi s"ezd K.D. Partii," Vestnik Partii Narodnoi Svobody (St. Petersburg), (1907), 1981–89, 2041–60, 2088–2100, 2133–63.

POLIANSKII, V. (ed.). "Marksistskaia pechat' 1896–1906 gg.," *Krasnyi Arkhiv* (Moscow), XVIII(1926), 226–68.

POLIVANOV, A. *Iz vospominanii i dnevnikov.* Moscow, 1924.

Postanovleniia II-go s"ezda 5–11 ianvaria 1906 g. i programma. St. Petersburg: Konstitutsionno-Demokraticheskaia Partiia, 1906.

"Postanovleniia III-go s"ezda partii Narodnoi Svobody 21–25 aprelia 1906 g.," *Vestnik Partii Narodnoi Svobody* (St. Petersburg), 1906, pp. 593–600.

"Postanovleniia IV-go s"ezda partii Narodnoi Svobody," *ibid.*, pp. 1585–91.

"Postanovleniia V-go s"ezda K.D. partii," *ibid.*, 1907, pp. 1829–33.

Prigovor moskovskoi dumy 18-go avgusta 1915 g. Moscow, 1915.

"Privetstvia F. I. Rodichevu," *Vestnik Partii Narodnoi Svobody* (St. Petersburg), 1907, pp. 1974–76; 2018–19.

"Protokoly doprosa Admirala Kolchaka chrezvychainoi sledstvennoi kommissiei v Irkutske v ianvare–fevrale 1920 g.," *Arkhiv Russkoi Revoliutsii* (Berlin), X(1923), 177–312.

PROTOPOPOV, D. *Ocherk deiatel'nosti St. Peterburgskoi gorodskoi gruppy partii Narodnoi Svobody.* St. Petersburg, 1908.

RADKEY, O. *The Agrarian Foes of Bolshevism.* New York, 1958.

————. *The Election to the Russian Constituent Assembly of 1917.* Cambridge, Mass., 1950.

RAEFF, M. "Some Reflections on Russian Liberalism," *Russian Review* (Hanover, N.H.), July, 1959, pp. 218–30.

RAKHMETOV, V. (ed.). "Aprel'skie dni 1917 g. v Petrograde," *Krasnyi Arkhiv* (Moscow), XXXIII(1929), 34–82.

Report of the International Commission To Inquire into the Causes and Conduct of the Balkan Wars. Washington, D.C.: Carnegie Endowment for International Peace, 1914.

Revoliutsionnoe dvizhenie v Rossii posle sverzheniia samoderzhaviia. Moscow: Velikaia Oktiabrskaia Sotsiolisticheskaia Revoliutsiia— Dokumenty i Materialy, 1957.

REZANOV, A. *Shturmovoi signal' P. N. Miliukova.* Paris, 1924.

RIHA, T. "Miliukov and the Progressive Bloc in 1915," *Journal of Modern History* (Chicago), XXXII(1960), 16–24.

————. "Riech': A Portrait of a Russian Newspaper," *Slavic Review* (Seattle), XXII(1963), 663–82.

RODZIANKO, M. "Gosudarstvennaia duma i fevral'skaia Revoliutsiia," *Arkhiv Russkoi Revoliutsii* (Berlin), VI(1922), 5–80.

————. "Krushenie Imperii," ibid., XVII(1926), 5–169.

Sbornik sekretnykh dokumentov iz arkhiva byvshego ministerstva inostranykh del. 7 vols. Petrograd: Ministerstvo Inostranykh Del, 1917–18.

SCHAPIRO, L. "The Vekhi Group and the Mystique of Revolution," Slavonic and East European Review (London), XXXIV(1955–56), 56–76.

SERGEEV, A. (ed.). "Pervaia gosudarstvennaia duma v Vyborge," Krasnyi Arkhiv (Moscow), LVII(1933), 85–99.

S"ezd 12–18 oktiabria 1905 g. Moscow: Konstitutsionno Demokraticheskaia Partiia, 1905.

"S"ezd partii Narodnoi Svobody," Riech', March 26, 1917, pp. 3–4; March 28, 1917, pp. 3–5; March 29, 1917, pp. 2–4.

"S"ezd zemskikh i gorodskikh deiatelei," Pravo (St. Petersburg), (1905), 3601–30, 3699–3727.

SHAKHOVSKOI, D. "Avtobiografiia," in Russkiia Vedomosti, 1863–1913: Sbornik statei. Moscow, 1913. Pp. 196–200.

————. "Soiuz osvobozhdeniia," Zarnitsy (St. Petersburg), 1909, No. 2, Part 2, pp. 81–171.

SHCHEGOLEV, P. (ed.). Padenie tsarskogo rezhima. 7 vols. Moscow, 1926–27.

SHIPOV, D. Vospominaniia i dumy o perezhitom. Moscow, 1918.

SHLIAPNIKOV, A. Kanun semnadtsatogo goda. 2 vols. Moscow, 1920.

————. Semnadtsatyi god. 4 vols. Moscow, 1923–31.

SHUL'GIN, V. Dni. Leningrad, 1926.

SIDEL'NIKOV, S. Obrazovanie i deiatel'nost pervoi gosudarstvennoi dumy. Moscow, 1962.

SIDOROV, A. "Bor'ba s krizisom vooruzhenii russkoi armii v 1915–16 gg.," Istoricheskii Zhurnal (Moscow), (1944) No. 10–11, pp. 37–57.

SKIF, N. (pseud.) "G. Miliukov i Slavianofil'stvo," Russkii Vestnik (St. Petersburg), (1903) No. 1, pp. 269–317.

SMIRNOV, A. Kak proshly vybory v 2-iu gosudarstvennuiu dumu: So vstupitel'noi statei i zakliucheniem P. N. Miliukova. St. Petersburg, 1907.

SMIRNOV, S., et al. P. N. Miliukov: Sbornik materialov po chestvovaniiu ego semidesiatiletiia, 1859–1929. Paris, 1929.

SMITH, C. J. The Russian Struggle for Power, 1914–1917. New York, 1956.

_____. "The Russian Third State Duma: An Analytical Profile," *Russian Review* (Hanover, N. H.), XVII(1958), 201–10.

SOLOV'EV, V. "Zamechaniia na lektsiiu P. N. Miliukova," *Sobranie Sochinenii* V. S. Solov'eva. St. Petersburg, n.d. Vol. V, pp. 458–62.

Stenograficheskie otchety [Gosudarstvennaia Duma]. St. Petersburg, 1906–7.

STOROZHEV, V. "Diplomatiia i revoliutsiia," *Vestnik Narodnogo Kommisariata Inostrannykh Del* (Moscow), 1920, No. 4–5, pp. 69–104.

_____. "Istoricheskaia Khronika," *Istoricheskoe Obozrenie* (St. Petersburg), V(1892), 198–215.

"Sudebnye Otchety," *Pravo* (St. Petersburg), 1906, pp. 1854–60.

SUKHANOV, N. *Zapiski o revoliutsii*, 7 vols. Berlin, 1922–23.

TREADGOLD, D. *Lenin and his Rivals*. New York, 1955.

"Tretii S"ezd Delegatov Partii Narodnoi Svobody," *Pravo* (St. Petersburg), 1906, pp. 1667–97.

TROTSKII, L. "Otkrytoe pis'mo Professoru P. N. Miliukovu," *Nasha Revoliutsiia*. St. Petersburg, n.d. Pp. 136–48.

_____. *The History of the Russian Revolution*. 3 vols. in one. New York, 1936.

TRUBETSKOI, E. "Otkrytoe pis'mo P. N. Miliukovu," *Riech'*, June 28, 1907.

TSERETELLI, I. *Vospominaniia o fevral'skoi revoliutsii*. 2 vols. Paris, 1963.

TUCK, R. "Paul Miliukov and Negotiations for a Duma Ministry," *American Slavic and East European Review* (New York), X(1951), 117–29.

VANAG, N. (ed.). "Russkaia 'parliamentskaia' delegatsiia zagranitsei v 1916 g.," *Krasnyi Arkhiv* (Moscow), LVIII(1933), 3–23.

VASIL'EV, N. *Pravda o Kadetakh*. St. Petersburg, 1912.

VERNADSKII, G. *Pavel Nikolaevich Miliukov*. Petrograd, 1917.

VINAVER, M. *Istoriia vyborgskogo vozvaniia*. Petrograd, 1917.

_____. "Konflikty v pervoi dume," in N. BORODIN, et al. *Pervaia gosudarstvennaia duma*. St. Petersburg, 1907. Vol. I, pp. 184–279.

VISHNIAK, M. *Dan' proshlomu*. New York, 1954.

_____. "Russkii Evropeets," *Sovremennyia Zapiski* (Paris), XXXVIII(1929), 461–67.

VLADIMIROVA, V. *Kontrrevoliutsiia v 1917 godu*. Moscow, 1924.

VOITINSKII, V. *Gody pobed i porazhenii*. 2 vols. Berlin, 1923–24.

VON LAUE, T. *Sergei Witte and the Industrialization of Russia*. New York, 1963.

VRANGEL', L. "Russkoe Bogatstvo i Mir Bozhii," Novyi Zhurnal (New York, LXIX(1962), 161–69.

"Vtoroi vserossiiskii delegatskii s"ezd K. D. partii," Pravo (St. Petersburg), 1906, Supplement to No. 4, pp. 1–22; Supplement to No. 7, pp. 25–56.

Vyborgskii Protsess. St. Petersburg, 1908.

WALSH, W. "Political Parties in the Russian Dumas," Journal of Modern History (Chicago), XXII(1950), 144–50.

WARTH, R. The Allies and the Russian Revolution. Durham, N. C., 1954.

WITTE, S. Vospominaniia. 3 vols. Moscow, 1960.

WUORINEN, J. Nationalism in Modern Finland. New York, 1931.

Zapiska fraktsii progressistov ob vozniknovenii progressivnogo bloka. Petrograd: Fraktsiia Progressistov, 1915.

ZEMAN, Z. (ed.). Germany and the Revolution in Russia, 1915–1918. London, 1958.

INDEX